Teacher's Edition
Level Two

Español para ti

Elena Steele
K–12 Foreign Language Specialist
Clark County, Nevada, Public Schools

Holly Johnson
Español para ti Video Teacher

National Textbook Company
a division of NTC/Contemporary Publishing Group
Lincolnwood, Illinois USA

Editorial Director: Cindy Krejcsi
Executive Editor: Mary Jane Maples
Director, World Languages Publishing: Keith Fry
Design Manager: Ophelia Chambliss
Cover and Interior Design: Karen Christofferson
Production Manager: Margo Goia
Editorial and Production Management: Elm Street Publications, Wellesley, MA
Composition: Jan Ewing, Ewing Systems, New York, NY

ISBN: 0-8442-0209-6

Published by National Textbook Company,
a division of NTC/Contemporary Publishing Group,
4255 West Touhy Avenue
Lincolnwood (Chicago), Illinois 60649-1975 U.S.A.
© 1998 NTC/Contemporary Publishing Group

All rights reserved. No part of this book may be reproduced, stored in a retrieval system, or transmitted in any form or by any means, electronic, mechanical, photocopying, recording or otherwise, without the prior permission of the publisher.

Manufactured in the United States of America.

890 ML 0987654321

ESPAÑOL PARA TI, Level Two

TABLE OF CONTENTS

A Message from the Authors   v

Español para ti Components   vii

Introduction to the Program   ix

Introduction to a Lesson   xii

Sample Lesson Pages   xv

Audiovisual Techniques   xxi

Timing, Pacing, and Articulation   xxv

Integrating Spanish with the Curriculum   xxvii

Assessment   xxix

Family and Community   xxxi

Heritage Speakers   xxxiii

Content-Based Topics   xxxiv

Topics and Language Covered   xxxvi

Lessons 1–66   1

Teacher's Manual

A Message from the Authors

Bienvenidos a *Español para ti*. (*Welcome to **Español para ti**.*)

We are happy to welcome you to a new language adventure! It is our hope that you are excited about giving your students the gift of learning a second language. Relax and enjoy the experience! You don't need to speak Spanish in order to use ***Español para ti***. The program offers you an abundance of support so that you can successfully join with your students in learning the language and the cultures of the Spanish-speaking world.

As experienced Spanish teachers, we have designed an interactive program offering you, our colleagues, the very best and easiest approach to teaching Spanish through the rich medium of video in a fun, exciting, and non-threatening way. Everything you need to facilitate instruction is provided for you in convenient kits. You and your students will enjoy the puppet characters, music, mimes, excursions, activities, and games that make learning Spanish through ***Español para ti*** a real treat.

For us, the creation of ***Español para ti*** has been a labor of love and a dream come true, and you are our partners in the realization of this dream. With your help, we can bring Spanish instruction to every child at the elementary school level. Your enthusiastic implementation of ***Español para ti*** will make your students successful language learners, and you will experience that Spanish truly is **para ti** (*for you*) and for everyone!

Our best wishes for a wonderful experience with ***Español para ti***.

Mil gracias y muy buena suerte. (*Many thanks and best wishes.*)

Elena Steele
Doña Elena
Elena Steele

Holly Johnson
La maestra
Holly Johnson

Teacher's Manual

ESPAÑOL PARA TI COMPONENTS

Materials Center

Videocassettes

The videos serve as the core of instruction. The programs for Levels 1 and 2 consist of 17 videocassettes containing 66 fifteen-minute video lessons. The programs for Levels 3–5 consist of 20 videocassettes containing 60 fifteen-minute video lessons. With the help of puppets, a mime, and a variety of visitors, the vivacious video teacher (**la maestra** in Spanish) introduces and practices Spanish. The interaction between the teacher and the other characters is lively and often results in humorous situations.

Teacher's Manual

The Teacher's Manual makes no assumptions that teachers speak Spanish, so any teacher can easily follow the step-by-step directions for presenting each lesson of *Español para ti* and coordinating the use of the many support materials. The Teacher's Manual for Level 2 provides a self-contained lesson plan for each of the 66 lessons. Each lesson plan includes:

- learning objectives for the lesson
- key vocabulary items with English translations, teaching tips, and cultural information
- miniature reproductions of the Blackline Masters used in the lesson
- activities and games that reinforce the language presented on the video

In addition, there are guidelines for formal and informal assessments and audiovisual techniques.

Teacher's Resource Book

This valuable resource contains:

- patterns to make the Rosco flag, which can be used in many activities throughout the year
- a course completion certificate, which can be duplicated for each child
- four letters to send home to parents, which explain the program and suggest ways that families can help and encourage children
- formal assessments to be used at the end of the semester and at the end of the year, and a rubric for holistic evaluations
- large Number Cards for 1–20 and 10–100 by tens
- 51 Blackline Masters to use in a variety of ways—for vocabulary practice, as masks or puppets, in games, and as aids to remembering songs

Teacher's Manual

Activity Cassettes 1, 2, and 3

These three cassettes provide listening and speaking activities that coordinate with and reinforce the video lessons. These activities either practice what was taught in the related video lesson or review previously learned vocabulary. They also contain the formal assessment activities.

Song Cassette

All the songs taught by the video teacher are included on this cassette. A listing of the songs as they appear on the Song Cassette can be found on page xxiv. These songs are lively and fun, but are also instructional and teach vocabulary. Lyrics and translations for all the songs appear in the appropriate lessons of the Teacher's Manual.

Visuals Package

Puppets

Español para ti includes hand puppets for the two characters who appear most frequently on the videos—the adorable but sometimes outrageous Rosco, a wolf, and the ever-lovable Dora, a cow. The video teacher talks to the puppets to model words, questions, and answers, and the puppets frequently provide further modeling by talking to one another. Sometimes the puppets ask the children questions or answer the video teacher's questions along with the children. Classroom teachers can use the puppets in similar ways. Some children may find speaking through or to the puppets less threatening than talking as themselves. The Teacher's Manual provides suggestions for using these delightful characters.

Flashcards

Two sets of Flashcards are provided for use in activities and for vocabulary reinforcement. The video teacher introduces vocabulary and expressions with the same large, colorful Flashcards, providing continuity between the videos and the classroom. Since they are on heavy paper and are large enough to be seen from a distance, they are ideal for use in classroom activities.

Posters

There are two large posters—the classroom and the animals' party. The classroom poster shows examples of the classroom vocabulary presented in the lessons. The colorful poster of the animals' party shows the animals for which the children learn Spanish names. The posters are also useful for practicing colors and numbers. Both posters can be used to brighten up the classroom.

ESPAÑOL PARA TI, Level Two

Introduction to the Program

Why teach foreign languages in elementary school?

Improved academic performance

There are many benefits to early foreign language learning. It's been shown that children who have studied a foreign language in the elementary grades achieve higher scores on standardized testing. Learning a second language also improves children's understanding of their native language. In addition, children who study a foreign language show greater cognitive development than many of their peers. Finally, as educator Gladys Lipton points out in her book *Practical Handbook to Elementary Foreign Language Programs*,[1] "children who have studied a foreign language have an improved self-concept and sense of achievement in school."

Ease of learning

Research shows that children are most receptive and more able to learn a language before the age of ten. In a *Time Magazine* article about brain research, J. Madeleine Nash[2] wrote:

> There appears to be a series of windows for developing language. The window for acquiring syntax may close as early as five or six years of age, while the window for adding new words may never close. The ability to learn a second language is highest between birth and the age of six, then undergoes a steady and inexorable decline. . . .

Young children learn languages with great enthusiasm. They are willing to imitate the new sounds in a foreign language, to sing and play with it, unlike older students who may be more self-conscious about such efforts.

Young children also have time to master a second language. Think about the young children you know, and how many years of extended practice they need to learn English. These resources—a long period of time and repeated practice—are required to learn any language. This is particularly true if fluency—speaking, reading, and writing like or almost like a native speaker—is the goal. Starting language learning in the early grades enables children to achieve that fluency.

A jump on the future

Learning a foreign language fosters tolerance and appreciation of different cultures. When Americans of different cultural backgrounds live and work together amicably, society's efforts can be directed toward creativity and productivity.

> "Children who have studied a foreign language in elementary school achieve expected gains and score higher on standardized tests of reading, language arts, and mathematics than children who have not studied a foreign language."
>
> –U.S. Congress

> "I wish I had had the chance to take Spanish in elementary school. As it was, it wasn't until high school; and I think if we can start our children earlier, they'll have a better grasp [of a foreign language] and they'll be much more competitive in today's society."
>
> –A parent

---

[1] Gladys Lipton, *Practical Handbook to Elementary Foreign Language Programs*, Lincolnwood, IL: NTC/Contemporary Publishing Company, in preparation.

[2] J. Madeleine Nash, "Fertile Minds" (*Time Magazine,* February 3, 1997; pages 55–56).

Teacher's Manual

> "Four out of five new jobs in the United States are created from foreign trade."
> –U.S. Congress

> "The age of ten is a crucial time in the development of attitudes toward nations and groups perceived as 'other' . . . The awareness of a global community can be enhanced when children have the opportunity to experience involvement with another culture through a foreign language."
> –Barbara Wing, Educator[3]

In addition, businesses in the United States are now involved in increased competition with foreign companies on the one hand and in more cooperative ventures in foreign countries on the other. American workers in areas such as manufacturing, marketing, product development, and engineering, for example, find themselves interacting increasingly with representatives of foreign subsidiaries or holding companies. The ability to speak the language of these representatives gives those workers both a personal and an economic advantage.

How does *Español para ti* work?

The videos are the heart of the program. You, the classroom teacher, are the facilitator who watches the video with the children and responds along with them. And don't worry if you don't speak Spanish. The on-screen video teacher (**la maestra** in Spanish) introduces small amounts of information at a time, and she explains in English what is happening or what is going to happen. She frequently uses a gesture, a picture, or an object to help the children, and you, understand what is being said. She repeatedly models any language that the children are supposed to say or react to. And, when **la maestra** asks a question, she or one of the puppet characters always models the answer. Watch and listen with the class. Before long, you'll discover one of the great benefits of *Español para ti*. You'll be learning Spanish along with your students!

Teaching techniques

Español para ti employs a "spiral" method of teaching. Material is usually introduced in one lesson, practiced in several succeeding lessons, dropped for a while, and then practiced again. New material is always introduced in the context of known vocabulary. Explanations are always given in English so no one is ever lost.

Throughout the program, the video teacher uses a technique called Total Physical Response (TPR) in which children respond physically to a command or direction to help them learn vocabulary and concepts. First, she states a command and models the accompanying activity several times. Second, she repeats the command and has the children respond as a group. Then she gives commands to individuals who respond, and finally, children give commands to classmates. As facilitator, you may enjoy following the commands along with the children.

Support materials

Vocabulary and language concepts are reinforced with Flashcards, Blackline Masters, and the activities on the three

---

[3] Barbara H. Wing, "Starting Early: Foreign Languages in the Elementary and Middle Schools," in Barbara H. Wing, ed., *Northeast Conference Reports: Foreign Languages for All, Challenges and Choices*, copyright 1996, Lincolnwood, IL: National Textbook Company, p. 41.

ESPAÑOL PARA TI, Level Two

Activity Cassettes. The audio teacher (**la maestra** again or her friends doña Elena and Mr. Hale) explains each activity in English and provides all the necessary Spanish. He or she also supplies responses. During the video, he or she often uses songs to provide a framework for learning vocabulary. These songs also appear on the Song Cassette, so that **la maestra** can continue to practice singing them with the children in your class.

Think of the video teacher as someone with whom you are team teaching. Her job is to model, teach, and practice Spanish whether on the videotape, the Activity Cassette, or the Song Cassette. Your job is to facilitate what she is choreographing. So relax and have fun. Seeing that you are participating and learning will make your students even more eager to master their new language.

What are the goals of *Español para ti?*

By the end of Level 2, children will be able to

- understand more basic vocabulary and structures that are essential for everyday communication
- respond to simple questions and commands using words, phrases, and in some instances short sentences
- describe or demonstrate more customs from Spanish-speaking countries

For a complete list of the language and vocabulary taught at this level, see Topics and Language Covered on pages xxxvi–xlii of this Teacher's Manual.

In Level 2, there is continued emphasis on listening and speaking skills. Then in Level 3, the scope of *Español para ti* widens to include the Spanish alphabet and exploration of how different sounds are spelled. In Levels 4 and 5, children begin to read and write in Spanish.

"I speak a little bit of Spanish and I've learned a lot more with the children. We've both learned a lot from this experience with *Español para ti*. I've been using it now for four years and it's wonderful. The program is just wonderful."

–Tracy Wright,
Second grade teacher

"Learning a foreign language at a very young age can clearly benefit children's reading abilities, and hopefully parents and educators can help to provide resources for this to happen."

–Ellen Bialystok,
Psychologist

Teacher's Manual

Introduction to a Lesson

How do I use the materials provided?

The Teacher's Manual is your guide to the program. In it is a self-contained lesson plan for each of the video segments or lessons in *Español para ti*. Each lesson plan is made up of six pages.

The Lesson Opener

The first two pages of each lesson plan contain:

- a list of *Objectives* outlining the language, culture, and vocabulary that will be presented by the video teacher
- a list of *Materials to gather* that you will want to collect prior to watching the video or doing the activities with the children
- simple *Warm-up* and *Review* activities that you can do with the class to prepare them to watch the video
- a brief *Introduction to the video*

The Video Lesson

The next two pages of each lesson plan contain an outline of what occurs on the video. The interactions among the video teacher, the puppets, and their guests are described. The vocabulary, expressions, songs, stories, and cultural items with which children work are listed, explained, and translated into English.

The Activity Lesson

The final two pages of each lesson plan contain the Activity Lesson. Each Activity Lesson includes at least three activities that practice the content of the Video Lesson or review materials from earlier lessons. Many of the activities require the use of one of the three Activity Cassettes and/or the Song Cassette and are intended to provide additional opportunity for the children to practice listening, speaking, or singing in Spanish. Other materials required for doing an activity, such as crayons, pencils, or scissors, are listed at the beginning of the activity. The Blackline Masters and Number Cards used in certain activities are located in the Teacher's Resource Book and may be duplicated. Miniature reproductions of the Blackline Masters appear in the margin next to the activity where they are needed, so you always know exactly what to have on hand.

What do I do when?

Day 1: A Video Lesson

To prepare for a lesson, you might glance through the lesson plan for the Video Lesson. This will give you a quick overview of the content of the video. In addition, the notes in the margins give information and suggestions to help you introduce and follow up on the video more effectively.

Remember, in *Español para ti* you and the video teacher are team teaching. She teaches, models, and practices Spanish with the class. You facilitate instruction. In that role, it is important that you cue the videotape before gathering children to watch it. Have the class seated and quiet before beginning the video. Be sure everyone can see and hear. You may want to introduce a special seating arrangement for video watching to make the Spanish class a special experience.

View the video segment or lesson with the class and participate if possible. Repeat after the video teacher and have patience with your mistakes. These modeled behaviors show children that learning a language requires practice and that making mistakes is all right and a natural part of learning.

Monitor class reaction to the video. Is the class paying attention to **la maestra**? Are children following directions by repeating after her, answering questions, raising their hands? If most children do not seem to understand what is happening, stop the tape, discuss the problem, and then continue with the lesson.

Do some shy children seem hesitant to participate? Keep an eye on them to see if the problem persists. Sometimes a child is willing to speak if he or she uses a puppet. Also bear in mind that some children need to listen for a longer time before they start talking. Do not force a child to speak Spanish.

After viewing the video, you and the children may choose to discuss a particular part of the lesson. Perhaps it relates to something that they are learning in another content area. Perhaps a heritage speaker has something to share. The notes in the margins of the lesson plan offer cultural and cross-curricular information you may want to share with the class.

Day 2: An Activity Lesson

Each Activity Lesson contains at least three activities, numbered according to the lesson. The instruction for each activity contains:

- a list of materials needed to do the activity—Activity Cassette, Song Cassette, Blackline Master, Flashcards, crayons, etc.
- an explanation of any preparation that needs to be done in advance, such as duplicating and cutting out Blackline Masters or distributing crayons

Some activities are structured as games, others require the use of the Activity Cassette or Song Cassette, while still others are craft activities. Note that all materials related to an activity have the same number as the activity. For example, for Activity 1B, you will use Activity 1B on the Activity Cassette and Blackline Master 1B. In a few cases a Blackline Master may get reused later in the level. In that instance it will be labeled with its original number. A listing of the songs as they appear on the Song Cassette can be found on page xxiv.

To prepare for an Activity Lesson, read over the descriptions of the activities and gather any materials you need. You may want to preview the activities on the Activity Cassette before

> "The materials for *Español para ti* are excellent. I don't have to be a Spanish teacher to teach the program. All I need to do is to facilitate. All the materials are there for you. It's very, very good . . . very teacher friendly."
> –Yumi Arai,
> Fourth grade teacher

playing them for the children. (They are very short!) Describe the activity to the class before starting the tape. In this way, you can be sure that children understand the directions. The audio teacher will explain the activity in English, work through the activity in Spanish, and usually supply answers. Answers are provided as needed in the Teacher's Manual.

These activities practice vocabulary or concepts that have already been taught. By reading an activity's description and listening to the audio teacher, you can identify what is being practiced, even if you don't understand Spanish. Monitor the class's responses to the tape. Are children holding up the correct picture? Are they responding appropriately to commands? On the basis of your observations, decide if the class would benefit from repeating the activity or go on to another activity.

When choosing among the other activities, keep your observations in mind. What did the class do well? What might children need more practice with? What kinds of activities did your class particularly like to do? Learning is easier when the process is enjoyable!

Most Activity Lessons also include an optional activity called *If you have time . . .* if, indeed, you do have time left over in Spanish class. This activity follows the same format as the others.

Annotated sample lesson pages follow. These pages are from Level 1 and are taken from a variety of lessons.

ESPAÑOL PARA TI, Level Two

Lesson 5

Each lesson plan is numbered and consists of six pages. The first two pages list the Objectives *and the* Materials to gather, *and contain the* Warm-up, Review, *and* Introduce the video *activities.*

The Objectives *list goals of the lesson.*

Materials to gather

- VCR and Video Lesson 5 on Tape 2
- Cassette player
- Activity Cassette 1
- Song Cassette
- Hand puppet Rosco
- World map or globe
- Gold Flashcards 1 and 2
- Poster "**El salón de clase**" (*The classroom*)
- Blackline Master 5A (things/people found in the classroom)
- Blackline Master 5B (José and Rosita)
- Scissors, one pair per student
- Crayons
- Glue
- *Optional:* paper cutter

OBJECTIVES

Language

- Match the correct pictures to the words **maestra** (*female teacher*), **maestro** (*male teacher*), and **calendario** (*calendar*)
- Respond to the command **Toca** _____ (*Touch* _____)

Language—student behaviors that indicate comprehension of the language

Culture

- Sing "The Finger Play Song"

Culture—customs, body language, stories, and songs that are native to Spanish-speaking countries.

Review

- Sing "**Buenos días a ti**" ("*Good Morning to You*") and "**Buenas tardes a ti**" ("*Good Afternoon to You*")
- Ask and respond to the questions ¿**Cómo te llamas tú?** (*What is your name?*) and ¿**Cómo se llama?** (*What is his/her name?*)
- Recall that **la maestra** means *female teacher* and **el maestro** means *male teacher*
- Review the meaning of **Muéstrame** _____ (*Show me* _____), using classroom objects

Vocabulary

José es el amigo.	*José is the (male) friend.*
Rosita es la amiga.	*Rosita is the (female) friend.*
el calendario	*calendar*
Toca _____.	*Touch* _____.
el escritorio	*desk*

Review—previously learned language and culture concepts that are practiced again.

Vocabulary—new words and expressions that are presented in the lesson. Vocabulary from Level 1 is reintroduced in Level 2.

The list always begins with audiovisual materials. The part labeled Optional *names materials needed for the* If you have time . . . *activity, or lists materials that are not essential for an activity but would make it more enjoyable, such as a small bell or laminating machine.*

Teacher's Manual

In Level 2, this Warm-up includes practice with greetings, farewells, the opening conversation, songs, and questions and answers on various topics.

This icon stands for the Rosco flag, and it appears before any activity in which the Rosco flag is employed. One frequent use is to designate players in a game or other activity.

The puppets icon means that one or both of the hand puppets are used in this activity.

Warm-up

Greet the hand puppet Rosco with **Hola, Rosco** (*Hello, Rosco*). Have him respond to you with **Hola** and then to the class with **Hola, clase**. Encourage the children to say **Hola, Rosco**.

Review

Review some of the classroom objects by pointing to the objects in your classroom and asking the children what they are called in Spanish. Vocabulary practiced: **el calendario** (*calendar*), **el escritorio** (*desk*), **el globo** (*globe*), **el lápiz** (*pencil*), **la mesa** (*table*), **la pizarra** (*chalkboard*), **la regla** (*ruler*), **el reloj** (*clock*), **la silla** (*chair*), **la tiza** (*chalk*).

Introduce the video

Remind the children that in the last lesson they learned the names of some colors in Spanish. Introduce Video Lesson 16 by inviting children to listen, watch, and take part as **la maestra** and Ñico teach them the names of more colors.

FYI Although **rosado** is the standard word for *pink* in Spanish-speaking countries, **rosita** is an accepted regionalism in many parts of Mexico. There are many words for brown, but **café** is understood everywhere. If heritage speakers question the usage or pronunciation of a word taught in these lessons, tell them that they are fortunate to now know two ways of saying the same thing. The Spanish taught in these lessons is standard American Spanish—the vocabulary and pronunciation of all the Spanish-speaking countries except Spain.

This activity is a quick review of a topic or vocabulary from a previous lesson. The selected items are often used in the video for this lesson.

This section explains the focus of the up-coming Video Lesson. If relevant, there is also a description of how topics in this lesson are connected to material learned in previous lessons.

The letters *FYI* mean *For Your Information.* FYIs include additional information on the Spanish language or a cultural topic. These are included primarily for your own information. You may wish to share the information with the class.

ESPAÑOL PARA TI, Level Two

xvii

In the first activity, the video teacher and the puppet characters or the class usually say the opening conversation.

The Video Lesson is an outline of the video segment. The Video Lesson describes what occurs on the videotape and what is taught.

VIDEO LESSON

1. Greeting the children

La maestra has the opening conversation with Rosco, then with the children (**M** = Maestra, **R** = Rosco, **C** = class):

M: Buenos días, Rosco/clase.	Good morning, Rosco/class.
R/C: Buenos días, Maestra.	Good morning, Teacher.
M: ¿Cómo estás tú?	How are you?
R/C: Muy bien, gracias. ¿Y usted?	Very well/Fine, thank you. And you?
M: Muy bien, gracias.	Very well/Fine, thank you.

2. Reviewing numbers

La maestra and Rosco review the numbers 1 to 20.

Numbers 1 to 20:

1	uno	11	once
2	dos	12	doce
3	tres	13	trece
4	cuatro	14	catorce
5	cinco	15	quince
6	seis	16	dieciséis
7	siete	17	diecisiete
8	ocho	18	dieciocho
9	nueve	19	diecinueve
10	diez	20	veinte

The Spanish and English for previously taught vocabulary is provided in different ways, sometimes in the description of the segment and other times in a sidebar. In some instances, a cross-reference to such vocabulary may be made.

3. Discussing the number 20

La maestra and Rosco discuss different combinations of numbers: **diez y diez son veinte** (*ten and ten are twenty*); **cinco y cinco son diez** (*five and five are ten*); **diez y cinco son quince** (*ten and five are fifteen*); **quince y cinco son veinte** (*fifteen and five are twenty*).

4. Comparing *las banderas* (*flags*)

La maestra reminds the children that there are 20 Spanish-speaking countries. She and Rosco compare the colors of **la bandera de los Estados Unidos de América** (*the flag of the United States of America*) with those of **la bandera de Cuba** (*the flag of Cuba*), **la bandera de México** (*the flag of Mexico*), and **la bandera de Ecuador** (*the flag of Ecuador*).

HERITAGE SPEAKERS

If heritage speakers have brought in pictures of the flags of their countries, display them for the class and ask the heritage speakers to tell the class what country they come from and to name in Spanish the colors in their flags.

The flags of the U.S. and Cuba have the colors **rojo** (*red*), **blanco** (*white*), and **azul** (*blue*). The flag of Mexico is **rojo** (*red*), **blanco** (*white*), and **verde** (*green*). The flag of Ecuador is **amarillo** (*yellow*), **azul** (*blue*), and **rojo** (*red*).

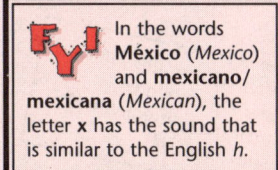

5. Reviewing questions

La maestra reviews two useful questions and responses for making friends:

¿Cómo te llamas tú?	What is your name?
Me llamo _____.	My name is _____.
¿Cómo se llama?	What is his/her name?
Se llama _____.	His/Her name is _____.

The video teacher presents and reviews several topics during a video. These changes in topic correspond to the numbered sections.

6. Playing a game

La maestra shows pictures of puppet characters (Rosco, Dora, Ñico, and Jorge) and asks the children **¿Cómo se llama?** (*What is his/her name?*). Children respond with **Se llama _____**.

FYI In the words **México** (*Mexico*) and **mexicano/mexicana** (*Mexican*), the letter **x** has the sound that is similar to the English *h*.

These sections contain suggestions for how to use to advantage the expertise of students who are native Spanish speakers. There are also suggestions for dealing with regional varieties of Spanish.

CROSS-CULTURAL CONNECTIONS

The information in *Cross-cultural connections* points out how people are alike and different. They offer opportunities to explore similarities and differences based upon what was learned on the video.

Teacher's Manual

xviii

A description of the context within which an activity is taking place is provided for your convenience in previewing and reviewing the lesson.

Both Spanish and English are provided for the reviewed vocabulary.

The checkmark icon points out a way to informally assess children's progress.

9. Introducing new words

La maestra introduces two new words for the classroom: **la regla** (*ruler*) and **la silla** (*chair*).

10. Playing *Muéstrame* _____ (*Show me* _____)

La maestra again plays **Muéstrame** _____ with the children, this time occasionally pointing to a picture and waiting for the children to name it. **La maestra** reviews the following vocabulary in the order given: **el calendario** (*calendar*), **la maestra** (*female teacher*), **el maestro** (*male teacher*), **el escritorio** (*desk*), **la mesa** (*table*), **el globo** (*globe*), **el lápiz** (*pencil*), **la pizarra** (*chalkboard*), **la silla** (*chair*), **la bandera** (*flag*), **la tiza** (*chalk*), **el libro** (*book*), **el reloj** (*clock*), **el mapa** (*map*), **la regla** (*ruler*), **la tiza** (*chalk*). (*Chalk* was mentioned twice.) After the game, Rosco says he feels **Muy bien** (*Very well*).

✓ Because in this activity the children are sometimes expected to reply without prompting, you have an ideal opportunity to gauge their progress in learning the classroom vocabulary.

11. Reviewing numbers 1 to 10

¡Vamos a contar! (*Let's count!*), says Rosco before helping **la maestra** count blocks forward and backward.

12. Singing a song

Rosco says eagerly, **¡Vamos a cantar!** (*Let's sing!*). **La maestra** leads the children in singing both verses of **"Uno, dos, tres niñitos"** ("*One, Two, Three Little Children*").

Uno, dos, tres niñitos,	One, two, three little children,
Cuatro, cinco, seis niñitos,	Four, five, six little children,
Siete, ocho, nueve niñitos,	Seven, eight, nine little children,
Diez niñitos son.	There are ten little children.
Diez, nueve, ocho niñitos,	Ten, nine, eight little children,
Siete, seis, cinco niñitos,	Seven, six, five little children,
Cuatro, tres, dos niñitos,	Four, three, two little children,
Un niñito es.	There is one little child.

Song lyrics are given in both Spanish and English.

LANGUAGE ACROSS THE CURRICULUM

Include counting in Spanish in physical education classes. For example, children can count the number of players on a team, the number of hops or jumps, the number of sit-ups, and so on.

These sections suggest ways to use Spanish in other subject areas and vice versa. The lessons in *Español para ti* are tied directly into many content areas, such as health, math, science, social studies, and career awareness. (See the list called Content-Based Topics on page xxxiv–xxxv of the Teacher's Manual for Level 2.)

13. Reviewing expressions for feelings

Using the face masks, **la maestra** and Rosco review the expressions **Muy bien** (*Very well*); **Así, así** (*So-so*); and **Muy mal** (*Very bad*).

14. Closing

La maestra and Rosco bid the children **Adiós** (*Good-bye*) and **Hasta luego** (*See you later*).

After viewing the video, praise the children for their good listening and watching skills.

Lesson Twelve

This section describes how the video teacher sums up the lesson and brings closure. Sometimes the summary includes the entire lesson. At other times the video teacher and the puppets just use various expressions to say good-bye. You may wish to end your own lesson in a similar manner.

Tipped boxes offer you teaching "tips" and instructional techniques for Spanish class.

ESPAÑOL PARA TI, Level Two

Blackline Masters are located in the Teacher's Resource Book. The number of the activity and the Blackline Master are usually the same. For example, Blackline Master 38A is to be used with Activity 38A. When a Blackline Master is used in a later activity, it retains the original number.

The Activity Lesson includes at least three activities and a closing. The activities mainly practice what was taught in the Video Lesson and often review topics from previous lessons. Sometimes activities are based on the Activity Cassettes and/or the Song Cassette. Sometimes there are art activities and optional activities called *If you have time . . . .*

228

ACTIVITY LESSON

Activity 38A: Make a balloon bouquet

Materials: Cassette player; Activity Cassette 2, Side A; Blackline Master 38A, one per child; pink, yellow, red, orange, brown, blue, purple, black, and green crayons for each child.

Preparation: Give each child a copy of Blackline Master 38A and the nine crayons.

Point out that each balloon on Blackline Master 38A has a number on it. **La maestra** will say a number and a color twice. The children should color the balloons according to these directions. Assure the children that they simply need to color part of the balloon in the time given. They can color the rest of the balloons after the tape has stopped.

All the materials needed for an activity are listed. If any advance preparation is required, it is also explained.

Blackline Master 38A

Answers to Activity 38A:

(21) pink   (22) yellow
(23) red   (24) orange
(25) black (26) brown
(27) blue   (28) purple
(29) black (30) green

When the children talk about the answers to this activity, a colored overhead transparency of this page would make the discussion easier.

Activity 38B: Act out feelings

Materials: Cassette player; Activity Cassette 2,

You may want to have children sit in a circle for this Tell the children that they are going to pretend to fe ways. When **la maestra** states a feeling, they should The feelings are stated in the following order: **Tengo** (*I'm hungry*), **Tengo sed** (*I'm thirsty*), **Tengo calor** (*I'm Tengo frío* (*I'm cold*).

The activity number in the Teacher's Manual matches the number of the activity on the tape. Activity 38B uses audio Activity 38B, which is on Activity Cassette 2, Side A.

Activity 38C: Sing about the ranc

Materials: Cassette player; "**Vengan a ver** ("*Come See My Ranch*") on the Song Cassette; G 20-22 and 24-27.

Turn the Gold Flashcards facedown. Explain to t that they are going to sing "**Vengan a ver mi ra** *See My Ranch*") with **la maestra**. Ask for seven v the volunteers to each take a Flashcard and to k hidden. Ask them to line up in front of the class. In the song, the animals are named in this order: cat, dog, cow, chicken, rooster, horse, pig. When the class comes to the part of the song that names an animal, the child with that Flashcard should step forward and show it to everyone. For the song lyrics, see Lesson 36, Activity 36C.

A cassette player and the Song Cassette are used with this activity. A listing of the songs as they appear on the Song Cassette can be found on page xxiv.

There is a summary of the activity on the Activity Cassette.

EN ESPAÑOL

In several lessons, you have heard **la maestra** say, **Te toca a ti** (*It's your turn*) to Rosco or Dora. Rosco often excitedly insists, **Me toca a mí** (*It's my turn*). If you feel comfortable with these expressions, try to incorporate them into daily activities and games.

The video teacher and the puppets sometimes say Spanish words and expressions that are frequently used in daily life but are not part of the core vocabulary. **En español** sidebars point out these expressions so that you may use them yourself if you feel comfortable doing so.

This kind of activity may include ideas for practicing a song or for using a song in a different way.

LEVEL ONE

The audio teacher usually supplies answers for the Activity Cassettes directly on the cassettes. Occasionally she does not. In such cases, the answers are provided in the lesson plan of the Teacher's Manual.

The cassette icon indicates that a cassette player and an Activity Cassette are needed for this activity.

Teacher's Manual

This section helps you bring closure to the lesson. It also provides you with information to preview the next lesson for the class. There may also be a short activity, such as the closing conversation.

The hourglass points out that *If you have time . . .* is an optional activity.

CLOSING

Tell the children that Spanish class is finished for today. Next time the children will learn more weather expressions and sing some songs they know. Put on the hand puppet Dora and ask the children what kind of animal Dora is (a cow) and what the word is in Spanish (**la vaca**). Then hold the good-bye conversation with the hand puppet Dora and the class (D = Dora, C = class):

D: Adiós, clase.   *Good-bye, class.*
C: Adiós, Dora.   *Good-bye, Dora.*

FAMILY CONNECTION

To foster a friendly link between home and school, you may want to send home Family Letter 3 found in the Teacher's Resource Book. The letter informs parents about what their children are learning in Spanish and suggests enrichment and practice activities.

There are four Family Connection letters. This section reminds you to send them home after Lessons 1, 22, 44, and 66, if you wish to do so. The letters are located in the Teacher's Resource Book.

IF YOU HAVE TIME . . .

Materials: Gold Flashcards 41–43.

Put the Flashcards facedown where everyone can see them. Ask a volunteer to choose a Flashcard and tell what the weather is like—in Spanish preferably, but English is fine. Then have the child tell in Spanish how he or she feels. If the volunteer did not know the weather expression, allow classmates to state it once the volunteer has finished. Continue in the same way until all the Flashcards are turned over. You may want to repeat this activity several times. Flashcard 41: **Hace calor** (*It's hot*) and **Hace sol** (*It's sunny*) / **Tengo calor** (*I'm hot*); Flashcard 42: **Hace frío** (*It's cold*) / **Tengo frío** (*I'm cold*); Flashcard 43: **Hace buen tiempo** (*It's good weather*) / **Estoy muy bien** (*I'm very well/fine*).

Any needed materials and advance preparation are described here. The materials necessary for this activity are also listed under the *Optional* section in *Materials to gather* in the Lesson Opener.

These optional activities always practice and/or review previously introduced materials.

Lesson Forty-Four

This icon points out activities in which children make and use art to learn Spanish.

ESPAÑOL PARA TI, Level Two

Audiovisual Techniques

Video Viewing Strategies

For the teacher:

- Before watching a video segment or lesson with the class, we encourage you to read through the corresponding Lesson in the Teacher's Manual (that is, the *Objectives,* the *Video Lesson,* and the *Activity Lesson*). This preview will provide you with the goals and content of the lesson.
- Cue the video lesson before seating the class in front of the television.
- During the video lesson, take an active part along with your class. Your example encourages children to participate.
- Once in a while, the video teacher is going to ask you to facilitate an activity for her. Whether this request involves handing the Rosco flag to a child you select to participate or something else, you will want to have any necessary materials available beforehand. **La maestra** moves quickly through the lesson, and you don't want to be left behind!
- In the first lesson, the video teacher introduces hand gestures to signal children when to listen and when to respond. Throughout the lessons, she gives the "respond" signal and allows time for students to answer. However, **la maestra** sometimes asks a question without indicating what the children should do. If she pauses, encourage the students to answer. However, try to train the children not to speak while **la maestra** is talking because they will miss important information.
- In some lessons, visitors read picture-book stories to the children. The stories are intentionally a mixture of known and unknown vocabulary. Before children hear a story, reassure them by telling them they won't understand everything. Explain that every story is repeated later in the year and they'll be surprised at how much more they understand then.

  Listen to the story along with the class. Your reaction is important since children may take their cue from you. If you are learning Spanish, you are going to experience some frustration. Show some, but try not to overreact. Be pleased at what you do understand. After the video, do some sharing and mutual "wondering" with the class.
- Congratulate the children on their good watching, listening, and participatory skills.

For the children:

- Tell the children that the video takes fifteen minutes.
- Ask them if they are seated so that they can see and hear the video clearly.

Teacher's Manual

- Tell them to listen and watch closely, imitating and responding to the video teacher as she indicates. Tell them they will discover they can mimic new sounds and use them and that they may want to use Spanish in real-life situations.

Activity Cassette Strategies

For the teacher:

- The cassette activities are extremely important because they provide needed practice in hearing and speaking Spanish. The tapes practice material that has already been introduced. Spanish, like math and handwriting, requires practice for mastery. Please use each activity at least once. If possible, repeat it so that many children have the opportunity to participate.
- Read the description of the activity before playing the cassette for the class. This description lists all needed materials and any required advance preparations. It also includes the goals and content of the activity.
- If possible, listen to cassette activities before your class does. They are very short.
- Have all the needed/prepared materials at hand before gathering the class to take part in an activity. Sometimes the audio teacher is going to ask you to facilitate an activity for her. Be prepared to move quickly.
- Cue the Activity Cassette to the appropriate activity before gathering the class to take part in it.
- Describe the tape activity to your class before turning on the tape. With this preview, children are prepared for the audio teacher's description. She will practice the activity with the class before asking them to participate.
- During the tape activity, you may want to take an active part. By all means do so, especially if you are learning Spanish along with the class. Your example encourages children to participate. At other times, you may simply want to observe. Watching the children's physical and verbal reactions provides you with valuable information about how well they understand and can perform the relevant skills.
- If children are having difficulty doing an exercise, stop the tape and discuss what the problem is. Sometimes the class may not understand the directions or may not understand the concept in English. Giving children a point of reference, such as where the class/the video teacher did the same kind of activity on the video, is often helpful. Be sure to explain that the tape activities are for practice. Children are not expected to get everything right the first time nor all the time.
- In some cassette activities, the audio teacher may make a request or ask a question and a harp-like sound will follow. Please pause the tape at the sound of the harp to allow children time to respond. Then continue the activity.

Children may enjoy playing this role once they understand the harp's function.

- Usually the audio teacher provides an immediate reply to each exercise. Emphasize that children should pay attention to her answers. Once in a while you are going to give them the answers. They are listed for you in the Teacher's Manual.
- Congratulate the children on using the relevant skills for a particular activity—watching, listening, and/or speaking.
- For activities that require the children to color objects in specific colors, have them color only a piece of the object (fish, puppet, or piece of clothing) while the tape is running. Afterwards they can finish coloring their activity sheet.

For the children:

- Tell the children to follow the directions.
- Let them know that sometimes the audio teacher is going to ask them something and then they will hear a short musical sound. They need to say their answer then.
- Usually they are going to hear the correct answers on the tape. It is very, very important to listen carefully and check their answers against the teacher's. This checking is an extra chance to practice their Spanish.

Song Cassette Strategies

For the teacher:

- Before having children do an activity that includes the Song Cassette, read the description in the Activity Lesson. This description lists all needed materials and any required advance preparations. It also includes the goals and content of the activity.
- Have all the needed/prepared materials on hand before gathering the class to take part in the song activity. Sometimes children need to make props or take out previously made materials before singing a song.
- Cue the cassette to the appropriate song before gathering the class to sing it. In a few instances this is only partly possible because there is more than one song in an activity. A listing of the songs as they appear on the Song Cassette can be found on page xxiv.
- Children will have heard, and usually practiced, all or part of a song before they practice it with the cassette. Depending on the length of a song or the portion that you are practicing, play it at least once or twice before inviting the children to join in.
- As you know, children love to sing, and these songs are fun. Initially children may be able to sing only a few words here and there. Let them know that's all right. The more often the children hear the tape and watch the videos, the more they are going to pick up.

Teacher's Manual

- Depending on the length and complexity of a song, you may want to practice a few lines or a stanza with the tape until the class can sing most of it so they have a sense of accomplishment. Then go on to the next part. The songs are lively and fun and singing them should always be fun.
- Sing along with the class. Your example encourages children to participate. It doesn't matter if you make a mistake or two. At other times, you may simply want to observe. Watching and listening provides you with valuable information about how well children know and understand the song.

For the children:

- Tell the children to sing as much of a song as they can. Practicing helps them learn more.
- Have them act out the words as they are singing or listening to the tape. That will help them remember the words.
- Have them ask you to replay the particular parts of a song, so they learn the words or music better.

Song Cassette Contents:

SIDE A
"Español para ti" ("*Spanish Is for You, and for Me*") (short version)
"Uno de enero" ("*January First*")
"Buenos días a ti" ("*Good Morning to You*")
"Buenas tardes a ti" ("*Good Afternoon to You*")
"Buenas noches a ti" ("*Good Evening to You*")
"Months Rap"
"The Finger Play Song"
"Calendar Rap"
"Uno, dos, tres niñitos" ("*One, Two, Three Little Children*")
"La ropa" ("*Clothing*")
"Las estaciones" ("*The Seasons*")
"Uno, dos, tres burritos" ("*One, Two, Three Little Donkeys*")
"Vengan a ver mi rancho" ("*Come See My Ranch*")
"Vamos a contar" ("*Let's Count*")
"Dulce canta el burro" ("*Sweetly Sings the Donkey*")
"Las vocales" ("*The Vowels*")
"Ojos, orejas, boca, nariz" ("*Eyes, Ears, Mouth, Nose*")
"Manos, dedos, piernas, pies" ("*Hands, Fingers, Legs, Feet*")
"El picnic" ("*The Picnic*")
"Fray Felipe" ("*Friar Phillip*")
"Español para ti" ("*Spanish Is for You, and for Me*") (long version)
"Let's March #1"
"Let's March #2"

SIDE B
Midyear Assessments
End-of-Year Assessments

ESPAÑOL PARA TI, Level Two

Timing, Pacing, and Articulation

How much time does it take?

The *Español para ti* program consists of five levels—one level per school year. Levels 1 and 2 have 66 lessons each and Levels 3 to 5 have 60 lessons each. Level 2 provides for two 15-minute Video Lessons and two 15-minute Activity Lessons per week. It is possible to teach two complete lessons in one hour!

The Video Lessons are imaginative and fun and have a variety of activities and experiences that will appeal to every learning style. Depending on the interests of the children in your class, you may not wish to do all of the activities provided in an Activity Lesson. When working through an Activity Lesson, however, the exercises on the Activity Cassette should take priority so that the children are given as much opportunity as possible to hear and react to the language.

As you would expect, the instruction at each level builds on what was taught in earlier levels. For example, children learn the numbers 1 to 50 in Level 1. In Level 2, children review the numbers 1 to 50 and then learn 51 to 100. But since learning a language, like learning math, requires much repeated practice, instruction within each level is also spiraled—topics are repeatedly reviewed and integrated with new content. Consider the vocabulary for rooms or places in the school, such as *the classroom, the library,* and *the playground:* in the Video lessons for Level 2, six places in the school are introduced in Lesson 13 with a tour of a school. They are reviewed in Lessons 14 and 15, then reviewed and expanded in Lesson 21. They are reviewed again by means of games and other activities in Lessons 22, 23, and 24, then connected to the names of school personnel in Lesson 32. They get reintroduced in Lesson 41, then reviewed one last time in Lesson 65. These words are also practiced in several Warm-ups, and lesson activities.

What do I do with children who join the class later in the year?

Spiraling helps the entire class learn Spanish, but it also addresses another issue—what to do with children who join the class later in the year. Such a child may have some difficulty at first, but spiraling, with its continual reviewing, helps a great deal. *Español para ti* provides many opportunities for children to catch up. In addition, the video teacher (**la maestra**) uses pictures, objects, and body language to demonstrate and reinforce the meaning of Spanish words and expressions as she reviews. Whether the videos and Activity Cassettes are in the classroom or in the media center, they provide a team teacher who can present any part of the program before school, after school, during recess, or during those times when children self-select activities. In addition, parents can check out videos from the classroom or media center and help children to catch up at

---

"I really enjoy the videos. They're very organized . . . structured well, so it's easy to put them in a video machine and get them started. I really love the music tapes. They're wonderful. The children enjoy singing the music. And the interactive activity sheets are delightful. The children do a lot with them."

–Jeffrey Hybarger,
First grade teacher

"As a first generation Hispanic who does not speak my native language, Spanish, I am glad to know that my children have the opportunity to learn a foreign language in the elementary school."

–A parent

home. Since the video teacher employs the same Flashcards as are provided for you in the Visuals Package, newcomers may use them to practice vocabulary with classmates.

Where do children go after *Español para ti?*

The programs *¡Hola!* (*Hello!*), *¿Qué tal?* (*What's Happening?*), and *¡Adelante!* (*Onward!*) lead students from *Español para ti* through to a first year high-school proficiency in Spanish. *¡Hola!* provides a multi-level approach to Spanish. It may be used both with students who have completed *Español para ti* and with those who have no knowledge of Spanish. *¡Hola!* begins with the world of the student at school and spirals out to the family. While using *¿Qué tal?* and *¡Adelante!*, students continue to extend their Spanish listening, speaking, reading, and writing skills. In *¿Qué tal?* students focus first on home life and gradually expand their focus to the community. *¡Adelante!* explores the world in general. The use of *¿Qué tal?* and *¡Adelante!* over a two-year period provides students with the opportunity for repeated language practice in a variety of situations, a critical factor in language acquisition.

Integrating Spanish with the Curriculum

Why should I spend precious time teaching Spanish?

As was pointed out earlier, *Español para ti* requires only one hour of instruction a week. Moreover, the program is not an add-on to your curriculum; the lessons are tied in directly to other content areas. Spanish becomes an integral part of the curriculum, reinforcing and adding new dimensions to what is already being taught. Math, science, social studies, health, and career awareness are all woven into the lessons of *Español para ti.* During the course of the year, for example, your class is going to learn the numbers 1 to 100 in Spanish. Among other mathematical strategies, the video teacher is going to use children's knowledge of how to count; how to add; and how to count by twos, fives, and tens to introduce and practice numbers from 1 to 100. As a result the class is going to have more practice in number order and addition in Spanish class.

Before the children actually read Spanish in Level 3 of *Español para ti*, they are going to hear and discuss stories told in Spanish. Since the tales are in picture-book format and involve both known and unknown vocabulary, children will use context and pictures to help determine meaning—strategies they also employ while learning to read in English. (For specifics regarding the correlation between Spanish and other content areas, see the Content-Based Topics listed on pages xxxiv–xxxv.)

Since the Video Lesson and Activity Lesson take only 15 minutes each and provide review in each lesson, *Español para ti* is also suitable for use in Spanish language enrichment courses that meet before or after school as infrequently as once per week.

How much preparation time does *Español para ti* require?

Very little. The Teacher's Resource Book has all the reproducible Blackline Masters that teachers need for the student activities, as well as assessment pages. Prior to showing Lesson 1, we suggest that you laminate frequently handled items such as the Number Cards (found in the Teacher's Resource Book), so that they have a longer life. We also suggest that you make the Rosco flag right away as it will be used frequently throughout the program for classroom management (see Lesson 4, page 21). There are some props, such as feeling masks and a "rap roll" that each child makes and reuses throughout the year. It is helpful to designate some permanent place where you or children may keep these items.

Since the *Warm-up* and *Review* are done prior to the Video Lesson, you may sometimes need to gather program components, such as Flashcards or Number Cards, for these

> "Children, by starting second language study early, advance in the development of an intelligent understanding of language concepts, which will help in learning additional languages."
> –Gladys C. Lipton, Educator

> "The *Español para ti* materials are very easy to use. They are all laid out for you. Where you leave off one day, you pick up the next day. And it's ready to go every day."
> –Tracy Wright, Second grade teacher

Teacher's Manual

activities. It is also helpful to cue the videotape before it is time for the lesson.

The Activity Lessons often require gathering one or more program components, such as an Activity Cassette and/or the Song Cassette, cueing an audiovisual component before class begins, and copying Blackline Masters for the class. Occasionally an activity may need additional craft supplies. Materials you need to assemble prior to doing an activity are outlined in the "Materials" and "Preparation" sections of the activity and in the "Prepare ahead" section in some of the lessons.

Assessment

How can I tell how my class is doing when I don't speak Spanish?

For a start, you're watching the same video as your class. If most children are watching the video, repeating when asked, and answering questions without hesitation, you can assume that everything is going all right. Perhaps it's the other times you're wondering about, and for those, we offer the following suggestions.

- Whenever the video teacher asks the children a question, she allows time for them to respond, and then she or one of the puppets answers it. She wants children to know what the right answer is. Compare her answer with theirs.
- What if most children do not answer a question or answer incorrectly? Frequently the same question is immediately asked again or within a couple of minutes. Watch if more children attempt to answer or answer correctly the next time. Learning a language, like learning math facts, requires practice. Watch for cumulative improvement rather than perfection.
- Follow the video teacher's lead. If something is difficult, she often reassures children that they are going to have many opportunities to practice it. Don't worry.
- It is just as possible to have a bad Spanish day as it is to have a bad hair day. If most children are not involved in a video or a cassette activity, stop the tape and find out what the problem is. Sometimes children are not paying attention at the beginning, and as the lesson becomes more complicated, they cannot continue because they've missed a key element. Perhaps the children are having difficulty with a concept instead of the language. Pinpointing the problem enables the class to finish the lesson.
- If the class is singing, notice if the children have learned more of the lyrics or melody than the last time they sang the song.
- Ask small groups or pairs to sing a song or demonstrate an activity.
- As children play games, check that they are following directions and using Spanish words or phrases.
- After the video teacher has taught multiple answers to a question, check if children are using any of the newer responses.
- Note individual and/or group responses to cassette activities.
- When the video teacher stresses similarities or differences between pairs of words, listen for the accuracy of children's responses.
- From time to time, ask children to explain why their answers are correct.

> "I tell them all the time, 'This is new to me too, so I'm learning right with you.'"
> –Laura Schumacher, First grade teacher

> "When we first started the program, I think teachers were a bit nervous because they did not speak Spanish. But as they were in-serviced into the program, they saw the ease of working with the videos that were already done for them and when they actually used them in the classroom with the children and saw the enthusiasm of the children, I felt that they became quite confident."
> –Nadine Nielsen, Principal

Teacher's Manual

- Make a copy of the rubric for holistic assessment (in the Teacher's Resource Book) for each child. You might want to complete the rubric for each child while they are watching a Video Lesson, or you may wish to observe them while they watch a Video Lesson and take part in an Activity Lesson and complete the rubric at a later time. The rubric is designed to be used at any time and as often as you feel necessary throughout the year.

What can I use for formal assessments?

Español para ti, Level 2, provides two formal assessments—one for the midyear and one for the end of the year. The directions and questions for each exam are located at the end of Activity Cassette 2, Side B, and the reproducible student assessment pages are in the Teacher's Resource Book. Children are going to follow **la maestra**'s and doña Elena's directions and mark their answers on the Blackline Masters. You can give the first exam after Lesson 33 and the final exam after Lesson 66.

If you need frequent formal assessments so that you can give grades, reuse activities on Activity Cassettes 1, 2, and 3 with their accompanying Blackline Masters.

FAMILY AND COMMUNITY

Parents, guardians, and other members of the community can play a vital role in motivating children to learn and use Spanish, and in reinforcing the value of learning about and understanding other cultures.

Laying the groundwork for support and participation starts with communication. It is very important to begin the school year by sharing the goals of the Spanish program with parents and guardians and by explaining how parents and guardians may assist their children. Use the Introduction to the Program (pages ix–xi) and Video Lessons as resources to explain to families the reasons for teaching Spanish at this grade and the methods that are being used.

In the Teacher's Resource Book, there are four letters that you may want to send home during the school year. Family Letter 1 introduces the year, what children will do, and encourages caretakers to ask—but not pressure—children to share with them what they're learning. Family Letter 2 updates families on what children have been learning and will be doing next. Family Letter 3 suggests ways that caretakers may help children practice what they are learning in Spanish with similar topics in English, e.g., songs that exist in both English and Spanish. Family Letter 4 stresses the large amount of Spanish that children have learned over the year and suggests ways to help them maintain their language skills over the summer.

Within the school, parents can also do many things to encourage interest in Spanish.

- Talk to the class about experiences (trips and/or jobs) in Spanish-speaking cultures.
- Speak to the children in Spanish.
- Share foods, videos or audiotapes, and souvenirs or gifts from Spanish-speaking countries.
- Help with the decorations, food, or clean-up during a Spanish-related event.

Many people are willing to visit classes and/or participate in school events. Drawing on people from the community unites all participants in a shared experience. Consider the following possibilities:

- Community service: paramedic, librarian, police officer, firefighter, postal worker
- Recreation: athlete, disc jockey, travel agent
- Health: exercise instructor, nurse or nurse's aide, physician, dietitian, pharmacist
- Science: florist, conservationist, programmer, scientist
- Labor: construction worker, custodian, mechanic, painter
- Other: baker, banker, musician, photographer, secretary, television or radio personality, reporter

> "The children go home and speak Spanish with their parents. The parents love the fact that their children are learning a second language."
> –Tracy Wright,
> Second grade teacher

Teacher's Manual

Which of these people might be volunteers for your children as they investigate topics such as "What do our community workers do?"; "What do plants need in order to live?"; and "How do you make bread?" What is fascinating is that language does not live in a vacuum! Language is always being used by someone for something. Any of these individuals may also be native speakers of Spanish who would be willing to talk to your children about what they do, how they use Spanish on the job, or even about non-work-related topics, such as family life and schools in other countries. An enthusiastic class-written thank-you note, and perhaps some drawings of the event, earns goodwill for the school and the program.

So far the discussion has centered on people and events in the classroom, but don't forget field trips, which are valuable experiences in the real world. Does your class want to see what happens behind the scenes at a television station or to know how a gift shop owner knows what to order? Anywhere you take your class—to a bank, a hospital, or a grocery store—you or someone else may possibly make a connection to a language other than English. Each time this connection occurs, it shows the value of learning another language.

HERITAGE SPEAKERS

This section contains ideas for enriching the course with the experiences of children whose native language is Spanish. The language and customs of Spanish speakers are particularly relevant to this course, but heritage speakers of other languages offer children unique opportunities to hear about how various cultural groups deal with daily needs, relationships, and important events. If speakers of Spanish question the usage or pronunciation of a word or expression, tell them that they are fortunate to now know two ways of saying the same thing. The Spanish taught here is standard American Spanish—the vocabulary and pronunciation of all the Spanish-speaking countries except Spain. The following list suggests guidelines for drawing on the expertise of heritage speakers in your class.

- Some children are proud of their non-English background and are glad to share information about their birth countries and native languages. Other children may feel sensitive about "being different." Invite children to share their experiences, but don't single them out too often.

- Ask for help with pronunciation, as needed. Keep in mind that children from different countries may have slightly different pronunciations.

- During the year, the children are going to discuss some specific areas where Spanish is spoken. Children from these locations might tell what they know about them. If necessary, point out that these comments only partly describe what these places are like.

- *Español para ti* treats many topics related to daily life—family members, colors, greetings, birthdays, clothing, seasons, weather, numbers, and so forth. The course also includes vocabulary and scenes related to transportation and animals—but all within an American context. Encourage non-English speakers to compare these topics and locations with those in their birth countries.

- Songs and stories are an integral part of *Español para ti.* Invite heritage speakers to share the same or comparable ones from their cultures.

- In the lessons that involve reading stories, allow heritage speakers to explain maybe one or two parts that everyone is curious about. Perhaps they might teach the class a couple of words or expressions. Do *not* have them translate the whole story!

Try to include adult heritage speakers as classroom visitors. They bring a wider perspective and often have surprising experiences in the United States that point out cultural similarities and differences with their countries of origin. While it's not likely that you'll have bullfighters or **vaqueros** (*cowboys*) as guests, children also enjoy learning about the kinds of work adults have done and are doing. In addition, children simply enjoy hearing stories about when adults were themselves young children.

> "*Español para ti* has, I think, brought cultural joy into the classroom. It's given the children an opportunity to see another culture, to hear the language, to hear the celebrations.
>
> –Jeffrey Hybarger, First grade teacher

Teacher's Manual

Content-Based Topics

Art

Draw with various media
Cut and paste
Observe art works

Language arts

Demonstrate characteristics of a good listener
Follow a one-step oral direction
Compare and contrast sounds
Recall presented material
Identify a purpose for listening
Listen for a variety of purposes
Activate prior knowledge
Describe objects/pictures
Communicate in complete sentences
Obtain information by asking questions
Participate in various forms of oral communication
Interact verbally in informal situations
Make introductions
Listen to different types of literature
Expand vocabulary
Recall sequence of events
Identify/Restate details
Respond to different types of literature
Demonstrate an active interest in reading

Mathematics

Sort objects in a variety of ways
Recognize/Develop patterns
Reason/Connect mathematical understandings
Observe/Compare by measurable attributes
Count objects
Represent quantities
Model number composition
Investigate number relationships
Develop numeration concepts

Music

Explore differences between speaking and singing
Sing songs in a limited range
Perform a repertoire of songs

Reading

Identify/Form plurals

ESPAÑOL PARA TI, Level Two

Science

Observe weather conditions
Explore the effects of weather
Observe the life cycle of animals
Construct criteria for classifying animals
Observe the interaction between living things/environment
Infer that living things have changed over time

Social Studies

Identify self by name and birthday
Recognize similarities between self and others
Describe personal feelings
Demonstrate the relationship of feelings to actions
Demonstrate an understanding of the concept of rule
Demonstrate courteous behavior when interacting
Apply appropriate personal decision-making skills
Recognize the importance of each individual to the group
Evaluate the consequences of decisions
Determine reasons why communities require laws
Define earth as being made up of land and water
Be introduced to other people and places
Recognize human needs
Define family in various ways
State how people are more alike than different
Evaluate the exchange of ideas between cultures
Describe the relationship of the United States to other countries
Identify features which make a culture unique
Recognize the different kinds of people in the United States

Topics and Language Covered

These lists show only those items that the children practice, not the many others that the video teacher (**la maestra**) introduces as enrichment and to develop children's listening and comprehension skills. The English equivalents are what an English-speaking person would ordinarily say in a comparable situation. They are not word-for-word translations.

The topics listed below are introduced in Level 2. Within each topic, words and expressions are usually in alphabetical order. Some sections are divided into Vocabulary items and functional expressions in the form of questions and answers.

Greetings, farewells, introductions

Vocabulary

Adiós.	Good-bye.		
Buenas noches.	Good evening.		
Buenas tardes.	Good afternoon.		
Buenos días.	Good morning.		
Hasta la vista.	Until we meet again.		
Hasta luego.	See you later.		
Hasta mañana.	Until tomorrow.		
Hola.	Hello./Hi.		

Asking about names

¿Cómo te llamas (tú)?	What is your name (informal)?
¿Cómo se llama usted?	What is your name (formal)?
Me llamo ___.	My name is ___.
¿Cómo se llama?	What is his/her name?
Se llama ___.	His/Her name is ___.

Expressions of feeling

Vocabulary

Así, así.	So-so.
Muy bien.	Fine/Very well.
Muy mal.	Very bad.

Asking about feelings

¿Cómo estás (tú)?	How are you?
¿Y tú?	And you?
¿Y usted?	And you (formal)?
Estoy contento/contenta.	I am happy.
Estoy enojado/enojada.	I am angry.
Estoy triste.	I am sad.
Tengo calor.	I'm hot.
Tengo dolor.	I'm hurt.
Tengo frío.	I'm cold.
Tengo hambre.	I'm hungry.
Tengo miedo.	I'm afraid.
Tengo sed.	I'm thirsty.
Tengo sueño.	I'm sleepy.

Age-related expressions

el cumpleaños	birthday
¿Cuándo es tu cumpleaños?	When is your birthday?
¿Cuántos años tienes (tú)?	How old are you?
Tengo ___ años.	I'm ___ years old.

ESPAÑOL PARA TI, Level Two

Classroom objects

Vocabulary

la bandera	*flag*
los bolígrafos	
(los bolis)	*pens*
el calendario	*calendar*
los colores	*crayons*
el cuaderno	*notebook*
el escritorio	*desk*
la goma	*eraser*
las gomas	*erasers*
el globo	*globe*
el lápiz	*pencil*
los lápices	*pencils*
el libro	*book*
los libros	*books*
el mapa	*map*
la mesa	*table*
la mochila	*book bag, backpack*
el papel	*paper*
los papeles	*papers*
la pizarra	*chalkboard*
la regla	*ruler*
el reloj	*clock*
el sacapuntas	*pencil sharpener*
la silla	*chair*
las tijeras	*scissors*
la tiza	*chalk*

Asking about a person or object

¿Qué es?	*What is it?*
¿Qué es esto?	*What is this?*
¿Qué son?	*What are they?*
¿Es ___ o es ___?	*Is it ___ or is it ___?*
Es ___.	*It is ___.*
¿Dónde está ___?	*Where is ___?*
Aquí está(n) ___.	*Here is (are) ___.*
¿Estas listo/a?	*Are you ready?*
¿Necesitas ___?	*Do you need ___?*
Necesito ___.	*I need ___.*
¿Qué tienes?	*What do you have?*
Tengo ___.	*I have ___.*
No tengo ___.	*I don't have ___.*
¿Cuál falta?	*What's missing?*

Rooms in the school

el baño	*bathroom*
la biblioteca	*library*
la cafetería	*cafeteria*
la clase	*classroom*
la clase de español	*Spanish class*
la oficina	*office*
el patio	*playground*

School personnel

la directora	*(female) principal*
el director	*(male) principal*
la enfermera	*(female) nurse*
el enfermero	*(male) nurse*
la maestra	*(female) teacher*
el maestro	*(male) teacher*
la secretaria	*(female) secretary*
el secretario	*(male) secretary*

Teacher's Manual

Positive commands

Anda.	*Walk.*
Busca ___.	*Look for, search for ___.*
Colorea.	*Color.*
Corre.	*Run.*
Cuenta.	*Count.*
Dame ___.	*Give me ___.*
Dale ___.	*Give him/her ___.*
Muéstrame ___.	*Show me ___.*
Párate.	*Stand up.*
Pon.	*Put.*
Salta.	*Jump.*
Siéntate.	*Sit down.*
Toca ___.	*Touch ___.*

Negative commands

¡No andes!	*Don't walk!*
¡No corras!	*Don't run!*
¡No saltes!	*Don't jump!*
¡No toques!	*Don't touch!*

Colors
Vocabulary

amarillo	*yellow*
anaranjado	*orange*
azul	*blue*
blanco	*white*
café	*brown*
gris	*gray*
morado	*purple*
negro	*black*
rojo	*red*
rosado	*pink*
verde	*green*

Asking about colors

¿De qué color es ___?	*What color is ___?*
Es de color ___.	*It is ___.*
Es ___.	*It is (the color) ___.*
¿De qué color son ___?	*What color are ___?*
Son (de color) ___.	*They are ___.*

Days of the week[1]
Vocabulary

lunes	*Monday*
martes	*Tuesday*
miércoles	*Wednesday*
jueves	*Thursday*
viernes	*Friday*
sábado	*Saturday*
domingo	*Sunday*

---

[1] Given in calendar order for Spanish-speaking countries.

ESPAÑOL PARA TI, Level Two

Months
Vocabulary

enero	*January*
febrero	*February*
marzo	*March*
abril	*April*
mayo	*May*
junio	*June*
julio	*July*
agosto	*August*
septiembre	*September*
octubre	*October*
noviembre	*November*
diciembre	*December*

Asking about the date, month, and day of the week

¿Cuál es la fecha?	*What is the date?*
¿Qué día es?	*What day of the week is it?*
¿Qué mes es?	*What month is it?*
Es ___.	*It is ___.*

Seasons of the year
Vocabulary

el invierno	*winter*
la primavera	*spring*
el verano	*summer*
el otoño	*autumn, fall*

Asking about the seasons

¿Qué estación es?	*What season is it?*
Es ___.	*It is ___.*

Weather expressions
Vocabulary

Hace buen tiempo.	*It's good weather.*
Hace mal tiempo.	*It's bad weather.*
Hace calor.	*It's hot.*
Hace frío.	*It's cold.*
Hace sol.	*It's sunny.*
Hace viento.	*It's windy.*
Llueve.	*It's raining.*
Nieva.	*It's snowing.*

Asking about the weather

¿Qué tiempo hace?	*What's the weather like?*
¿Qué tiempo hace en ___?	*What is the weather like in ___?*
En ___, ¿qué tiempo hace?	*In ___, what is the weather like?*
En ___, hace viento.	*In ___, it is windy.*
Hace ___.	*It's ___.*

Parts of the body

la boca	*mouth*
los brazos	*arms*
la cabeza	*head*
la cara	*face*
los dedos	*fingers*
las manos	*hands*
la nariz	*nose*
las orejas	*ears*
los ojos	*eyes*
el pelo	*hair*
las piernas	*legs*
los pies	*feet*

Teacher's Manual

Animals
Vocabulary

el burro	*donkey*
el caballo	*horse*
el cerdo	*pig*
el conejo	*rabbit*
la gallina	*chicken, hen*
el gallo	*rooster*
el gato	*cat*
el perro	*dog*
la vaca	*cow*

Asking about animals

¿Quién dice "___"?	*Who says "___"?*
¿Qué dice el/la ___?	*What does the ___ say?*

Family members

la abuela	*grandmother*
el abuelo	*grandfather*
la familia	*family*
la hermana	*sister*
el hermano	*brother*
la hija	*daughter*
el hijo	*son*
la mamá	*mother*
el papá	*father*

Articles of clothing

el abrigo	*coat*
la blusa	*blouse*
las botas	*boots*
las calcetines	*socks*
la camisa	*shirt*
la chaqueta	*jacket*
la falda	*skirt*
los pantalones	*pants*
el pijama	*pajamas*
la ropa	*clothing*
el sombrero	*hat*
los sombreros	*hats*
el suéter	*sweater*
el traje de baño	*bathing suit*
el vestido	*dress*
los zapatos	*shoes*

Rooms in a house

el baño	*bathroom*
la cocina	*kitchen*
el comedor	*dining room*
el cuarto	*bedroom*
la sala	*living room*

ESPAÑOL PARA TI, Level Two

Means of transportation
Vocabulary

el autobús	bus
el avión	airplane
la bicicleta	bicycle
el bote	boat
el coche	car
el jipi	jeep
la motocicleta	motorcycle
el taxi	taxi
el transporte	transportation
el tren	train

Asking about transportation

¿Adónde vas (tú)?	Where are you going?
Aquí viene ___.	Here comes ___.
¿Cómo vas?	How are you going?
Va en ___.	He/She goes by ___.
Vamos a ___.	Let's go to ___.
Voy a ___.	I'm going to ___.
Voy a ___ en ___.	I'm going to ___ by ___.
Voy en ___.	I'm going by ___.

Traffic-related expressions

la calle	street
las luces del tráfico	traffic lights
el policía	(male) police officer
la policía	(female) police officer
el perro policía	police dog
Verde: ¡Sigue!	Green: Go!
Amarillo: ¡Espera!	Yellow: Wait!
Rojo: ¡Alto!	Red: Stop!

Destinations in the city

el aeropuerto	airport
la casa	house/home
la escuela	school
el lago	lake
el parque	park
la piscina	swimming pool
la playa	beach
el restaurante	restaurant
el supermercado	supermarket
la tienda	store
el zoológico	zoo

Sports and other activities
Vocabulary

dormir	to sleep
hacer un viaje	to take a trip
ir de campo	to go on a picnic
jugar	to play
jugar al béisbol	to play baseball
jugar al fútbol	to play soccer
jugar al vólibol	to play volleyball
leer	to read
montar en bicicleta	to ride a bicycle
nadar	to swim
saltar la cuerda	to jump rope

Asking about sports and activities

¿Qué vas a hacer?	What are you going to do?
Voy a ___.	I'm going to ___.

Teacher's Manual

Telephone-related expressions

el teléfono	*telephone*
Diga.	*Hello?*
¿Qué haces?	*What are you doing?*
Hablo por teléfono.	*I'm talking on the telephone.*

Miscellaneous

despacio	*slowly*
rápido	*quickly*
No.	*No.*
¡Olé!	*Hurray!*
Sí.	*Yes.*
Gracias.	*Thank you.*
Lo siento.	*I'm sorry.*

Numbers 1–100

Vocabulary

uno	*one*	veinte	*twenty*
dos	*two*	veintiuno	*twenty-one*
tres	*three*	veintidós	*twenty-two*
cuatro	*four*	veintitrés	*twenty-three*
cinco	*five*	veinticuatro	*twenty-four*
seis	*six*	veinticinco	*twenty-five*
siete	*seven*	veintiséis	*twenty-six*
ocho	*eight*	veintisiete	*twenty-seven*
nueve	*nine*	veintiocho	*twenty-eight*
diez	*ten*	veintinueve	*twenty-nine*
once	*eleven*	treinta	*thirty*
doce	*twelve*	cuarenta	*forty*
trece	*thirteen*	cincuenta	*fifty*
catorce	*fourteen*	sesenta	*sixty*
quince	*fifteen*	setenta	*seventy*
dieciséis	*sixteen*	ochenta	*eighty*
diecisiete	*seventeen*	noventa	*ninety*
dieciocho	*eighteen*	cien	*one hundred*
diecinueve	*nineteen*		

Asking about numbers

¿Qué número es?	*What number is it?*
Es ___.	*It's ___.*
¿Cuántos son?	*How many are there?*
Son ___.	*There are ___.*

ESPAÑOL PARA TI, Level Two

Lessons
1 - 66

Lesson 1

Materials to gather

- VCR and Video Lesson 1 on Tape 1
- Hand puppets Rosco and Dora
- Blackline Master 1A (sunrise)
- *Optional materials:* crayons or colored markers

OBJECTIVES

Language

- Practice the opening conversation
- Practice classroom vocabulary

Culture

- Understand that many teachers in Spanish-speaking countries wear smocks

Vocabulary

Hola.	*Hi. Hello.*
Adiós.	*Good-bye.*
Hasta luego.	*See you later.*
¿Cómo estás tú?	*How are you?*
Muy bien.	*Very well.*
la mochila	*book bag, backpack*
el papel	*paper*
los colores	*crayons*
los lápices	*pencils*
la regla	*ruler*
las gomas	*erasers*
las tijeras	*scissors*
los bolígrafos	*pens*
los bolis	*pens*
el cuaderno	*notebook*
el sacapuntas	*pencil sharpener*

Warm-up

Remind children that they learned how to say many things in Spanish last year—say hello and good-bye, give their name and their age, say how they feel, and say numbers 1 to 50 among other items. They also learned many songs, including one about a picnic, one about animals on a farm, a holiday in Spain, and the days of the week. Now they are going to use what they already know to learn more Spanish.

Introduce the video

Point out that children are going to hear many words and expressions that they learned last year, plus new ones. In this video, they are going to practice the opening conversation and words for classroom objects. Children are also going to meet three old friends—**la maestra**, their teacher from last year; Rosco, the wolf; and Dora, the cow.

VIDEO LESSON

1. Starting another year of Spanish

La maestra notices how the children have changed. She reminds them that teachers in Spanish-speaking countries wear smocks.

2. Reviewing hand gestures and the opening conversation

La maestra demonstrates the gestures for listening and speaking. Then she and the children practice the opening conversation (**M** = Maestra, **C** = class):

M: Buenos días, clase.	*Good morning, class.*
C: Buenos días, Maestra.	*Good morning, Teacher.*
M: ¿Cómo estás tú?	*How are you?*
C: Muy bien, gracias. ¿Y usted?	*Very well, thank you. And you?*
M: Muy bien, gracias.	*Very well, thank you.*

3. Meeting Dora again

La maestra and Dora say the opening conversation and then talk about school (**M** = Maestra, **D** = Dora):

M: Dora, ¿estás lista?	*Dora, are you ready?*
D: Sí, estoy lista para la escuela.	*Yes, I'm ready for school.*
M: ¿Qué tienes para la escuela?	*What do you have for school?*
D: Tengo muchas cosas.	*I have lots of things.*

4. Practicing classroom vocabulary

La maestra asks about the contents of Dora's book bag.

¿Qué tienes en la mochila?	*What do you have in your backpack?*
¿Qué es?	*What is it?*
¿Qué son?	*What are they?*

5. Meeting Rosco again

La maestra, Rosco, and Dora greet each other. Then **la maestra** tells Rosco about Dora's school supplies.

Dora tiene ___.	*Dora has ___.*

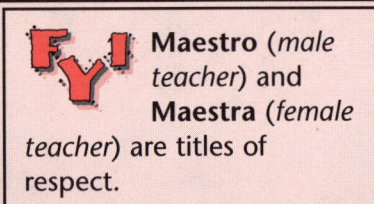

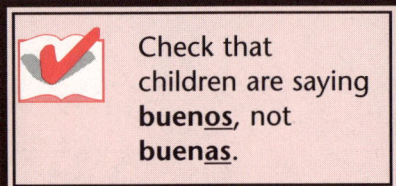

FYI **Maestro** (*male teacher*) and **Maestra** (*female teacher*) are titles of respect.

Check that children are saying **buenos**, not **buenas**.

Classroom objects:

la mochila	book bag, backpack
el papel	paper
los colores	crayons
los lápices	pencils
la regla	ruler
las gomas	erasers
las tijeras	scissors
los bolígrafos	pens
los bolis	pens
el cuaderno	notebook

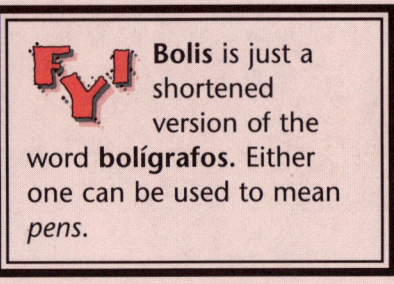

FYI **Bolis** is just a shortened version of the word **bolígrafos**. Either one can be used to mean *pens*.

LEVEL TWO

An embarrassed Rosco admits he's not ready for school. **La maestra** says **Vamos de compras** (*Let's go shopping*).

¿Tienes una regla?	*Do you have a ruler?*
No tengo una regla.	*I don't have a ruler.*
¿No tienes papel?	*Don't you have any paper?*
¿No estás listo?	*Aren't you ready?*
No estoy listo.	*I'm not ready.*
No tengo nada.	*I have nothing.*
	I don't have anything.

6. Shopping for school items

In the store, **la maestra** and Rosco discuss his needs.

¿Necesitas ___?	*Do you need ___?*
Sí, necesito ___.	*Yes, I need ___.*
Rosco necesita ___.	*Rosco needs ___.*

La maestra reviews vocabulary in the order given: **los colores** (*crayons*), **los bolígrafos** (*pens*), **el cuaderno** (*notebook*), **el papel** (*paper*), **una regla** (*ruler*), **los lápices** (*pencils*), **las gomas** (*erasers*). She also introduces **un cuaderno de papel** (*notebook*) and **el sacapuntas** (*pencil sharpener*).

7. Discussing Rosco's purchases with Dora

La maestra asks about Rosco's purchases.

¿Qué hay en la mochila?	*What's in the backpack?*
¿Qué es?	*What is it?*
¿Qué son?	*What are they?*
Rosco tiene ___.	*Rosco has ___.*
Tengo ___.	*I have ___.*

8. Singing "Español para ti" (*"Spanish Is for You, and for Me"*)

La maestra models a new song and the class sings with her.

Español para ti.	*Spanish for you.*
Español para mí.	*Spanish for me.*
Para ti, para mí.	*For you, for me.*
Y así todos sentir	*And so, everyone feels*
Una nueva sensación.	*A new sensation.*

9. Closing

La maestra bids everyone **Adiós** (*Good-bye*) and **Hasta luego** (*See you later*).

EN ESPAÑOL

La maestra exclaims **Mira** (*Look*) while she is shopping. Use the expression with your class if you feel comfortable.

La maestra often uses these expressions:

Aquí está ___.   *Here is ___.*
Aquí están ___.   *Here are ___.*

See section 4 for a list of the classroom objects. In addition, **el sacapuntas** means *pencil sharpener*.

FYI To state *I am ready*, Rosco says **Estoy listo**, but Dora says **Estoy lista**.

After viewing the video, praise the children for their good listening and watching skills.

Lesson One

Blackline Master 1A

If children are paying attention during the video and class activities but are hesitant to speak, do not force them to speak Spanish. Just as some young children begin speaking later than others, some children need to hear more Spanish before they are ready to say anything.

ACTIVITY LESSON

Activity 1A: Say good morning and hello

Materials: Blackline Master 1A.

Preparation: Make a copy of Blackline Master 1A for each child (found in the Teacher's Resource Book).

Discuss with the class how to say *Good morning* (**Buenos días**) and *Hello* (**Hola**). Replay section 2 of the Video Lesson if children are having trouble remembering the expressions. Divide the class in half. Have the groups practice saying **Buenos días** and then **Hola** to each other. When the children are practicing **Buenos días**, have them hold Blackline Master 1A in front of themselves. If the class seems comfortable with these expressions, ask for pairs of volunteers to exchange greetings using the puppets.

Buenos días, Rosco.	*Good morning, Rosco.*
Buenos días, Dora.	*Good morning, Dora.*
Hola, Rosco.	*Hello, Rosco.*
Hola, Dora.	*Hello, Dora.*

Finally, have pairs of volunteers exchange greetings with classmates, using their real names.

Activity 1B: Discuss how children have changed

Remind children that **la maestra** commented on how they had changed over the summer. Discuss what she may have noticed. For example, some of the children may be taller, have different hair styles, or may have lost baby teeth. Then connect the discussion of changes over time to topics for which the class learned Spanish words and expressions last year, such as how to say your age, how to describe the weather, and how to talk about the people who are in your family. For a list of topics from Level 1, see the Level 1 Teacher's Manual, pages xxxvii-xli. Allow children to make these comparisons in English. Tell the children that this year they will learn even more ways to talk about these and other topics in Spanish.

LEVEL TWO

Activity 1C: Prepare for school

Point out that during the Video Lesson, **la maestra** mentioned the importance of getting ready for school—the need to plan ahead. Talk about what Rosco and Dora did to get ready. Integrate Spanish into the discussion by talking about the mixture of words for classroom objects that children already know in Spanish—*paper* (**el papel**), *pencil* (**el lápiz**), *ruler* (**la regla**)—and the words that are new—*book bag, backpack* (**la mochila**), *crayons* (**los colores**), *erasers* (**las gomas**), *scissors* (**las tijeras**), *pens* (**los bolígrafos**), *notebook* (**el cuaderno**), *pencil sharpener* (**el sacapuntas**). Explain that the class will continue to work with the words from last year and learn new ones.

Expand the discussion about preparing for school to what is relevant for your class. Also include topics beside buying school supplies, such as finding out when and where the school bus will stop.

IF YOU HAVE TIME...

Materials: Blackline Master 1A; crayons or colored markers.

Have the children color Blackline Master 1A.

CLOSING

Tell the children that Spanish class is finished for today. Next time they are going to learn more words for classroom objects and a new song.

FAMILY CONNECTION

To foster a friendly link between home and school, you may want to send out Family Letter 1 (found in the Teacher's Resource Book). This letter suggests how families can be involved in their children's learning of Spanish.

Lesson One

Lesson 2

Materials to gather

- VCR and Video Lesson 2 on Tape 1
- Cassette player
- Activity Cassette 1
- Song Cassette

Objectives

Language
- Practice saying **Buenos días** (*Good morning*)
- Practice the singular and plural for some classroom objects

Culture
- Sing a new song, **"Español para ti"** (*"Spanish Is for You, and for Me"*)
- Describe or use the Spanish method for waving farewell

Review
- Practice the opening conversation
- Recall appropriate behavior for ¡Olé! (*Hurray!*)

Vocabulary

el globo	*globe*
el libro	*book*
los libros	*books*
el lápiz	*pencil*
los papeles	*papers*

Warm-up

Ask a volunteer how to say **Buenos días** (*Good morning*). Divide the class in half and have the groups say good morning to each other.

Review

Ask a volunteer how to say good-bye in Spanish (**Adiós**). If the child responds **Hasta luego** (*See you later*), explain that **Adiós** is a more definite good-bye, while **Hasta luego** means *I'll see you later*. Acknowledge that people do use both these expressions when leaving each other. Next, divide the class in half and have the groups say good-bye to each other. Then divide the class into two groups in three or four different additional ways. Each time have the groups say farewell to one another.

Introduce the video

Explain that in this video, the class is going to learn more words for classroom objects and practice a new song. Point out that **la maestra** always says farewell to the children at the end of a video. Ask them to return her politeness by saying farewell in Spanish (**Adiós** or **Hasta luego**).

> Many activities specify using volunteers. In this way, children who are ready to speak Spanish individually may do so. Children who are more hesitant, on the other hand, have more opportunities to listen and to speak with the whole class and in groups before talking as individuals.

VIDEO LESSON

1. Practicing the opening conversation

La maestra first practices the opening conversation with Rosco, then with the class. Finally, they all say the conversation together (**M** = Maestra, **C** = class):

M: Buenos días, clase.	*Good morning, class.*
C: Buenos días, Maestra.	*Good morning, Teacher.*
M: ¿Cómo estás tú?	*How are you?*
C: Muy bien, gracias. ¿Y usted?	*Very well, thank you. And you?*
M: Muy bien, gracias.	*Very well, thank you.*

2. Reacting to ¡Olé! (Hurray!)

La maestra and Rosco talk about singing.

¿Te gusta cantar?	*Do you like to sing?*
Me gusta cantar.	*I like to sing.*
Vamos a cantar.	*Let's sing.*

Then **la maestra** reminds the children that they are supposed to be quiet and pay special attention when they hear the word **¡Olé!**

3. Practicing "Español para ti" ("*Spanish for Is You, and for Me*")

La maestra and Rosco decide to sing "**Español para ti.**" She uses hand gestures to demonstrate the meaning of the first three lines as she models each line and then the whole song. The class should repeat with her as Rosco does.

Español para ti.	*Spanish for you.*
Español para mí.	*Spanish for me.*
Para ti, para mí.	*For you, for me.*
Y así todos sentir	*And so, everyone feels*
Una nueva sensación.	*A new sensation.*

EN ESPAÑOL

La maestra says **Muy bien** (*Very good*) to compliment the children on their participation and to encourage them. Try to do the same, if you feel comfortable.

FYI

La maestra often asks:

¿<u>Te</u> gusta <u>cantar</u>?
(*Do <u>you</u> like <u>to sing</u>?*)

The usual answer is:

<u>Me</u> gusta <u>cantar</u>.
(*<u>I</u> like <u>to sing</u>.*)

Encourage children to use the same hand gestures to help them remember the lyrics.

LEVEL TWO

4. Practicing classroom vocabulary

La maestra models classroom vocabulary and asks the class to repeat after her. As part of the practice, **la maestra** introduces and contrasts the difference in sound between the singular and plural of some of the nouns.

Estos son libros. *These are books.*

Singular		**Plural**	
el globo	*globe*	los globos	*globes*
el libro	*book*	los libros	*books*
la regla	*ruler*	las reglas	*rulers*
el lápiz	*pencil*	los lápices	*pencils*
el papel	*paper*	los papeles	*papers*
el cuaderno	*notebook*	los cuadernos	*notebooks*

5. Closing

La maestra bids the class **Adiós** (*Good-bye*).

FYI Spanish nouns are masculine or feminine. Notice what **el, los, la,** and **las** tell about the nouns they accompany.

el libro: *masculine singular*
los libros: *masculine plural*
la regla: *feminine singular*
las reglas: *feminine plural*

EN ESPAÑOL

Remind children to say farewell—**Adiós** (*Good-bye*) or **Hasta luego** (*See you later*)—to **la maestra**.

After viewing the video, praise the children for their good listening and watching skills.

Lesson Two

ACTIVITY LESSON

Activity 2A: Cooperative learning—Greet your partner

Materials: Cassette player; Activity Cassette 1, Side A.

La maestra will ask you to pause the tape in the middle of this activity. Divide the class into pairs. Next, explain that **la maestra** and Rosco are going to say the opening conversation. When they have finished, **la maestra** will ask you to pause the tape and tell partners to say the opening conversation. The harp sound indicates that children should speak before **la maestra** goes on to the next part of the activity. Then the class should listen as **la maestra** and Rosco repeat the opening conversation.

Point out that **la maestra** and Rosco repeat the opening conversation for two reasons: so that children can then check that they said the words correctly, and that they can hear any parts that they forgot. Emphasize that it is very important for the class to listen to the correct answers on the tape.

Depending on how well the class knows the opening conversation, you may want to repeat this activity several times. To provide some variety, have the children take the part of **la maestra** or Rosco.

Activity 2B: Singular and plural of classroom objects

Materials: Cassette player; Activity Cassette 1, Side A.

Point out that the class is going to hear an old friend—Mr. Hale—in this activity. Remind children that he learned Spanish from his playmates while he was growing up in Kansas. Explain that Mr. Hale is going to say each word twice. If the word names one thing, children should raise one hand. If he says a word that names more than one thing, children should raise both hands. You may want to repeat this activity because identifying the difference between singular and plural is a new skill for the class.

Strategy:

To impress on children the importance of listening to these repetitions, stop from time to time at the end of a tape activity and ask volunteers to tell how listening to the repetition has helped them. This technique is particularly effective when a tape activity has improved performance.

IF YOU HAVE TIME . . .

Discuss with children the expressions that **la maestra** has said at the end of class—**Adiós** (*Good-bye*) and **Hasta luego** (*See you later*). Have a volunteer describe what **la maestra** does as she says them: She waves good-bye and her fingers look as if they are asking someone to come back.

Divide the class in half. Have the two groups say the expression to each other. Make sure that they mimic **la maestra**'s wave. Then have pairs of volunteers, with or without the puppets, demonstrate how to say farewell to one another.

LEVEL TWO

Activity 2C: Sing "Español para ti" (*"Spanish Is for You, and for Me"*)

Materials: Cassette player; Song Cassette, Side A.

Tell the children that on this recording, **la maestra** has added a little bit more at the end of **"Español para ti."** You may choose to say the Spanish and English or just explain what the extra line means—**¡Viva! ¡Viva! ¡Viva! "Español para ti." ¡Olé!** (*May "Spanish Is for You, and for Me" live forever! Hurray!*). Explain that the class should just listen to these extra words but not worry about them. Play the song through a couple of times before the class sings it. Mimic **la maestra**'s gestures to help the class remember what they are saying and what to say.

(*Point to the children.*)

Español para ti. *Spanish for you.*

(*Point to yourself.*)

Español para mí. *Spanish for me.*

(*Point to the children and then to yourself.*)

Para ti, para mí. *For you, for me.*

Y así todos sentir *And so, everyone feels*

Una nueva sensación. *A new sensation.*

When you play the song another couple of times, encourage children to sing the parts they know and to use the hand gestures. Explain that there will be many more opportunities to sing this song.

CLOSING

Tell the children that Spanish class is finished for today. Next time they are going to talk about colors, numbers, and more classroom objects. In addition, another old friend will visit the class to speak Spanish.

LANGUAGE ACROSS THE CURRICULUM

Many words in English and Spanish sound alike and have similar meanings. Being aware of such similarities helps children remember the meaning of Spanish words. Tell the children that the last word in the song (**sensación**—*sensation*) sounds like an English word. Play the end of the song several times. Ask volunteers to say the word and explain its meaning. If children have difficulty identifying it, give them a clue, such as the English word.

Lesson Two

Lesson 3

Materials to gather

- VCR and Video Lesson 3 on Tape 1
- Cassette player
- Activity Cassette 1
- Song Cassette
- Blackline Master 3A (Ñico)
- Red, yellow, blue, black, orange, and green crayons
- Classroom objects: pencil, paper, book, eraser, notebook, ruler, scissors
- *Optional materials:* Number Cards 1–6

Objectives

Language
- Count from 1 to 6
- Answer questions about some colors
- Play a game using classroom objects

Culture
- Sing along with **"Español para ti"** (*"Spanish Is for You, and for Me"*)

Review
- Participate in the opening conversation
- Review some vocabulary for classroom objects

Vocabulary

uno	*one*	verde	*green*
dos	*two*	rojo	*red*
tres	*three*	anaranjado	*orange*
cuatro	*four*	amarillo	*yellow*
cinco	*five*	la bandera	*flag*
seis	*six*	el escritorio	*(teacher's) desk*
negro	*black*	la mesa	*table*
azul	*blue*	la silla	*chair*

Warm-up

Begin Spanish class by exchanging the greetings below, using **Hola** (*Hello*) (**T** = Teacher, **C** = class):

   M: Hola, clase.   *Hello, class.*

   C: Hola, Maestro/Maestra.   *Hello, Teacher.*

Review

Place examples of the classroom objects where everyone can see them. For items such as *pencil* and *pencils,* make sure that there are multiples available. If you do not have an item, such as a globe, in your classroom, use a picture instead.

Explain that each volunteer may choose one of the object(s) and name it for the class. If a volunteer makes a mistake, he or she may have a second try but, if necessary, may ask other volunteers to name the item. Once an object has been identified, the rest of the class repeats its Spanish name and the volunteer removes it from the playing area. Encourage the children to name as many items as possible, but point out that it is all right if no one chooses some objects since the class is going to continue practicing all these words.

Introduce the video

Explain that in this video, the children are going to practice some of the numbers and colors they learned last year and their new song. In addition Ñico, the toucan, is back to learn Spanish with them. Once again remind children to say farewell to **la maestra** at the end of the Video Lesson.

Classroom objects:

la mochila	book bag, backpack
el papel	paper
los papeles	papers
los colores	crayons
el lápiz	pencil
los lápices	pencils
la regla	ruler
las gomas	erasers
las tijeras	scissors
los bolígrafos	pens
los bolis	pens
el cuaderno	notebook
el sacapuntas	pencil sharpener
el globo	globe
el libro	book
los libros	books

VIDEO LESSON

1. Opening the lesson with Rosco and Ñico

La maestra models the opening conversation line-by-line and has the class and the puppets repeat after her. Then, they all say the conversation (**M** = Maestra, **C** = class):

M: Buenos días, clase.	*Good morning, class.*
C: Buenos días, Maestra.	*Good morning, Teacher.*
M: ¿Cómo estás tú?	*How are you?*
C: Muy bien, gracias. ¿Y usted?	*Very well, thank you. And you?*
M: Muy bien, gracias.	*Very well, thank you.*

2. Reviewing numbers and colors

La maestra asks Ñico about his appearance.

¿Cuántos colores tienes tú?	*How many colors do you have?*
Tengo muchos colores.	*I have many colors.*
¿Cuántos son?	*How many are they?*
Vamos a contar.	*Let's count.*

Numbers: **uno** (*1*), **dos** (*2*), **tres** (*3*), **cuatro** (*4*), **cinco** (*5*), **seis** (*6*).

¿De qué color es?	*What color is it?*
Es de color ___.	*It's ___.*

Colors: **negro** (*black*), **azul** (*blue*), **verde** (*green*), **rojo** (*red*), **anaranjado** (*orange*), **amarillo** (*yellow*).

3. Singing "Español para ti" (*"Spanish Is for You, and for Me"*)

Rosco and Ñico both want to sing. **La maestra** comments:

A Ñico le gusta cantar.	*Ñico likes to sing.*
A Rosco le encanta cantar.	*Rosco loves to sing.*

La maestra says **Vamos a cantar** (*Let's sing*) and then models "**Español para ti**" for the class. The children and the puppets follow her lead.

Español para ti.	*Spanish for you.*
Español para mí.	*Spanish for me.*
Para ti, para mí.	*For you, for me.*
Y así todos sentir	*And so, everyone feels*
Una nueva sensación.	*A new sensation.*

FYI

The **los** in **los colores** shows that **colores** is masculine and plural. An adjective shows gender (masculine or feminine) and number (singular or plural) like the noun it describes. In **muchos** and **cuántos**, the **-o** indicates masculine and the **-s** indicates plural.

EN ESPAÑOL

Use the following expressions with your class, if you feel comfortable:

Me toca a mí.
(*It's my turn.*)

Te toca a ti.
(*It's your turn.*)

Le toca a [*child's name*].
(*It's ___'s turn.*)

LEVEL TWO

4. Preparing for a new game

La maestra comments **Nosotros estamos contentos** (*We are happy*) before everyone begins practicing for a new game. Then Rosco chooses classroom objects in response to her questions.

¿Qué tienes (tú)?	*What do you have?*
(Yo) tengo ___.	*I have ___.*
¿Qué más tienes?	*What else do you have?*
¿Qué más tenemos?	*What else do we have?*
¿Qué tengo yo?	*What do I have?*
¿Qué más tengo yo?	*What else do I have?*

La maestra models Rosco's answers and children repeat them. Answers: **las tijeras** (*scissors*), **el cuaderno** (*notebook*), **la goma** (*eraser*), **la regla** (*ruler*), **el papel** (*paper*), **el lápiz** (*pencil*), **el libro** (*book*), **la bandera** (*flag*), **el escritorio** (*teacher's desk*), **la mesa** (*table*), **la silla** (*chair*).

5. Playing *Sí o no* (*Yes or no*)

La maestra holds an object in her hand and asks about it. If she correctly names the item, players should say **sí** (*yes*). If she names it incorrectly, children should say **no** (*no*).

¿Qué tengo yo?	*What do I have?*
¿Tengo ___?	*Do I have ___?*

6. Closing

La maestra tells children that they will play the game again. Then she wishes them **Adiós** (*Good-bye*).

FYI **Qué** has a couple of different meanings.

In a question:
¿Qué tienes tú?
(*What do you have?*)
¿De qué color es?
(*What color is it?*)

In an exclamation:
¡Qué bueno!
(*What a good job!*)
¡Qué bonita!
(*What a pretty one [ruler]!*)

EN ESPAÑOL

If you feel comfortable, use these expressions with children in various classes.

Vamos a jugar. *Let's play.*
Vamos a cantar. *Let's sing.*
Vamos a contar. *Let's count.*

After viewing the video, praise the children for their good listening and watching skills.

Lesson Three

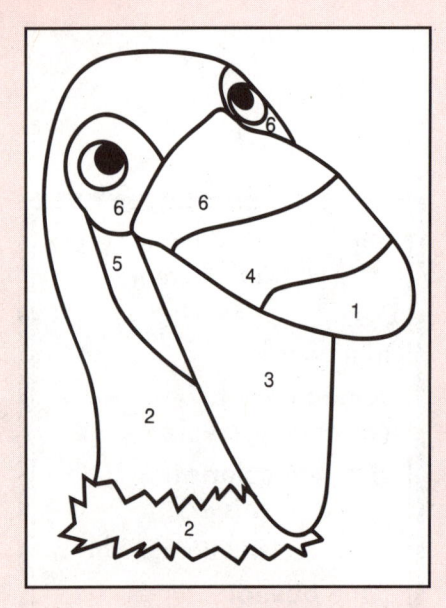

Blackline Master 3A

LANGUAGE ACROSS THE CURRICULUM

Many words in Spanish and English sound alike and have similar meanings. Becoming aware of these similarities may help increase children's English vocabulary.

The class now knows the Spanish words **verde** (*green*) and **azul** (*blue*); in the future, if they encounter the unknown words *verdant* and *azure*, children are more likely to make accurate guesses about the meaning of these words because of their background in Spanish. These words are examples of the kind of language transfer that often happens.

LEVEL TWO

ACTIVITY LESSON

Activity 3A: Color Ñico

Materials: Cassette player; Activity Cassette 1, Side A; Blackline Master 3A; red, yellow, blue, black, orange, and green crayons.

Preparation: Make a copy of Blackline Master 3A for each child (found in the Teacher's Resource Book). Distribute a set of crayons to everyone.

The goal of this activity is to check children's recall of some colors. Stop the tape momentarily after each harp sound. This pause will give children time to select the correct crayon and color the appropriate area(s) of the picture.

Ask the class to tell where each number (1–6) appears on Ñico. Be sure that children are aware that the number 2 appears in two places and 6 in three places. Explain that doña Elena will give the class directions for coloring Ñico. She is going to say each number and each color twice. Children should color the corresponding sections. Assure them that they simply need to color a small portion of each area in the time given. The class will have time to color the rest of the picture later.

Activity 3B: Tell what you have

Materials: Cassette player; Activity Cassette 1, Side A; classroom objects that include pencil, paper, book, eraser, notebook, ruler, scissors.

Give each object to a different volunteer. Have the class sit in a circle. Explain that Mr. Hale is going to ask who has different classroom objects (¿**Quién tiene** ___ ?). He will repeat each question twice. The child who is holding the named object should hold it up for everyone to see and say **Yo tengo** ___ (*I have* ___).

Activity 3C: Sing "Español para ti" (*"Spanish Is for You, and for Me"*)

Materials: Cassette player; Song Cassette, Side A.

Play the song once and mimic **la maestra**'s gestures for the lyrics.

(*Point to children.*)

| Español <u>para ti</u>. | *Spanish <u>for you</u>.* |

(*Point to yourself.*)

| Español <u>para mí</u>. | *Spanish <u>for me</u>.* |

(*Point to the children, then to self.*)

Para ti, para mí.	*For you, for me.*
Y así todos sentir	*And so, everyone feels*
Una nueva sensación.	*A new sensation.*

Play the song again. Stop after each line and ask volunteers what the lyrics mean. Accept reasonable answers. Next, tell the children that they are going to practice this song as a whole class and then in groups. Divide the class into two groups. Replay the first line. Have the whole class use **la maestra**'s gesture and *say* the words with the rhythm of the song. Ask each group to do the same. Play the tape again as needed. Follow the same process with the second line and then ask the class to say the two lines together. Repeat the same procedure for the third line. Your class may also find it helpful to simply say **para ti** and **para mí** and point appropriately several times. Replay the song and encourage children to mouth the words with the music. Then have the class sing along with the music a few times.

CLOSING

Tell the children that Spanish class is finished for today. Next time they are going to sing their new song, play a game, and follow commands. Still another surprise is waiting for them. Someone is coming back to see them.

Learning a song should be fun, not drudgery. Praise the children frequently for their efforts and/or increased fluency. Use English if necessary, but say **Muy bien** (*Very good*) or **¡Qué bueno!** (*What a good job!*) if you feel comfortable speaking Spanish.

IF YOU HAVE TIME . . .

Materials: VCR and Video Lesson 3 on Tape 1; Number Cards 1–6 (found in the Teacher's Resource Book).

Display the Number Cards where everyone can see them. Point to each Number Card as the class counts from 1 to 6.

1	uno
2	dos
3	tres
4	cuatro
5	cinco
6	seis

Repeat this process a couple of times. If the children are having difficulty, play section 2 of Video Lesson 3 in which **la maestra** models these numbers. Have the class repeat them. If children appear confident about these numbers, point to the Number Cards in random order and ask the class to name the numbers.

Lesson Three

Lesson 4

Materials to gather

- VCR and Video Lesson 4 on Tape 1
- Cassette player
- Activity Cassette 1
- Poster "**El salón de clase**" (*The classroom*)
- 2 Rosco flags
- Blackline Master 4B (classroom objects)
- Blackline Master 4C (classroom)
- Red, yellow, blue, black, orange, and green crayons
- *Optional materials:* Song Cassette

OBJECTIVES

Language
- Play games using vocabulary for classroom objects
- Respond to **Anda** (*Walk*) and **Toca** ___ (*Touch* ___)
- Identify classroom objects on "**El salón de clase**" (*The classroom*) poster
- Recognize that **Tengo** means *I have*

Culture
- Say **Adiós** (*Good-bye*) or **Hasta luego** (*See you later*) as a farewell

Review
- Say the opening conversation
- Practice vocabulary for classroom objects
- Sing "**Español para ti**" (*"Spanish Is for You, and for Me"*)

Vocabulary

el mapa	*map*
Anda.	*Walk.*
Toca.	*Touch.*
Tengo ___.	*I have ___.*

Warm-up

Say **Buenos días** (*Good morning*) or **Hola** (*Hello*) to the children. Ask them to respond to your greeting.

Review

Materials: Cassette player; Activity 2A on Activity Cassette 1, Side A.

Divide the class into pairs. Within each pair, let children decide who will play **la maestra** and who will be himself or herself. Then have the class listen to **la maestra** and Rosco model the opening conversation and ask pairs to say it.

Introduce the video

Explain that the class is going to say the opening conversation and sing "**Español para ti**" (*"Spanish Is for You, and for Me"*) with Jorge, who is visiting the class. They will also play some games. Display the poster "**El salón de clase**" (*The classroom*) before starting the Video Lesson. **La maestra** will ask you to use it during section 6.

Make the Rosco flag from the pattern found in the Teacher's Resource Book. Duplicate one or more copies of the flag, and paste each one on a stick or a ruler. For variety, photocopy them on different colored paper. You may want to make at least two since you can use multiple flags to keep an activity moving quickly. Have the Rosco flag(s) ready. You may use them during section 6 of the Video Lesson and you will need at least one flag during Activity 4A. Keep them available for use during the year.

VIDEO LESSON

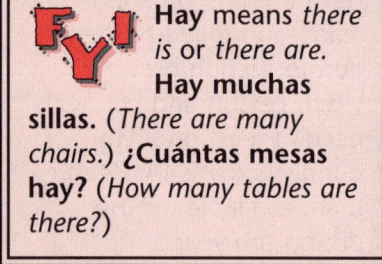

1. Greeting Jorge and the children

La maestra reintroduces Jorge to the class. She holds the opening conversation with Jorge, then with the children (**M** = Maestra, **J** = Jorge, **C** = class):

M: Buenos días, Jorge/clase.	*Good morning, Jorge/class.*
J/C: Buenos días, Maestra.	*Good morning, Teacher.*
M: ¿Cómo estás tú?	*How are you?*
J/C: Muy bien, gracias. ¿Y usted?	*Very well, thank you. And you?*
M: Muy bien, gracias.	*Very well, thank you.*

2. Singing "Español para ti" (*"Spanish Is for You, and for Me"*)

La maestra asks Jorge ¿Recuerdas la canción "Español para ti"? (*Do you remember the song "Spanish Is for You, and for Me"?*) She then asks the class to help her teach Jorge the song. After some practicing, everyone sings together.

Jorge va a cantar.	*Jorge is going to sing.*
Toda la clase va a cantar.	*The whole class is going to sing.*
Vamos a cantar con la música.	*Let's sing with music.*

For song lyrics, see Lesson 3, Video Lesson, section 3.

3. Practicing classroom vocabulary

La maestra states **Estamos en la clase de español** (*We are in Spanish class*). Then she models **Tengo ___** (*I have ___*) plus classroom objects.

el papel	*paper*
el cuaderno	*notebook*
las tijeras	*scissors*
la regla	*ruler*
el lápiz	*pencil*
la goma	*eraser*
el libro	*book*
la bandera	*flag*
el escritorio	*(teacher's) desk*
la mesa	*table*
la silla	*chair*
el boli	*pen*
el sacapuntas	*pencil sharpener*
el globo	*globe*

FYI **Estoy aquí con mi amigo Jorge** means *I'm here with my friend Jorge.*

EN ESPAÑOL

If you are comfortable, use these expressions with your class during the day.

To a boy: ¿**Estás listo, ___?** (*Are you ready, ___?*) and to a girl: ¿**Estás lista, ___?** **Una vez más.** (*One more time.*)

FYI **Hay** means *there is* or *there are.* **Hay muchas sillas.** (*There are many chairs.*) ¿**Cuántas mesas hay?** (*How many tables are there?*)

LEVEL TWO

4. Playing a game of *Sí o no* (*Yes or no*)

La maestra holds an object in her hand and asks the children:

¿Tengo ___?   *Do I have ___?*

If she is correct, children should answer **sí**. If she is incorrect, children should answer **no**.

La maestra holds up a book and asks whether she has a **bandera** (*flag*). Then she asks if she has a **sacapuntas** (*pencil sharpener*). Finally, she asks whether she has a **libro** (*book*). Next, she holds up a pencil sharpener and asks if she has a **globo** (*globe*), **tijeras** (*scissors*), a **boli** (*pen*), or a **sacapuntas** (*pencil sharpener*). The last item she holds up is a pair of scissors; does she have a **regla** (*ruler*), a **cuaderno** (*notebook*), a **bandera** (*flag*), or **tijeras** (*scissors*)?

5. Playing a choosing game

La maestra holds an object and asks Jorge and the class to choose:

¿Es ___ o es ___?   *Is it ___ or is it ___?*
Es ___.   *It's ___.*

Choices: **sacapuntas** (*pencil sharpener*) o **cuaderno** (*notebook*)
    papel (*paper*) o **bandera** (*flag*)
    libro (*book*) o **tijeras** (*scissors*)
    goma (*eraser*) o **regla** (*ruler*)
    sacapuntas (*pencil sharpener*) o **papel** (*paper*)

6. Practicing the commands *Anda* (*Walk*) and *Toca ___* (*Touch ___*)

La maestra and the mime demonstrate the meaning of **Anda** and **Toca**. Next, she carries out the command **Anda y toca el mapa** (*Walk and touch the map*) by using the poster "**El salón de clase**" (*The classroom*). Then **la maestra** asks you to select three children to carry out her commands by touching items on the poster—**el escritorio** (*teacher's desk*), **el libro** (*book*), **la regla** (*ruler*).

> Make sure the poster is displayed for this portion of the video, and be ready to choose three children to follow **la maestra**'s commands.

7. Closing

La maestra says **Adiós** (*Good-bye*) and **Hasta luego** (*See you later*) to the children.

> After viewing the video, praise the children for their good listening and watching skills.

Lesson Four

24

IF YOU HAVE TIME...

Materials: Cassette player; Song Cassette, Side A.

Play **"Español para ti"** (*"Spanish Is for You, and for Me"*) twice. Have children sing with the tape. Next, focus on what they need to practice. For the first three lines, use suggestions in Activity 3C. For the last two lines, have children listen for **sentir** (*sense*) and **sensación** (*sensation*)—synonyms for *feel* and *feeling*—as you play the last part twice. Then practice the song with the tape. End with the class singing the entire song. For song lyrics, see Lesson 3, Video Lesson, section 3.

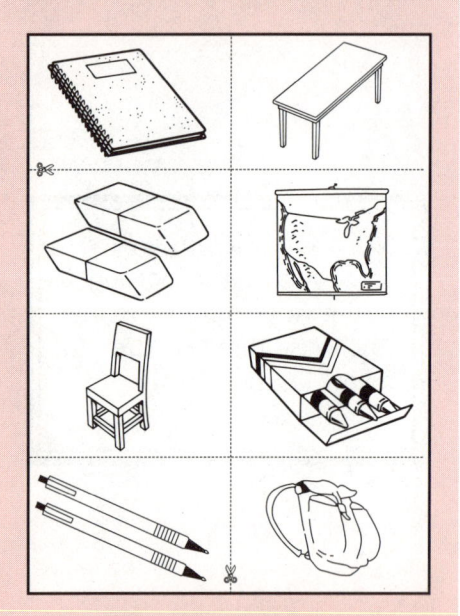

Blackline Master 4B

ACTIVITY LESSON

Activity 4A: Play with *"El salón de clase"* (*The classroom*) poster

Materials: Cassette player; Activity Cassette 1, Side A; 2 Rosco flags; and **El salón de clase** (*The classroom*) poster.

Preparation: Construct two Rosco flags if you have not already done so, and display the **"El salón de clase"** poster where everyone can see it.

If you are going to employ the Rosco flags, explain their use to the children. Tell them that before an activity begins, you will hand a flag to the first and second players. When a child has finished, he or she should return the flag to you, so that you may hand it on to another child. In the meantime, the second player and the rest of the class continue with the activity. In this way, children may keep playing without interruption.

Before the activity begins, select one child to follow Mr. Hale's directions. A total of five children will participate during the tape activity. Explain that Mr. Hale is going to ask different children to walk (**anda**) to the poster of the classroom and touch (**toca**) an object. He will say each direction once. To give the class more practice hearing the names for these classroom objects in Spanish, you may want to repeat this activity.

Activity 4B: Follow commands to *Toca* ___ (*Touch* ___)

Materials: Blackline Master 4B.

Preparation: Make a copy of Blackline Master 4B for each child (found in Teacher's Resource Book).

Ask the class to name the objects on Blackline Master 4B in English and in Spanish: *notebook* (**el cuaderno**), *table* (**la mesa**), *erasers* (**las gomas**), *map* (**el mapa**), *chair* (**la silla**), *crayons* (**los colores**), *pens* (**los bolis** or **los bolígrafos**), *backpack* (**la mochila**). Then ask a volunteer to tell the class to touch (**toca**) three or four different objects on the Blackline Master. After each command, the child must show the answer to classmates. Encourage classmates to listen carefully to what the volunteer says. Is the child using **el, los, la,** and **las** correctly? Are they naming the objects correctly? If a mistake is made, allow the volunteer to correct himself or herself or have fellow classmates do so. Emphasize that children should follow **la maestra**'s example. She helps; she doesn't criticize. Repeat the activity with other volunteers.

LEVEL TWO

Activity 4C: Color the classroom

Materials: Blackline Master 4C; red, yellow, blue, black, orange, and green crayons.

Preparation: Make a copy of Blackline Master 4C for each child (found in Teacher's Resource Book). Make sure that children have the appropriate crayons.

Give the class time to color the Blackline Master. Next, choose one of the objects in the list of classroom objects, and ask volunteers how to ask and answer the following question:

What color is [the object]?   ¿De qué color es ___?
It's ___.   Es de color ___.

The possible colors are **rojo** (*red*), **amarillo** (*yellow*), **azul** (*blue*), **negro** (*black*), **anaranjado** (*orange*), and **verde** (*green*). Then have volunteers ask the same question about self-selected items and encourage several children to respond and show what color they made it. If individuals make a mistake using **el** or **la** (the Spanish word for *the*) with an object, encourage them to self-correct or allow classmates to state the correct word *and* the name of the item before continuing. It is very important that children automatically know the gender of a noun. Some children may try to ask about plural objects, such as **los libros** (*books*). Congratulate them on their initiative, but explain that they have not yet learned all they need to know.

CLOSING

Tell the children that Spanish class is finished for today. Next time children are going to use other answers for *How are you?* and follow another command.

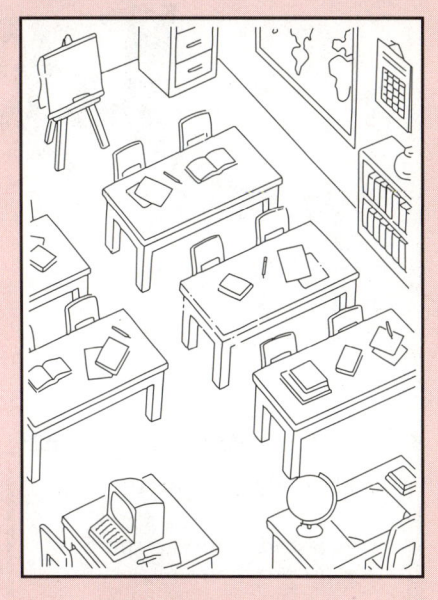

Blackline Master 4C

Classroom objects:

el papel	paper
el lápiz	pencil
el globo	globe
el libro	book
el escritorio	(teacher's) desk
la mesa	table
la silla	chair
el mapa	map

Lesson Four

Lesson 5

Materials to gather

- VCR and Video Lesson 5 on Tape 2
- Cassette player
- Activity Cassette 1
- Blackline Master 5A (classroom objects)
- Paper cutter or scissors

OBJECTIVES

Language

- Practice additional expressions for feelings
- Respond to the command **Muéstrame** ___ (*Show me* ___)
- Recognize that **Necesito** means *I need*

Culture

- Use the Spanish hand wave when saying farewell

Review

- Recall expressions for classroom objects

Vocabulary

Así, así.	*So-so.*
Muy mal.	*Very bad.*
el reloj	*clock*
la pizarra	*chalkboard*
el calendario	*calendar*
la tiza	*chalk*
Muéstrame ___.	*Show me ___.*
Necesito ___.	*I need ___.*

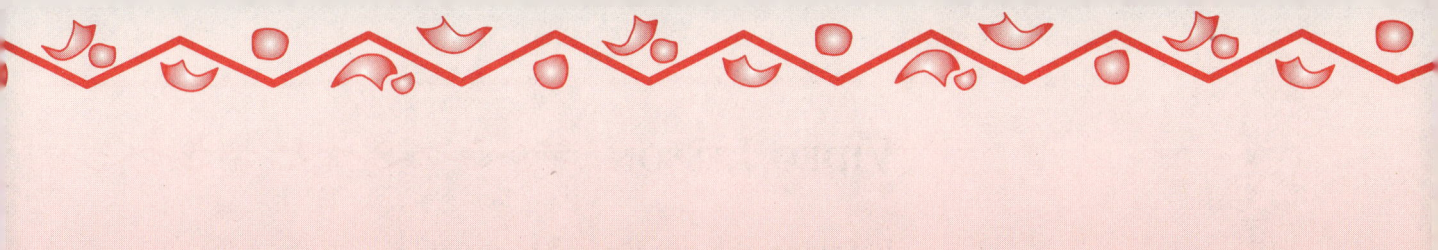

Warm-up

Exchange greetings with the class (T = Teacher, C = class):

    T: Buenos días, clase.   *Good morning, class.*
    C: Buenos días,   *Good morning, Teacher.*
       Maestro/Maestra.

Exchange farewells with the class. Wave good-bye Spanish style—with your palm toward yourself and fingers moving as if to say *come back*. Remind children to do the same. Use either **Adiós** (*Good-bye*) or **Hasta luego** (*See you later*).

Review

Ask the children to select one classroom object that they own, such as a pencil or a notebook, and to place it on top of their desks. Then go around the class and ask several students to say what item they have chosen, using **Tengo** (*I have*) and the name of the object in Spanish.

Introduce the video

Invite the class to play games using the words for classroom objects and to sing their new song as they view the video. Remind children to say farewell to **la maestra** at the end of the video.

Classroom vocabulary:

el cuaderno	*notebook*
el mapa	*map*
la goma	*eraser*
los colores	*crayons*
el boli	*pen*
el bolígrafo	*pen*
la mochila	*backpack*
el papel	*paper*
las tijeras	*scissors*
el sacapuntas	*pencil sharpener*
la bandera	*flag*

VIDEO LESSON

1. Saying the opening conversation

La maestra begins by saying **Estoy aquí con nuestra amiga Dora** (*I'm here with our friend Dora*). Next, **la maestra** says the opening conversation with Dora and then the class (**M** = Maestra, **D** = Dora, **C** = class):

M: Buenos días, Dora/clase.	*Good morning, Dora/class.*
D/C: Buenos días, Maestra.	*Good morning, Teacher.*
M: ¿Cómo estás tú?	*How are you?*
D/C: Muy bien, gracias. ¿Y usted?	*Very well, thank you. And you?*
M: Muy bien, gracias.	*Very well, thanks.*

2. Recalling other expressions for feelings

La maestra uses additional expressions for feelings.

Así, así.	*So-so.*
Muy mal.	*Very bad.*

3. Practicing words for classroom objects

La maestra asks about Dora's things.

Tengo muchas cosas aquí.	*I have many things here.*
Son cosas de la clase de español.	*They are things from Spanish class.*
¿Qué (más) necesitas?	*What (more) do you need?*
¿Necesitas ___?	*Do you need ___?*
Necesito ___.	*I need ___.*
Tengo ___.	*I have ___.*
Aquí está ___.	*Here is ___.*
Aquí están ___.	*Here are ___.*

La maestra reviews vocabulary in the order given: **un lápiz** (*pencil*), **un libro** (*book*), **un cuaderno** (*notebook*), **(el) papel** (*paper*), **(las) tijeras** (*scissors*), **un sacapuntas** (*pencil sharpener*), **(los) bolis** (*pens*), **(la) goma** (*eraser*), **(la) regla** (*ruler*), **una bandera** (*flag*), **(el) reloj** (*clock*), **(la) pizarra** (*chalkboard*), **(el) calendario** (*calendar*), **el globo** (*globe*), **(la) mesa** (*table*), **(la) silla** (*chair*), **la clase de español** (*Spanish class*). As part of the review, she says the following sentences.

Es una bandera de tres colores—azul, rojo, blanco.	*It's a three-colored flag—blue, red, white.*
¿Cuántas sillas hay?	*How many chairs are there?*
Hay nueve sillas.	*There are nine chairs.*

FYI: **Me siento muy bien** is another way of saying *I feel very well.*

FYI: Both **Necesito** and **Yo necesito** mean *I need*. Both **¿Qué necesitas?** and **¿Qué necesitas tú?** mean *What do you need?*

La maestra does not have to use **yo** (*I*) or **tú** (*you*) in the above questions. In Spanish, subject pronouns are often omitted because verb endings, such as **-o** and **-as**, tell what the subject is.

FYI: **el lápiz** (*the pencil*), **un lápiz** (*a pencil*), **la bandera** (*the flag*), **una bandera** (*a flag*). **El** (*the*) and **un** (*a, an*) are masculine. **La** (*the*) and **una** (*a, an*) are feminine.

LEVEL TWO

4. Reintroducing *Muéstrame* ___ (*Show me* ___)

The mime demonstrates the meaning of **Muéstrame**. Then **la maestra** asks children to point out the classroom objects she names.

    Muéstrame ___.   *Show me* ___.
    Sí, es ___.   *Yes, it's* ___.

5. Reviewing *Muéstrame* ___ (*Show me* ___), *Necesito* (*I need*) and *Tengo* (*I have*)

La maestra and Dora discuss what these expressions mean.

6. Singing "Español para ti" (*"Spanish Is for You, and for Me"*)

La maestra invites Dora and the class to sing along with her. Dora requests **Vamos a practicar las palabras** (*Let's practice the words*) and **la maestra** says, instead of sings, the words. For lyrics to the song, see Lesson 3, Video Lesson, Section 3.

7. Closing

La maestra says *Good-bye* (**Adiós**) and *See you later* (**Hasta luego**) to the class.

Classroom objects in order mentioned:

el calendario	calendar
el globo	globe
el reloj	clock
el escritorio	(teacher's) desk
el libro	book
el papel	paper
el mapa	map
la bandera	flag
la pizarra	chalkboard
el libro	book
el maestro	(male) teacher
la mesa	table
la maestra	(female) teacher
el lápiz	pencil
el escritorio	(teacher's) desk
la tiza	chalk

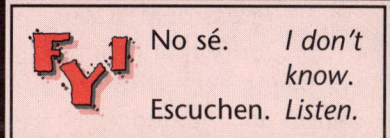

FYI

No sé.   *I don't know.*
Escuchen. *Listen.*

After viewing the video, praise the children for their good listening and watching skills.

Lesson Five

Blackline Master 5A

> Watch that children are responding with the correct pictures.

> Walk around the classroom. Make sure that children are saying **Yo tengo** or **Tengo** and pointing to the appropriate pictures. Check that children are following doña Elena's example and are using **el** and **la** correctly.

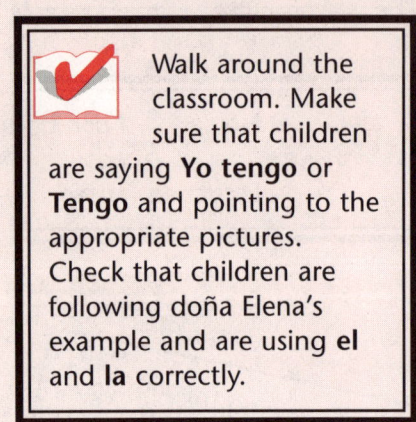

ACTIVITY LESSON

Activity 5A: Show me ___.

Materials: Cassette player; Activity Cassette 1, Side A; Blackline Master 5A; and paper cutter or scissors.

Preparation: Make copies of Blackline Master 5A (one per child). Then cut out the eight pictures or have children do so. They will use the pictures again in Activities 5B and 5C.

Have children place their pictures faceup *in random order* on their desks. Ask the class to pretend that you are Mr. Hale. Explain that he is going to ask the children to show (hold up) their pictures of a classroom object after he names it two times.

Repeat this exercise if you have time. Some children may need additional practice. Other children may simply enjoy demonstrating what they know.

Activity 5B: Who has ___?

Materials: Cassette player; Activity Cassette 1, Side A; Blackline Master 5A; and paper cutter or scissors.

Preparation: Make copies of Blackline Master 5A (one per child), if you have not already done so, and cut out the eight pictures or have children do so.

Doña Elena is going to ask a series of questions in this activity. You may wish to stop the tape after each one to allow children time to answer without speaking over the next question. Do keep the pace moving, however, so that the activity does not drag out. Tell the class that each child should choose three favorite classroom objects and place the pictures faceup on their desks. Children should then turn the other pictures facedown and put them aside. Doña Elena is going to ask **¿Quién tiene ___?** (*Who has ___?*) and say the name of a classroom object two times. Anyone who has that picture showing should point to it and say **Yo tengo** (*I have*) and its name. If you have time, allow children to choose different classroom objects and replay this activity.

LEVEL TWO

Activity 5C: Who needs ___?

Materials: Cassette player; Activity Cassette 1, Side A; Blackline Master 5A; and paper cutter or scissors.

Preparation: Make copies of Blackline Master 5A (one per child). Then cut out the eight pictures or have children do so.

Mr. Hale, the on-tape teacher, assumes that your class has done Cassette Activity 5B. If this is true, children may work with the same pictures that they used for it. If this is not true, tell the class that each child should select three favorite classroom objects and place the pictures faceup on their desks. Children should then turn over the other pictures and put them aside.

Explain that Mr. Hale is going to ask **¿Quién necesita ___?** (*Who needs ___?*) and say the name of a classroom object two times. Anyone who does not have that picture showing should say **Necesito** (*I need*) and its name. If you have time, ask children to choose different classroom objects and replay this activity.

CLOSING

Tell the children that Spanish class is finished for today. Explain that in the next video, the class will practice additional greetings and sing some more songs.

IF YOU HAVE TIME . . .

Materials: VCR and Video Lesson 5 on Tape 2.

Preparation: Cue the VCR to Video Lesson 5, section 6.

During this activity, you and the class should use **la maestra**'s hand gestures as in Activity 3C. Using the videotape, encourage children to sing along with **la maestra**. Next, have the class repeat each line of the lyrics after **la maestra** *says* it. If the class is having difficulty with any line, practice it several times before proceeding to the next one. Finish by having children sing with **la maestra** again and congratulate them on their increased fluency.

Lesson Five

Lesson 6

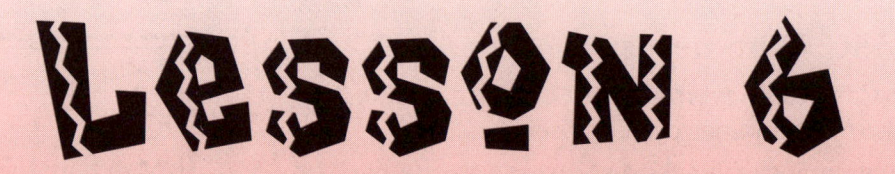

Materials to gather

- VCR and Video Lesson 6 on Tape 2
- Cassette player
- Activity Cassette 1
- Blackline Master 6A (classroom objects)
- Paper cutter or scissors
- *Optional materials:* Blackline Masters 4B, 5A, and 6A

Objectives

Language

- Sing **"Buenos días a ti"** (*"Good Morning to You"*), **"Buenas tardes a ti"** (*"Good Afternoon to You"*), **"Buenas noches a ti"** (*"Good Evening to You"*)

Culture

- Use appropriate greetings for different times of the day

Review

- Practice vocabulary for classroom objects
- Name numbers for 1 to 9
- Use **Necesito** (*I need*) and **Tengo** (*I have*)
- Sing **"Español para ti"** (*"Spanish Is for You, and for Me"*)

Vocabulary

Buenos días.	*Good morning.*
Buenas tardes.	*Good afternoon.*
Buenas noches.	*Good evening.*

Warm-up

Exchange greetings with a few students (**T** = Teacher, **C** = child):

    T: Buenos días, [*child's name*].

    C: Buenos días, Maestro/Maestra.

Then ask for a few pairs of volunteers to greet each other. They should use each other's names in the greeting (**S1** = Student 1, **S2** = Student 2):

    S1: Buenos días, [Mary].

    S2: Buenos días, [Peter].

Review

Materials: Cassette player; Activity Cassette 1, Activity 2B.

Explain that the teacher on the tape will say each word twice. If the word names one thing, children should raise one hand. If the word names more than one thing, children should raise both hands. After the cassette activity, discuss how the class knows if a word names one or more than one object.

Introduce the video

Point out that in this video, children are going to sing some songs they know from last year and they are going to play games with the words for classroom objects. Remind children to say farewell and wave good-bye to **la maestra** at the end of the video.

Video Lesson

1. Saying the opening conversation

La maestra says the opening conversation with Rosco and the class (**M** = Maestra; **R** = Rosco; **C** = class):

M:	Buenos días, Rosco/clase.	Good morning, Rosco/class.
R/C:	Buenos días, Maestra.	Good morning, Teacher.
M:	¿Cómo estás tú?	How are you?
R/C:	Muy bien, gracias. ¿Y usted?	Very well, thank you. And you?
M:	Muy bien, gracias.	Very well, thank you.

2. Reintroducing more greetings

La maestra asks Rosco what to say in three different situations.

Buenos días.	Good morning.
Buenas tardes.	Good afternoon.
Buenas noches.	Good evening.

> ✓ Make sure that children are distinguishing between **buenos** and **buenas**. **Buenos** is masculine like **días**. **Buenas** is feminine like **tardes** and **noches**.

3. Singing about greetings for various times of the day

La maestra invites Rosco and the class to sing three songs.

Buenos días a ti.	Good morning to you.
Buenos días a ti.	Good morning to you.
Buenos días, amigo.	Good morning, friend.
Buenos días a ti.	Good morning to you.
Buenas tardes a ti.	Good afternoon to you.
Buenas tardes a ti.	Good afternoon to you.
Buenas tardes, amigo.	Good afternoon, friend.
Buenas tardes a ti.	Good afternoon to you.
Buenas noches a ti.	Good evening to you.
Buenas noches a ti.	Good evening to you.
Buenas noches, amigo.	Good evening, friend.
Buenas noches a ti.	Good evening to you.

4. Reviewing words for classroom objects

As **la maestra** points to objects on "**El salón de clase**" (*The classroom*) poster, she asks the class questions and makes comments.

¿Qué es esto?	What is this?
Hay ___.	There is/are ___.
¿Qué es?	What is it?
Es ___.	It's ___.

La maestra also reviews numbers: *1* (**uno**), *2* (**dos**), *3* (**tres**), *4* (**cuatro**), *5* (**cinco**), *6* (**seis**), *7* (**siete**), *8* (**ocho**), *9* (**nueve**).

Classroom objects:

el calendario	calendar
el reloj	clock
la pizarra	chalkboard
el mapa	map
el libro	book
(el) escritorio	(teacher's) desk
el globo	globe
el lápiz	pencil
la regla	ruler
la mesa	table
la silla	chair

5. Playing *Muéstrame* ___ (*Show me* ___)

La maestra has children point to objects that she names and also asks the class to name items that she indicates.

6. Using *Tengo* (*I have*) and *Necesito* (*I need*)

Rosco teases **la maestra** about a picture he has drawn.

¿Qué tienes?	*What do you have?*
Tengo papel.	*I have a piece of paper.*
¿Quién es?	*Who is she?*
Es la maestra.	*She's the teacher.*
Necesito boli.	*I need a pen.*
¿Necesitas boli?	*Do you need a pen?*
¿Qué necesitas hacer?	*What do you need to do?*

As she looks for a pen, **la maestra** names classroom objects.

Tengo ___.   *I have ___.*

After a frustrated Rosco finally lets her draw the teacher's mouth, **la maestra** reviews parts of the face. Vocabulary: **los ojos** (*eyes*); **la nariz** (*nose*); and **la boca** (*mouth*).

7. Identifying classroom objects

La maestra wants Rosco and the class to name various items.

¿Qué es esto?	*What is this?*
Es ___.	*It's ___.*

8. Singing "Español para ti" ("*Spanish Is for You, and for Me*")

La maestra invites Rosco and the class to sing with her. For song lyrics, see Lesson 3, Video Lesson, section 3.

9. Closing

La maestra says **Adiós** (*Good-bye*) and **Hasta luego** (*See you later*).

Classroom vocabulary:

el boli	*pen*
la regla	*ruler*
las tijeras	*scissors*
el sacapuntas	*pencil sharpener*
la goma	*eraser*
el cuaderno	*notebook*
el papel	*paper*

After viewing the video, praise the children for their good listening and watching skills.

Lesson Six

Blackline Master 6A

> Check that children are holding up the correct pictures.

> Make sure that children are saying **Necesito**. Check that children are following Mr. Hale's example and are using **el** and **la** correctly.

LEVEL TWO

ACTIVITY LESSON

Activity 6A: *Muéstrame* ___ (*Show me* ___)

Materials: Cassette player; Activity Cassette 1, Side A; Blackline Master 6A; and paper cutter or scissors.

Preparation: Make copies of Blackline Master 6A (one per child). Then cut out the eight pictures or have children do so. You will need this Blackline Master for Activities 6B and 6C.

Have the children place their pictures faceup in random order on their desks. In this activity, as in Activity 5A, Mr. Hale will ask the children to show (hold up) a picture of a classroom object after he names it two times. Repeat this exercise if you have time.

Activity 6B: *¿Quién tiene?* (*Who has* ___?)

Materials: Cassette player; Activity Cassette 1, Side A; Blackline Master 6A; and paper cutter or scissors.

Preparation: Make copies of Blackline Master 6A (one per child), if you haven't already done so, and cut out the eight pictures or have children do so.

Tell the class that each child should choose three classroom objects and place the pictures faceup on their desks. Children should then put aside the other pictures.

Explain that Mr. Hale is going to ask **¿Quién tiene** ___**?** (*Who has* ___?) and say the name of a classroom object two times. Anyone who has that picture should stand, hold up the picture, and say **Tengo** (*I have*) and its name. If you have time, allow children to choose different classroom objects and replay this activity.

Activity 6C: *Yo necesito* (*I need*)

Materials: Cassette player; Activity Cassette, Side A; Blackline Master 6A; and paper cutter or scissors.

Preparation: Make copies of Blackline Master 6A (one per child), if you haven't already done so, and cut out the eight pictures or have children do so.

As in Lesson 5, Mr. Hale assumes that your class has already done Cassette Activity 6B and has picked out three favorite classroom objects from those on Blackline Master 6A. If this is not true, tell the class to select the three objects now and place the pictures faceup on their desks. The remaining pictures can be put aside.

Explain that Mr. Hale is going to ask **¿Quién necesita** ___**?** (*Who needs* ___?) and say the name of a classroom object two times. Anyone who does not have that picture showing should say **Necesito** (*I need*) and its name. If you have time, ask children to choose different classroom objects and replay this activity.

Closing

Tell the children that Spanish class is finished for today. In the next class, they will play more games and talk about the months of the year.

> **IF YOU HAVE TIME . . .**
>
> Materials: Blackline Masters 4B, 5A, and 6A.
>
> Preparation: Make enough copies so that each child has a cutout picture. Depending on the size of your class, some children may have duplicate pictures.
>
> Have the class sit in a circle. Select the first two players. Have the second player show his or her picture to the rest of the class. Explain that the first player should look at the other child's picture and say **Necesito** (*I need*) and name the object. The second child should answer **Tengo** (*I have*), name it, and hand the picture to the first player. Continue in the same way around the circle.
>
> The classroom vocabulary is listed in the Video Lesson for this lesson. If a player cannot name an object or misnames it, encourage the other children to assist him or her just as **la maestra**, Rosco, and Dora help each other.

Lesson Six

Lesson 7

Materials to gather

- VCR and Video Lesson 7 on Tape 2
- Cassette player
- Activity Cassette 1
- Hand puppets Dora and Rosco
- Blackline Masters 6A, 7A (classroom objects)
- Gold Flashcards 48–50, 62
- Paper cutter or scissors
- *Optional materials:* Song Cassette

OBJECTIVES

Language
- Practice the months January through July in Spanish

Culture
- Sing "**Uno de enero**" (*"January First"*)

Review
- Practice classroom vocabulary
- Use classroom vocabulary in games

Vocabulary

enero	*January*
febrero	*February*
marzo	*March*
abril	*April*
mayo	*May*
junio	*June*
julio	*July*
Gracias.	*Thank you.*

Warm-up

Select two volunteers to use puppets to exchange the appropriate greeting, depending on the time of day (**D** = Dora, **R** = Rosco):

D: Buenos días/Buenas tardes, Rosco. *Good morning/afternoon, Rosco.*

R: Buenos días/Buenas tardes, Dora. *Good morning/afternoon, Dora.*

Review

Materials: Gold Flashcards 48–50 and 62.

Preparation: You may wish to cut these cards in half as **la maestra** has, so that you show only one month at a time.

Ask the class to name the first seven months of the year in English. Remind children that **la maestra** used Flashcards last year to help them remember these names in Spanish. Show the Gold Flashcards and quickly review what each one represents. Encourage the class to name the months in English and explain the illustrations, but provide any necessary information.

#48: January—snow because January is a cold month in most places in the United States

February—valentines for Valentine's Day

#49: March—shamrocks for St. Patrick's Day

April—kites for the windy days of spring

#50: May—flowers because they are starting to bloom

June—mortar board and diploma for graduation

#62: July—fireworks for July 4, Independence Day

Remind children that **la maestra** uses different Flashcards for May and June. For May, she has flowers that are just starting to bloom. For June, she has flowers that are in full bloom.

Introduce the video

Tell children that they are going to play games and sing a song.

> **FYI** The months of the year are not capitalized in Spanish.

> **La <u>mochila</u> es muy bonit<u>a</u>.**
> (The book bag is very <u>pretty</u>.)
> **Tengo mucha<u>s</u> <u>cosas</u>.**
> (I have <u>many</u> <u>things</u>.)
> **La mochila es de mucho<u>s</u> <u>colores</u>.**
> (The book bag has <u>many</u> <u>colors</u>.)
>
> Adjectives agree with the nouns they describe. **Mochila** is feminine and singular, so **bonita** ends in **-a**. **Cosas** is feminine and plural, so **muchas** ends in **-as**. **Colores** is masculine and plural, so **muchos** ends in **-os**.

Video Lesson

1. Saying the opening conversation

La maestra says the opening conversation with Rosco and the class (**M** = Maestra, **R** = Rosco, **C** = class):

M: Buenos días, Rosco/clase.	*Good morning, Rosco/class.*
R/C: Buenos días, Maestra.	*Good morning, Teacher.*
M: ¿Cómo estás tú?	*How are you?*
R/C: Muy bien, gracias. ¿Y usted?	*Very well, thank you. And you?*
M: Muy bien, gracias.	*Very well, thanks.*

2. Reviewing classroom objects

As **la maestra** talks about her school supplies, she expects Rosco and the class to repeat the words after her.

Tengo ___.	*I have ___.*
No tengo ___.	*I don't have ___.*
¿No tienes ___?	*You don't have ___?*
Tienes ___.	*You have ___.*

La maestra reviews vocabulary in the order given: **colores** (*crayons*), **gomas** (*erasers*), **regla** (*ruler*), **papel** (*paper*), **lápiz** (*pencil*), **boli** (*pen*), **cuaderno** (*notebook*).

3. Playing ¿Cuál falta? (What's missing?)

La maestra models vocabulary practiced earlier plus **la mochila** (*book bag*), **la goma** (*pen*), and **las tijeras** (*scissors*) and has children repeat after her. Then she asks ¿**Cuál falta**? After children respond, she models the answers.

4. Reintroducing the months January through July

La maestra asks Rosco, ¿**Recuerdas los meses del año**? (*Do you remember the months of the year?*). Next, she models the first seven months and has Rosco and the children repeat after her.

enero	*January*
febrero	*February*
marzo	*March*
abril	*April*
mayo	*May*
junio	*June*
julio	*July*

> **LANGUAGE ACROSS THE CURRICULUM**
>
> Discuss the months whose names are similar in Spanish and English—**febrero** (*February*), **marzo** (*March*), **abril** (*April*), and **mayo** (*May*).

LEVEL TWO

5. Reintroducing "Uno de enero" ("January First")

La maestra prepares the class for singing **"Uno de enero"** by modeling each line up to the chorus. Then she and the children sing the entire song and she reminds them what the chorus means.

Uno de enero, dos de febrero,	*January first, February second,*
Tres de marzo, cuatro de abril.	*March third, April fourth.*
Cinco de mayo, seis de junio,	*May fifth, June sixth,*
Siete de julio, San Fermín.	*July seventh, Saint Fermín.*

Chorus:

Tra la la la la la la.	*Tra la la la la la la.*
¿Quién ha roto la pandereta?	*Who broke the tambourine?*
Tra la la la la la la.	*Tra la la la la la la.*
El que la ha roto la pagará.	*Whoever broke it will pay for it.*
El que la ha roto la pagará.	*Whoever broke it will pay for it.*

6. Playing ¿Quién tiene ___? (Who has ___?)

La maestra asks about objects practiced earlier in the lesson plus two additional ones—**la bandera** (*flag*) and **el libro** (*book*).

¿Quién tiene ___?	*Who has ___?*
Yo tengo ___.	*I have ___.*
(Yo) no tengo ___.	*I don't have ___.*

7. Playing ¿Cuál falta? (What's missing?) with la maestra

La maestra models vocabulary practiced earlier plus additional ones, and has the children repeat them. Then she asks **¿Cuál falta?** After children respond, she models the answers.

8. Playing ¿Quién tiene ___? (Who has ___?) again

Rosco and Dora play a hotly contested **¿Quién tiene ___?**

Yo quiero jugar.	*I want to play.*
Yo tengo ___.	*I have ___.*
No, yo tengo ___.	*No, I have ___.*
Rosco y Dora tienen el boli.	*Rosco and Dora have the pen.*

9. Singing "Español para ti" ("Spanish Is for You, and for Me")

La maestra asks **¿Qué canción quieren ustedes?** (*What song do you want to sing?*). Then everyone says the words to **"Español para ti"** in addition to singing it. For the lyrics to the song, see Lesson 3, Video Lesson, section 3.

10. Closing

La maestra bids the class **Adiós** (*Good-bye*).

FYI July 7 is the feast of Saint Fermín in Pamplona, Spain. During this festival the Running of the Bulls takes place. Bulls run through particular streets and men run in front of them to prove their courage.

Classroom vocabulary:

la maestra	(*female*) *teacher*
el maestro	(*male*) *teacher*
el calendario	*calendar*
el escritorio	*teacher's desk*
la tiza	*chalk*
la mochila	*book bag*
el reloj	*clock*

FYI In this game, the puppets say **yo tengo** and not **tengo** because they are emphasizing the *I* in *I have.*

After viewing the video, praise the children for their good listening and watching skills.

Lesson Seven

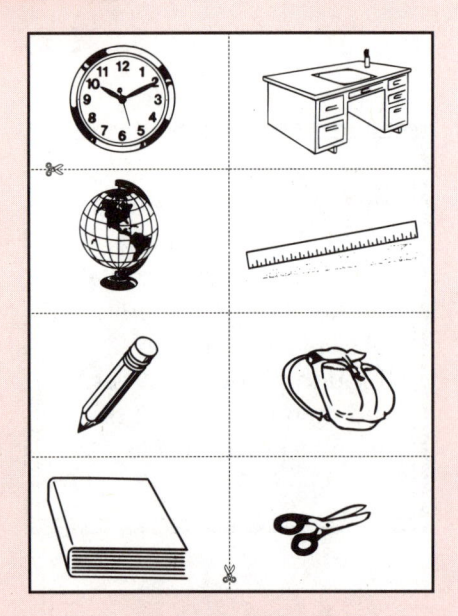

Blackline Master 6A

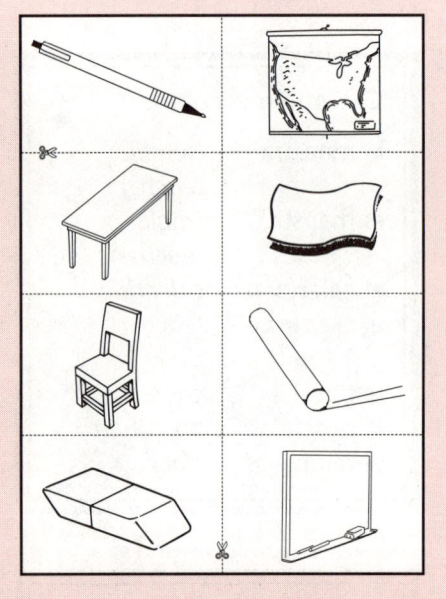

Blackline Master 7A

LEVEL TWO

ACTIVITY LESSON

Activity 7A: *Tengo* ___ (*I have* ___)

Materials: Cassette player; Activity Cassette 1, Side A; Blackline Masters 6A and 7A; and paper cutter or scissors.

Preparation: Make enough copies of Blackline Masters 6A and 7A, so that there is one picture per child. Depending on your class size, there may be some duplicates. Cut the pictures apart.

Explain that Mr. Hale is going to ask about classroom objects. For each item, he is going to say **¿Quién tiene ___?** (*Who has ___?*) and the name of an object two times. Whoever has a picture of that object should hold it up and say **tengo** (*I have*) and the item's name. Point out that the class should listen very carefully because Mr. Hale is only going to name some of the pictures. Children could trade pictures before you repeat this activity.

Activity 7B: Which month comes next?

Materials: Cassette player; Activity Cassette 1, Side A; and Gold Flashcards 48–50 and 62.

Display the Flashcards where everyone can see them. As the class says the names for the first seven months of the year in English and in Spanish, point to the appropriate picture.

Ask the children to name the months on the Flashcards in English. Explain that Mr. Hale first wants them to repeat these months after him. He is only going to say each name once. Then they are going to say the months with him. Since the last five months are introduced in the next lesson, you may want to repeat this activity at that point.

Activity 7C: How can we be polite in Spanish?

Materials: Cassette player; Activity Cassette 1, Side A.

Point out to the children that they and **la maestra** say thank you to each other in the opening conversation; they thank one another for asking how they are feeling. Explain that in this activity, doña Elena is going to have them practice saying thank you in Spanish.

Closing

Tell the children that Spanish class is finished for today. In the next video, the class is going to sing the song about the months again and learn the rest of the months in Spanish. Children are also going to hear a story.

LANGUAGE ACROSS THE CURRICULUM

You may wish to discuss various times when it is appropriate for the children to say thank you in their daily lives, including in the classroom.

IF YOU HAVE TIME...

Materials: Cassette player; Song Cassette, Side A.

Play each song through once and have a volunteer summarize its meaning. Then have children sing along with the cassette.

Buenos días a ti.
(*Good morning to you.*)
Buenos días a ti.
(*Good morning to you.*)
Buenos días, amigo.
(*Good morning, friend.*)
Buenos días a ti.
(*Good morning to you.*)

Buenas tardes a ti.
(*Good afternoon to you.*)
Buenas tardes a ti.
(*Good afternoon to you.*)
Buenas tardes, amigo.
(*Good afternoon, friend.*)
Buenas tardes a ti.
(*Good afternoon to you.*)

Buenas noches a ti.
(*Good evening to you.*)
Buenas noches a ti.
(*Good evening to you.*)
Buenas noches, amigo.
(*Good evening, friend.*)
Buenas noches a ti.
(*Good evening to you.*)

Lesson Seven

Lesson 8

Materials to gather

- VCR and Video Lesson 8 on Tape 2
- Cassette player
- Activity Cassette 1
- Song Cassette
- Gold Flashcards 48–50, 62–64
- 7 small self-stick notes
- Colored marker

- *Optional materials:* Blackline Masters 4B, 5A, 6A; scissors or paper cutter

- *Prepare ahead:* Masks for Activity 9B

OBJECTIVES

Language

- Practice the months August through December
- Play games using the months of the year
- Understand sustained conversation in Spanish about activities at a school

Culture

- Sing **"Uno de enero"** (*"January First"*)
- Associate holidays with the months in which they occur

Review

- Practice the months January through July

Vocabulary

agosto	*August*
septiembre	*September*
octubre	*October*
noviembre	*November*
diciembre	*December*

Warm-up

Greet the class with **Buenos días** (*Good morning*), **Buenas tardes** (*Good afternoon*), or **¡Hola!** (*Hello*). After their response, ask several pairs of volunteers to greet each other by name.

Review

Remind children that there were times last year when they heard quite a bit of Spanish being said all at once. This usually happened when they heard stories, such as "The Three Little Pigs." Point out that the stories were always a mixture of known and unknown Spanish words. Then try to elicit some methods that children used to understand what was going on— listening for words that they knew, looking at the pictures for clues, and listening for Spanish words that sounded like English words. Suggest these procedures if the class has forgotten them.

Emphasize that no one is expected to understand everything when they hear a lot of Spanish at once. Children should just do their best and enjoy what is being told.

Introduce the video

Tell children that they are going to learn more names for months of the year and play some games. In addition, **la maestra** is going to take them on a visit to a school and tell them what she sees. She is introducing them to many topics that they are going to study in Spanish during the year.

Video Lesson

1. Saying the opening conversation

In turn, **la maestra** says the conversation with Ñico, Rosco, and the class (**M** = Maestra, **Ñ** = Ñico, **R** = Rosco, **C** = class):

M:	Buenos días, Ñico/Rosco/clase.	*Good morning, Ñico/Rosco/class.*
Ñ/R/C:	Buenos días, Maestra.	*Good morning, Teacher.*
M:	¿Cómo estás tú?	*How are you?*
Ñ/R/C:	Muy bien, gracias. ¿Y usted?	*Very well, thank you. And you?*
M:	Muy bien, gracias.	*Very well, thanks.*

2. Reviewing January through July

La maestra asks, ¿Recuerdan ustedes los meses del año? (*Do you remember the months of the year?*). Then she models the name for each month, shows the accompanying Flashcard, and has children repeat after her. **La maestra** reviews vocabulary in the order given: **enero** (*January*), **febrero** (*February*), **marzo** (*March*), **abril** (*April*), **mayo** (*May*), **junio** (*June*), **julio** (*July*).

3. Singing "Uno de enero" (*"January First"*)

Using the Flashcards, **la maestra** models the lyrics through July and has the puppets and class repeat after her. Then she has everyone sing the entire song with her.

Uno de enero, dos de febrero,	*January first, February second,*
Tres de marzo, cuatro de abril.	*March third, April fourth.*
Cinco de mayo, seis de junio,	*May fifth, June sixth,*
Siete de julio, San Fermín.	*July seventh, Saint Fermín.*

Chorus:

Tra la la la la la la.	*Tra la la la la la la.*
¿Quién ha roto la pandereta?	*Who broke the tambourine?*
Tra la la la la la la.	*Tra la la la la la la.*
El que la ha roto la pagará.	*Whoever broke it will pay for it.*
El que la ha roto la pagará.	*Whoever broke it will pay for it.*

4. Introducing August through December

La maestra models each of the months after July and shows the corresponding the Flashcard. The puppets and the class take turns repeating after her. During this practice, **la maestra** discusses the illustrations on the Flashcards and related weather expressions.

agosto	*August*	noviembre	*November*
septiembre	*September*	diciembre	*December*
octubre	*October*		

FYI

La maestra introduces another command.

Repitan.   *Repeat.*

CROSS-CULTURAL CONNECTIONS

This Spanish song is linked with a particular holiday celebrated in Spain. In a similar way, "Yankee Doodle" is often played in the U.S.A. on July 4 because it was a popular song during the American Revolution and is associated with the United States becoming an independent country.

Weather expressions:

Hace mucho calor.	*It's very hot.*
Hace viento.	*It's windy.*
Hace mucho frío.	*It's very cold.*

5. Playing *Sí o no* (Yes or no)

La maestra takes turns showing Rosco and Ñico a Flashcard. She asks if it represents a particular month and the player says **sí** or **no**. **La maestra** verifies the correct answer.

¿Es ___?	Is it ___?
Sí, es ___.	Yes, it's ___.
No, no es ___.	No, it's not ___.
Es ___.	It's ___.

6. Touring a school

La maestra takes the class on a visit to a school. Here is some of the information she gives.

Vamos a la escuela.	Let's go in the school.
Aquí está la oficina.	Here is the office.
Aquí trabajan la secretaria y la directora.	The secretary and the principal work here.
Estoy en la biblioteca.	I am in the library.
A todos los niños les gustan los libros.	All children like books.

7. Playing a game, using the command *Toca ___* (*Touch ___*)

La maestra models all the months. She has the puppets and the class repeat after her. Then she shows Flashcards for two months. **La maestra** tells a puppet to touch a particular month and she confirms the answer.

Toca ___.	Touch ___.
___ está aquí.	___ is this one.

8. Closing

La maestra promises to practice the months more. Then she says **Adiós** (*Good-bye*) and **Hasta luego** (*See you later*) to the class.

HERITAGE SPEAKERS

Ask children when school begins and ends in their countries. If some children come from nations that are south of the equator, their answers will surprise classmates.

After viewing the video, praise the children for their good listening and watching skills.

Lesson Eight

> Just as we all know to stop when we see a red octagonal sign, visuals help children remember the meaning of what they are saying *without* having to consciously translate English into Spanish or vice versa.

ACTIVITY LESSON

Activity 8A: The months of the year

Materials: Cassette player; Activity Cassette 1, Side A; and Gold Flashcards 48–50 and 62–64.

Preparation: Arrange the Gold Flashcards in calendar order and place them where everyone can see them, or be ready to show each month as it is named on the tape.

Explain that after Mr. Hale names each month once, the class should repeat after him. Repeat this activity several times if possible. To prevent boredom, you could do this activity a couple of times, then do Activity 8B, and then return to this one again.

Activity 8B: Which Flashcard means August?

Materials: Gold Flashcards 48–50 and 62–64.

Preparation: Display the Flashcards in calendar order.

Ask the class to name the months of the year in English, and point to each one as it is mentioned. If you have already reviewed the meaning of the illustrations for January through July, have volunteers quickly name the months and explain the pictures. If not, use the information in the Review for Lesson 7.

For August through December, name each month and point to the illustration. Ask what the Flashcard shows and why an artist might use that picture to stand for the selected month. Provide answers where necessary.

- #62: August—Often the hottest weather occurs at that time in the United States and people go to the beach to cool off.
- #63: September—Many children go back to school.
    October—In many parts of the United States, the leaves change color as the weather gets colder.
- #64: November—The horn of plenty or cornucopia shows the fruits and vegetables from a good harvest ready for a Thanksgiving feast.
    December—The weather gets cold and winter snows begin in many areas of the United States.

After discussing these months, quickly name them again and have the class briefly summarize the meaning of the illustrations.

Activity 8C: Remember July 7

Materials: Cassette player; **"Uno de enero"** (*"January First"*) on the Song Cassette, Side A; Gold Flashcards 48–50, 62; 7 small self-stick removable notes; and a colored marker.

Preparation: To help the children remember the number for each month, write 1–7 on the self-stick notes. Place the notes within view of the class.

Ask children to listen as you play the song through once and point to the months on the Flashcards.

Uno de enero, dos de febrero,	*January first, February second,*
Tres de marzo, cuatro de abril.	*March third, April fourth.*
Cinco de mayo, seis de junio,	*May fifth, June sixth,*
Siete de julio, San Fermín.	*July seventh, Saint Fermín.*

Chorus:

Tra la la la la la la.	*Tra la la la la la la.*
¿Quién ha roto la pandereta?	*Who broke the tambourine?*
Tra la la la la la la.	*Tra la la la la la la.*
El que la ha roto la pagará.	*Whoever broke it will pay for it.*
El que la ha roto la pagará.	*Whoever broke it will pay for it.*

Then replay the song line by line and ask volunteers to tell which day of each month the song describes. After a volunteer explains, have him or her attach the appropriate self-stick note to the relevant Flashcard.

Play the song a couple more times and have the class sing along. As each day and month is named, point to the note and the illustration.

CLOSING

Tell the children that Spanish class is finished for today. In the next video, the class is going to add more numbers, practice the months, and talk about the weather.

IF YOU HAVE TIME . . .

Materials: Blackline Masters 4B, 5A, 6A; scissors or paper cutter.

Preparation: Make two copies of the Blackline Masters for each small group. Cut them into pictures for cards.

Divide the class into small groups. Tell the groups to turn the pictures face down and mix them thoroughly. Each player then takes four cards.

In each group, Player A asks another player for a card by saying **Necesito** (*I need*) and an object's name. If Player B has it, he or she says **Tengo** (*I have*) and its name and gives Player A the card. Player A then lays down the pair and asks for another picture. If Player B does not have the object, he or she says **No tengo** (*I don't have*) and its name. Player A draws a card from the pile. It is then the next player's turn. Play continues until one child no longer has any cards left.

Lesson Eight

Lesson 9

Materials to gather

- VCR and Video Lesson 9 on Tape 3
- Cassette player
- Song Cassette
- Gold Flashcards 48–50, 62–64
- Basketball or other large ball
- Blackline Master 9B-1, 9B-2, 9B-3 (masks)
- Blackline Master 9C-1, 9C-2, 9C-3 (times of day)
- Scissors
- Glue
- Craft sticks

Objectives

Language

- Sing the "Finger Play Song"
- Count from 1 to 20
- Practice eight weather expressions

Culture

- Understand that seasons are reversed in most of South America

Review

- Practice the months of the year
- Sing **"Uno de enero"** (*"January First"*)

Vocabulary

siete	*seven*	catorce	*fourteen*
ocho	*eight*	quince	*fifteen*
nueve	*nine*	dieciséis	*sixteen*
diez	*ten*	diecisiete	*seventeen*
once	*eleven*	dieciocho	*eighteen*
doce	*twelve*	diecinueve	*nineteen*
trece	*thirteen*	veinte	*twenty*

Hace sol.	*It's sunny.*
Hace calor.	*It's hot.*
Hace frío.	*It's cold.*
Hace buen tiempo.	*It's good weather.*
Llueve.	*It's raining.*
Hace viento.	*It's windy.*
Nieva.	*It's snowing.*
Hace mal tiempo.	*It's bad weather.*

Warm-up

Exchange both types of greetings with the class (T = Teacher, C = class):

T: Buenos días/Buenas tardes, clase.	*Good morning/Good afternoon, class.*
C: Buenos días/Buenas tardes, Maestro/Maestra.	*Good morning/Good afternoon, Teacher.*
T: Hola, clase.	*Hello, class.*
C: Hola, Maestro/Maestra.	*Hello, Teacher.*

Ask volunteers to explain what the greetings mean.

Review

Materials: Gold Flashcards 48–50, 62–64

Display the Flashcards where everyone can see them. Remind children that they have already talked about the months in Spanish. Tell the class to name the months of the year and the seasons in English. Then ask them to briefly describe what the weather is like during the summer and winter. Explain that they'll be talking more about the seasons later.

Introduce the video

As children practice with this video, ask them to notice how much Spanish they already know—another song, counting, months of the year, and expressions that describe the weather.

HERITAGE SPEAKERS

Ask children from other cultures to say comparable greetings in their native languages.

Video Lesson

1. Exchanging greetings

La maestra greets everyone (**M** = Maestra, **C** = class, **R** = Rosco, **Ñ** = Ñico):

M:	Buenos días, clase/Rosco/Ñico.	*Good morning, class/Rosco/Ñico.*
C/R/Ñ:	Buenos días, Maestra.	*Good morning, Teacher.*
M:	¿Cómo estás tú?	*How are you?*
C/R/Ñ:	Muy bien, gracias. ¿Y usted?	*Very well, thank you. And you?*
M:	Muy bien, gracias.	*Very well, thanks.*

2. Reintroducing the "Finger Play Song"

La maestra sings the "Finger Play Song." Next, she models it line by line and has the class repeat after her. Then they all sing it.

Buenos días, buenos días.	*Good morning, good morning.*
¿Cómo estás tú?	*How are you?*
¿Cómo estás tú?	*How are you?*
Muy bien, gracias.	*Very well, thank you.*
Muy bien, gracias.	*Very well, thank you.*
Adiós. Adiós.	*Good-bye. Good-bye.*

3. Counting numbers 1–20

La maestra models counting two ten-block trains. First, she has the puppets and the class repeat after her and then they count together. **La maestra** also asks for the sum of 10 and 10.

1	uno	*6*	seis	*11*	once	*16*	dieciséis
2	dos	*7*	siete	*12*	doce	*17*	diecisiete
3	tres	*8*	ocho	*13*	trece	*18*	dieciocho
4	cuatro	*9*	nueve	*14*	catorce	*19*	diecinueve
5	cinco	*10*	diez	*15*	quince	*20*	veinte

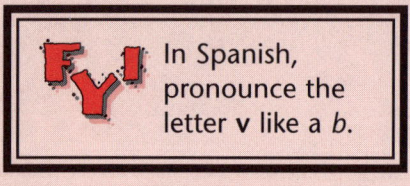

You may wish to have volunteers summarize these lyrics to check that children still remember what they are saying in this song.

FYI In Spanish, pronounce the letter **v** like a *b*.

Notice how **la maestra** is always encouraging the class. In this lesson she is focusing on how much the children already know.

4. Practicing the months of the year

La maestra models each month and has the class repeat them.

enero	*January*	julio	*July*
febrero	*February*	agosto	*August*
marzo	*March*	septiembre	*September*
abril	*April*	octubre	*October*
mayo	*May*	noviembre	*November*
junio	*June*	diciembre	*December*

La maestra counts the months and the others repeat after her.

¿Cuántos son?   *How many are there?*
Hay doce meses del año.   *There are twelve months in a year.*

5. Singing "Uno de enero" (*"January First"*)

La maestra and the class review numbers and months.

Uno de enero, dos de febrero,   *January first, February second,*
Tres de marzo, cuatro de abril.   *March third, April fourth.*
Cinco de mayo, seis de junio,   *May fifth, June sixth,*
Siete de julio, San Fermín.   *July seventh, Saint Fermín.*

6. Changing months, changing seasons

La maestra points out that as the months change so do the weather and the seasons. She explains that in South America the summer months are December, January, and February and the winter months are June, July, and August.

7. Reintroducing weather expressions

La maestra practices two groups of weather expressions. She models each and has the class repeat them. **La maestra** also asks children to provide information about weather conditions.

Muéstrame ___.   *Show me ___.*
¿Qué tiempo hace?   *What's the weather like?*
¿Hace ___ o ___?   *Is it ___ or ___?*
¿Hace ___?   *Is it ___?*
No, no hace ___.   *No, it's not ___.*
Hace ___.   *It's ___.*

8. Saying weather expressions with months of the year

La maestra uses a month and a weather condition together.

En enero hace frío.   *In January it's cold.*

9. Closing

La maestra says **Adiós** (*Good-bye*) to the class.

LANGUAGE ACROSS THE CURRICULUM

If you have a globe or a map showing the relative positions of North and South America, point out the location of these continents to the class. Explain that seasons are reversed in countries that fall below the equator.

Weather expressions:

Hace sol.
(*It's sunny.*)
Hace calor.
(*It's hot.*)
Hace frío.
(*It's cold.*)
Hace buen tiempo.
(*It's good weather.*)
Llueve.
(*It's raining.*)
Hace viento.
(*It's windy.*)
Nieva.
(*It's snowing.*)
Hace mal tiempo.
(*It's bad weather.*)

After viewing the video, praise the children for their good listening and watching skills.

Lesson Nine

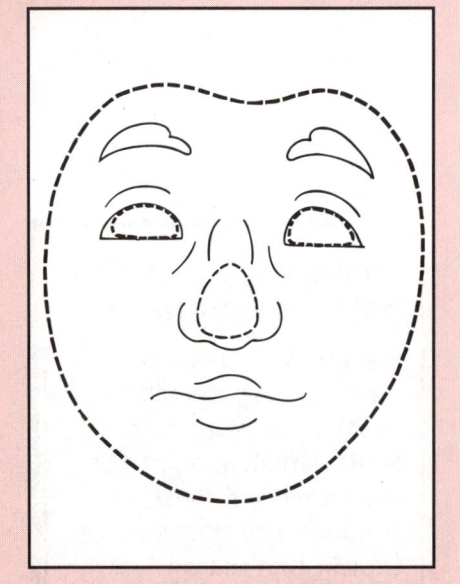

Blackline Master 9B-1

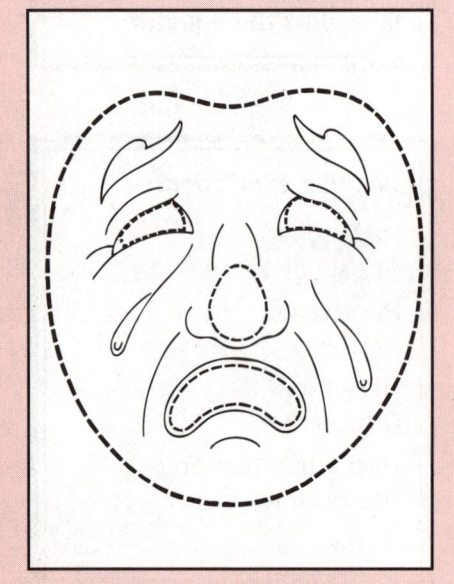

Blackline Master 9B-2

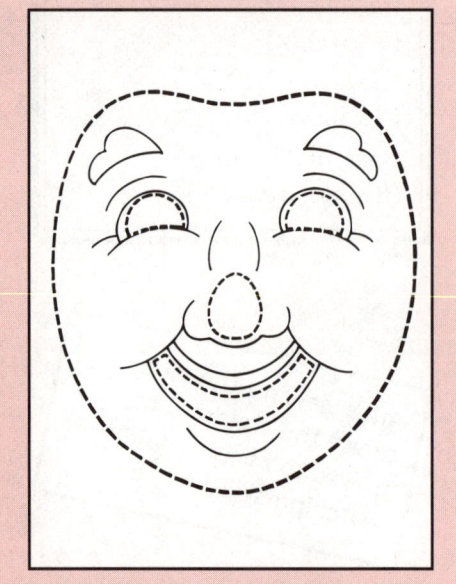

Blackline Master 9B-3

LEVEL TWO

ACTIVITY LESSON

Activity 9A: Cooperative Learning—Bounce and count

Materials: Basketball or other large-size ball.

Divide the class into two groups. Explain that each group is going to have an opportunity to play with the ball. Next, ask half the class to stand and form a circle. Tell the other half to remain seated. Then give the ball to a player in the circle. This player and the seated children are going to say **uno** (*1*) as the player bounces the ball to another child in the circle. The second player and the seated children say **dos** (*2*) as the ball is bounced to still another player. Tell the children to continue in this way until they reach **veinte** (*20*). Then have the two groups change places and replay the game. To maintain interest in the game, encourage players to keep the ball moving as quickly as is reasonable.

1	uno	*6*	seis	*11*	once	*16*	dieciséis
2	dos	*7*	siete	*12*	doce	*17*	diecisiete
3	tres	*8*	ocho	*13*	trece	*18*	dieciocho
4	cuatro	*9*	nueve	*14*	catorce	*19*	diecinueve
5	cinco	*10*	diez	*15*	quince	*20*	veinte

Activity 9B: Look at our masks!

Materials: Cassette player; "Let's March #1" on Song Cassette, Side A; Blackline Masters 9B-1, 9B-2, 9B-3; scissors; glue; and craft sticks.

Preparation: Make approximately equal numbers of the Blackline Masters. Each child should have one mask. If possible, duplicate the Blackline Masters in different colors and laminate them, so that children may use the masks throughout the year.

Have the class sit in a circle. Discuss what feeling each picture represents—**Así, así** (*So-so*); **Muy mal** (*Very bad*); and **Muy bien** (*Very well*). Next, explain that the class is going to hear some familiar music and that **la maestra** is going to take turns saying **así, así; muy mal;** and **muy bien.** When children hear the expression that matches their picture, they should march to the center of the circle with the picture and then return to their seat.

Tell children that they are going to use these pictures to make masks that they are going to use throughout the year. Ask children to follow the dotted lines to cut out the mask, the eyes, and the nose. Then demonstrate how to put glue on the stick and attach the stick to the mask. Allow time for the glue to dry and save the masks in a safe place.

Activity 9C: How do you greet friends?

Materials: Cassette player; **"Buenos días a ti"** (*"Good Morning to You"*), **"Buenas tardes a ti"** (*"Good Afternoon to You"*), and **"Buenas noches a ti"** (*"Good Evening to You"*) on Song Cassette, Side A; and two copies each of Blackline Masters 9C-1, 9C-2, 9C-3.

Show children the three Blackline Masters and discuss the times of day they represent—morning, afternoon, and evening. Next, display the appropriate Blackline Master as you play each song. Remind the class that the word **amigo** in the songs means *friend*. Then replay each song and have children sing along, again showing the appropriate Blackline Master.

Buenos días a ti.	*Good morning to you.*
Buenos días a ti.	*Good morning to you.*
Buenos días, amigo.	*Good morning, friend.*
Buenos días a ti.	*Good morning to you.*
Buenas tardes a ti.	*Good afternoon to you.*
Buenas tardes a ti.	*Good afternoon to you.*
Buenas tardes, amigo.	*Good afternoon, friend.*
Buenas tardes a ti.	*Good afternoon to you.*
Buenas noches a ti.	*Good evening to you.*
Buenas noches a ti.	*Good evening to you.*
Buenas noches, amigo.	*Good evening, friend.*
Buenas noches a ti.	*Good evening to you.*

Then have several pairs of volunteers each choose a set of Blackline Masters, show them to the class, and say the appropriate greeting to each other. Be sure that volunteers practice **Buenas noches** since this is the greeting with which children have the least practice.

CLOSING

Tell the children that Spanish class is finished for today. Next time they are going to sing a rap and play games.

Blackline Master 9C-1

Blackline Master 9C-2

Blackline Master 9C-3

Lesson Nine

Lesson 10

Materials to gather

- VCR and Video Lesson 10 on Tape 3
- Cassette player
- Activity Cassette 1
- Song Cassette
- Blackline Master 9C-1, 9C-2, 9C-3 (times of day)
- Gold Flashcards 48–50, 62–64
- Blackline Master 10A (weather expressions)
- Scissors
- Blackline Master 10B (weather expressions)
- Blackline Masters 10C-1, 10C-2 (months and numbers 1–12)
- Paste or tape
- Paper clips or rubber bands
- *Prepare ahead:* rap roll for Activity 10C

OBJECTIVES

Language
- Sing the "Months Rap"
- Recognize appropriate weather expressions for specific months

Culture
- Learn the order of months in the year

Review
- Practice the names for months of the year
- Practice weather expressions
- Sing **"Español para ti"** (*"Spanish Is for You, and for Me"*)

Vocabulary

No new vocabulary is introduced in this lesson.

Warm-up

Materials: Blackline Masters 9C-1, 9C-2, 9C-3.

Exchange appropriate greetings, considering the time of day when this Spanish class meets. Then show a Blackline Master for another time of day and exchange the relevant greetings with the class (T = Teacher, C = class):

    T: Buenos días/Buenas tardes/Buenas noches, clase.
        Good morning/Good afternoon/Good evening, class.

    C: Buenos días/Buenas tardes/Buenas noches, Maestro/Maestra.
        Good morning/Good afternoon /Good evening, Teacher.

Review

Materials: Cassette player; Activity 8A on Activity Cassette 1, Side A; and Gold Flashcards 48–50, 62–64.

Display the Flashcards where everyone can see them. Next, explain that the class should repeat the months with Mr. Hale. Point to each month as he names it.

Introduce the video

Tell the class that in this video, they are going to begin learning a new rap song and play games with the weather expressions.

> **FYI** **Estoy aquí con Ñico y con Rosco y con ustedes, mis amigos especiales** means *I am here with Ñico, Rosco, and you, my special friends.*
>
> Children already know two words for *you*—**tú** for a friend and **usted** for someone older. **La maestra** is gradually introducing the plural of *you*—**ustedes**.

Months of the year:

enero	January
febrero	February
marzo	March
abril	April
mayo	May
junio	June
julio	July
agosto	August
septiembre	September
octubre	October
noviembre	November
diciembre	December

LEVEL TWO

VIDEO LESSON

1. Saying *Buenas tardes* (Good afternoon) to each other

The class, Rosco, and Ñico respond as **la maestra** greets them (**M** = Maestra, **C** = class, **R** = Rosco, **Ñ** = Ñico):

M: Buenas tardes, clase/Rosco/Ñico.	*Good afternoon, class/Rosco/Ñico.*
C/R/Ñ: Buenas tardes, Maestra.	*Good afternoon, Teacher.*
M: ¿Cómo estás tú?	*How are you?*
C/R/Ñ: Muy bien, gracias. ¿Y usted?	*Very well, thank you. And you?*
M: Muy bien, gracias.	*Very well, thanks.*

2. Reviewing the months of the year

La maestra has everyone name the months.

¿Recuerdan ustedes los meses del año?	*Do you remember the months of the year?*
¿Recuerdas tú los meses del año, Rosco?	*Do you remember the months of the year, Rosco?*
¿Qué mes es éste?	*What month is this?*
Es ___.	*It's ___.*

La maestra counts the Flashcards and the class repeats after her to confirm the number of months in a year.

¿Cuántos son?	*How many are there?*
Son doce.	*There are twelve.*
Hay doce meses del año.	*There are twelve months in a year.*

1	uno	4	cuatro	7	siete	10	diez
2	dos	5	cinco	8	ocho	11	once
3	tres	6	seis	9	nueve	12	doce

3. Introducing the "Months Rap"

La maestra sings the entire rap while showing numbers for the months. Next, she models the rap in groups of three lines and has the class sing them. Then she encourages the children to sing the song.

Uno, enero.	*1, January.*
Dos, febrero.	*2, February.*
Tres, marzo.	*3, March.*
Cuatro, abril.	*4, April.*
Cinco, mayo.	*5, May.*
Seis, junio.	*6, June.*
Siete, julio.	*7, July.*
Ocho, agosto.	*8, August.*

Nueve, septiembre.	9, September.
Diez, octubre.	10, October.
Once, noviembre.	11, November.
Doce, diciembre.	12, December.

4. Playing a game with numbers and months

La maestra shows several numbers in turn and asks everyone to guess the month. Sometimes she comments on the weather as an indirect way of reintroducing that vocabulary.

| Hace viento. | *It's windy.* |
| Hace frío. | *It's cold.* |

5. Matching weather expressions with months

La maestra describes the weather on different Flashcards and asks if the weather describes particular months.

Llueve.	*It's raining.*
En abril llueve.	*It rains in April.*
Hace frío y nieva.	*It's cold and it's snowing.*
Hace frío y nieva en diciembre.	*It's cold and it snows in December.*

> Notice how the meaning of the verb changes when a month and a weather expression are combined.

6. Reintroducing weather expressions

La maestra models each weather expression and has the class repeat it. Next, she asks **¿Qué tiempo hace?** (*What's the weather like?*) and plays **¿Cuál falta?** (*What's missing?*).

Hace sol.	*It's sunny.*
Hace buen tiempo.	*It's good weather.*
Hace calor.	*It's hot.*
Hace frío.	*It's cold.*
Llueve.	*It's raining.*
Hace viento.	*It's windy.*
Nieva.	*It's snowing.*
Hace mal tiempo.	*It's bad weather.*

7. Singing "Español para ti" (*"Spanish Is for You, and for Me"*)

La maestra asks everyone to sing **"Español para ti"** with her. For song lyrics, see Lesson 3, Video Lesson, section 3.

8. Closing

La maestra reassures children that they'll have more practice with these Spanish words. Then she says **Adiós** (*Good-bye*).

> After viewing the video, praise the children for their good listening and watching skills.

Lesson Ten

Blackline Master 10A

Blackline Master 10B

ACTIVITY LESSON

Activity 10A: *Muéstrame* ___ (*Show me* ___) the weather

Materials: Cassette player; Activity Cassette 1, Side A; Blackline Master 10A; and scissors.

Preparation: Make a copy of Blackline Master 10A for each child.

Talk about the weather that each picture represents.

Top left: It's sunny.   *Top right:* It's cold.
Bottom left: It's hot.   *Bottom right:* It's nice weather.

Have children cut their Blackline Masters into the four pictures. Ask the class to mix up the order of the pictures before starting the cassette activity. Then explain that after Mr. Hale says each weather expression twice, children should hold up the picture that matches what he said.

Activity 10B: What's the weather like?

Materials: Cassette player; Activity Cassette 1, Side A; and Blackline Master 10B.

Preparation: Make a copy of Blackline Master 10B for each child.

Talk about the weather that each picture represents.

Top left: It's raining.   *Top right:* It's snowing.
Bottom left: It's windy.   *Bottom right:* It's bad weather.

Then point out that Mr. Hale is going to ask the class to touch (**toca**) the pictures that match weather expressions. He is only going to say each expression once.

LEVEL TWO

Activity 10C: Make a rap roll

Materials: Cassette player; "Months Rap" on Song Cassette, Side A; Blackline Masters 10C-1 and 10C-2; scissors or paper cutter; paste or tape; paper clips or rubber bands; and crayons.

Preparation: Make a copy of Blackline Masters 10C-1 and 10C-2 for each child. Cut along the dotted lines to make rows of calendar pictures and numbers or have children do so.

Have the class describe how to put the pictures end-to-end in calendar order. As children explain, have them glue or tape the pictures together. Next, ask the class to listen carefully as you play the "Months Rap." Explain that there's a part at the beginning and the end that they may not understand yet.

Uno, enero.	1, January.
Dos, febrero.	2, February.
Tres, marzo.	3, March.
Cuatro, abril.	4, April.
Cinco, mayo.	5, May.
Seis, junio.	6, June.
Siete, julio.	7, July.
Ocho, agosto.	8, August.
Nueve, septiembre.	9, September.
Diez, octubre.	10, October.
Once, noviembre.	11, November.
Doce, diciembre.	12, December.

Then ask what the lyrics mean and have children explain the first couple of lines. Ask children how these pictures and numbers might be useful—as a help for remembering the lyrics to the "Months Rap." Next, have individuals write their names on the back of their "rap rolls." If possible, allow children time to color them.

Finally, show children how they can roll the assemblage into a coil and hold the ends in place with a paper clip or rubber band. Keep these memory aids in a safe place, so that children may use them periodically throughout the year.

Make sure you make a "rap roll" for yourself ahead of time, so you can show the children what the finished product should look like.

CLOSING

Tell the children that Spanish class is finished for today. Next time they are going to play a game with the months and sing the "Months Rap."

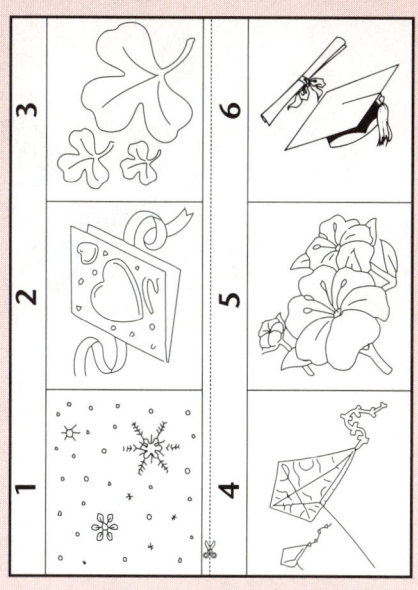

Blackline Master 10C-1

Blackline Master 10C-2

IF YOU HAVE TIME...

Materials: Cassette player; "Months Rap" on Song Cassette, Side A; and rap rolls.

Ask children to silently "read" their rap rolls for January through December as you play the "Months Rap" once or twice. Then have the class sing along with the cassette. Encourage children to use their rap rolls for help.

Lesson Ten

Lesson 11

Materials to gather

- VCR and Video Lesson 11 on Tape 3
- Cassette player
- Activity Cassette 1
- Song Cassette
- Gold Flashcards 48–50, 62–64
- Blackline Masters 9B-1, 9B-2, 9B-3 (feeling masks)
- Rosco flag(s)
- Blackline Master 11B (months)

Objectives

Language

- Use number clues to name months according to their calendar order
- Recognize that **Dame** means *Give me*

Culture

- Use appropriate greetings for different times of the day

Review

- Review expressions for feelings
- Sing songs to recall greetings
- Sing the "Months Rap"

Vocabulary

Dame.   *Give me.*

Warm-up

Exchange an appropriate greeting with your class (**T** = Teacher, **C** = class):

T: Buenos días/Buenas tardes, clase.   *Good morning/Good afternoon, class.*

C: Buenos días/Buenas tardes, Maestro/Maestra.   *Good morning/Good afternoon, Teacher.*

Then ask volunteers to name the current month in English and in Spanish—**septiembre** (*September*) or **octubre** (*October*). Discuss how knowing the name of the month in one language can help them remember it in the other language.

Review

Materials: Cassette player; Activity 8A on Activity Cassette 1, Side A; and Gold Flashcards 48–50, 62–64.

Explain that the children should say the months along with Mr. Hale. During this activity, show the appropriate Flashcard for each month. Then divide the class in half. Starting with **enero** (*January*), have groups alternate saying the months. Show the Flashcards at a pace that keeps the activity moving.

> Notice if children have improved their skill in naming the months and where they are having difficulties, if any.

Introduce the video

Tell the class that in this video they are going to play games with the months and sing the "Months Rap."

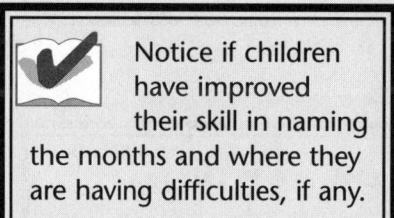

Video Lesson

1. Exchanging greetings

La maestra says the opening conversation with Rosco and then the class (**M** = Maestra, **R** = Rosco, **C** = class):

M:	Buenos días, Rosco/clase.	*Good morning, Rosco/class.*
R/C:	Buenos días, Maestra.	*Good morning, Teacher.*
M:	¿Cómo estás tú?	*How are you?*
R/C:	Muy bien, gracias. ¿Y usted?	*Very well, thank you. And you?*
M:	Muy bien, gracias.	*Very well, thanks.*

2. Reviewing expressions for feelings

La maestra uses the feeling masks to practice three answers to ¿Cómo estás tú? (*How are you?*).

Así, así.	*So-so.*
Muy mal.	*Very bad.*
Muy bien.	*Very well.*

3. Reviewing greetings

La maestra uses some modeling and singing to review greetings with the class.

Buenos días.	*Good morning.*
Buenas tardes.	*Good afternoon.*
Buenas noches.	*Good evening.*
Buenos días a ti.	*Good morning to you.*
Buenos días a ti.	*Good morning to you.*
Buenos días, amigo.	*Good morning, friend.*
Buenos días a ti.	*Good morning to you.*
Buenas tardes a ti.	*Good afternoon to you.*
Buenas tardes a ti.	*Good afternoon to you.*
Buenas tardes, amigo.	*Good afternoon, friend.*
Buenas tardes a ti.	*Good afternoon to you.*
Buenas noches a ti.	*Good evening to you.*
Buenas noches a ti.	*Good evening to you.*
Buenas noches, amigo.	*Good evening, friend.*
Buenas noches a ti.	*Good evening to you.*

✓ Check that children are saying **buenos días**, **buenas tardes**, and **buenas noches**.

EN ESPAÑOL

If you feel comfortable, use these expressions with your class.

Vamos a contar.
(*Let's count.*)

Vamos a cantar.
(*Let's sing.*)

Vamos a mirar.
(*Let's watch.*)

Vamos a jugar.
(*Let's play.*)

LEVEL TWO

4. Playing Dame ___ (Give me ___) with months

La maestra models the first six months in the "Months Rap." Everyone repeats the months and then the numbers and the months. Next, the mime demonstrates the meaning of **dame**, and then Rosco and **la maestra** play **Dame** ___. He names the months aloud until he finds the one he wants.

Dame ___.	Give me ___.
Éste es el mes de ___.	This is the month of ___.

5. Playing Dame ___ (Give me ___) again

La maestra and Rosco repeat the same process for the last six months.

6. Singing the "Months Rap"

La maestra begins by saying **Los meses del año son** (*The months of the year are*) and then invites the class to join in as they sing the whole song.

Uno, enero.	1, January.
Dos, febrero.	2, February.
Tres, marzo.	3, March.
Cuatro, abril.	4, April.
Cinco, mayo.	5, May.
Seis, junio.	6, June.
Siete, julio.	7, July.
Ocho, agosto.	8, August.
Nueve, septiembre.	9, September.
Diez, octubre.	10, October.
Once, noviembre.	11, November.
Doce, diciembre.	12, December.
Y no más.	And that's all.

7. Integrating numbers with months of the year

Using Flashcards, **la maestra** asks Rosco to name the months.

¿Qué mes es éste?	What month is this?
Es ___.	It's ___.
¿Cuál es el mes número ___?	Which is the ___ month?
Es el mes de ___.	It's the month of ___.

8. Closing

To reassure children, **la maestra** reminds them that learning Spanish takes practice and more practice. Then she says **Adiós** (*Good-bye*) and **Hasta luego** (*See you later*).

Months of the year:

enero	January
febrero	February
marzo	March
abril	April
mayo	May
junio	June
julio	July
agosto	August
septiembre	September
octubre	October
noviembre	November
diciembre	December

LANGUAGE ACROSS THE CURRICULUM

Remind the class that people often use body language, such as hand signals and facial expressions, to express an idea instead of saying words. In the "Months Rap," **la maestra** spreads her hands apart in front of her to explain that **Y no más** means *That's all* or *There aren't any more*. Adults often use this same gesture to show babies that there's nothing left.

After viewing the video, praise the children for their good listening and watching skills.

Lesson Eleven

> Although **la maestra** models a sentence as the answer in Activity 11A, a phrase is also correct. You could explain the difference in meaning between pairs of answers if children are confused. Suggest that they use the longer statement just for the practice.

> Check that children are answering the questions according to the masks they have. Also encourage children to listen to each other's answers as a way of practicing their Spanish.

Blackline Master 11B

LEVEL TWO

ACTIVITY LESSON

Activity 11A: How do you feel?

Materials: Cassette player; Activity Cassette 1, Side A; face feeling masks (one per child) from Activity 9B or Blackline Masters 9B-1, 9B-2, 9B-3; and Rosco flag(s).

Preparation: If your class made masks in Lesson 9, distribute them. If not, make approximately equal numbers of the Blackline Masters. There should be one for each child.

Discuss the pictures with the class. Make sure that children associate the correct feeling with each mask. Then explain that **la maestra** is going to ask ¿Cómo estás tú? (*How are you?*) five times. Each time you will hand a Rosco flag to someone. The selected child should answer according to the mask that he or she is holding.

Estoy muy bien./Muy bien.	*I'm fine./Very well.*
Estoy así, así./Así, así.	*I'm so-so./So-so.*
Estoy muy mal./Muy mal.	*I'm very bad./Very bad.*

If possible, repeat the activity so that many children may participate.

Activity 11B: Touch the month

Materials: Cassette player; Activity Cassette 1, Side A; and Blackline Master 11B.

Discuss the meaning of each picture before the class listens to the tape activity. Then explain that **la maestra** is going to ask the class to **Toca** (*touch*) the pictures of different months. She is only going to say each command one time.

Activity 11C: Let's pretend to be José and Rosita

Materials: Cassette player; "Finger Play Song" on Song Cassette, Side A.

Play the song once as the class listens. Remind children that last year José and Rosita used to sing the "Finger Play Song" to each other. Next, divide the class in half. Replay the song twice and have the groups take turns singing first and then responding.

Buenos días, buenos días.	*Good morning, good morning.*
¿Cómo estás tú? ¿Cómo estás tú?	*How are you? How are you?*
Muy bien, gracias. Muy bien, gracias.	*Very well, thank you. Very well, thank you.*
Adiós. Adiós.	*Good-bye. Good-bye.*

CLOSING

Tell the children that Spanish class is finished for today. Next time they are going to talk about days of the week and birthdays.

IF YOU HAVE TIME...

Materials: Cassette player; Activity 8A on Activity Cassette 1, Side A; and Gold Flashcards 48–50, 62–64.

Preparation: Put the Gold Flashcards in calendar order and display them.

In English, discuss what the local weather is like for each month. Next, help children categorize the months according to seasons. As each one is named, group the Flashcards appropriately.

Explain that on the tape, Mr. Hale is going to name the months and children should say them with him. Point to each month as Mr. Hale names it. You may want to repeat this cassette activity.

Lesson Eleven

Lesson 12

Materials to gather

- VCR and Video Lesson 12 on Tape 3
- Cassette player
- Activity Cassette 1
- Hand puppets Rosco and Dora
- Rosco flag
- Gold Flashcards 48–50, 62–64
- *Optional materials:*
  Song Cassette; rap roll from Activity 10C
- *Prepare ahead:*
  dates of children's birthdays (Activity 12C)

OBJECTIVES

Language

- Practice the names for the days of the week
- Answer the question ¿**Cuándo es tu cumpleaños?** (*When is your birthday?*) with the month of birth
- Sing "**Adiós a ti**" ("*Good-bye to You*")

Culture

- Understand that calendars in Spanish-speaking countries are different from those in the United States

Review

- Sing the "Calendar Rap"
- Sing the "Months Rap"
- Count from 1 to 12
- Practice the names of the months

Vocabulary

lunes	*Monday*
martes	*Tuesday*
miércoles	*Wednesday*
jueves	*Thursday*
viernes	*Friday*
sábado	*Saturday*
domingo	*Sunday*

Warm-up

Exchange an appropriate greeting with a child (T = Teacher, C = child):

    T: Buenos días/Buenas tardes, [child's name].   *Good morning/Good afternoon, [child's name].*

    C: Buenos días/Buenas tardes, Maestro/Maestra.   *Good morning/Good afternoon, Teacher.*

Then have that child greet a second child. Continue until five or six children have exchanged greetings.

Review

Materials: Cassette player; Activity 2A on Activity Cassette 1, Side A; and the hand puppets Rosco and Dora.

Tell the class to listen to **la maestra** and Rosco. Ask a volunteer to explain why Rosco said **¿Y usted?** when he asked **la maestra**—*And you?* (Children say **usted** to grown-ups, such as a teacher, as a way of showing respect.)

Next, ask what the puppets Rosco and Dora would say to each other instead of **¿Y usted?** If children have forgotten, say **¿Y tú?** (*And you?*) because **tú** is for friends. Have volunteers use the puppets to ask one another how they are (**R** = Rosco, **D** = Dora):

    R: ¿Cómo estás tú, Dora?   *How are you, Dora?*

    D: Muy bien, gracias. ¿Y tú?   *Fine, thanks. And you?*

    R: Muy bien, gracias.   *Fine, thanks.*

Alternate responses: **Así, así** (*So-so*) and **Muy mal** (*Very bad*).

Finally, have a couple pairs of volunteers ask one another comparable questions.

Introduce the video

Point out that in this video children are going to talk about one of their favorite events—their birthdays.

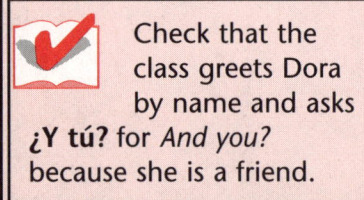

Video Lesson

> Check that the class greets Dora by name and asks ¿Y tú? for *And you?* because she is a friend.

1. Using ¡Hola! (Hello!) to greet the class

Dora and **la maestra** say hello and then Dora greets the children (**D** = Dora, **C** = class):

Los niños están aquí.	*The children are here.*
D: Hola, clase.	*Hello, class.*
C: Hola, Dora.	*Hello, Dora.*
D: ¿Cómo estás tú?	*How are you?*
C: Muy bien, gracias. ¿Y tú?	*Very well, thank you. And you?*
D: Muy bien, gracias.	*Very well, thanks.*

2. Reintroducing the calendar and the days of the week

La maestra reminds the class that Spanish-speaking people use a calendar in which Monday is the first day of the week. Then she models the days of the week and the class repeats them.

En el mes de septiembre hay treinta días.	*In the month of September, there are thirty days.*

Days of the week:

lunes	Monday
martes	Tuesday
miércoles	Wednesday
jueves	Thursday
viernes	Friday
sábado	Saturday
domingo	Sunday

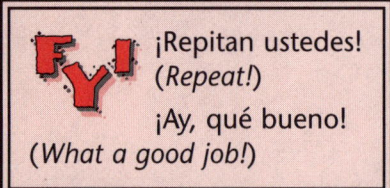

3. Singing the "Calendar Rap"

La maestra sings the "Calendar Rap." Then she suggests **Vamos a practicar los días de la semana** (*Let's practice the days of the week*) and the class sings along with her.

Lunes, martes, miércoles, tres.	*Monday, Tuesday, Wednesday, three.*
Uno, dos, tres.	*One, two, three.*
Jueves, viernes, sábado, seis.	*Thursday, Friday, Saturday, six.*
Uno, dos, tres, cuatro, cinco, seis.	*One, two, three, four, five, six.*
Y domingo siete es.	*And Sunday is seven.*
Uno, dos, tres, cuatro, cinco, seis, siete.	*One, two, three, four, five, six, seven.*

> Check if children are saying **junio** (*June*) and **julio** (*July*).

4. Reviewing the months

Using the Flashcards, **la maestra** models the months and has the class repeat them. Then she and the class sing the "Months Rap."

Hay doce meses del año.	*There are twelve months in a year.*
Uno, enero.	*1, January.*
Dos, febrero.	*2, February.*
Tres, marzo.	*3, March.*
Cuatro, abril.	*4, April.*
Cinco, mayo.	*5, May.*
Seis, junio.	*6, June.*

> **FYI** ¡Repitan ustedes! (*Repeat!*)
> ¡Ay, qué bueno! (*What a good job!*)

LEVEL TWO

Siete, julio.	7, July.
Ocho, agosto.	8, August.
Nueve, septiembre.	9, September.
Diez, octubre.	10, October.
Once, noviembre.	11, November.
Doce, diciembre.	12, December.
Y no más.	And that's all.

La maestra and the class count the months and she announces **Hay doce meses del año** (*There are 12 months in a year*). See the "Months Rap" if you need to refer to the months of the year and/or numbers 1–12.

5. Connecting months and birthdays

Talking about months leads **la maestra** to ask Dora and the children about their birthdays.

¿Cuándo es tu cumpleaños?	*When is your birthday?*
¿En cuál mes?	*In what month?*
Mi cumpleaños es en ___.	*My birthday is in ___.*

6. Playing ¿Cuál falta? (*What's missing?*)

Working with groups of four months, **la maestra** challenges Dora to find the missing months. **La maestra** also encourages children to name the months before Dora does.

7. Singing "Adiós a ti" (*"Good-bye to You"*)

La maestra sings "**Adiós a ti**" and has children join her.

Adiós a ti.	*Good-bye to you.*
Adiós a ti.	*Good-bye to you.*
Adiós, amigo.	*Good-bye, friend.*
Adiós a ti.	*Good-bye to you.*

8. Closing

La maestra compliments the children on their Spanish.

EN ESPAÑOL

If you feel comfortable, try to use these expressions.

¡No mires!
(*Don't look!*)

Otra vez.
(*Again.*)

Una vez más.
(*One more time.*)

After viewing the video, praise the children for their good listening and watching skills.

Lesson Twelve

Activity Lesson

Activity 12A: Let's get some exercise

Materials: Cassette player; Activity Cassette 1, Side A.

Tell children that **la maestra** is going to ask them to walk (**anda**), jump (**salta**), and run (**corre**) in place. She will only say the command once each time. Try to repeat this activity.

Activity 12B: Where's that month?

Materials: Cassette player; Activity Cassette 1, Side A; Rosco flag; and Gold Flashcards 48–50, 62–64.

Display the Flashcards where everyone can see them. Explain that **la maestra** wants children to **anda y toca** (walk and touch) Flashcards for different months. She will say each command twice. Tell the class that as **la maestra** finishes speaking, you are going to give the Rosco flag to someone and also pause the tape recorder while he or she follows **la maestra**'s request. You may wish to repeat this activity to allow more than five children to participate.

✔ Note that this is the first time children will be following the commands **corre** (run) and **salta** (jump) this year. Make sure they remember what the words mean.

This activity requires children to identify the months out of sequence. Follow **la maestra**'s example and, if necessary, allow children time to recite the months as Dora did.

IF YOU HAVE TIME . . .

Materials: Cassette player; "Months Rap" on Song Cassette, Side A; and rap roll from Activity 10C.

Play the "Months Rap" and have the class follow along on their rap rolls. Replay **la maestra**'s statement in Spanish at the beginning of the song—**Los meses del año son . . .** (*The months of the year are . . .*). Ask a volunteer to explain it. Accept any reasonable answer. Then replay the song itself a couple of times and have the class sing it, using the rap rolls for help.

LEVEL TWO

Activity 12C: When is your birthday?

Materials: Cassette player; Activity Cassette 1, Side A; Rosco flag; and dates of children's birthdays (optional).

Preparation: Have a list of children's birthdays handy, so that you can help anyone who does not remember the month in which his or hers falls.

Remind the class that **la maestra** and Dora talked about their birthdays. Explain that **la maestra** is now going to ask children about theirs. As she asks *When is your birthday?* (¿**Cuándo es tu cumpleaños?**) you are going to hand the Rosco flag to someone. You will also stop the tape, so he or she has time to answer. The tape only asks for five responses, but give as many children as possible the opportunity to participate in this activity.

CLOSING

Tell the children that Spanish class is finished for today. In the next class, children are going to tell how old they are and begin talking about different places in the school building.

Months of the year:

enero	*January*
febrero	*February*
marzo	*March*
abril	*April*
mayo	*May*
junio	*June*
julio	*July*
agosto	*August*
septiembre	*September*
octubre	*October*
noviembre	*November*
diciembre	*December*

HERITAGE SPEAKERS

If there are any heritage speakers in your class, ask them to share how birthdays are celebrated in their countries of origin.

Lesson Twelve

Lesson 13

Materials to gather

- VCR and Video Lesson 13 on Tape 4
- Cassette player
- Activity Cassette 1
- Rosco flag
- Paper
- Pens or pencils
- Gold Flashcards 48–50, 62–64
- *Optional materials:* Song Cassette and rap roll from Activity 10C

OBJECTIVES

Language

- Ask and answer questions about birthdays
- Ask and answer questions about age
- Practice vocabulary related to places in the school

Culture

- Learn about similarities and differences between schools in different parts of the country
- Sing the "Months Rap"

Review

- Practice the months of the year

Vocabulary

el cumpleaños	*birthday*
¿Cuándo es tu cumpleaños?	*When is your birthday?*
¿Cuántos años tienes tú?	*How old are you?*
Tengo ___ años.	*I'm ___ years old.*
la oficina	*office*
el baño	*bathroom*
la biblioteca	*library*
la cafetería	*cafeteria*
la clase	*classroom*
el patio	*playground*

Warm-up

Open the class by exchanging an appropriate greeting with your class (T = Teacher, C = class):

    T: Buenos días/Buenas tardes, clase.   *Good morning/Good afternoon, class.*

    C: Buenos días/Buenas tardes, Maestro/Maestra.   *Good morning/Good afternoon, Teacher.*

Ask volunteers to tell when their birthdays are and how old they are.

Review

Remind children that **la maestra** took them on a tour of a school in an earlier lesson. Then build contextual knowledge for a repeat visit by asking children to name some of the places they visited and/or to describe what people were doing. Remind the class that **la maestra** knows she used some Spanish words that the class doesn't know yet. Encourage children to listen for words they know, look at the pictures for clues, and try to enjoy the trip when they visit the school again in this video.

Introduce the video

Tell the children that in this video they are going to talk more about their birthdays and discuss how old they are. In addition, they are going to start learning words that describe a school.

VIDEO LESSON

1. Saying the opening conversation

La maestra greets Jorge and the class (**M** = Maestra, **J** = Jorge, **C** = class):

M: Buenos días, Jorge/clase.	*Good morning, Jorge/class.*
J/C: Buenos días, Maestra.	*Good morning, Teacher.*
M: ¿Cómo estás tú?	*How are you?*
J/C: Muy bien, gracias. ¿Y usted?	*Very well, thank you. And you?*
M: Muy bien, gracias.	*Very well, thanks.*

2. Reviewing the months of the year

La maestra talks about the months. Then she says each one and Jorge and the class repeat after her.

Aprendemos los meses del año.	*We are learning the months of the year.*
Hay doce meses del año.	*There are twelve months in a year.*

3. Practicing birthdays and months

La maestra models expressions related to birthdays and the class repeats them. To lend variety to the exercise, the children ask Jorge, **la maestra**, and then each other about their birthdays.

¿Cuándo es tu cumpleaños?	*When is your birthday?*
Mi cumpleaños es en ___.	*My birthday is in ___.*
Tu cumpleaños es en ___.	*Your birthday is in ___.*

4. Singing the "Months Rap"

La maestra and the class sing the "Months Rap." For lyrics to the rap, see Lesson 12, Video Lesson, section 4.

5. Asking and answering questions about age

Since the class knows that the answer to ¿**Tienes tú?** is **Tengo**, **la maestra** first asks children about their age and then practices how to ask about age.

Tengo ___ años.	*I'm ___ years old.*
¿Cuántos años tienes tú?	*How old are you?*

FYI

Estoy muy bien porque estoy aquí con mi amigo Jorge means *I'm fine because I'm here with my friend Jorge.*

Months of the year:

enero	January
febrero	February
marzo	March
abril	April
mayo	May
junio	June
julio	July
agosto	August
septiembre	September
octubre	October
noviembre	November
diciembre	December

FYI

The question ¿**Cuántos años tienes tú?** literally translates as "*How many years do you have?*" The verb *to have* is also used in the answer: "*I have ___ years.*" The children may notice the use of **tengo** here now that they know that **tengo** means *I have.*

LEVEL TWO

6. Introducing vocabulary for rooms in a school

La maestra models the words and the class repeats them:

la oficina	*office*	la cafetería	*cafeteria*
el baño	*bathroom*	la clase	*classroom*
la biblioteca	*library*	el patio	*playground*

7. Visiting the school again with *la maestra*

La maestra repeats her tour of the school with the class.

Estoy en la cafetería.	*I am in the cafeteria.*
Los niños comen en la cafetería.	*Children eat in the cafeteria.*
Les gusta comer.	*They like to eat.*

After the tour she exclaims **Es muy divertido visitar la escuela** (*It's a lot of fun to visit the school*). Then **la maestra** and Jorge play a game of **Sí o no** (*Yes or no*). She asks him if he would go to different places if he wanted to do something in particular. He answers **sí** or **no**.

8. Closing

La maestra says **Adiós** (*Good-bye*) and **Hasta luego** (*See you later*).

> After viewing the video, praise the children for their good listening and watching skills.

Lesson Thirteen

The videos alone do not give your class enough practice using Spanish. The cassette activities can provide that needed extra practice. When choosing activities, remember that the cassette activities are the most important ones.

Activity Lesson

Activity 13A: How old are you?

Materials: Cassette player; Activity Cassette 1, Side A; Rosco flag; paper; and pencils or pens.

Preparation: Have each child write his or her age in a large number on a sheet of paper. Explain that **la maestra** is going to ask several children their ages. As she finishes saying **¿Cuántos años tienes tú?** (*How old are you?*), you will hand the Rosco flag to a child. That child should hold up his or her age and answer **Tengo ___ años** (*I am ___ years old*).

Tengo siete años.	*I am seven years old.*
Tengo ocho años.	*I am eight years old.*
Tengo nueve años.	*I am nine years old.*

La maestra only asks the question four times. If possible, replay the tape several times to include most children in the activity.

Activity 13B: Can you find the month?

Materials: Cassette player; Activity Cassette 1, Side A; Rosco flag; and Gold Flashcards 48–50, 62–64.

Display the Gold Flashcards where everyone can see and touch them. Explain that **la maestra** is going to give directions about walking and touching (**anda y toca**) Flashcards for different months. She will say each command two times. As she finishes each direction, you will hand the Rosco flag to a child. He or she should then follow her command. Consider repeating this activity a couple of times since **la maestra** only gives directions three times.

Activity 13C: Let's compare schools

Ask children to compare the school in **la maestra**'s tour with theirs. Organize the discussion around similarities and differences. For example, name places that **la maestra** shows the class—the outside of the school, the school office, a classroom, the library, a bathroom, the cafeteria, and the playground. Which of these places does your school have? Which ones doesn't your school have? What activities seem to take place in each? How are they the same or different in your school? Do the buildings look the same or different? How?

CLOSING

Tell the children that Spanish class is finished for today. In the next class, they are going to visit the school again and use numbers.

> **IF YOU HAVE TIME...**
>
> Materials: Cassette player; "Months Rap" on Song Cassette, Side A; and rap roll from Activity 10C.
>
> Display your open rap roll where everyone can see it. Then point to each number and month as it is mentioned on the tape. Next, try to keep a rhythm as you point to the numbers and pictures, and the class names them. Notice how well children know the various lines and use this knowledge to determine what to practice.
>
> Replay the tape three or four times, stopping periodically to practice particular lines. Ask the class to use their rap rolls as they are singing. Encourage children by reminding them that the goals are to improve their singing and to have fun. No one is expected to know the song perfectly. For lyrics to the rap, see Lesson 12, Video Lesson, section 4.

Lesson Thirteen

Lesson 14

Materials to gather

- VCR and Video Lesson 14 on Tape 4
- Cassette player
- Activity Cassette 1
- Song Cassette
- Blackline Masters 9C-1, 9C-2, 9C-3 (times of day)
- Blackline Master 14A (places in a school)
- Rosco flag
- Number Cards for 10, 20, 30, 40, 50
- *Optional materials:* Song Cassette

Objectives

Language

- Learn a new way of saying good-bye
- Sing "**Uno, dos, tres niñitos**" (*"One, Two, Three Little Children"*)
- Practice the numbers 10, 20, 30, 40, 50

Culture

- Recall that adding **-ito** or **-ita** to the end of a noun or a name is a way of saying *little*

Review

- Review vocabulary for places in the school
- Review the numbers 1–20
- Sing "**Español para ti**" (*"Spanish Is for You, and for Me"*)

Vocabulary

Hasta la vista. *Until we meet again.*

Warm-up

Materials: Blackline Masters 9C-1, 9C-2, 9C-3.

Exchange greetings that correspond to the time of day with your class. Then show a Blackline Master for another time of day and exchange the appropriate greetings for that time (T = Teacher, C = class):

T: Buenos días/Buenas tardes/Buenas noches, clase.
Good morning/Good afternoon/Good evening, class.

C: Buenos días/Buenas tardes/Buenas noches, Maestro/Maestra.
Good morning/Good afternoon/Good evening, Teacher.

Review

Ask children to describe what happened on **la maestra**'s school tour. Encourage them to use Spanish words for the various rooms when they feel comfortable doing so. Reassure the class that there's going to be much more practice with these words.

Have children mention any new information they may have understood when **la maestra** again toured the school. Point out that they're going to see the tour again in this video. Remind children that their job is to listen closely for words they know and to look for picture clues to what's happening. No one—not even you, the teacher—is expected to understand everything.

Introduce the video

Tell the class that in this video, **la maestra** moves very quickly in some places. She and Dora are going to quickly count to 20 and then immediately start singing the song about counting children—"**Uno, dos, tres niñitos.**" Children should be ready to jump in and do these activities with **la maestra**.

Places in the school:

la oficina	*office*
el baño	*bathroom*
la biblioteca	*library*
la cafetería	*cafeteria*
la clase	*classroom*
el patio	*playground*

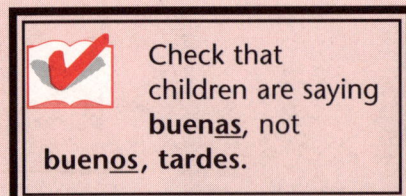

> ✓ Check that children are saying **buenas**, not bue**nos**, tardes.

VIDEO LESSON

1. Saying *Buenas tardes* (Good afternoon)

La maestra, Dora, and the class exchange greetings (**M** = Maestra, **D** = Dora, **C** = class):

M: Buenas tardes, Dora/clase.	*Good morning, Dora/class.*
D/C: Buenas tardes, Maestra.	*Good morning, Teacher.*
M: ¿Cómo estás tú?	*How are you?*
D/C: Muy bien, gracias. ¿Y usted?	*Very well, thank you. And you?*
M: Muy bien, gracias.	*Very well, thanks.*

The teacher goes on to say **Estoy perfecta porque estoy aquí con Dora y con ustedes**, which means *I'm perfect because I am here with Dora and with you.*

2. Reviewing vocabulary for places in a school

La maestra models words for places in a school and the class repeats them. Then **la maestra** asks Dora where she goes if she wants to do certain things. For vocabulary for places in the school, see Review section in this lesson.

Voy a la cafetería.	*I go to the cafeteria.*
Voy a la oficina.	*I go to the office.*
Voy a la biblioteca.	*I go to the library.*

3. Touring the school with *la maestra*

Once more **la maestra** visits the school. Part of the narrative follows.

Estoy en el patio con los niños.	*I am on the playground with the children.*
Los niños juegan en el patio.	*The children play on the playground.*

4. Playing games with names for places in the school

La maestra reviews the words for places in a school. Next, she and Dora play **Sí o no** (*Yes or no*) and then **Muéstrame ___** (*Show me ___*).

¿Es ___ o es ___?	*Is it ___ or is it ___?*
Es ___.	*It's ___.*
¿Es ___?	*Is it ___?*
No, no es ___.	*No it isn't ___.*

LEVEL TWO

5. Reviewing the numbers 1–20

La maestra proudly talks about all the things "we do" in school. Next, she quickly counts from 1 to 10 and Dora counts from 11 to 20.

1	uno	6	seis	11	once	16	dieciséis
2	dos	7	siete	12	doce	17	diecisiete
3	tres	8	ocho	13	trece	18	dieciocho
4	cuatro	9	nueve	14	catorce	19	diecinueve
5	cinco	10	diez	15	quince	20	veinte

6. Singing "Uno, dos, tres niñitos" ("One, Two, Three Little Children")

La maestra bursts into song and wants everyone to join her.

Uno, dos, tres niñitos,	One, two, three little children,
Cuatro, cinco, seis niñitos,	Four, five, six little children,
Siete, ocho, nueve niñitos.	Seven, eight, nine little children,
Diez niñitos son.	There are ten little children.
Diez, nueve, ocho niñitos,	Ten, nine, eight little children,
Siete, seis, cinco niñitos,	Seven, six, five little children,
Cuatro, tres, dos niñitos,	Four, three, two little children,
Un niñito es.	There is one little child.

7. Recalling numbers

La maestra models the numbers 10, 20, 30, 40, and 50, and children repeat them. Next, she asks questions about the numbers. Then **la maestra**, Dora, and the class play a game of **¿Cuál falta?** (*What's missing?*), followed by a choice game (**¿Es ___ o es ___?**).

10	diez	30	treinta	50	cincuenta
20	veinte	40	cuarenta		

¿Qué número es?   What number is it?
Es ___.   It's ___.

8. Singing "Español para ti"

La maestra and the class sing **"Español para ti"** (*"Spanish Is for You, and for Me"*). For song lyrics, see Lesson 3, Video Lesson, section 3.

9. Closing

La maestra says **Hasta la vista** (*Until we meet again*).

FYI
En la cafetería comemos.
(*We eat in the cafeteria.*)
En la biblioteca leemos.
(*We read in the library.*)
En el patio jugamos.
(*We play on the playground.*)
En la escuela contamos.
(*We count in school.*)

You may want to remind the class that **niñitos** means *little children*. The endings *-ito* and *-ita* mean *little* and are terms of endearment.

FYI
Cant*as* muy bien, Dora.
(*You sing very well, Dora.*)
Todos los niños cant*an* muy bien.
(*All the children sing very well.*)
La maestra is getting the class accustomed to hearing endings on verbs change to agree (go) with the subject.

After viewing the video, praise the children for their good listening and watching skills.

Lesson Fourteen

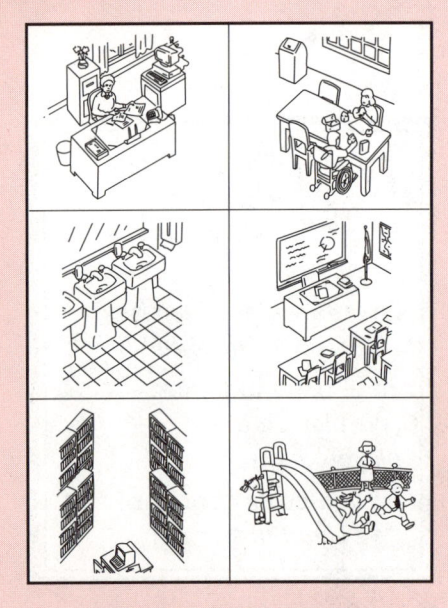

Blackline Master 14A

Note how well children are matching the words and the pictures in Activity 14A. Watch for words that most of the class seem to recognize and for those that are more problematic.

ACTIVITY LESSON

Activity 14A: Find the room

Materials: Cassette player; Activity Cassette 1, Side B; and Blackline Master 14A.

Preparation: Make one copy of Blackline Master 14A for each child.

Discuss the illustrations on Blackline Master 14A to make sure children understand which rooms are represented. Next, explain that doña Elena is going to ask them to **toca** (*touch*) different places in the school. She will say each command two times.

Repeat this activity, if possible. It is excellent for practicing comprehension of this newly introduced vocabulary.

Activity 14B: Follow the commands

Materials: Cassette player; Activity Cassette 1, Side B; Rosco flag; and Number Cards 10, 20, 30, 40, 50.

Display the Number Cards where everyone can see and reach them. You will need to choose children for the practice exercise as well as the three exercises.

Tell the class that doña Elena is going to ask children to follow directions—walk (**anda**), run (**corre**), or jump (**salta**) and then touch (**toca**) a number. She will say the commands two times apiece. As she is giving each direction, you will give the Rosco flag to a child. Explain that you will also stop the cassette player after a command to give the selected child time to carry it out. Repeat this activity as time allows.

Activity 14C: Say farewell

Materials: Cassette player; Activity Cassette 1, Side B.

Explain to children that they are going to practice three different ways to say farewell—**Adiós** (*Good-bye*), **Hasta luego** (*See you later*), and the new expression **Hasta la vista** (*Until we meet again*). Doña Elena simply wants them to listen and then repeat.

As usual, try to do this activity more than once. After children have practiced it the first time, encourage them to wave farewell in the Spanish manner. This action will help them remember the meaning of the different expressions.

LEVEL TWO

CLOSING

Tell the children that Spanish class is finished for today. In the next class, they will see all the things they have learned in Spanish!

> **IF YOU HAVE TIME...**
>
> Materials: Cassette player; **"Español para ti"** (*"Spanish Is for You, and for Me"*) on the Song Cassette, Side A. For song lyrics, see Lesson 3, Video lesson, section 3.
>
> Play the song once, and ask the class to sing along. Watch for lines with which children are having difficulty. Then rewind the tape to such a section and replay it two or three times. Have children join in as they feel comfortable. Try to *improve* performance on particular lyrics, so that the class feels a sense of accomplishment. As the final part of the activity, play the entire song, with the class singing as much as possible. If children know the song well, do it a couple of times for sheer enjoyment. Celebrate what they have learned.

Lesson Fourteen

Lesson 15

Materials to gather

- VCR and Video Lesson 15 on Tape 4
- Cassette player
- Activity Cassette 1
- Blackline Masters 9C-1, 9C-2, 9C-3 (times of day)
- Five blank index cards
- Black marker
- Rosco flag
- Balls

- *Optional materials:* Blackline Master 14A (places in a school)

OBJECTIVES

Language
- Practice the numbers 21–30

Culture
- Recall various ways to say farewell

Review
- Review expressions for feelings
- Name the numbers 10, 20, 30, 40, 50
- Review the numbers 11–19
- Respond to **Dame** ___ (*Give me* ___)
- Practice vocabulary for places in a school

Vocabulary

veintiuno	twenty-one
veintidós	twenty-two
veintitrés	twenty-three
veinticuatro	twenty-four
veinticinco	twenty-five
veintiséis	twenty-six
veintisiete	twenty-seven
veintiocho	twenty-eight
veintinueve	twenty-nine
treinta	thirty

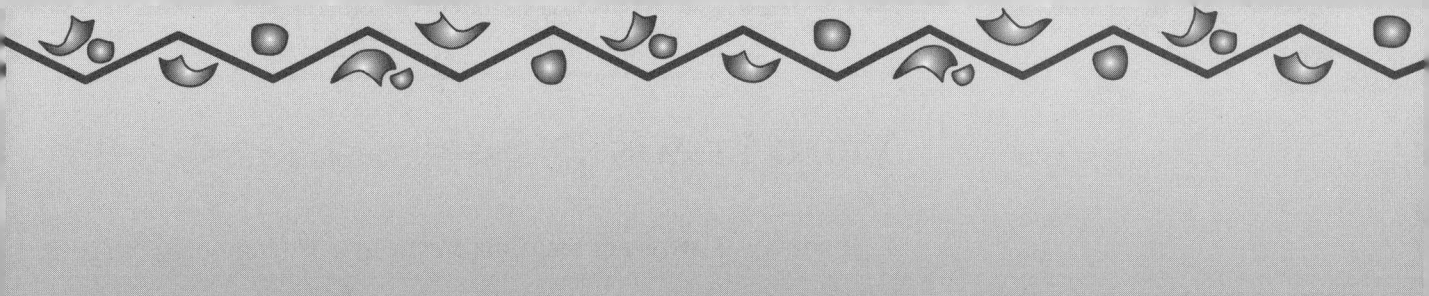

Warm-up

Materials: Blackline Masters 9C-1, 9C-2, 9C-3.

Exchange greetings that correspond to the actual time of day. Next, show a Blackline Master for another time of day and exchange appropriate greetings for that time (**T** = Teacher, **C** = class):

T: Buenos días/Buenas tardes/Buenas noches, clase.   *Good morning/Good afternoon/Good evening, class.*

C: Buenos días/Buenas tardes/Buenas noches, Maestro/Maestra.   *Good morning/Good afternoon/Good evening, Teacher.*

Then ask children for some ways to say farewell—**Adiós** (*Goodbye*) and **Hasta luego** (*See you later*). Someone may remember **Hasta la vista** (*Until we meet again*) from the previous lesson.

Review

Materials: Blackline Master 14A (optional).

Ask children to name in English the places in the school for which they have learned Spanish names. Write them on the chalkboard. You may want to use Blackline Master 14A to help the class remember all the places.

Then ask volunteers to explain ways they have used to help them remember the Spanish words for these places. For words such as **la oficina** and **la cafetería**, children may say that they sound almost the same in English and Spanish. They may say the same for **la clase**, or perhaps knowing the Spanish phrase **la clase de español** is a help. For **el patio**, maybe there is an association with the English meaning of an outdoor place. Children may not have ideas for **la biblioteca** and that is fine. Accept all reasonable answers.

Introduce the video

Tell children that in this lesson, they are going to play games with numbers and places in the school.

LANGUAGE ACROSS THE CURRICULUM

When possible, make children aware of ways in which English and Spanish are similar or different. In the Review activity, children look for similarities between the two languages. In the *If you have time . . .* activity for this lesson, the class searches for similarities within English and then within Spanish. Making these kinds of comparisons promotes sensitivity to language in general and helps children build vocabulary.

Video Lesson

1. Reviewing answers to ¿Cómo está usted? (How are you?)

Using masks as clues to how she feels, **la maestra** answers Rosco's question ¿**Cómo está usted?** three different ways—**Estoy muy mal** (*I feel very bad*), **Estoy así, así** (*I feel so-so*), and **Estoy muy bien** (*I feel very well/I feel fine*). Then she has the opening conversation with the class with Rosco as spokesperson (**M** = Maestra, **R** = Rosco, **C** = class):

M: Buenos días, clase.	*Good morning, class.*
R/C: Buenos días, Maestra.	*Good morning, Teacher.*
M: ¿Cómo estás tú?	*How are you?*
R/C: Muy bien, gracias. ¿Y usted?	*Very well, thank you. And you?*
M: Yo también estoy muy bien.	*I'm very well, too.*

2. Reviewing the numbers 10, 20, 30, 40, and 50

La maestra alternates between asking Rosco and the class to identify numbers. Then she models the numbers and has the class repeat them.

10	diez	30	treinta	50	cincuenta
20	veinte	40	cuarenta		

¿Qué número es?	*What number is it?*
Si, es ___.	*Yes, it's ___.*

3. Recalling the numbers 11–19

La maestra and Rosco discuss where the numbers 11–19 belong in the range 10–50. Then she models 11–19 and has the class repeat the numbers.

11	once	14	catorce	17	diecisiete
12	doce	15	quince	18	dieciocho
13	trece	16	dieciséis	19	diecinueve

4. Playing *Muéstrame* ___ (*Show me* ___)

La maestra models numbers 21–30 and children repeat them. Then **la maestra** plays **Muéstrame** ___ with the class. For numbers 21–30, see the Vocabulary section in this lesson.

¿Qué número es?	*What number is it?*
¿Es ___?	*Is it ___?*
No, no es ___. Es ___.	*No, it isn't ___. It's ___.*
¿Dónde está ___?	*Where is ___?*

EN ESPAÑOL

If you feel comfortable, use these expressions.

Yo también.	*Me, too.*
Mira.	*Look.*
No mires.	*Don't look.*
Lo siento.	*I'm sorry.*
Está bien.	*That's all right.*

LANGUAGE ACROSS THE CURRICULUM

La maestra uses the terms **números grandes** (*big numbers*) for numbers 10, 20, 30, etc., and **números pequeños** (*small numbers*) for the numbers in between. Ask the class if they know any other name for those numbers (children may be familiar with the terms *greater* and *lesser numbers*, which are often used to refer to those two types of numbers in math class).

5. Adding numbers to 10, 20, 30, 40, 50

Working with Rosco, **la maestra** demonstrates how the name for a double-digit number is composed of a name for the ten and for the ones. Then they play a game with double-digit numbers.

| ¿Qué número es? | *What number is it?* |
| ¿Es ___ o ___? | *Is it ___ or ___?* |

6. Reintroducing *Dame* ___ (*Give me* ___)

La maestra says **Vamos a mirar** (*Let's watch*) and then the mime demonstrates the meaning of **Dame**.

7. Playing *Dame* ___ (*Give me* ___) with numbers

La maestra asks Rosco to give her selected numbers from those shown—**treinta y ocho** (*38*), **diecinueve** (*19*), **doce** (*12*).

8. Practicing vocabulary for places in the school

La maestra models vocabulary for rooms in the school and the class repeats them. Then she and the children play **¿Cuál falta?** (*What's missing?*).

la oficina	*office*
el baño	*bathroom*
la biblioteca	*library*
la cafetería	*cafeteria*
la clase	*classroom*
el patio	*playground*

9. Closing

La maestra reminds the class that there are many ways to say farewell—**Adiós** (*Good-bye*), **Hasta la vista** (*Until we meet again*), and **Hasta luego** (*See you later*).

CROSS-CULTURAL CONNECTIONS

Point out that the same type of system for organizing numbers is used in both Spanish- and English-speaking countries.

LANGUAGE ACROSS THE CURRICULUM

La maestra points out ways to use numbers in different places in the school. You may want to ask children for additional suggestions.

After viewing the video, praise the children for their good listening and watching skills.

Lesson Fifteen

ACTIVITY LESSON

Activity 15A: What should we do?

Materials: Cassette player; Activity Cassette 1, Side B; five blank index cards; black marker; and Rosco flag.

Preparation: Using the marker, write one of these numbers on each of the index cards—24, 17, 36, 49, 52. Display the cards where everyone can see and reach them.

At the beginning of this activity, **la maestra** is going to say each number in Spanish. Be prepared to point to each one as she names it—**veinticuatro** (*24*), **diecisiete** (*17*), **treinta y seis** (*36*), **cuarenta y nueve** (*49*), **cincuenta y dos** (*52*).

Explain that **la maestra** is going to tell individuals to *walk* (**anda**), *run* (**corre**), or *jump* (**salta**). She is also going to say *give me* (**dame**) and one of the numbers on the cards. As **la maestra** is giving each command, you are going to hand the Rosco flag to someone. Then turn off the cassette tape, so that the selected child has time to follow **la maestra**'s directions and give you the number. Repeat this activity if you have time.

Activity 15B: Where would you go to . . . ?

Materials: Cassette player; Activity Cassette 1, Side B.

Tell the children that **la maestra** is first going to ask them to repeat words for places in the school. Then she is going to ask children where they would go to do particular things, just as she did with Dora and Rosco. Explain that **la maestra** wants the class to respond in Spanish.

Goal	Destination
• to visit principal or school secretary	**la oficina**
• to study with classmates	**la clase**
• to check out a book	**la biblioteca**
• to play jump rope or tetherball	**el patio**
• to wash your hands	**el baño**
• to eat lunch	**la cafetería**

Activity 15C: Play ball

Materials: Cassette player; Activity Cassette 1, Side B; and as many balls as groups.

Have the class count in English from 10 to 50 by tens. Then divide the class into smaller groups and ask each one to stand in a circle. Choose the starting player in each group.

Explain that **la maestra** is going to count to 50 by tens—**diez** (*10*), **veinte** (*20*), **treinta** (*30*), **cuarenta** (*40*), **cincuenta** (*50*)—and she wants the class to count with her. When she says **diez** (*10*), the class should repeat **diez** and the starting player should bounce the ball to another child within the same group. When **la maestra** says **veinte** (*20*), the second player bounces the ball to another player and so forth. She is going to count this way two times.

Depending on the skills of your class, you may want to pause the cassette player after **la maestra** says each number. On the other hand, children may be able to keep up with the count after they have played the game three or four times.

CLOSING

Tell the children that Spanish class is finished for today. The next video practices names and colors.

IF YOU HAVE TIME . . .

Write these numbers on the chalkboard.

3   4   5
30 40 50

First, ask the class to name the pairs of numbers—3/30, 4/40, 5/50—in English. Ask children to explain how knowing the name of the one-digit number in a pair can help them remember the name of the two-digit number. Accept all reasonable answers.

Then have the class name the same pairs of numbers in Spanish—**tres/treinta, cuatro/cuarenta, cinco/cincuenta.** Ask children to analyze these numbers in the same way. Accept all reasonable answers.

Lesson Fifteen

Lesson 16

Materials to gather

- VCR and Video Lesson 16 on Tape 4
- Cassette player
- Activity Cassette 1
- Blackline Masters 9C–1, 9C–2, 9C–3 (times of day)
- Blackline Master 16A (fish)
- Scissors or paper cutter
- Number Cards 1–10
- Blackline Master 16C (heads of 4 puppets)

- *Optional materials:* laminating machine

- *Prepare ahead:* colored fish for Review and Activity 16A

OBJECTIVES

Language

- Ask and answer questions about names
- Practice names for five colors
- Respond appropriately to the commands **siéntate** (*sit down*) and **párate** (*stand up*)

Culture

- State appropriate greetings for different times of day
- Understand that there are two ways to pronounce the letter **ll** in Spanish

Review

- Recall names for six colors
- Sing **"Español para ti"** (*"Spanish Is for You, and for Me"*)

Vocabulary

¿Cómo te llamas tú?	*What is your name?*
Me llamo ___.	*My name is ___.*
¿Cómo se llama?	*What is his/her name?*
Se llama ___.	*His/Her name is ___.*
morado	*purple*
gris	*gray*
blanco	*white*
rosado	*pink*
café	*brown*
Siéntate.	*Sit down.*
Párate.	*Stand up.*

Warm-up

Materials: Blackline Masters 9C-1, 9C-2, 9C-3.

Ask volunteers to say the appropriate greeting—**Buenos días** (*Good morning*), **Buenas tardes** (*Good afternoon*), **Buenas noches** (*Good evening*) as you show the Blackline Masters in random order.

Review

Materials: Blackline Master 16A; scissors; paper in different colors and laminating machine.

Preparation: Cut out and make color copies of Blackline Master 16A so that you have a fish in each of these colors: red, orange, yellow, green, blue, and black. If possible, laminate them so you can reuse them throughout the year. Note that for Activity 16A, you will need two sets of these fish, plus other colors. You may wish to make them all at once.

Remind children that they have practiced many colors in Spanish. One-by-one, show them a red, orange, yellow, green, blue, and black fish. Ask them to name as many as they can. Tell the class to listen carefully to the video for any colors they have forgotten.

Introduce the video

Explain that this video deals with names, colors, and commands.

Colors:

rojo	red
anaranjado	orange
amarillo	yellow
verde	green
azul	blue
negro	black

Blackline Master 16A

Video Lesson

1. Saying the opening conversation

Rosco and Dora say the opening conversation with the class (**M** = Maestra, **R** = Rosco, **D** = Dora, **C** = class):

M: Buenos días, clase.	*Good morning, class.*
R/D/C: Buenos días, Maestra.	*Good morning, Teacher.*
M: ¿Cómo estás tú?	*How are you?*
R/D/C: Muy bien, gracias. ¿Y usted?	*Very well, thank you. And you?*
M: Muy bien, gracias.	*Very well, thanks.*

2. Reintroducing questions and answers about names

Before practicing with the class, **la maestra** uses the puppets to model asking and answering about someone's name.

¿Cómo te llamas tú?	*What is your name?*
Me llamo ___.	*My name is ___.*
¿Cómo se llama?	*What is his/her name?*
Se llama ___.	*His/Her name is ___.*

3. Reintroducing eleven colors

Using the **sombreros** from Level 1, **la maestra** reviews colors through a mixture of modeling the names and asking **¿De qué color es?** (*What color is it?*).

rojo	*red*	gris	*gray*
anaranjado	*orange*	blanco	*white*
amarillo	*yellow*	rosado	*pink*
verde	*green*	café	*brown*
morado	*purple*	negro	*black*
azul	*blue*		

4. Playing *Muéstrame* ___ (*Show me* ___) with colors

La maestra models all the colors and has the class repeat them before and after playing **Muéstrame** ___.

5. Practicing colors

La maestra asks the class to identify the colors of several hats.

¿De qué color es?   *What color is it?*

FYI: In Spanish, **ll** may be pronounced [y] or soft [j]. **La maestra** has chosen the soft [j] sound used in Chile and Argentina. Rosco and Dora use the [y] sound that is used in most of the other Spanish-speaking countries.

FYI: Notice how the **-os** on **muchos** shows that **peces** and **colores** are masculine and plural.

con much**os** peces
(*with many fish*)

de much**os** colores
(*in many colors*)

LEVEL TWO

6. Introducing new commands

La maestra and the mime demonstrate the new commands.

Siéntate.	*Sit down.*
Párate.	*Stand up.*

But when Rosco practices them with **la maestra**, he gets carried away as usual. Then **la maestra** makes sure that all your children are seated, and she has them practice following the commands.

7. Reviewing colors

La maestra quickly asks Rosco and the class ¿De qué color es? (*What color is it?*) about different **sombreros**. Then she models each color and has Rosco and the class repeat them.

8. Practicing commands and colors

You are now going to choose a child and give him or her one of the colored fish you made for the Review activity. **La maestra** asks the selected child to sit down, stand up, and name the color he or she is holding. Check that the child answers correctly.

9. Singing "Español para ti" (*"Spanish Is for You, and for Me"*)

La maestra leads the class in singing **"Español para ti."** For song lyrics, see Lesson 3, Video Lesson, section 3.

10. Closing

La maestra says Adiós (*Good-bye*) and **Hasta la vista** (*Until we meet again*).

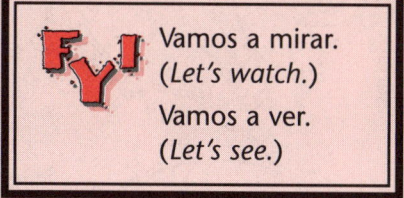

FYI
Vamos a mirar. (*Let's watch.*)
Vamos a ver. (*Let's see.*)

EN ESPAÑOL
Use this command if you feel comfortable.
Repitan, clase. (*Repeat, class.*)

After viewing the video, praise the children for their good listening and watching skills.

Lesson Sixteen

Blackline Master 16A

Blackline Master 16C

ACTIVITY LESSON

Activity 16A: Stand up with the red fish

Materials: Cassette player; Activity Cassette 1, Side B; and Blackline Master 16A.

Preparation: Make at least two sets of eleven colored fish from Blackline Master 16A, if you have not already done so. Each set should include white, black, blue, brown, red, orange, pink, green, yellow, purple, and gray. If possible, laminate the pages so you can reuse the fish throughout the year.

Give each child one colored fish, using all the colors. Explain that **la maestra** is going to tell the children to **párate** (*stand up*) or **siéntate** (*sit down*) if the fish they're holding is a certain color. Before repeating the activity, have children trade fish to get a different color.

Activity 16B: ¿Cómo te llamas tú? (*What is your name?*)

Materials: Cassette player; Activity Cassette 1, Side B.

Explain that **la maestra** is going to ask children to tell her their names in this activity.

Children *do* need additional practice with this activity, but you may want to alternate between Activities 16B and 16C, so that the class must listen more closely to distinguish between **¿Cómo te llamas tú?** (*What is your name?*) and **¿Cómo se llama?** (*What is his/her name?*) and their respective answers.

Activity 16C: Name that puppet

Materials: Cassette player; Activity Cassette 1, Side B; and Blackline Master 16C.

Preparation: Make a copy of Blackline Master 16C for each child and make sure children understand the meaning of **vaca** (*cow*), **lobo** (*wolf*), **jirafa** (*giraffe*), and **tucán** (*toucan*).

Have the class quickly identify the puppets on the Blackline Master by name. Explain that **la maestra** is going to ask children each puppet's name: **¿Cómo se llama la vaca?** (*What is the cow's name?*).

Answers: Rosco, the wolf; Dora, the cow; Jorge, the giraffe, and Ñico, the toucan.

LEVEL TWO

Closing

Tell the children that Spanish class is finished for today. In the next lesson, they are going practice months and learn how to say the date.

> **IF YOU HAVE TIME . . .**
>
> Have children sit in a circle. Select a child and have him or her say **Me llamo ___** (*My name is ___*). That child should then turn to the one sitting at his or her left and ask **¿Cómo te llamas tú?** (*What is your name?*). If a child asks **¿Cómo te llamas?** instead, accept that variation. Have children continue in the same way around the circle.

Lesson Sixteen

Lesson 17

Materials to gather

- VCR and Video Lesson 17 on Tape 5
- Cassette player
- Activity Cassette 1
- Song Cassette
- 11 colored fish from Lesson 16
- Gold Flashcards 1–2, 35–36, 39–40, 48–50, 62–64
- 7 small self-stick notes
- marker
- *Optional materials:* rap rolls from Activity 10C

OBJECTIVES

Language
- Answer the question **¿Cuál es la fecha?** (*What is the date?*)

Culture
- Use **tú** and **usted** appropriately

Review
- Practice the months of the year
- Respond appropriately to **siéntate** (*sit down*), **párate** (*stand up*), and **dame** (*give me*)
- Sing the "Months Rap" and **"Uno de enero"** (*"January First"*)

Vocabulary
No new vocabulary is introduced in this lesson.

Warm-up

Exchange greetings with the class (**T** = Teacher, **C** = class):
    T: Hola, clase.   *Hello, class.*
    C: Hola, Maestro/Maestra.   *Hello, Teacher.*

Review

Materials: Fish from Lesson 16 in all 11 colors.

Display the fish where everyone can see them. Ask volunteers to each choose a fish and name its color. Tell them to remain standing until all the colors are named. Next, have each volunteer name his or her color and ask the class to repeat it.

Introduce the video

Tell children that **la maestra** is going to talk about months and dates and sing the "Months Rap" in this video.

Colors:

rojo	*red*
anaranjado	*orange*
amarillo	*yellow*
verde	*green*
morado	*purple*
azul	*blue*
gris	*gray*
blanco	*white*
rosado	*pink*
café	*brown*
negro	*black*

Months:

enero	January
febrero	February
marzo	March
abril	April
mayo	May
junio	June
julio	July
agosto	August
septiembre	September
octubre	October
noviembre	November
diciembre	December

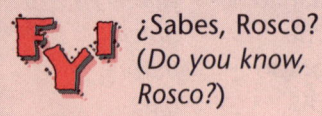

FYI

¿Sabes, Rosco?
(*Do you know, Rosco?*)

¡Qué rápido!
(*That was fast!*)

EN ESPAÑOL

If you feel comfortable, use these expressions and encourage children to do the same.

Otra vez.
(*Let's do it once more.*)

Otra vez más.
(*One more time.*)

Me toca a mí.
(*It's my turn.*)

Te toca a ti, [child's name].
(*It's your turn, [child's name].*)

Le toca a [child's name].
(*It's [child's name] turn.*)

LEVEL TWO

VIDEO LESSON

1. Saying the opening conversation

In a change of pace, Rosco says the opening conversation with the class. **La maestra** is part of the class, so that he can say **¿Y tú?** (*And you?*) to **la maestra** (**R** = Rosco, **M** = Maestra, **C** = class):

R: Buenos días, clase.	*Good morning, class.*
M/C: Buenos días, Rosco.	*Good morning, Rosco.*
R: ¿Cómo estás tú?	*How are you?*
M/C: Muy bien, gracias. ¿Y tú?	*Very well, thank you. And you?*
R: Muy bien, gracias.	*Very well, thanks.*

2. Discussing different words for *you*

La maestra reminds children that they should use **tú** for *you* with friends and with people they call by their first name. They should use **usted** for *you* with grown-ups.

3. Reviewing the months of the year

La maestra practices the months with Rosco and the class.

¿Recuerdas tú los meses del año?	*Do you remember the months of the year?*
¿Qué mes es éste?	*What month is this?*

4. Singing the "Months Rap"

La maestra and the class sing the "Months Rap." For lyrics to the rap, see Lesson 12, Video Lesson, section 4.

5. Naming the months while using Flashcards

La maestra asks Rosco and the class to name months according to the Flashcards she shows in random order.

Hay doce meses del año.	*There are 12 months in a year.*
¿Qué [mes] es?	*What [month] is it?*

6. Reviewing commands

The mime demonstrates three commands.

Siéntate.	*Sit down.*
Párate.	*Stand up.*
Dame.	*Give me.*

La maestra and Rosco name **los primeros seis meses del año** (*the first six months of the year*). Next, they take turns giving commands about these months. Then **la maestra** and Rosco review the remaining months and play the same game with them.

7. Practicing dates

La maestra talks about the number of days in each month. Then she asks Rosco to name random dates.

¿Cuál mes tiene veintiocho días?	What month has 28 days?
¿Cuál es la fecha?	What is the date?
El ___ de ___.	The ___ of ___.

8. Singing "Uno de enero" ("*January First*")

La maestra explicitly connects the words in the song to how dates are expressed in Spanish. For song lyrics, see Lesson 8, Video Lesson, section 3.

9. Closing

La maestra and friends say **Adiós** (*Good-bye*) and **Hasta luego** (*See you later*).

> After viewing the video, praise the children for their good listening and watching skills.

Lesson Seventeen

ACTIVITY LESSON

> When children physically respond to a verbal statement, they remember its meaning better.

Activity 17A: *Siéntate* (Sit down) and *Párate* (Stand up)

Materials: Cassette player; Activity Cassette 1, Side B; and Gold Flashcards 48–50, 62–64.

Give the Flashcards to six volunteers. Explain that **la maestra** is going tell someone who has the Flashcard for two particular months to stand up (**párate**) and then sit down (**siéntate**). She will repeat each direction two times. Explain that as **la maestra** names a volunteer's card, he or she should hold up the card so that the class can see it, and follow the direction. Repeat the activity a few times, so that many children have the opportunity to take part in this activity.

Activity 17B: How are you?

Materials: Cassette player; Activity 2A on Activity Cassette 1, Side A; and Gold Flashcards 1–2, 35–36, 39–40.

Play Activity 2A and then discuss with the class why Rosco asked ¿**Y usted?** and not ¿**Y tú?** for *And you?* (He was talking to an adult, **la maestra**.) Next, choose six or eight pairs of volunteers. Give one person in some of the pairs a Flashcard to indicate that he or she is an adult. Explain that each adult should be called *Mr.* or *Mrs.* and have a last name. If a pair includes an adult and a child, the adult should speak first. Then have members of each pair exchange greetings.

Between an adult (A) and a child (C):

A: ¿Cómo estás tú?   How are you?

C: Muy bien, gracias.   Fine, thank you.
    ¿Y usted?   And you?

A: Muy bien, gracias.   Very well, thank you.

Between two children (C1 and C2):

C1: ¿Cómo estás tú?   How are you?

C2: Muy bien, gracias.   Fine, thank you.
    ¿Y tú?   And you?

C1: Muy bien, gracias.   Very well, thank you.

LEVEL TWO

Activity 17C: What's the date?

Materials: Cassette player; Song Cassette, Side A; Gold Flashcards 48–50, 62; 7 small self-stick notes; and a marker.

Preparation: The months January through July should each have a small piece of self-stick paper at the left of the picture on the Flashcard. Consecutively number the months 1–7.

Place the Flashcards where everyone can see them. Then play **"Uno de enero"** (*"January First"*) down to the words **San Fermín**. Point to each number and month as it is named.

Uno de enero, dos de febrero,	*January first, February second,*
Tres de marzo, cuatro de abril.	*March third, April fourth.*
Cinco de mayo, seis de junio,	*May fifth, June sixth,*
Siete de julio, San Fermín.	*July seventh, Saint Fermín.*

Replay the song, stopping after each day and month. Ask volunteers to name the dates.

Then simply point to number 1 and the picture for January. If you or a child feel comfortable doing so, ask **¿Cuál es la fecha?** (*What is the date?*). If no one feels comfortable, ask it in English and have a volunteer answer in Spanish. Continue in the same way through July.

CLOSING

Tell the children that Spanish class is finished for today. In the next class, children are going to talk about days, numbers, and weather.

IF YOU HAVE TIME...

Materials: Cassette player; "Months Rap" on Song Cassette, Side A; Gold Flashcards 48–50, 62–64; and rap rolls from Activity 10C.

Display your rap roll. Ask children to follow along on their rap rolls as everyone listens to the "Months Rap." Next, have the class sing the rap once or twice with the cassette while following along with their rap rolls. For lyrics to the rap, see Lesson 12, Video Lesson, section 4.

Then point to different months on the Flashcards in random order and ask volunteers to name them in Spanish. If children have any difficulties, tell them to use the song for help like Rosco.

Months:

enero	*January*
febrero	*February*
marzo	*March*
abril	*April*
mayo	*May*
junio	*June*
julio	*July*
agosto	*August*
septiembre	*September*
octubre	*October*
noviembre	*November*
diciembre	*December*

Lesson Seventeen

Lesson 18

Materials to gather

- VCR and Video Lesson 18 on Tape 5
- Cassette player
- Activity Cassette 1
- Song Cassette
- Blackline Masters 9C-1, 9C-2, 9C-3 (times of day)
- Hand puppets Rosco and Dora
- Gold Flashcards 41–50, 62–64
- Rosco flag

OBJECTIVES

Language

- Ask and answer the question **¿Qué día es?** (*What day is it?*)
- Answer the question **¿Qué tiempo hace?** (*What's the weather like?*)

Culture

- Recall that Spanish speakers consider Monday the first day of the week while English speakers consider it to be Sunday

Review

- Practice the days of the week
- Ask and answer the question **¿Cuál es la fecha?** (*What's the date?*)
- Review numbers 1–30
- Sing the "Month Rap," the "Calendar Rap," and **"Español para ti"** (*"Spanish Is for You, and for Me"*)

Vocabulary

¿Cuál es la fecha?	*What's the date?*
¿Qué día es?	*What day is it?*
¿Qué tiempo hace?	*What's the weather like?*

Warm-up

Materials: Blackline Masters 9C-1, 9C-2, 9C-3; hand puppets Rosco and Dora.

Greet the class, using Rosco and Dora. Exchange greetings that correspond to the time of day. Then show a Blackline Master for another time of day and exchange appropriate greetings for that time (**R** = Rosco, **D** = Dora, **C** = class):

R/D: Buenos días/Buenas tardes/Buenas noches, clase.
Good morning/Good afternoon/Good evening, class.

C: Buenos días/Buenas tardes/Buenas noches, Rosco/Dora.
Good morning/Good afternoon/Good evening, Rosco/Dora.

Review

Materials: Gold Flashcards 48–50, 62–64.

Preparation: Make a copy of each Flashcard, so that there is only one month on each sheet of paper. Divide the copies into two piles, alternating months. For example, Pile A has January, March, May, and so forth, while Pile B includes February, April, June, and so on. Display the months in Pile A in calendar order where the class can see them. Show the months in Pile B in a separate group.

Divide the class in half. Next, ask for a volunteer to lead each group in naming the months. Tell the leader of Group A (who has January) to start. Have the groups alternate naming the months in calendar order as leaders point to each one. Then ask the leaders to change sides and tell Group B to begin. You may wish to repeat this process.

Introduce the video

Tell children that in this video they are going to talk about the days of the week, numbers to 30, and the weather.

105

Video Lesson

1. Saying the opening conversation

La maestra exchanges greetings with Rosco, Dora, and the class (**M** = Maestra, **R** = Rosco, **D** = Dora, **C** = class):

M:	Buenas tardes, Rosco/Dora/clase.	Good afternoon, Rosco/Dora/class.
R/D/C:	Buenas tardes, Maestra.	Good afternoon, Teacher.
M:	¿Cómo estás tú?	How are you?
R/D/C:	Muy bien, gracias. ¿Y usted?	Very well, thank you. And you?
M:	Muy bien, gracias.	Very well, thanks.

2. Reviewing days of the week

La maestra models the days and the class repeats them.

Hay siete días de la semana.	There are seven days in a week.
la diferencia entre un calendario en inglés y un calendario en español	the difference between an English calendar and a Spanish calendar
En español el día número uno es lunes.	In Spanish the first day of the week is Monday.
En español el día número siete es domingo.	In Spanish the seventh day of the week is Sunday.
En inglés el día número uno es domingo.	In English the first day of the week is Sunday.
En inglés el día número siete es sábado.	In English the seventh day of the week is Saturday.

3. Singing the "Calendar Rap"

La maestra and the class sing the "Calendar Rap." For lyrics to the rap, see the *If you have time . . .* activity in this lesson.

4. Asking questions about the calendar

La maestra varies who asks and answers questions. Then she carefully contrasts how to say the day and the date.

¿Qué día es?	What day is it?
Es ___.	It's ___.
¿Cuál es la fecha?	What is the date?
Es el ___ de ___.	It's ___.

Days of the week:

lunes	Monday
martes	Tuesday
miércoles	Wednesday
jueves	Thursday
viernes	Friday
sábado	Saturday
domingo	Sunday

CROSS-CULTURAL CONNECTIONS

Point out that the months are in the same order in Spanish- and English-speaking countries. In contrast, the days of the week start with **lunes** (*Monday*) in Spanish-speaking countries and Sunday in English-speaking countries.

EN ESPAÑOL

If you feel comfortable, use these expressions that both mean *Of course* — ¡Claro! and ¡Cómo no!

LEVEL TWO

5. Singing the "Months Rap"

La maestra and the class sing this rap. For lyrics to the rap, see Lesson 12, Video Lesson, section 4.

Hay doce meses del año. *There are 12 months in a year.*

6. Reviewing the numbers

La maestra reviews random numbers by asking **¿Qué número es?** (*What number is it?*).

30	treinta	16	dieciséis	13	trece	13	trece
12	doce	17	diecisiete	19	diecinueve	11	once
10	diez	15	quince	15	quince	20	veinte
18	dieciocho	14	catorce				

7. Linking months of the year with weather

La maestra asks about dates and the weather. In addition, she models different kinds of weather and has the class repeat them.

¿Cuál es la fecha?	*What is the date?*
el ___ de ___	*the ___ of ___*
¿Qué tiempo hace?	*What's the weather like?*
En ___, ¿___ o ___?	*In ___, is it ___ or is it ___?*
Hace sol.	*It's sunny.*
Hace calor.	*It's hot.*
Llueve.	*It's raining.*
Hace viento.	*It's windy.*
Hace frío.	*It's cold.*
Hace buen tiempo.	*It's good weather.*
Nieva.	*It's snowing.*
Hace mal tiempo.	*It's bad weather.*

8. Singing "Español para ti" (*"Spanish Is for You, and for Me"*)

La maestra and the class sing **"Español para ti."** For song lyrics, see Lesson 3, Video Lesson, section 3.

9. Closing

La maestra recalls the days, dates, and weather practiced during class. Everyone says **Adiós** (*Good-bye*).

Answers to questions:
Jan. 15
el quince de enero
Feb. 20
el veinte de febrero
Mar. 11
el once de marzo
Apr. 13
el trece de abril
Nieva en enero.
(*It snows in January.*)
Hace frío en febrero.
(*It's cold in February.*)
Hace viento en abril.
(*It's windy in April.*)

After viewing the video, praise the children for their good listening and watching skills.

Lesson Eighteen

Activity Lesson

Activity 18A: *Toca* ___ (*Touch* ___)

Materials: Cassette player; Activity Cassette 1, Side B; Gold Flashcards 41–47; and Rosco flag.

Display the Flashcards where everyone can see and touch them. Point out that you have displayed the Gold Flashcards for weather expressions. Explain that **la maestra** is going to say each command twice. She will use **anda** (*walk*), **corre** (*run*), or **salta** (*jump*), plus the command **toca** (*touch*). As she is speaking, you are going to hand the Rosco flag to someone. That child should then follow **la maestra**'s directions concerning a Flashcard for a weather expression. You are going to give the Rosco flag to a total of five children, including the child who does the practice exercise. Select new players each time the class plays the game.

Activity 18B: Follow those directions

Materials: Cassette player; Activity Cassette 1, Side B; and Gold Flashcards 41–47.

Distribute all the Flashcards even though the activity only uses four of them. Tell the class that **la maestra** is going to ask children holding some of the weather expressions to **párate** (*stand up*) and then **siéntate** (*sit down*). When someone hears the matching weather expression for his or her Flashcard, that child should show it to the class and follow **la maestra**'s directions. If possible, play this game several times and use different participants. You may want to alternate this activity with Activity 18A, so that children must listen to the directions on the tape and not simply remember what happened.

IF YOU HAVE TIME . . .

Materials: Cassette player; "Calendar Rap" on Song Cassette, Side A.

Play the song once, and then ask children to sing along two or three times. Encourage children to count on their fingers while singing as **la maestra** does.

Lunes, martes, miércoles, tres.
(*Monday, Tuesday, Wednesday, three.*)

Uno, dos, tres.
(*One, two, three.*)

Jueves, viernes, sábado, seis.
(*Thursday, Friday, Saturday, six.*)

Uno, dos, tres, cuatro, cinco, seis.
(*One, two, three, four, five, six.*)

Y domingo siete es.
(*And Sunday is seven.*)

Uno, dos, tres, cuatro, cinco, seis, siete.
(*One, two, three, four, five, six, seven.*)

Activity 18C: Put yourselves in calendar order

Materials: Cassette player; "Months Rap" on Song Cassette, Side A; and Gold Flashcards 41–47.

Display the Gold Flashcards in calendar order. Play the "Months Rap" a couple of times and have children sing along as you point to the appropriate months. For lyrics to the rap, see Lesson 12, Video Lesson, section 4.

Next, put the Flashcards facedown in a pile. Ask six volunteers to come to the front of the class, take a card, and hold it so that the class can see it. Have them stand in a group.
Tell the volunteers that they are going to arrange themselves in calendar order by doing what their classmates sing. Ask children to sing along as you replay the first pair of lines from the song. Have the child holding **enero** and **febrero** identify him- or herself and start a line at the left. Continue in the same way until all the months are in order.

As an alternative when repeating the activity, ask volunteers to first arrange themselves in calendar order. Then have everyone sing along with the tape. As each pair of months is mentioned, the appropriate child should hold up his or her Flashcard.

> **FYI** In English, the days of the week and the months are capitalized. In Spanish, they are not.

CLOSING

Tell the children that Spanish class is finished for today. In the next video, they are going to practice the dates, weather, and learn a new command.

Lesson 19

Materials to gather

- VCR and Video Lesson 19 on Tape 5
- Cassette player
- Activity Cassette 1
- Song Cassette
- Gold Flashcards 41–50, 62–64
- Calendar
- Blackline Master 19C (Guide to Days)
- Tape or glue
- *Optional materials:* marker; 7 small pieces of self-adhesive paper; crayons
- *Prepare ahead:* Guide to Days (Activity 19C)

OBJECTIVES

Language
- Understand the meaning of **pon** (*put*)

Culture
- Understand that art can be culture specific

Review
- Ask and answer questions about the day, date, and weather
- Review the commands **siéntate** (*sit down*), **párate** (*stand up*), and **dame** (*give me*)

Vocabulary

Pon.   Put.

Warm-up

Materials: Gold Flashcards 41–47.

Exchange greetings that correspond to the time of day (**T** = Teacher, **C** = class):

T: Buenos días/Buenas tardes, clase. *Good morning/Good afternoon, class.*

C: Buenos días/Buenas tardes, Maestro/Maestra. *Good morning/Good afternoon, Teacher.*

Then have a volunteer ask the class **¿Qué tiempo hace?** (*What's the weather like?*). Accept all reasonable answers, based on the weather in your area. Show the corresponding Gold Flashcards, so all children know which expressions are being used.

Review

Materials: Cassette player; "Calendar Rap" on Song Cassette, Side A.

Preparation: On the chalkboard, draw the outline of the upper part of a calendar with spaces for the days of the week and blocks for the seven days. Number the blocks 1–7. Play the "Calendar Rap" and ask the class to sing along. For the rap lyrics, see Lesson 12, Video Lesson, section 3.

Point to the names for the days and the numbers as they are mentioned. Next, ask volunteers to name the days without any music. If necessary, encourage children to say the rap to help themselves remember the days just as Rosco has been saying the "Months Rap" to himself.

Introduce the video

Explain that this video is about days, dates, and weather.

Weather expressions:

Hace sol.
(*It's sunny.*)

Hace calor.
(*It's hot.*)

Llueve.
(*It's raining.*)

Hace viento.
(*It's windy.*)

Hace frío.
(*It's cold.*)

Hace buen tiempo.
(*It's good weather.*)

Nieva.
(*It's snowing.*)

Hace mal tiempo.
(*It's bad weather.*)

Video Lesson

1. Saying the opening conversation

La maestra greets Rosco, Dora, and the class (**M** = Maestra, **R** = Rosco, **D** = Dora, **C** = class):

M:	Buenos días, Rosco/Dora/clase.	*Good morning, Rosco/Dora/class.*
R/D/C:	Buenos días, Maestra.	*Good morning, Teacher.*
M:	¿Cómo estás tú?	*How are you?*
R/D/C:	Muy bien, gracias. ¿Y usted?	*Very well, thank you. And you?*
M:	Muy bien, gracias.	*Very well, thanks.*

2. Practicing various questions and answers

La maestra talks about the calendar she is displaying.

Miro el calendario.	*I look at the calendar.*
En el calendario, tenemos el mes de septiembre.	*The month of September is showing on the calendar.*
Siete días de la semana: lunes, martes, miércoles, jueves, viernes, sábado, domingo.	*The seven days of the week: Monday, Tuesday, Wednesday, Thursday, Friday, Saturday, Sunday.*
Tenemos muchos días de la semana.	*There are many days in a week.*
Si estamos aquí, ¿cuál es la fecha?	*If we are here, what is the date?*

La maestra models questions and answers for the puppets and the class to repeat.

¿Cuál es la fecha?	*What is the date?*
El ___ de ___.	*The ___ of ___.*
¿Qué día es?	*What day of the week is it?*
Es ___.	*It's ___.*
¿Qué tiempo hace?	*What's the weather like?*
Hace sol.	*It's sunny.*
Hace buen tiempo.	*It's good weather.*

3. Reviewing commands

The mime demonstrates the meaning of three commands.

Siéntate.	*Sit down.*
Párate.	*Stand up.*
Dame ___.	*Give me ___.*

FYI Notice how the same date is expressed in numbers in English and Spanish.

April 15   4/15
el quince de abril   15/4

LEVEL TWO

4. Reviewing the months of the year

La maestra models questions for the class to repeat. Then using a calendar, she asks Rosco and Dora to answer these questions.

¿Cuál es la fecha?	*What is the date?*
¿Qué día es?	*What day of the week is it?*
¿Qué tiempo hace?	*What's the weather like?*

Next, **la maestra** models the months and has the class repeat them. She also comments on various holidays, such as **el cuatro de julio** (*July 4*) and asks questions. For months, see Lesson 17, Video Lesson, section 3.

Son doce meses del año.	*There are 12 months in a year.*
¿Qué mes es este?	*What month is this?*

5. Introducing the command *pon* (*put*)

The mime demonstrates the meaning of **pon**.

6. Using *pon* (*put*) with weather expressions

La maestra asks Rosco and Dora to pair Flashcards for months and weather.

Pon diciembre en hace frío.	*Put December on it's cold.*
Pon agosto en hace calor.	*Put August on it's hot.*
Pon enero en nieva.	*Put January on it's snowing.*

7. Closing

La maestra says **Hasta la vista** (*Until we meet again*).

HERITAGE SPEAKERS

Remind the class that on the Flashcards for the months, July is represented by fireworks for Independence Day. Point out that this picture would *not* help people from Spain (Spaniards) remember July. Discuss why the picture of a bull chasing men would be more helpful to them. (The running of the bulls during the feast of San Fermín is an important event in Pamplona, Spain.) Then ask heritage speakers what illustrations they would want for different months and why.

After viewing the video, praise the children for their good listening and watching skills.

Lesson Nineteen

Since listening and speaking practice are so important, have as many children as possible take part in each activity. Encourage children to be active listeners by:

- listening to the Spanish even when it is not their turn.
- figuring out answers to all questions.
- checking their answers against those given.

Blackline Master 19C

ACTIVITY LESSON

Activity 19A: Pair months and weather

Materials: Cassette player; Activity Cassette 1, Side B; and Gold Flashcards 41–46, 48–50, 62–64.

Distribute the Flashcards to twelve volunteers. Discuss the meaning of **párate** (*stand up*) and **siéntate** (*sit down*) with the class. Explain that **la maestra** is going to name two months and the child with that Flashcard should stand up, show the card to the rest of the class, and remain standing. Next, she is going to describe typical weather during those months. The person with that weather card should also stand up and show it to the class. Then **la maestra** will tell both of them to sit down and go on to other months and weather. Since she only asks twelve children to take part in this activity, repeat it a couple of times, so that many children may participate.

Activity 19B: Ask questions

Materials: Cassette player; Activity Cassette 1, Side B; calendar; and Gold Flashcard 47.

In this tape activity, doña Elena is going to ask the class to repeat three questions. Help the class by giving visual clues. As she is working with **¿Qué día es hoy?**, point to the names of the days on a calendar. For **¿Cuál es la fecha?** indicate different dates on the calendar. When **la maestra** asks **¿Qué tiempo hace?** (*What's the weather like?*), show the Gold Flashcard for *It's bad weather.*

Explain that doña Elena is going to ask the class to listen and then repeat questions about the day, the date, and the weather.

Activity 19C: ¿Qué día es hoy? (*What day is today?*)

Materials: Cassette player; "Calendar Rap" on Song Cassette, Side A; calendar for speakers of English; Blackline Master 19C; tape or glue; and crayons (optional).

Preparation: Make a copy of Blackline Master 19C for each child and yourself. Construct a "Guide to Days," so that you may use it for demonstration purposes.

Display your "Guide to Days" where everyone can see it. Ask the class to cut Blackline Master 19C in half and tape or glue the pieces end to end, so that the numerals are in number order like yours. Explain that you call this strip a "Guide to Days" because it shows where the days are on a calendar for Spanish-speaking people.

LEVEL TWO

On the calendar for speakers of English, point to the names of the days and discuss what this row represents. Next, point out the equivalent row on the children's strips. Explain that it only shows the first letter of each day because the class has not yet learned how to read Spanish.

Point to the name of each day and the numbers as children sing along with the cassette to the "Calendar Rap." For words to the "Calendar Rap," see Lesson 12, Video Lesson, section 3.

Beginning with **lunes**, have children point to each day on their guides, and name it in Spanish. Where possible, briefly mention school activities that usually take place on a particular day, such as going to the library or having art.

Have volunteers take turns pointing to a day on your strip and then ask the class ¿**Qué día es hoy?** (*What day is today?*). Encourage the class to sing the "Calendar Rap" and to point to the appropriate spaces on their strips when they don't know an answer.

If you have time, have children draw pictures in the boxes for the days for repeated school activities, such as a trip to the library or having art. Keep these Guides to Days for use in additional activities.

CLOSING

Tell the children that Spanish class is finished for today. In their next class, they are going to talk more about dates and weather and play games with colors.

Days of the week:

lunes	*Monday*
martes	*Tuesday*
miércoles	*Wednesday*
jueves	*Thursday*
viernes	*Friday*
sábado	*Saturday*
domingo	*Sunday*

IF YOU HAVE TIME

Materials: Cassette player; "Uno de enero" (*"January First"*) on Song Cassette, Side A; Gold Flashcards 48–50, 62; 7 small, self-adhesive pieces of paper; and marker.

Preparation: Number the pieces of paper 1–7 and attach them to the left of each month, 1 for January, 2 for February, and so forth. Display the months in calendar order.

Play the song two or three times and have children sing along. Point to the numbers and the months as they are named in the song. Repeat and practice the sections with which the class is having difficulty. For song lyrics, see Lesson 8, Video Lesson, section 3.

For variety, divide the class in half. Have groups take turns singing the lyrics about the months, e.g., Group A sings **Uno de enero** and Group B sings **Dos de febrero,** and so forth. They all sing the refrain together.

Lesson Nineteen

Lesson 20

Materials to gather

- VCR and Video Lesson 20 on Tape 5
- Cassette player
- Activity Cassette 1
- Blackline Masters 9C-1, 9C-2, 9C-3 (times of day)
- Calendar
- Gold Flashcards 41–47
- Green, blue, yellow, white, black, orange, and red crayons
- Blackline Master 20A (numbered fish)
- 11 colored fish from Lesson 16 (Review and Activity 16A)
- Rosco flag
- Construction paper
- Blackline Master 20C (blank calendar)
- *Optional materials:* green, blue, yellow, black, white, orange, and red chalk; calendar for English speakers

OBJECTIVES

Language
- Understand the meaning of **colorea** (*color*)

Culture
- Compare calendars used by speakers of English and Spanish and understand the difference

Review
- Ask and answer questions about the date and weather
- Ask and answer the questions ¿**Cómo te llamas?** (*What is your name?*) and ¿**Cómo se llama?** (*What is his/her name?*)
- Practice the names of eleven colors
- Understand the commands **pon** (*put*) and **dame** (*give me*)

Vocabulary

Colorea. *Color.*

Warm-up

Materials: Blackline Masters 9C-1, 9C-2, 9C-3 and a calendar.

Display a calendar. Exchange greetings that correspond to the time of day. Then show a Blackline Master for another time of day and exchange appropriate greetings for that time (T = Teacher, C = class):

    T: Buenos días/Buenas tardes/Buenas noches, clase.   *Good morning/Good afternoon/Good evening, class.*

    C: Buenos días/Buenas tardes/Buenas noches, Maestro/Maestra.   *Good morning/Good afternoon/Good evening, Teacher.*

Have volunteers ask and answer *What day is today?* (**¿Qué día es hoy?**) as you point to the appropriate day on the calendar. Next, point to today's date and tell volunteers to ask and answer *What is the date?* (**¿Cuál es la fecha?**).

Review

Materials: Gold Flashcards 41–47.

Place the Flashcards facedown in random order in a pile. Have volunteers each draw a Flashcard and name the weather. Then have other volunteers ask and answer *What's the weather like?* (**Qué tiempo hace?**) about today's weather. Accept all reasonable answers. Show the appropriate Flashcard for each child's answer.

For weather expressions, see Lesson 19, Warm-up section.

Introduce the video

Explain that during this video, children are going to work with the calendar and names, and play games with colors.

Days of the week:

lunes	*Monday*
martes	*Tuesday*
miércoles	*Wednesday*
jueves	*Thursday*
viernes	*Friday*
sábado	*Saturday*
domingo	*Sunday*

Months of the year:

enero	*January*
febrero	*February*
marzo	*March*
abril	*April*
mayo	*May*
junio	*June*
julio	*July*
agosto	*August*
septiembre	*September*
octubre	*October*
noviembre	*November*
diciembre	*December*

Video Lesson

1. Saying the opening conversation

La maestra greets Jorge, Ñico, and the class (M = Maestra, J = Jorge, Ñ = Ñico, C = class):

M: Buenas tardes, Jorge/Ñico/clase.	Good afternoon, Jorge/Ñico/class.
J/Ñ/C: Buenas tardes, Maestra.	Good afternoon, Teacher.
M: ¿Cómo estás tú?	How are you?
J/Ñ/C: Muy bien, gracias. ¿Y usted?	Very well, thank you. And you?
M: Muy bien, gracias.	Very well, thanks.

2. Reviewing the calendar and weather

La maestra asks the puppets and the class questions about the date, the day, and the weather.

¿Cuál es la fecha?	What is the date?
El tres de septiembre.	The third of September.
¿Qué día es?	What day is it?
Es lunes.	It's Monday.
¿Qué tiempo hace?	What's the weather like?
Nieva y hace frío.	It's snowing and it's cold.

Next, **la maestra** models each of the previous questions and has the class repeat them.

3. Reviewing names

La maestra asks the puppets and children their names. Then she has the puppets tell each other's names. Finally, she asks children the puppet's names.

¿Cómo te llamas?	What is your name?
Me llamo ___.	My name is ___.
¿Cómo se llama?	What is his/her name?
Se llama ___.	His/Her name is ___.

LEVEL TWO

4. Reviewing colors

La maestra discusses Ñico's colors with him.

¿De qué color es?	*What color is it?*
negro	*black*
azul	*blue*
verde	*green*
rojo	*red*
anaranjado	*orange*

Then the mime plays with several colors:

morado	*purple*
anaranjado	*orange*
verde	*green*
rosado	*pink*
blanco	*white*
café	*brown*
gris	*gray*

5. Playing ¿Cuál falta? (*What's missing?*) with colors

La maestra models each color and then plays **¿Cuál falta?** with the class. She comments that there are **muchos peces de muchos colores** (*many fish in many colors*).

Additional color:

amarillo   *yellow*

6. Coloring and playing *Dame* ___ (*Give me* ___)

La maestra asks Ñico to give her different-colored crayons. Then, the mime demonstrates the command **colorea** (*color*) and **la maestra** tells Jorge to color in various colors.

7. Closing

La maestra says **Hasta la vista** (*Until we meet again*) to the children.

After viewing the video, praise the children for their good listening and watching skills.

Lesson Twenty

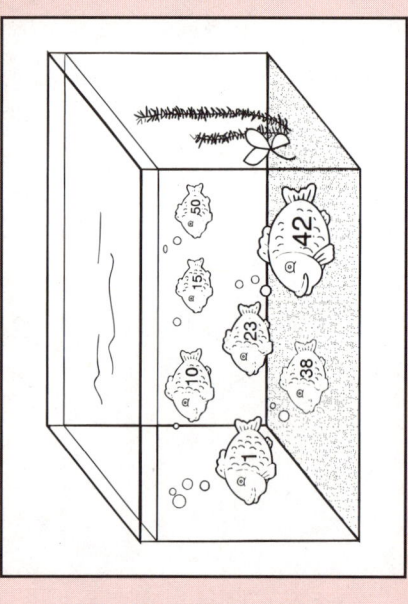

Blackline Master 20A

IF YOU HAVE TIME . . .

Ask three volunteers to come to the front of the class. Have Child A ask Child B the name of Child C:

A: ¿Cómo se llama? (*What's his/her name?*)

B: Se llama [Child C's name]. (*His/Her name is ___.*)

Demonstrate how the group can switch positions, each time asking about the name of a different member. Then divide the class into trios. Have each group follow the same process.

ACTIVITY LESSON

Activity 20A: *Colorea* (Color)

Materials: Cassette player; Activity Cassette 1, Side B; green, blue, yellow, white, black, orange, and red crayons; Blackline Master 20A; and yellow, black, orange, green, white, blue, and red chalk (optional).

Preparation: Make a copy of Blackline Master 20A for everyone in the class. Give each child all the listed crayons.

The chart below includes all the numbers and colors that doña Elena uses in this activity, in the order she calls them out. As she names the numbers on the fish, you may want to stop the cassette player and make sure that children can identify the correct fish. While numbers are part of this activity, the main purposes are to practice the names for colors and the new command **colorea** (*color*).

uno—amarillo	1—yellow
diez—negro	10—black
quince—anaranjado	15—orange
treinta y ocho—verde	38—green
veintitrés—blanco	23—white
cuarenta y dos—azul	42—blue
cincuenta—rojo	50—red

Tell the children to follow along as doña Elena names the numbers and the colors. She will repeat each number and color two times. Ask children to color only part of a fish when doña Elena calls its number. They may go back later and finish coloring the picture.

To repeat this activity, draw outlines of seven fish on the chalkboard and write one of these numbers in random order above each fish—1, 10, 15, 23, 38, 42, 50. Replay the cassette activity and have volunteers color the fish with chalk. By simply erasing the fish and putting the numbers in different order, you create a new version of the activity.

Activity 20B: Put the color on the weather

Materials: Cassette player; Activity Cassette 1, Side B; Gold Flashcards 41–47; 11 colored fish from Lesson 16; and Rosco flag.

Put the fish and the Gold Flashcards where everyone can see them. Explain that doña Elena is going to tell children to put (**pon**) the colored fish on weather cards. She will repeat each color and each weather expression two times. Give the Rosco flag to a child and have him/her follow her command. Since there are only five commands including the practice one, try to repeat this activity a couple of times. For colors, see section 4 of this Video Lesson.

LEVEL TWO

Activity 20C: Make a Spanish calendar

Materials: Large-size monthly calendar for speakers of English; Blackline Master 20C; and crayons for each child.

Preparation: Make a copy of Blackline Master 20C for every child. Draw Blackline Master 20C on the chalkboard. To the left of your drawing, display the current month on a calendar for speakers of English, or draw the current month on the chalkboard.

Discuss with the class how the displayed calendars are alike and different, being sure to include that on an "English" calendar Sunday is the first day but that on a "Spanish" calendar **lunes** (*Monday*) is the first day.

Explain that you want children to make Spanish calendars. Use the English calendar to help children locate where the first day of the current month should go on the Spanish calendar. Write it on the blank calendar on the chalkboard as the children fill in theirs. Continue in the same way until the tenth. For 8, 9, and 10, encourage children to add or count on from 7 to make sure they have numbers correctly positioned. Children haven't reviewed the number 31 yet this year. If you need it for the month you're working with, you can either provide it or ask if anyone in the class remembers it from last year.

If you feel comfortable, use a mixture of Spanish with English equivalents as you and the class discuss what's happening. Assist the class as necessary until the calendar is complete. If necessary, point out that although on the Spanish calendar the week begins with Monday instead of Sunday, it does not change either the date any day falls on or the number of days in the month.

Have children save this calendar so that at appropriate points they can say what the date is using a Spanish calendar. You may also want to complete a copy of Blackline Master 20C for yourself, and make a transparency of it for use in future lessons. For months and days of the week, see the Warm-up section of this lesson.

CLOSING

Tell the children that Spanish class is finished for today. Next time children are going talk about the calendar and the weather again.

Blackline Master 20C

Numbers 1–31:

1	uno
2	dos
3	tres
4	cuatro
5	cinco
6	seis
7	siete
8	ocho
9	nueve
10	diez
11	once
12	doce
13	trece
14	catorce
15	quince
16	dieciséis
17	diecisiete
18	dieciocho
19	diecinueve
20	veinte
21	veintiuno
22	veintidós
23	veintitrés
24	veinticuatro
25	veinticinco
26	veintiséis
27	veintisiete
28	veintiocho
29	veintinueve
30	treinta
31	treinta y uno

Lesson Twenty

Lesson 21

Materials to gather

- VCR and Video Lesson 21 on Tape 6
- Cassette player
- Activity Cassette 1
- Gold Flashcards 1–2, 41–47, 48–50, 62–64
- 11 colored fish from Lesson 16
- Bag or box
- 14 sheets of 8½" x 11" paper
- Several large balls
- Calendar with all twelve months
- Blackline Master 20C (blank calendar)
- Pencils
- Markers or crayons

- *Optional materials:*
  Song Cassette; 7 small self-adhesive pieces of paper marked 1–7; and rap rolls from Activity 10C

- *Prepare ahead:*
  list of children's birthdays (Activity 21C)

Objectives

Language
- Practice vocabulary for places in the school

Culture
- Recall that dates in Spanish follow the opposite order of dates in English

Review
- Ask and answer questions about the calendar and weather
- Respond appropriately to **párate** (*stand up*) and **siéntate** (*sit down*)
- Listen to a tour of a school
- Practice months and dates related to birthdays
- Sing the "Months Rap"

Vocabulary

la escuela   *school*

Warm-up

Materials: Gold Flashcards 1–2, 41–47.

Say the opening conversation with your class if you feel comfortable doing so. If not, ask a volunteer to play the role of the teacher. Have the child show a Flashcard to denote his or her role (**T** = Teacher, **C** = class):

T: Buenos días/Buenas tardes, clase.	*Good morning/Good afternoon, class.*
C: Buenos días/Buenas tardes, Maestro/ Maestra.	*Good morning/Good afternoon, Teacher.*
T: ¿Cómo estás tú?	*How are you?*
C: Muy bien, gracias. ¿Y usted?	*Very well, thank you. And you?*
T: Muy bien, gracias.	*Very well, thanks.*

Then ask, or have a volunteer ask, **¿Qué tiempo hace?** (*What's the weather like?*). Accept all reasonable answers and display Flashcards to accompany appropriate responses.

Review

Materials: 11 colored fish from Lesson 16; bag or box.

Preparation: Put the fish into a bag or box, so that children cannot see what they are going to pull out.

Have volunteers reach into the bag, pull out a fish, and ask the class **¿De qué color es?** (*What color is it?*). Tell the class to identify the color. To keep the Review moving, have each volunteer ask about three or four colors before changing to another volunteer.

Introduce the video

Explain that children are going to practice words for places in a school.

Weather flashcards:

41: Hace sol. Hace calor.
  (*It's sunny. It's hot.*)
42: Hace frío.
  (*It's cold.*)
43: Hace buen tiempo.
  (*It's good weather.*)
44: Llueve.
  (*It's raining.*)
45: Nieva.
  (*It's snowing.*)
46: Hace viento.
  (*It's windy.*)
47: Hace mal tiempo.
  (*It's bad weather.*)

Colors:

rojo	*red*
anaranjado	*orange*
amarillo	*yellow*
verde	*green*
morado	*purple*
azul	*blue*
gris	*gray*
blanco	*white*
rosado	*pink*
café	*brown*
negro	*black*

VIDEO LESSON

1. Saying the opening conversation

La maestra greets Rosco, Dora, and the class with **Buenos días** (*Good morning*). For the opening conversation, see the Warm-up in this lesson.

2. Reviewing the calendar and weather

La maestra questions the puppets.

¿Cuál es la fecha?	*What is the date?*
El cinco de septiembre.	*September 5th.*
¿Qué día es?	*What day of the week is it?*
Es miércoles.	*It's Wednesday.*
¿Qué tiempo hace?	*What's the weather like?*
Llueve.	*It's raining.*

The class practices asking and answering the same questions.

El dos de septiembre.	*September 2nd.*
Es jueves.	*It's Thursday.*
Llueve.	*It's raining.*

3. Reviewing *párate* (*stand up*) and *siéntate* (*sit down*)

The mime demonstrates the meaning of **párate** and **siéntate**. Then **la maestra** asks children to follow these commands.

4. Touring the school

La maestra takes the class on another visit to the school. Later she asks the puppets about school. Excerpts from the tour follow.

Estoy en la biblioteca.	*I am in the library.*
Y tengo libros.	*And I have books.*
Los libros son muy importantes.	*Books are very important.*
Y los libros son nuestros amigos.	*And books are our friends.*
A todos los niños les gustan los libros.	*All children like books.*
Los niños comen en la cafetería.	*Children eat in the cafeteria.*
Les gusta comer.	*They like to eat.*

EN ESPAÑOL

La maestra says **¡Escuchen!** (*Listen!*) to gain the children's attention. If you feel comfortable, use it too.

FYI

¿Te gusta la escuela? (*Do you like school?*)

Me gusta la escuela. (*I like school.*)

Me gusta la cafetería. (*I like the cafeteria.*)

A Rosco le gusta comer. (*Rosco likes to eat.*)

5. Reintroducing words for places in a school

La maestra models the three words—**la escuela** (*school*), **la clase** (*class*), **la biblioteca** (*library*)—and has everyone repeat them. Next, she asks each puppet and the class to say them after her. Then **la maestra** describes places in a school in English and wants the puppets and class to name them in Spanish. She also invites the puppets and children to go different places.

Vamos a la escuela.	*Let's go to school.*
Vamos a la clase.	*Let's go to class.*
Vamos a la biblioteca.	*Let's go to the library.*

6. Reviewing months and dates

La maestra comments on the months and models each one for everyone to repeat.

Muchos meses del año estamos en la escuela, en la clase y en la biblioteca.	*We are in school, class, and the library many months of the year.*

Rosco questions **la maestra** about her birthday. She then asks the puppets about theirs (**R** = Rosco, **M** = Maestra, **D** = Dora):

R: ¿Cuándo es su cumpleaños?	*When is your birthday?*
M: En enero.	*In January.*
R: ¿Cuál es la fecha?	*What is the date?*
M: La fecha es el veintiuno de enero.	*The date is January 21.*
M: ¿Cuándo es tu cumpleaños?	*When is your birthday?*
R/D: En julio./En mayo.	*In July./In May.*

For months, see Lesson 20, Warm-up section.

7. Singing the "Months Rap"

La maestra invites everyone to sing by saying **Vamos a cantar** (*Let's sing*). For lyrics to the rap, see Lesson 12, Video Lesson, section 4.

8. Reviewing vocabulary for places in the school

La maestra asks the puppets where in the school they would go to do certain things.

9. Closing

La maestra and the puppets say **Hasta la vista** (*Until we meet again*) and **Adiós** (*Good-bye*).

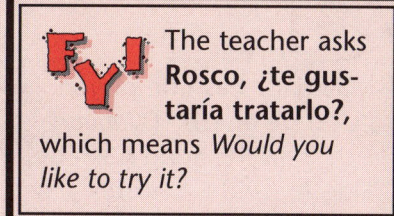

FYI The teacher asks **Rosco, ¿te gustaría tratarlo?**, which means *Would you like to try it?*

EN ESPAÑOL When Dora beats Rosco to an answer, he exclaims **¡Yo sé!** (*I know it!*). If you feel comfortable, teach children this expression.

After viewing the video, praise the children for their good listening and watching skills.

Lesson Twenty-One

IF YOU HAVE TIME...

Materials: Cassette player; "Uno de enero" ("January First") on the Song Cassette, Side A; Gold Flashcards 48–50, 62; 7 small self-adhesive pieces of paper marked 1–7; "Months Rap" on the Song Cassette, Side B; and rap roll from Activity 10C.

Preparation: Attach the self-adhesive pieces of paper at the left of the Flashcards. Display the Flashcards in calendar order.

As children sing along with the cassette to **"Uno de enero,"** point to the number and month as each is mentioned. For song lyrics, see Lesson 8, Video Lesson, section 3.

Next, have children follow along in their rap rolls as they sing the "Months Rap" with the cassette. For lyrics to the rap, see Lesson 12, Video Lesson, section 4.

Practice singing any parts with which the class may still have difficulties. Then discuss how the lyrics are the same and different. Lead children to discover that **"Uno de enero"** is about dates (*January first, February second*, and so forth) while the "Months Rap" is numbering the months (January is month number one, etc.).

ACTIVITY LESSON

Activity 21A: ¿Cuál es la fecha? (*What is the date?*)

Materials: Gold Flashcards 48–50, 62–64; 14 blank sheets of 8-1/2 x 11 paper; and a black marker.

Preparation: Using the marker, write one of the following numbers on each of the sheets of paper: 2, 6, 9, 10, 13, 14, 15, 18, 22, 23, 24, 26, 27, 30.

La maestra is going to give two sample dates and name them in Spanish before beginning the activity. You may want to show the appropriate number and Gold Flashcard for each sample as she explains it.

| Dec. 24 | el veinticuatro de diciembre |
| Feb. 10 | el diez de febrero |

When the class first begins identifying dates in the activity, it may be easier for children to name them if the months are in calendar order. Children may thus focus on the number and the way to say a date without also having to remember months in random order. Sample dates are included if you wish to use them in the activity.

Jan. 18	el dieciocho de enero
Feb. 22	el veintidós de febrero
Mar. 6	el seis de marzo
Apr. 27	el veintisiete de abril
May 30	el treinta de mayo
June 15	el quince de junio
July 26	el veintiséis de julio
Aug. 14	el catorce de agosto
Sept. 23	el veintitrés de septiembre
Oct. 13	el trece de octubre
Nov. 2	el dos de noviembre
Dec. 9	el nueve de diciembre

Explain that **la maestra** is going to ask the class **¿Cuál es la fecha?** (*What is the date?*). You are going to make the dates by using the numbers you prepared and the Flashcards, just as she did in the video. Stop the cassette between questions, so that children have time to answer.

Replay this activity several times if possible. Whether you decide to reuse the same dates in random order or to keep using new dates, children will benefit from a great deal of practice on dates.

LEVEL TWO

Activity 21B: Bounce to 30

Materials: As many balls as groups.

Divide the class into two or more groups, so that all children may take part in the counting. Select a starting player for each group. Explain that the starting player will bounce the ball to another child and count **uno** (*one*). As the second child bounces the ball to a third child, he or she will count **dos** (*two*). Children within each group should keep bouncing the ball and counting until they reach **treinta** (*thirty*). If there is enough time and children are enjoying themselves, play the game another time. For numbers 1–31, see Lesson 20, Activity 20C.

Activity 21C: ¿Cuándo es tu cumpleaños? (*When is your birthday?*)

Materials: Calendar with all twelve months; list of children's birthdays; Blackline Master 20C; pencils; and markers or crayons.

Preparation: Each child will need a pencil, markers or crayons, and a copy of Blackline Master 20C that is marked with the first of the month in which his or her birthday falls. Depending on how well your class knows the number of days in each month, you may also want to mark the last day of the month. Remember to use **lunes** (*Monday*) as the first day of the week.

Ask children whose birthdays are in January to raise their hands and give them the appropriate Blackline Masters. Follow the same process with the other months. Point out the date(s) you have marked the calendar pages. Ask children to complete the Blackline Masters by filling in the appropriate number of days for their birthday months. For numbers 1–31, see Lesson 20, Activity 20C.

Next, tell children to circle their birthdays in pencil. Explain that once you have checked that the dates are correct, the class may circle them with markers. In the meantime, have children decorate their calendar pages.

Ask, or select volunteers to ask, ¿Cuándo es tu cumpleaños? (*When is your birthday?*). Have other children answer the question as they point to the day and month on their calendar pages. Save these pages for use in Activity 22C.

Blackline Master 20C

EN ESPAÑOL

Ask children how to say 21 in Spanish—**veintiuno**.

Point out that this is 20 and 1—**veinte y uno**. Explain that 31 is formed the same way—**treinta y uno.**

CLOSING

Tell the children that Spanish class is finished for today. In the next video, **la maestra** is going to introduce more vocabulary for places in a school.

Lesson Twenty-One

Lesson 22

Materials to gather

- VCR and Video Lesson 22 on Tape 6
- Cassette player
- Activity Cassette 1
- Hand puppet Dora
- Blackline Master 19C (Guide to Days) or 20C (blank calendar)
- Gold Flashcards 48–50, 62–64
- Number Cards 1–20, 30
- Scissors
- Blackline Master 22A (rooms in school plus **la maestra**)
- Birthday calendars from Activity 21C
- *Optional materials:* Song Cassette

OBJECTIVES

Language
- Answer questions about what to wear in different weather conditions

Culture
- Understand that some Spanish words may be derived from other languages

Review
- Ask and answer questions about the date and weather
- Identify colors
- Practice vocabulary for places in a school

Vocabulary
No new vocabulary is introduced in this lesson.

Warm-up

Materials: Dora hand puppet; Blackline Master 19C or Blackline Master 20C filled in for this month.

Take the part of Dora and say the opening conversation with your class if you feel comfortable doing so. If not, ask a volunteer. Use an appropriate time of day (**D** = Dora, **C** = class):

D: Buenos días/Buenas tardes, clase.	*Good morning/Good afternoon, class.*
C: Buenos días/Buenas tardes, Dora.	*Good morning/Good afternoon, Dora.*
D: ¿Cómo estás tú?	*How are you?*
C: Muy bien, gracias. ¿Y tú?	*Very well, thank you. And you?*
D: Muy bien, gracias.	*Very well, thanks.*

Then ask, or have a volunteer ask, **¿Qué día es?** (*What day is it?*) while pointing to the day on Blackline Master 19C or 20C. For days of the week, see Lesson 20, Warm-up section.

> Be sure the class says **¿Y tú?** to Dora. If there is confusion about the change from **¿Y usted?**, remind the class that Dora is a friend.

Review

Materials: Cassette player; Activity 21A on Activity Cassette 1, Side B; Gold Flashcards 48–50, 62–64; and Number Cards 1–20, 30.

Preparation: Choose three dates for the class to name or use the following: *Mar. 7* (**el siete de marzo**), *Aug. 19* (**el diecinueve de agosto**), *Nov. 30* (**el treinta de noviembre**). Fold each Number Card so that the correct number is showing and put it with the selected month.

Explain that **la maestra** is going to ask **¿Cuál es la fecha?** (*What is the date?*). You will make dates by combining a Number Card with a Flashcard. Stop the cassette between questions to allow plenty of time for answers.

Introduce the video

Tell children that they are going to reuse much of their Spanish in this lesson.

Video Lesson

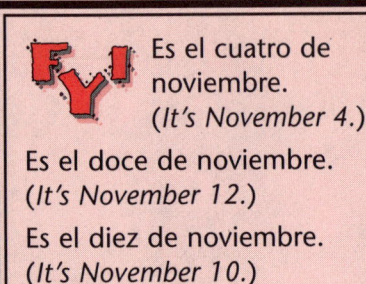

1. Saying the opening conversation

Using **buenos días** as the greeting, **la maestra** has the opening conversation with the class and then with Dora. For the opening conversation, see Lesson 20, Video Lesson, section 1.

2. Reviewing the calendar

La maestra, Dora, and the class take turns asking and answering questions (**M** = Maestra, **D** = Dora, **C** = class):

M:	Tengo una pregunta.	*I have a question.*
	¿Qué mes es?	*What month is it?*
D:	Es el mes de noviembre.	*It's November.*
M:	¿Cuál es la fecha?	*What's the date?*
D:	Es el nueve de noviembre.	*It's November 9.*
M:	¿Qué día es?	*What day of the week is it?*
D:	Es viernes.	*It's Thursday.*
	Es martes.	*It's Tuesday.*
M/C:	¿Qué tiempo hace?	*What's the weather like?*
D:	Hace mal tiempo.	*It's bad weather.*

3. Reviewing colors

Pointing to the **sombreros**, **la maestra** asks **¿De qué color es?** (*What color is it?*). Dora and the class answer **verde** (*green*) and **morado** (*purple*).

4. Practicing vocabulary for places in a school

La maestra reviews the three words for places in a school mentioned in the last lesson, and the class repeats them. Then **la maestra** describes places in English and Dora names them in Spanish.

la oficina	*office*
la clase	*classroom*
la biblioteca	*library*

5. Playing *Muéstrame* ___ (*Show me* ___)

La maestra models the three words for places in a school and the class repeats them. Next, she asks questions about the places before having the class show them to her.

¿Es ___?	*Is it ___?*
No, no es ___.	*No, it's not ___.*
Sí, es ___.	*Yes, it's ___.*

FYI

Es el cuatro de noviembre.
(*It's November 4.*)

Es el doce de noviembre.
(*It's November 12.*)

Es el diez de noviembre.
(*It's November 10.*)

6. Reviewing more places in a school

La maestra models three more words for places in a school and the children repeat them. She and Dora also comment on the places.

la cafetería	cafeteria
el baño	bathroom
el patio	playground
Tengo hambre.	I'm hungry.
Me gusta jugar.	I like to play.
El patio es para jugar.	The playground is for playing.

7. Playing more *Muéstrame* ___ (*Show me* ___)

La maestra models the new school vocabulary and then repeats the type of questions used in the earlier game of **Muéstrame** ___.

8. Reviewing ¿Qué tiempo hace? (*What's the weather like?*)

La maestra asks about the weather using the Flashcards. For weather expressions, see Lesson 19, Warm-up section.

9. Connecting weather conditions and clothing

La maestra and Dora talk about what is appropriate to wear when it's hot or cold.

Cuando hace calor, llevo el traje de baño.	When it's hot, I wear a bathing suit.
Cuando hace calor, ¿llevas (tú) la chaqueta?	When it's hot, do you wear a jacket?
No, no llevo la chaqueta.	No, I don't wear a jacket.
Cuando hace frío, llevo la chaqueta.	When it's cold, I wear a jacket.

10. Closing

La maestra and Dora say **Adiós** and **Hasta luego** (*See you later*).

CROSS-CULTURAL CONNECTIONS

Demonstrate how knowing what a word means in one language can help children figure out the meaning of an unknown word in another language. Point out that **biblioteca** means *library*, a place for books. Next, using a nonfiction book that relates to a topic that the class has been studying, show children its bibliography. Ask them if they can guess what a bibliography is—a list of books.

After viewing the video, praise the children for their good listening and watching skills.

Lesson Twenty-Two

Blackline Master 22A

Check that children are completing the activity correctly. Watch for the words that most children know and those that are more difficult. This knowledge will help you select which activities will best help your class.

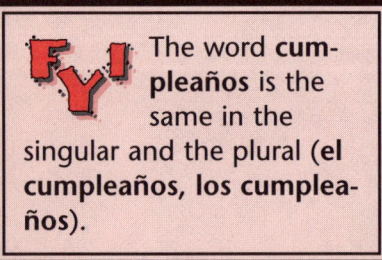

FYI The word **cumpleaños** is the same in the singular and the plural (**el cumpleaños, los cumpleaños**).

LEVEL TWO

ACTIVITY LESSON

Activity 22A: Put the teacher in the right room

Materials: Cassette player; Activity Cassette 1, Side B; Blackline Master 22A; and scissors for each child.

Preparation: Make a copy of Blackline Master 22A for each child. Give each child a pair of scissors.

Discuss the pictures with the class. Make sure children can identify each place. Then tell the class to cut out the shape containing the picture of the woman teacher. Explain that **la maestra** is going to tell children to **pon** (*put*) her in different rooms. **La maestra** will repeat each direction two times. Replay this game a couple of times if time allows.

Activity 22B: *Muéstrame* ___ (*Show me* ___)

Materials: Cassette player; Activity Cassette 1, Side B; Blackline Master 22A; and scissors for each child.

Preparation: Each child will need a copy of Blackline Master 22A and a pair of scissors.

Tell children to cut out the six boxes, each containing a place in a school. Explain that **la maestra** is going to ask the class to **muéstrame** (*show me*) different places in a school by holding up the pictures she calls out. She will repeat each direction twice. Repeat this activity a couple of times if possible.

Activity 22C: How many birthdays in . . . ?

Materials: Birthday calendars from Activity 21C; and Gold Flashcards 48–50, 62–64.

Children should have their birthday calendars visible. Ask, or have volunteers ask, several children **¿Cuándo es tu cumpleaños?** (*When is your birthday?*). Tell children to point to the date and month as they respond.

enero	*January*	julio	*July*
febrero	*February*	agosto	*August*
marzo	*March*	septiembre	*September*
abril	*April*	octubre	*October*
mayo	*May*	noviembre	*November*
junio	*June*	diciembre	*December*

Put the Gold Flashcards in calendar order across the bottom of the chalkboard. Next, use the birthday calendars to collect data for math activities. Have children form groups based on the months in which their birthdays fall. Ask each group to count off in Spanish and record the number of children for each month above its Flashcard. In which month were the most children born? When were the least children born? (**en ___** / *in ___*) For numbers 1–31, see Lesson 20, Activity 20C.

If children have had graphing, convert the information to a bar graph. If not, put the Flashcards for the months across the bottom of a bulletin board and make a pictograph with the calendar pages themselves. Summarize what the bar graph/pictograph shows by having volunteers tell how many birthdays there are in each month (**___ cumpleaños en ___**).

CLOSING

Tell the children that Spanish class is finished for today. In the next video, they are going to use the months in many activities.

FAMILY CONNECTION

To foster a friendly link between home and school, you may want to send out Family Letter 2 (see the Teacher's Resource Book). This letter suggests how families can be involved in their children's learning of Spanish.

IF YOU HAVE TIME . . .

Materials: Cassette player; "Uno, dos, tres niñitos" ("*One, Two, Three Little Children*") on the Song Cassette, Side A; Number Cards 1–10; and scissors.

Preparation: Make copies of the Number Cards. Cut them in half along the line.

Have ten volunteers stand in front of the class, holding Number Cards facedown. Play the song as the class sings along. When each number is named in ascending order, have the appropriate child show it. Tell children to turn the numbers facedown as each is named in descending order.

Uno, dos, tres niñitos,
(*One, two, three little children,*)
Cuatro, cinco, seis niñitos,
(*Four, five, six little children,*)
Siete, ocho, nueve niñitos.
(*Seven, eight, nine little children,*)
Diez niñitos son.
(*There are ten little children.*)
Diez, nueve, ocho niñitos,
(*Ten, nine, eight little children,*)
Siete, seis, cinco niñitos,
(*Seven, six, five little children,*)
Cuatro, tres, dos niñitos,
(*Four, three, two little children,*)
Un niñito es.
(*There is one little child.*)

Lesson Twenty-Two

Lesson 23

Materials to gather

- VCR and Video Lesson 23 on Tape 6
- Cassette player
- Activity Cassette 1
- Calendar, preferably a Spanish one
- Rosco flags
- Blackline Master 23B (places in a school)
- Scissors or paper cutter
- Marker
- **Optional materials:** Gold Flashcards 48–50, 62–64; 12 pieces of self-adhesive paper

OBJECTIVES

Language
- Understand suggestions to go to different places in a school

Culture
- Sing the "Months Rap"

Review
- Answer questions about the weather
- Review colors
- Recall the commands **corre** (*run*), **anda** (*walk*), and **salta** (*jump*)
- Practice the months
- Identify places in a school

Vocabulary

No new vocabulary is introduced in this lesson.

Warm-up

Materials: A calendar, preferably a Spanish one (perhaps one of the birthday calendars that the children made in Activity 21C).

Ask, or have volunteers ask, the class the questions below. For numbers 1–31, see Lesson 20, Activity 20C. For days of the week and months, see Lesson 20, Warm-up section. For weather expressions, see Lesson 19, Warm-up section.

¿Qué día es?	*What day is today?*
¿Cuál es la fecha?	*What is the date?*
¿Qué tiempo hace?	*What's the weather like?*

Review

Materials: Cassette player; Activity 21A on Activity Cassette 1, Side B; and calendar, preferably a Spanish one for the current month.

Explain that **la maestra** is going to ask **¿Cuál es la fecha?** (*What is the date?*) three times. You will stop the tape after each question to give volunteers time to name the date you are pointing to. Use the sample dates for the current month if you wish.

5th (el cinco de ___)
15th (el quince de ___)
25th (el veinticinco de ___)

Introduce the video

State that **la maestra** will play a game with places in the school.

Video Lesson

1. Saying the opening conversation

Using **buenas tardes** as the greeting, **la maestra** has the opening conversation with Rosco and with the class. She answers **así, así** (*so-so*) and later **muy bien** (*very well*) when asked how she is. For the opening conversation, see Lesson 20, Video Lesson, section 1.

2. Practicing questions for the calendar and weather

La maestra asks Rosco and the class questions.

¿Cuál es la fecha?	What is the date?
El veinticuatro de noviembre.	November 24.
¿Qué día es?	What day of the week is it?
Es sábado.	It's Saturday.
¿Vamos a la escuela los sábados?	Do we go to school on Saturdays?
No, no vamos a la escuela los sábados.	No, we don't go to school on Saturdays.
¿Qué tiempo hace?	What's the weather like?
Hace viento. (Hace frío y nieva.)	It's windy. (It's cold and it's snowing.)

3. Reviewing colors

La maestra asks about the color of several **sombreros**.

¿De qué color es?	What color is it?
Es de color ___.	It's ___.

4. Demonstrating commands

The mime shows the meaning of three commands—**corre** (*run*), **anda** (*walk*), and **salta** (*jump*).

5. Reviewing the months

La maestra models each month and the class repeats them.

¿Cuántos son?	How many are there?
Doce meses del año.	Twelve months in the year.

For months, see Lesson 22, Activity 22C.

6. Singing the "Months Rap"

La maestra invites everyone to sing with her. For song lyrics, see Lesson 12, Video Lesson, section 4.

7. Integrating months and weather

Using Flashcards, **la maestra** asks Rosco about weather.

FYI

Action that happens once or occasionally:

Voy al patio **el sábado**.
(*I'm going to the playground on Saturday.*)

Repeated action:

Voy al patio **los sábados**.
(*I go to the playground on Saturdays.*)

Colors:

amarillo	yellow
azul	blue
rojo	red

LEVEL TWO

En octubre, ¿qué tiempo hace?	In October, what's the weather like?
En octubre hace viento.	In October, it's windy.
En enero, ¿qué tiempo hace?	In January, what's the weather like?
En enero hace frío y nieva.	In January, it's cold and it snows.
En agosto, ¿qué tiempo hace?	In August, what's the weather like?
En agosto hace calor y hace sol.	In August, it's hot and sunny.

8. Integrating commands and months

Rosco gives different commands to **la maestra**.

Salta con enero.	Jump with January.
Corre con marzo.	Run with March.
Anda con abril.	Walk with April.

9. Reviewing vocabulary for places in a school

La maestra asks Rosco about what it is all right to do in school.

¿Corre en la escuela?	Do you run in school?
Corro en el patio.	I run on the playground.
¿Dónde salta?	Where can you jump?
En el patio.	On the playground.
¿Anda en la escuela?	Do you walk in school?
Sí, ando en la escuela.	Yes, I walk in school.

10. Touring a school

La maestra revisits the school with the children.

11. Playing games with words for places in a school

La maestra suggests going different places and models each place before playing **Muéstrame** ___ (*Show me* ___). Then she asks questions about various places in a school.

Vamos a la oficina.	Let's go to the office.
Vamos a la clase.	Let's go to class.
Vamos a la biblioteca.	Let's go to the library.
Vamos al patio.	Let's go to the playground.
Vamos al baño.	Let's go to the bathroom.
Vamos a la cafetería.	Let's go to the cafeteria.

12. Closing

La maestra says ¡Qué divertido! (*What a good time I had!*) and **Hasta la vista** (*Until we meet again*).

After viewing the video, praise the children for their good listening and watching skills.

Lesson Twenty-Three

ACTIVITY LESSON

Activity 23A: Follow the leader

Materials: Cassette player; Activity Cassette 1, Side B; and Rosco flag(s).

Have the class form a circle. Choose a leader, give him or her the Rosco flag, and tell the leader to stand in the center of the circle. Explain that **la maestra** is going to give the class six commands to follow and **el jefe** (*the male leader*) or **la jefa** (*the female leader*) will lead the class in following them. **La maestra** will say each command two times. Repeat this activity if possible, making sure that both boys and girls have turns as leaders. You should also consider doing the activity with two circles so that more children have an opportunity to lead.

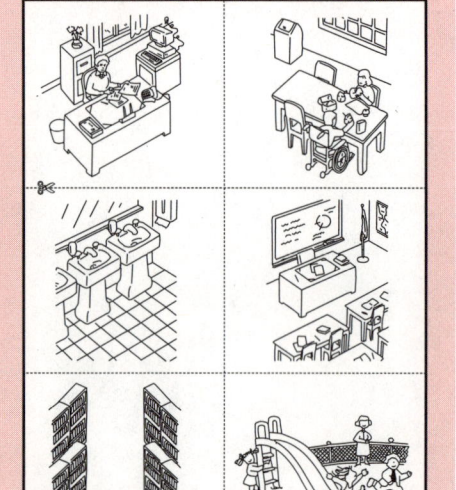

Activity 23B: Can you match the places?

Materials: Blackline Master 23B; scissors or paper cutter; and marker.

Preparation: Make two copies of Blackline Master 23B and cut the sections apart. If possible, enlarge the pictures. Turn them over in random order and write 1–12 on the backs of the pictures. Then tape the sections in a couple of rows and in numerical order where everyone can see them. Be careful to tape them so that when you flip the number back to show the picture underneath, the picture appears right-side-up.

Divide the class into two teams. Explain that teams will take turns trying to match pictures of places in a school by naming two numbers in Spanish. You will turn over the numbers called so everyone can see the pictures underneath. When a match is made, the pictures will remain showing *if* the player can correctly name the place in Spanish. When a player makes a match, his or her team has an extra turn. The game is over when all the pictures are visible.

Blackline Master 23B

LEVEL TWO

Activity 23C: Play *Dame* ___ (*Give me* ___)

Materials: Blackline Master 23B; scissors or paper cutter.

Preparation: Make two copies of Blackline Master 23B for each pair of children. Cut the pages into their six pictures.

Divide the class into pairs and give each pair their pictures. Have pairs turn over the pictures and mix them. Tell the class that each player should take three pictures from the pile and look at them. Then within each pair, Player A asks Player B for a picture in Spanish by saying **Dame el patio** (*Give me the playground*), for example. If Player B answers **Tengo el patio** (*I have the playground*) and gives the picture to Player A, Player A lays down the matching cards and has a chance to ask for another card. If Player B answers **No tengo el patio** (*I don't have the playground*), Player B may then ask for a picture. Play continues until one player is no longer holding any pictures.

Closing

Tell the children that Spanish class is finished for today. In the next video, they are going to answer many, many questions and play a game with places in a school.

IF YOU HAVE TIME . . .

Materials: Gold Flashcards 48–50, 62–64; and self-adhesive pieces of paper numbered 1–12.

Preparation: Arrange the Flashcards in calendar order where everyone can see them. Turn the pictures away from the class. Attach the numbered pieces of paper to the backs of the Flashcards to show the number order of the months.

Point to a number and ask **¿Qué mes es éste?** (*What month is this?*). Have a volunteer name the month. Show the picture of the month to confirm or deny the answer. Continue in the same way with other months. If you prefer, have volunteers ask the questions.

Lesson 24

Materials to gather

- VCR and Video Lesson 24 on Tape 6
- Cassette player
- Activity Cassette 2
- Song Cassette
- Rap rolls from Activity 10C
- Guide to Days from Activity 19C
- Spanish calendar or calendar for current month
- Blackline Master 22A (rooms in school plus **la maestra**)
- Scissors or paper cutter
- Overhead projector
- Blank transparency
- Crayons or markers
- Beans or other playing pieces
- *Optional materials:* 11 colored fish from Lesson 16

OBJECTIVES

Language
- Respond to visual cues to answer questions on many subjects

Culture
- Discuss weather in various geographic areas

Review
- Answer questions about the date and weather
- Recall the colors
- Tell one's own name and other people's names
- Sing the "Months Rap" and the "Calendar Rap"
- Practice words for places in a school
- Review a tour in a school

Vocabulary

No new vocabulary is introduced in this lesson.

Warm-up

Materials: Cassette player; "Months Rap" on Song Cassette, Side B; and rap rolls.

Ask children to sing the "Months Rap" with the cassette. Tell them to point to each month on their rap rolls as they sing. For lyrics to the rap, see Lesson 12, Video Lesson, section 4.

Review

Materials: Cassette player; "Calendar Rap" on Song Cassette, Side A; day guide from Activity 19C; and current Spanish calendar, if possible.

Have children sing the "Calendar Rap" with the cassette. Tell them to point to the days on their day guides as they sing. For lyrics to the rap, see Lesson 12, Video Lesson, section 3. Then ask, or have a volunteer ask, the following questions using a calendar:

| ¿Qué día es? | *What day is it?* |
| ¿Cuál es la fecha? | *What is the date?* |

For numbers 1–31, see Lesson 20, Activity 20C. For days and months, see Lesson 20, Warm-up section.

Introduce the video

Tell children that in this video they are going to answer many kinds of questions. Indeed, they may be surprised at how many they know how to answer!

VIDEO LESSON

1. Saying the opening conversation

Using **Buenos días** (*Good morning*) as the greeting, **la maestra** has the opening conversation with the class and with Rosco. For the opening conversation, see Lesson 20, Video lesson, section 1.

> **FYI**
> Estoy muy bien porque estoy aquí con Rosco y con Dora, mis amigos.
> (*I'm very well because I'm here with my friends Rosco and Dora.*)

2. Finding Dora

La maestra and Rosco search for Dora. Once they find her, the teacher greets Dora.

¿Dónde está Dora?	*Where is Dora?*
Aquí estoy.	*Here I am.*
Aquí está Dora.	*Dora is here.*

3. Reviewing previously taught questions

La maestra trades questions and answers with Dora, Rosco, and the class (M = Maestra, D = Dora, R = Rosco, C = class):

M: ¿Cuál es la fecha?	*What is the date?*
D: El dieciséis de noviembre.	*November 16.*
R: El ocho de noviembre.	*November 8.*
C: El diez de noviembre.	*November 10.*
El cinco de noviembre.	*November 5.*
M: ¿Qué tiempo hace?	*What's the weather like?*
R: Hace viento.	*It's windy.*
D: Hace frío y nieva.	*It's cold and it's snowing.*
C: Hace sol y hace calor.	*It's sunny and hot.*
Hace buen tiempo.	*It's good weather.*

> **FYI**
> Tengo una pregunta.
> (*I've got a question.*)
> Las preguntas son muy importantes.
> (*Questions are very important.*)

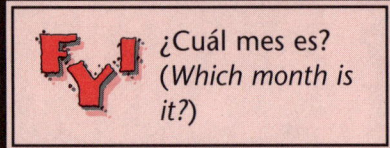

La maestra asks **¿Qué día es?** (*What day is it?*) and uses the "Calendar Rap" to show how to remember names for days of the week. For song lyrics, see Lesson 12, Video Lesson, section 3. Next, **la maestra** asks Rosco and Dora **¿De qué color es?** (*What color is it?*) about some **sombreros**, and the puppets answer with the colors **café** (*brown*), **negro** (*black*), and **rojo** (*red*). Then she asks about names.

¿Cómo te llamas tú?	*What is your name?*
Me llamo Dora/Rosco/___.	*My name is Dora/Rosco/___.*
¿Cómo se llama?	*What's her/his name?*
Se llama Dora/Rosco.	*Her name is Dora/Rosco.*

4. Singing the "Months Rap"

La maestra models the months and has the class repeat them. Next, she asks the class to sing the "Months Rap" with her. For lyrics to the rap, see Lesson 12, Video Lesson, section 4.

> **FYI**
> ¿Cuál mes es?
> (*Which month is it?*)

enero	January	julio	July
febrero	February	agosto	August
marzo	March	septiembre	September
abril	April	octubre	October
mayo	May	noviembre	November
junio	June	diciembre	December

5. Discussing the weather and months

La maestra asks about the weather.

¿Qué tiempo hace en enero?	What's the weather like in January?
En enero hace frío.	In January, it's cold.
¿Qué tiempo hace en agosto?	What's the weather like in August?
En agosto hace calor.	In August, it's hot.
¿Qué tiempo hace en diciembre?	What's the weather like in December?
En diciembre hace frío y nieva.	In December, it's cold and it snows.

La maestra then plays a game with Flashcards for these months.

¿Dónde está ___?	Where is ___?
Aquí está ___.	Here's ___.
Dame ___.	Give me ___.

6. Playing a game with words for places in a school

La maestra reviews the vocabulary. Then doña Elena asks the class to tell where **la maestra** is and models the answers.

¿Dónde está la maestra?	Where is the teacher?
La maestra está en ___.	The teacher is in ___.

7. Practicing places in a school

La maestra asks questions in English about where to go in the school to do certain things. The puppets answer in Spanish.

8. Touring the school

La maestra and the class visit the school again.

9. Closing

La maestra bids the class **Adiós** (*Good-bye*).

HERITAGE SPEAKERS

Invite children to talk about what the weather is like during these months in their countries of birth. If possible, discuss geographic reasons for these weather conditions.

Order of answers:

la biblioteca	library
el baño	bathroom
la oficina	office
la cafetería	cafeteria
el patio	playground
la clase	class

After viewing the video, praise the children for their good listening and watching skills.

Lesson Twenty-Four

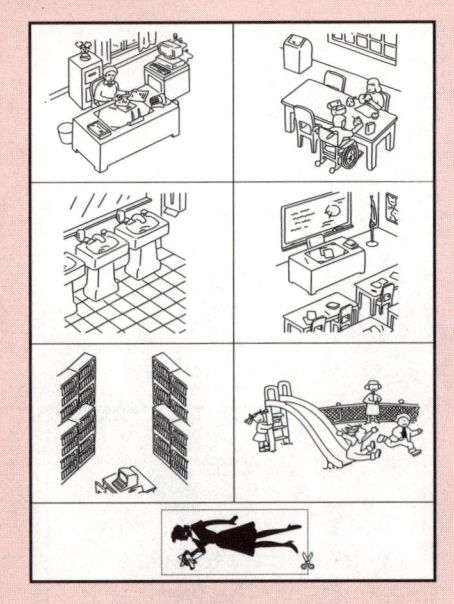

Blackline Master 22A

ACTIVITY LESSON

Activity 24A: Where is *la maestra*?

Materials: Cassette player, Activity Cassette 2, Side A; Blackline Master 22A; scissors or paper cutter; overhead projector; and blank transparency.

Preparation: Make a transparency of Blackline Master 22A if possible. Children will be better able to see the pictures. If not possible, display the Blackline Master where everyone can see it. Cut out **la maestra** along the dotted lines.

The cassette teacher is going to ask where **la maestra** is as you put her in different places in the school. Use the following order to match the answers on the cassette:

la oficina	office
la baño	bathroom
la biblioteca	library
la cafetería	cafeteria
la clase	class
el patio	playground

Explain that you and the children are going to play a game similar to the one they played with **la maestra** on the video tape. You are going to place **la maestra** in a place in the school and the cassette teacher will ask ¿**Dónde está la maestra?** (*Where is the teacher?*). Children should answer **Está en ___** (*She's in ___*) and the name of the place. The cassette teacher will ask each question two times.

Activity 24B: Cooperative learning—¿*Cómo te llamas (tú)?* (*What's your name?*)

Divide the class into pairs. Have partners take turns asking ¿**Cómo te llamas (tú)?** (*What's your name?*) and answering **Me llamo ___** (*My name is ___*). Have children trade partners three or four times.

LEVEL TWO

Activity 24C: Cooperative learning—Where are you?

Materials: Blackline Master 22A; crayons or markers; and beans or other objects that children can use for playing pieces.

Preparation: Make a copy of Blackline Master 22A for each child. Each player needs six playing pieces and a crayon or marker.

Divide the class into small groups of two to four players. Explain that children in each group will take turns being "it." As such, Player A secretly decides which place on the Blackline Master he or she is going to "hide" in, marks the place with an X, and turns over his or her playing card. The other players then take turns in random order asking ¿**Estás tú en** ___? (*Are you in* ___?) and the name of a place. Player A answers **Sí, estoy en** ___ (*Yes, I'm in* ___) or **No, no estoy en** ___ (*No, I'm not in* ___). After each place is named, players put a marker on that spot on their playing cards, eliminating it as a hiding place. Play continues until someone names the secret place and he or she then becomes "it." Players remove the markers from their playing cards and start over. If possible, play several rounds allowing all children in a group to have a turn being "it."

Closing

Tell the children that Spanish class is finished for today. In the next video, children are going to start working with words for clothing and go on a shopping trip.

IF YOU HAVE TIME . . .

Materials: 11 colored fish from Lesson 16.

Have children stand next to their desks or tables with individual sets of the colored fish spread out on the surface. Then give, or have a volunteer give, commands that include colors. Tell the class to follow them while standing in place.

- Salta con morado. (*Jump with purple.*)
- Anda con anaranjado. (*Walk with orange.*)
- Salta con blanco. (*Jump with white.*)
- Corre con verde. (*Run with green.*)
- Corre con café. (*Run with brown.*)
- Anda con amarillo. (*Walk with yellow.*)

Lesson 25

Materials to gather

- VCR and Video Lesson 25 on Tape 7
- Cassette player
- Activity Cassette 2
- Spanish calendar
- Gold Flashcards 41–64
- Rosco flag(s)
- Sets of colored fish from Lesson 16

- *Optional materials:* Guide to Days from Activity 19C

OBJECTIVES

Language

- Practice vocabulary for clothing
- Answer questions about colors to identify clothing
- Listen to sustained conversation about clothing

Culture

- Locate the days on a Spanish calendar

Review

- Practice answers to ¿Cómo estás tú? (*How are you?*)
- Answer questions about the calendar, weather, colors, and names

Vocabulary

la ropa	*clothing*
los pantalones	*pants*
el sombrero	*hat*
los sombreros	*hats*
los calcetines	*socks*
los zapatos	*shoes*
la camisa	*shirt*

Warm-up

Materials: Calendar (preferably a Spanish one); Gold Flashcards 41–50, 62–64; and Guide to Days from Activity 19C (optional).

Ask volunteers the questions below and use the visual materials to help children directly associate words and their meaning. If you have a Spanish calendar, the Guide to Days is not needed to name the day of the week.

¿Qué tiempo hace?	*What's the weather like?*
¿Cuál es la fecha?	*What is the date?*
¿Qué día es?	*What day of the week is it?*

For weather expressions, see Lesson 19, Warm-up section. For numbers 1–31, see Activity 20C. For months and days of the week, see Lesson 20, Warm-up section.

Review

Materials: Gold Flashcards 51–61.

After displaying the Flashcards where everyone can see them, ask children what kinds of clothing they buy when school starts and when the weather starts getting colder. Remind children that they learned some words for clothing last year and encourage them to use any Spanish words they remember in the discussion.

los zapatos	*shoes*	la falda	*skirt*
el vestido	*dress*	los pantalones	*pants*
el sombrero	*hat*	la blusa	*blouse*
el traje de baño	*bathing suit*	el pijama	*pajamas*
el suéter	*sweater*	los calcetines	*socks*
la chaqueta	*jacket*	la camisa	*shirt*

Introduce the video

Tell children that in this video they are going to hear words for clothing and visit a clothing store with **la maestra**.

Just as it is important that children associate the placement of the days on an English calendar with their names, so too is it important that they automatically go to the correct places on a Spanish calendar. It is *very* helpful if you keep a current monthly Spanish calendar—either a completed Blackline Master 20C, one done on tagboard like the one **la maestra** has, or one of the birthday calendars from Activity 21C. Consider asking volunteers to make them.

VIDEO LESSON

1. Saying the opening conversation

Using **buenos días** as a greeting, **la maestra** has the opening conversation with Ñico and later with the class. For the opening conversation, see Lesson 20, Video Lesson, section 1.

2. Responding to ¿Cómo estás tú? (How are you?)

La maestra uses the feeling masks to practice three possible answers to the question **¿Cómo estás tú?**—**muy bien** (*fine, very well*), **así, así** (*so-so*), and **muy mal** (*very bad*).

3. Reviewing the calendar, weather, colors, and names

La maestra asks Ñico and the class many questions (**M** = Maestra, **Ñ** = Ñico, **C** = class):

M: ¿Dónde está el calendario?	Where is the calendar?
Ñ: Aquí. El calendario está aquí.	Here. The calendar is here.
M: ¿Qué día es?	What day of the week is it?
Ñ: Es martes.	It's Tuesday.
Es jueves. No, no es jueves. Es viernes.	It's Thursday. No, it's not Thursday. It's Friday.
C: Es lunes.	It's Monday.
M: ¿Cuál es la fecha?	What is the date?
Ñ: El diez de noviembre.	November 10.
C: El dos de noviembre.	November 2.
M: ¿Qué tiempo hace?	What's the weather like?
Ñ: Llueve. Hace mal tiempo.	It's raining. It's bad weather.
Hace sol.	It's sunny.
M: Tengo otra pregunta. ¿De qué color es el calendario?	I have another question. What color is the calendar?
Ñ: Amarillo.	Yellow.
M: Tenemos muchos colores. ¿De qué color es?	We have many colors. What color is it?
Ñ: Es negro/rojo/anaranjado.	It's black/red/orange.
M: ¿Cómo te llamas?	What is your name?
Ñ: Me llamo Ñico.	My name is Ñico.
C: Me llamo ___.	My name is ___.

4. Reintroducing vocabulary for *la ropa* (clothing)

La maestra models and the class repeats words for clothing.

la ropa	clothing
los pantalones	pants
el sombrero	hat
los sombreros	hats
los calcetines	socks
los zapatos	shoes
la camisa	shirt

LEVEL TWO

5. Playing *Muéstrame* ___ (*Show me* ___) with clothing

La maestra models words for clothing, asks about colors, and then plays **Muéstrame** ___.

¿De qué color son los pantalones?	*What color are the pants?*
Son de color azul.	*They are blue.*
¿De qué color es el sombrero?	*What color is the hat?*
Es de color negro.	*It's black.*
¿De qué color es la blusa?	*What color is the blouse?*
Es de color rojo.	*It's red.*
¿De qué color son los calcetines?	*What color are the socks?*
Son de color amarillo.	*They are yellow.*

6. Shopping for clothes

La maestra suggests **Vamos de compras** (*Let's go shopping*). Excerpts from the shopping trip follow.

Aquí estoy en la tienda.	*Here I am in the clothing store.*
Voy de compras en la tienda.	*I'm going shopping in the clothing store.*
Y estoy en el departamento de los zapatos.	*And I'm in the shoe department.*
¿Qué zapatos compro?	*What shoes shall I buy?*
Aquí están los sombreros.	*Here are the hats.*
Hay muchos sombreros de muchos colores.	*There are many hats in many colors.*
¿Qué sombrero me gusta?	*Which hat do I like?*
Aquí está un sombrero de color azul con flores.	*Here's a blue flowered hat.*
¿Me gusta o no me gusta?	*Do I like it or not?*
No me gusta.	*I don't like it.*
Es muy divertido ir de compras a la tienda.	*It's a lot of fun to go shopping at a clothing store.*
Tengo mucha ropa de muchos colores.	*I have a lot of clothing in many colors.*
Tengo ropa para llevar a la escuela.	*I have clothes to wear to school.*

7. Closing

La maestra says **Es muy divertido ir de compras** (*It's a lot of fun to go shopping*) and **Adiós** (*Good-bye*).

FYI
¿De qué color es la blusa?
(*What color is the blouse?*)
¿De qué color son los pantalones?
(*What color are the pants?*)

FYI Because of the variation in individual monitors, some clothing colors may not match descriptions. Watch for these discrepancies and point them out to children. The sweater, for example, may look blue rather than purple.

FYI Aquí está el sombrero.
(*Here is the hat.*)
Aquí están los sombreros.
(*Here are the hats.*)

After viewing the video, praise the children for their good listening and watching skills.

Lesson Twenty-Five

> **FYI** **Una vez más** means *One more time.* The cassette teacher often uses this expression to advise you that she is now going to say the last item in the activity.

> **FYI** **Gustar** means *to be pleasing to.*
> Me gusta el sombrero.
> (*The hat is pleasing to me. I like the hat.*)
> No me gusta el sombrero. (*The hat is not pleasing to me. I don't like the hat.*)

> **EN ESPAÑOL**
> Point out that **la maestra** has often asked Rosco **¿Te gusta cantar?** (*Do you like to sing?*) and he has enthusiastically answered **Me gusta cantar** (*I like to sing*). If you feel comfortable, teach the class this question and answer.

ACTIVITY LESSON

Activity 25A: Play with clothing

Materials: Cassette player; Activity Cassette 2, Side A; Rosco flag(s); and Gold Flashcards 51–54.

Display the Gold Flashcards in random order where everyone can see them. Discuss with the class the meaning of **anda** (*walk*), **salta** (*jump*), **corre** (*run*), and **toca** (*touch*). Explain that you are going to hand the Rosco flag successively to three different children who should then follow doña Elena's commands. She will say each command two times. Repeat the activity a couple of times.

Activity 25B: Do I or don't I like it?

Materials: Cassette player; Activity Cassette 2, Side A; and one colored fish from Lesson 16 per child. (You may have to borrow some fish from the class in order to have enough for every child.) The fish should be in a variety of colors.

Ask children to name all 11 colors as you show each fish in a set to the class.

rojo	*red*	gris	*gray*
anaranjado	*orange*	blanco	*white*
amarillo	*yellow*	rosado	*pink*
verde	*green*	café	*brown*
morado	*purple*	negro	*black*
azul	*blue*		

Then divide the class into pairs. Explain that doña Elena is going to practice the expressions *I like* (**Me gusta**) and *I don't like* (**No me gusta**). She will say each expression two times and ask children to **repite** (*repeat*) afterward. Next, she is going to say each expression with a color—**blanco** (*white*) and then **rojo** (*red*)—and have the class repeat it. (You may want to hold up the colored fish and make an appropriate face as each statement is made to visually reinforce what is being said.) Finally, she will ask children to tell their partners how they feel about the colors they are holding.

Repeat the activity a couple of times, so children have several opportunities to hear and say **me gusta** and **no me gusta**. Have children use their sets of fish to change colors each time and be sure that the class practices both expressions.

Activity 25C: What happened at the clothing store?

Materials: Gold Flashcards 51–61.

When **la maestra** went shopping she talked about many kinds of clothing. Some have been reintroduced and others have not. **El abrigo** (*coat*) is new.

los zapatos	*shoes*	la falda	*skirt*
las botas	*boots*	los pantalones	*pants*
los sombreros	*hats*	la blusa	*blouse*
la ropa	*clothing*	el abrigo	*coat*
el suéter	*sweater*	los calcetines	*socks*
la chaqueta	*jacket*	la camisa	*shirt*

Display the Flashcards where everyone can see them and discuss what the class saw and heard during **la maestra**'s shopping trip.

- the kind of store—clothing store
- the departments she visited—shoes, hats, clothing
- the items considered—shoes, boots, hats, sweater, jacket, skirt, pants, blouse, coat
- characteristics—colors, tall and short, length, size

The goal is for children to have a real-life context for the clothing and shopping vocabulary. A general understanding with some details is sufficient. If possible, relate the discussion to the kinds of clothing children buy for school since **la maestra** was shopping for school clothes. Encourage children to use Spanish wherever possible.

CLOSING

Tell the children that Spanish class is finished for today. In the next class, they are going to practice words for clothing.

When the class has read a story, discussion helps children understand what happened, so that the next time they read the story they will have more context to help them do the actual reading. With the Spanish video, more context helps children understand more of what they hear.

IF YOU HAVE TIME...

Materials: 11 colored fish from Lesson 16; and Gold Flashcards 51, 53, 55.

Remind the children that they have just practiced saying **Me gusta** (*I like*) and **No me gusta** (*I don't like*). Hold up the colored fish in random order and have volunteers tell their opinions, such as:

Me gusta el café.
(*I like brown.*)
No me gusta el negro.
(*I don't like black.*)

Then, as you point to items on the Flashcards, ask volunteers to give opinions about **la blusa** (*blouse*), **el sombrero** (*hat*), **la camisa** (*shirt*).

If you or volunteers feel comfortable, ask ¿**Te gusta ___?**, in questions such as ¿**Te gusta el rojo?** (*Do you like red?*) and ¿**Te gusta la blusa?** (*Do you like the blouse?*).

Lesson Twenty-Five

Lesson 26

Materials to gather

- VCR and Video Lesson 26 on Tape 7
- Cassette player
- Activity Cassette 2
- Calendar (preferably Spanish)
- Gold Flashcards 41–54, 57, 62–64
- Blackline Master 26A (clothing)
- Gray, purple, pink, blue, black, red, yellow, orange, brown, and green crayons
- Number Cards 10, 20, 30, 40, 50
- *Optional materials:* Guide to Days from Activity 19C; Song Cassette

OBJECTIVES

Language

- Practice more vocabulary for clothing
- Use colors to identify clothing

Culture

- Discuss the similarities between the words **chaqueta** and *jacket,* **blusa** and *blouse*

Review

- Practice the numbers 10, 20, 30, 40, and 50
- Use colors to describe clothing
- Review **pon** (*put*)
- Sing "**Español para ti**" (*"Spanish Is for You, and for Me"*)

Vocabulary

la chaqueta	*jacket*
el vestido	*dress*
la blusa	*blouse*

Warm-up

Materials: Calendar (preferably a Spanish one); Guide to Days from Activity 19C (optional); and Gold Flashcards 41–50, 62–64.

Ask volunteers the questions that follow, or have classmates do so. If you have a Spanish calendar, you do not need the Guide to Days to find and name the day of the week. Follow **la maestra**'s example and point to appropriate parts of the visuals as questions are asked and answered.

¿Qué día es?	*What day of the week is it?*
¿Qué tiempo hace?	*What's the weather like?*
¿Cuál es la fecha?	*What is the date?*

For weather expressions, see Lesson 19, Warm-up section. For numbers 1–31, see Activity 20C. For months and days of the week, see Lesson 20, Warm-up section.

> Remind children that if they start with the first day of the week on a Spanish calendar, the "Calendar Rap" may help them remember the names of the days. For rap lyrics, see Lesson 12, Video lesson, section 3.

Review

Materials: Cassette player; Activity 27A on Activity Cassette 2, Side A; and Gold Flashcards 51–54.

Preparation: Copy Flashcard 54, so that socks and shoes are on different pieces of paper.

Display the Flashcards around the room and remind children that they have been using many words for clothing. Explain that doña Elena is going to model words two times and the class should simply say each word after her. Only use the *first five words* in the activity. When children repeat a word, they should point to its Flashcard picture.

> *Clothing:*
>
> | el sombrero | *hat* |
> | los pantalones | *pants* |
> | la camisa | *shirt* |
> | los calcetines | *socks* |
> | los zapatos | *shoes* |

Introduce the video

Explain that in this video, the class is going to learn how to ask **la maestra** her name and the words for more clothing.

154

> ✓ When children are responding to ¿Cómo estás tú?, listen for a variety of answers.

EN ESPAÑOL

There are two words in Spanish for *you* when it means one person.

Tú is used with family, close friends, children, and pets.

Usted is used with respected or older people, acquaintances, and with business associates.

Clothing:

la ropa	clothing
los zapatos	shoes
la chaqueta	jacket
el vestido	dress
la blusa	blouse

CROSS-CULTURAL CONNECTIONS

Point out two words for clothing that sound similar in English and Spanish and that have the same meaning:

chaqueta and *jacket*
blusa and *blouse*

LEVEL TWO

VIDEO LESSON

1. Saying the opening conversation

Using **buenas tardes** (*good afternoon*) as a greeting, **la maestra** has the opening conversation with Jorge and the class. She also discusses other answers to ¿**Cómo estás tú?** (*How are you?*)—**así, así** (*so-so*) and **muy mal** (*very bad*).

2. Using *tú* versus *usted* for *you*

La maestra and Jorge ask one another their names (**M** = Maestra, **J** = Jorge):

M: ¿Cómo te llamas tú?	*What is your name?*
J: Me llamo Jorge.	*My name is Jorge.*
J: ¿Cómo se llama usted?	*What is your name?*
M: Me llamo Maestra.	*My name is Teacher.*

3. Reviewing ¿Qué número es? (*What number is it?*)

La maestra models **diez** (*10*) and **veinte** (*20*) and children repeat. They follow the same process for **treinta** (*30*), **cuarenta** (*40*), and **cincuenta** (*50*). Next, they all count by tens to 50.

4. Reintroducing and practicing words for clothing

La maestra models each word and the class repeats it. She also asks about the shoes and jacket.

| ¿Cuántos [zapatos] son? | *How many [shoes] are there?* |

5. Playing games with clothing and colors

After **la maestra** models the clothing vocabulary, she asks about colors and plays **Muéstrame** _____ (*Show me ___*).

¿De qué color es la blusa?	*What color is the blouse?*
La blusa es de color rosado.	*The blouse is pink.*
¿De qué color es la chaqueta?	*What color is the jacket?*
La chaqueta es de color morado.	*The jacket is purple.*
¿De qué color es el vestido?	*What color is the dress?*
El vestido es de color anaranjado.	*The dress is orange.*
¿De qué color son los zapatos?	*What color are the shoes?*
Los zapatos son de color café.	*The shoes are brown.*

6. Practicing vocabulary for clothing

La maestra models clothing words and the class repeats them (**los pantalones**—*pants*, **el sombrero**—*hat*, **la camisa**—*shirt*).

7. Reviewing the command *pon* (*put*)

The mime demonstrates the meaning of **pon**.

8. Integrating colors and clothing

La maestra reverses her questioning strategy and asks the class to identify which object is a particular color.

¿Qué es azul?	*What is blue?*
Los pantalones son de color azul.	*The pants are blue.*
¿Qué es negro?	*What is black?*
El sombrero es de color negro.	*The hat is black.*
¿Qué es rojo?	*What is red?*
La camisa es de color rojo.	*The shirt is red.*
¿Qué es café?	*What is brown?*
Los zapatos son de color café.	*The shoes are brown.*
¿Qué es anaranjado?	*What is orange?*
El vestido es de color anaranjado.	*The dress is orange.*
¿Qué es morado?	*What is purple?*
La chaqueta es de color morado.	*The jacket is purple.*

FYI You may be interested in comparing section 5 with this one to see how **la maestra** manipulated essentially the same vocabulary to ask questions that required related but different answers.

9. Playing a game with *pon* (*put*) and clothing

La maestra models clothing words and the class repeats them. Jorge and **la maestra** tell each other where to put the Flashcards.

Pon la blusa aquí.	*Put the blouse here.*
Pon los pantalones en la blusa.	*Put the pants on the blouse.*
Pon la camisa en los pantalones.	*Put the shirt on the pants.*
Pon los sombreros en la camisa.	*Put the hats on the shirt.*

10. Singing "Español para ti" (*"Spanish Is for You, and for Me"*)

Everyone sings **"Español para ti."** For song lyrics, see Lesson 3, Video Lesson, section 3.

11. Closing

La maestra reviews what children have done and bids the class **Adiós** (*Good-bye*).

After viewing the video, praise the children for their good listening and watching skills.

Lesson Twenty-Six

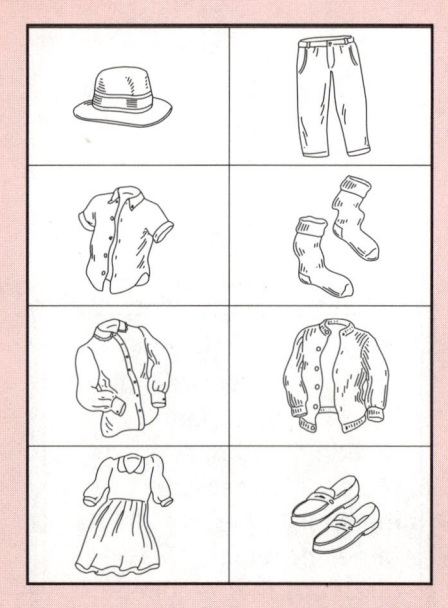

Blackline Master 26A

Check that children are coloring the clothing correctly and that they are making any necessary corrections. You may want to determine if the words for colors or for clothing primarily caused children's mistakes.

Using Blackline Master 26A in another activity may encourage the class to listen more closely to doña Elena's answers.

ACTIVITY LESSON

Activity 26A: What color shall we use?

Materials: Cassette player; Activity Cassette 2, Side A; Blackline Master 26A; and sets of gray, purple, pink, blue, black, red, yellow, orange, brown, and green crayons.

Preparation: Make a copy of Blackline Master 26A for each child. Every child will also need a set of crayons.

Discuss with children what each picture represents—hat, pants, shirt, socks, blouse, sweater, dress, and shoes. Explain that doña Elena is going to tell the class to **colorea** (*color*) various pieces of clothing in specific colors. She will repeat each direction two times. Tell children that they only need to color part of each item. They will have time to finish coloring later.

Emphasize that the class should listen carefully to doña Elena's answers. If anyone makes a mistake, he or she should make a small X in a corner of that picture. Point out that when the class listens to the tape for a second time, children can then correct any mistakes.

You may wish to stop the tape briefly after each direction to give the class time to color and then again later to make corrections. Since children will also use this Blackline Master for Activity 26C, accurate corrections are important.

Activity 26B: Where does the number go?

Materials: Cassette player; Activity Cassette 2, Side A; Number Cards for 10, 20, 30, 40, 50; and Gold Flashcards 51–52, 54, 57.

Preparation: Copy Gold Flashcard 54, putting the shoes and the socks on separate pieces of paper. Duplicate each Number Card and cut the copies in half, so that each number is on a separate sheet of paper.

Before starting the activity, display the Flashcard pictures where everyone can see them and give a number card to five different volunteers. Ask volunteers to stand in front of the class while showing their cards in number order. As each child raises his or her number, have the class count by tens to fifty.

Explain that doña Elena is going to tell volunteers to **pon** (*put*) their numbers on different pieces of clothing. She will repeat each direction two times. Repeat the activity a couple of times, so that more children have an opportunity to participate. Move the illustrations each time to keep the activity interesting.

LEVEL TWO

Activity 26C: What clothing is that color?

Materials: Blackline Master 26A.

Remind children that in the Video Lesson, **la maestra** played a game with them in which she asked **¿Qué es ___?** (*What is ___?*) and a color. The class named the clothing that matched the color.

Tell children that they are now going to play the same game with the paper they colored earlier (in Activity 26A). If you feel comfortable, ask questions in random order. If not, have volunteers do so. The questions and answers below follow the order on the page simply to help you verify their correctness.

¿Qué es verde?	*What is green?*
El sombrero.	*The hat.*
¿Qué es negro?	*What is black?*
Los pantalones.	*The pants.*
¿Qué es morado?	*What is purple?*
La camisa.	*The shirt.*
¿Qué es anaranjado?	*What is orange?*
Los calcetines.	*The socks.*
¿Qué es amarillo?	*What is yellow?*
La blusa.	*The blouse.*
¿Qué es azul?	*What is blue?*
El suéter.	*The sweater.*
¿Qué es rosado?	*What is pink?*
El vestido.	*The dress.*
¿Qué es café?	*What is brown?*
Los zapatos.	*The shoes.*

CLOSING

Tell the children that Spanish class is finished for today. In the next class, they are going to talk about clothing and the seasons and hear a new song.

IF YOU HAVE TIME...

Materials: Cassette player; **"La ropa"** (*"Clothing"*) on Song Cassette, Side A; and Gold Flashcards 51–54, 57.

Remind children that they learned a song about clothing. Play it through once to remind the class of the words and music. Show the Flashcards as the clothing is named (hat, pants, shirt, shoes, dress).

Play the first verse a couple more times before asking the class to sing. Depending on how well children do, either practice this verse a few more times or go on to the next verse. Follow the same process for the whole song.

Esto es mi sombrero.
(*This is my hat.*)
Esto es mi sombrero.
(*This is my hat.*)
Esto es mi sombrero.
(*This is my hat.*)
Tra la la la la.
(*Tra la la la la.*)
Éstos son mis pantalones.
(*These are my pants.*)
Ésta es mi camisa.
(*This is my shirt.*)
Éstos son mis zapatos.
(*These are my shoes.*)
Esto es mi vestido.
(*This is my dress.*)

Lesson Twenty-Six

Lesson 27

Materials to gather

- VCR and Video Lesson 27 on Tape 7
- Cassette player
- Activity Cassette 2
- Gold Flashcards 1–2, 41–47, 51–54, 56–61
- Blackline Master 27C (the seasons)
- Scissors or paper cutter
- Tape or paste
- Crayons or markers
- *Optional materials:* Song Cassette

Objectives

Language
- Practice vocabulary for the seasons

Culture
- Sing **"Las estaciones"** (*"The Seasons"*)

Review
- Respond to questions about names, the calendar, and the weather
- Practice words for articles of clothing
- Use color to identify clothing
- Practice vocabulary for months

Vocabulary

el invierno	*winter*
la primavera	*spring*
el verano	*summer*
el otoño	*fall, autumn*

Warm-up

Ask children to explain when to use **tú** and **usted** for *you*. (**Tú** is used with family, close friends, children, and pets. **Usted** is used with respected or older people, acquaintances, and business associates.)

Review

Materials: Gold Flashcards 1–2.

Have children tell how to:

    ask you your name   **¿Cómo se llama usted?**

    ask another child his/her name   **¿Cómo te llamas (tú)?**

Then have pairs of volunteers ask each other their names and answer the questions. Some children should pretend to be **la maestra** or **el maestro** and use the Flashcards for identification.

Introduce the video

Explain that in this lesson, children will talk about clothing and the seasons and then hear a new song.

Answers:

Me llamo ___.
(*My name is ___.*)

Se llama ___.
(*His/Her name is ___.*)

Video Lesson

1. Saying the opening conversation

Using **buenos días** (*good morning*) as a greeting, **la maestra** has the opening conversation with Rosco and then with the class.

2. Reviewing names, the calendar, and weather

La maestra asks many questions, including ones about weather.

¿Cómo te llamas?	What is your name (*informal*)?
¿Cómo se llama?	What is your name (*formal*)?
¿De qué color es el calendario?	What color is the calendar?
¿Qué día es?	What day of the week is it?
¿Cuál es la fecha?	What is the date?
¿Qué tiempo hace?	What's the weather like?

3. Reviewing articles of clothing

La maestra models the words and the class repeats them. She and Rosco comment on and ask questions about some words while pointing out the relation between weather and clothing.

¿Cuántos [sombreros] son?	How many [hats] are there?
Un sombrero de color blanco.	A white hat.
Un sombrero de color café.	A brown hat.
La camisa es para los niños.	Shirts are for boys.
¿De qué color son los pantalones?	What color are the pants?
La blusa es para las niñas.	Blouses are for girls.
Cuando llevamos la chaqueta hace frío.	When we wear jackets it's cold.
¿Cuántos [calcetines] son?	How many [socks] are there?
De qué color son los zapatos?	What color are the shoes?

4. Integrating colors and clothing

La maestra models the vocabulary for clothing for the class to repeat. Then she asks children to name items of clothing that are particular colors. For the complete text of this activity, see Lesson 26, Video Lesson, section 8.

FYI

Estoy contenta cuando tú estás muy bien.
(*I am happy when you are well.*)

EN ESPAÑOL

La maestra tells Rosco to **escucha** (*listen*). If you feel comfortable, teach your class this expression and use it to gain their attention.

FYI

La maestra teases Rosco that maybe he needs more than two socks. He seriously answers that he has **dos pies** (*two feet*). If children remember **pies,** they may understand the joke. Also, she comments that the Flashcard of the pants **está al revés**. This means that *it's upside down.*

Clothing and colors:

calcetines—amarillo
(*socks—yellow*)

blusa—rosado
(*blouse—pink*)

LEVEL TWO

5. Reviewing months

La maestra models the months and the class repeats them.

enero	January	julio	July
febrero	February	agosto	August
marzo	March	septiembre	September
abril	April	octubre	October
mayo	May	noviembre	November
junio	June	diciembre	December

6. Introducing the seasons

La maestra and Rosco talk about **las cuatro estaciones del año** (*the four seasons of the year*) before she models their names for the class to repeat.

el invierno	winter	el verano	summer
la primavera	spring	el otoño	autumn

7. Singing "Las estaciones" ("The Seasons")

La maestra says **Hace frío** (*It's cold*) and introduces the song.

En el invierno, en el invierno,	*In the winter, in the winter,*
diciembre, enero, febrero.	*December, January, February.*
La primavera, la primavera,	*The spring, the spring,*
marzo, abril y mayo.	*March, April, and May.*
En el verano, en el verano,	*In the summer, in the summer,*
junio y julio y agosto.	*June and July and August.*
Viene septiembre, octubre, noviembre,	*Come September, October, November,*
para el otoño.	*for the autumn.*

8. Integrating the seasons and weather

Using lyrics from **"Las estaciones,"** **la maestra** models the names of the seasons and everyone repeats them. Then she and Rosco discuss typical weather for each season.

el invierno	winter	Hace frío.	*It's cold.*
la primavera	spring	Llueve.	*It's rainy.*
el verano	summer	Hace sol.	*It's sunny.*
		Hace calor.	*It's hot.*
el otoño	autumn	Hace viento.	*It's windy.*

9. Closing

La maestra and Rosco say **Adiós** and **Hasta luego** (*See you later*).

LANGUAGE ACROSS THE CURRICULUM

When you are teaching about the months in science or social studies, refer to what the class has talked about in Spanish—the number of months, their names, and the number of days in each.

EN ESPAÑOL

Rosco asks ¿**Cómo se dice** *seasons*? (*How do you say "seasons"?*). If you feel comfortable, teach this expression to your class and encourage its use.

After viewing the video, praise the children for their good listening and watching skills.

Lesson Twenty-Seven

ACTIVITY LESSON

Activity 27A: Name that clothing

Materials: Cassette player; Activity Cassette 2, Side A; and Gold Flashcards 51–54, 56–61.

Before starting the activity, arrange the Flashcards in numerical order, so that they match the order of the words on the tape—hat, pants, shirt, socks, shoes, sweater, dress, skirt, jacket, pajamas, bathing suit.

Tell children that doña Elena is going to practice clothing words with them. She will say each word two times and then ask the class to repeat it. Explain that you are going to show a picture for the word at the same time to remind children what it means.

The class will probably benefit from repeating this activity two or three times. To keep the repetition from getting boring, however, you may want to alternate this activity with others. Note that three of these items of clothing—**la falda** (*skirt*), **el pijama** (*pajamas*), **el traje de baño** (*bathing suit*)—were presented last year, but will not get introduced formally this year until Lesson 28.

Activity 27B: ¿Qué tiempo hace? (*What's the weather like?*)

Materials: Cassette player; Activity Cassette 2, Side A; Gold Flashcards 41–47.

Arrange the Flashcards in numerical order, so that they match the order of the weather expressions on the tape—sunny/good weather, cold, hot, raining, snowing, windy, bad weather.

Tell children that you are going to show the class Flashcards illustrating various kinds of weather. For each Flashcard, doña Elena will ask ¿Qué tiempo hace? (*What is the weather like?*) two times and the class should answer. Then display Flashcard 43, for example, and point out that there are some Flashcards for which the class might be able to give many answers, such as *it's hot, it's sunny,* and even *it's bad weather* if someone didn't like hot weather. For this activity, however, children should respond with the answers they have practiced even if doña Elena does occasionally add extra information.

#41: Hace sol.	*It's sunny.*
Hace buen tiempo.	*It's good weather.*
#42: Hace frío.	*It's cold.*
#43: Hace calor.	*It's hot.*
#44: Llueve.	*It's raining.*
#45: Nieva.	*It's snowing.*
#46: Hace viento.	*It's windy.*
#47: Hace mal tiempo.	*It's bad weather.*

Repeat this activity if possible.

FYI Frequent practice literally acts as a reminder. The brain recognizes that it has heard at least part of this information before and retrieves it, which helps in the process of retaining information in long-term memory.

FYI La maestra adds this extra comment with Flashcard 45.
Hace mucho frío.
(*It's very cold.*)

✓ You can use this activity to check comprehension of weather expressions. Display the Gold Flashcards in random order. Tell the class to listen as doña Elena asks about the weather and then describes it. Stop the tape after each question and answer, and ask an individual to pick out the Flashcard that matches what she said.

Activity 27C: Make season circles

Materials: Blackline Master 27C; scissors or paper cutter; tape or paste; and crayons or markers.

Preparation: Make a copy of Blackline Master 27C for each child. You may also want to use a paper cutter to cut the rows on Blackline Master 27C instead of having children do it individually with scissors.

Ask the class what **la maestra**'s new song is about. Then discuss the illustrations on the Blackline Master. If children have difficulty identifying the seasons, remind them about the pictures behind **la maestra** while she was singing the song.

Row 1: winter, December, January, February
Row 2: spring, March, April, May
Row 3: summer, June, July, August
Row 4: fall, September, October, November

Tell children to cut along the dotted lines to make four strips of paper. Next, ask the class to tape or paste the strips end-to-end, so that the months are in calendar order in one row. To make the seasons stand out from the other pictures, have children color them.

Then tell the class to place the ends of the strip together to make a circle. (You may wish to have children permanently tape or paste them that way.) Discuss how the months and seasons make a "circle"—after the four seasons which include the twelve months pass, they start over again. Save the season circles to use in the *If you have time . . .* activity in this lesson and in other activities.

Blackline Master 27C

CLOSING

Tell the children that Spanish class is finished for today. Explain that next time, they are going to practice the song about the seasons.

IF YOU HAVE TIME . . .

Materials: Cassette player; "**Las estaciones**" ("*The Seasons*") on Song Cassette, Side A; and season circles from Activity 27C.

Make season circles available to children. Play "**Las estaciones**" once. Then replay the song, stopping after each pair of lines to talk about their meaning. Connect this discussion to the pictures on the season circle, so that children may use it as a tool for learning the song. Play "**Las estaciones**" again and ask the class to follow along with their season circles. For song lyrics, see section 7 of this Video Lesson.

Lesson Twenty-Seven

Lesson 28

Materials to gather

- VCR and Video Lesson 28 on Tape 7
- Cassette player
- Activity Cassette 2
- Song Cassette
- Gold Flashcards 48–50, 62–64
- Blackline Master 28A (clothes line)
- Red, pink, orange, yellow, green, blue, brown, purple, and black crayons or markers
- Rosco flag(s)
- Hundred Chart or chalkboard and chalk
- **Optional materials:** Activity Cassette 1; Spanish calendar; Rosco and Dora hand puppets; and Gold Flashcards 41–47.

OBJECTIVES

Language
- Practice additional vocabulary for clothing

Culture
- Sing **"Las estaciones"** (*"The Seasons"*)

Review
- Answer questions about names
- Review the months and the seasons
- Recall colors and vocabulary for clothing
- Practice vocabulary for weather

Vocabulary

la falda	*skirt*
el pijama	*pajamas*
el traje de baño	*bathing suit*
el abrigo	*coat*

Warm-up

Materials: Cassette player; "Months Rap" on Song Cassette, Side A; and Gold Flashcards 48–50, 62–64.

Divide the class into two groups. Have each half sing alternate lines along with the cassette. Show the Flashcards as the months are named on the song, or display them for the class. For song lyrics, see Lesson 12, Video Lesson, section 4.

Review

Ask the class to tell how many months there are, to name them, and to explain the relationship between the months and the seasons. Ask a volunteer to name the current season. Encourage children to use Spanish where possible.

Introduce the video

Tell children that in this video they are going to use the weather and clothing expressions together and sing the new song about the seasons.

---

invierno: diciembre, enero, febrero
(*winter: December, January, February*)

primavera: marzo, abril, mayo
(*spring: March, April, May*)

verano: junio, julio, agosto
(*summer: June, July, August*)

otoño: septiembre, octubre, noviembre
(*fall: September, October, November*)

Video Lesson

1. Saying the opening conversation

Using **Buenas tardes** (*Good afternoon*) as a greeting, **la maestra** has the opening conversation with the class, Dora, and Rosco.

2. Reviewing names and colors

La maestra asks the puppets and the class several questions.

¿Cómo te llamas (tú)?	What is your name?
Me llamo ___.	My name is ___.
¿Cómo se llama?	What is his/her name?
Se llama ___.	His/Her name is ___.
De qué color es [el sombrero]?	What color is [the hat]?
Es ___.	It's ___.

Colors:

anaranjado	orange
amarillo	yellow
gris	gray
blanco	white
negro	black

3. Reviewing the months

La maestra models the months and the class repeats them. For months, see the Review section in this lesson.

4. Reviewing the four seasons

La maestra talks about the seasons. Then she sings lyrics from "**Las estaciones**" (*"The Seasons"*) to model their names.

el invierno	winter
la primavera	spring
el verano	summer
el otoño	autumn

FYI

Cant<u>as</u> muy bien.
(*<u>You</u> <u>sing</u> very well.*)

Cant<u>o</u> muy bien.
(*<u>I</u> <u>sing</u> very well.*)

<u>Rosco y Dora</u> cant<u>an</u> muy bien.
(*<u>Rosco and Dora</u> <u>sing</u> very well.*)

5. Singing "Las estaciones" ("The Seasons")

La maestra invites the class to sing along with her.

En el invierno, en el invierno,	In the winter, in the winter,
diciembre, enero, febrero.	December, January, February.
La primavera, la primavera,	The spring, the spring,
marzo, abril y mayo.	March, April, and May.
En el verano, en el verano,	In the summer, in the summer,
junio y julio y agosto.	June and July and August.
Viene septiembre, octubre, noviembre,	Come September, October, November,
para el otoño.	for the autumn.

6. Playing *Sí o no* (*Yes or no*) with the seasons

Rosco and Dora take turns answering **la maestra**'s questions.

¿Es ___?	Is it ___?
No, no es ___.	No, it's not ___.
Es ___.	It's ___.

Additional questions:

¿Es ___?
(*Is it ___?*)
Sí, es ___.
(*Yes, it's ___.*)
¿Es ___ o ___?
(*Is it ___ or ___?*)
Es ___.
(*It is ___.*)

LEVEL TWO

7. Practicing clothing and colors

La maestra models the new words for clothing and asks about colors.

| la falda | *skirt* | el traje de baño | *bathing suit* |
| el pijama | *pajamas* | el abrigo | *coat* |

8. Playing games with clothing and colors

La maestra plays **Muéstrame** ___ (*Show me* ___), inquires about colors, and asks questions like those in section 6.

9. Connecting clothing and weather

La maestra models each word for clothing and then she and Rosco talk about the relation between clothing and weather.

¿Las niñas llevan la falda cuando hace frío?	*Do girls wear skirts when it's cold?*
Cuando hace frío y cuando hace calor llevamos la falda.	*When it's cold and when it's hot we wear skirts.*
¿Llevamos el pijama cuando hace frío?	*Do we wear pajamas when it's cold?*
Llevamos el pijama cuando hace frío y cuando hace calor.	*We wear pajamas when it's cold and when it's hot.*
¿Cuándo llevamos el traje de baño?	*When do we wear bathing suits?*
Cuando hace calor, llevamos el traje de baño.	*When it's hot, we wear bathing suits.*
Cuando hace frío, ¿llevamos la chaqueta/el abrigo?	*When it's cold, do we wear jackets/coats?*
Llevamos la chaqueta/el abrigo cuando hace frío.	*We wear jackets/coats when it's cold.*

10. Connecting weather and the seasons

La maestra talks about weather and the seasons.

En el invierno, hace frío.	*In winter, it's cold.*
En la primavera, llueve.	*In spring, it's rainy.*
En verano, hace sol y hace calor.	*In summer, it's sunny and it's hot.*
En otoño, hace viento.	*In autumn, it's windy.*

11. Closing

La maestra says **Adiós** (*Good-bye*) to the class.

Colors:

verde	green
rosado	pink
azul	blue
gris	gray
anaranjado	orange
blanco	white

FYI **Cuándo** (*When*) has an accent mark when it is used to ask a question, but not when it is used as a conjunction.

¿<u>Cuándo</u> llevamos el abrigo? (question—accent)
(*When do we wear coats?*)

¿Llevas abrigo <u>cuando</u> hace calor? (conjunction—no accent)
(*Do you wear a coat when it's hot?*)

After viewing the video, praise the children for their good listening and watching skills.

Lesson Twenty-Eight

Blackline Master 28A

You may want to begin with a whole-group activity and then break into groups of four.

LEVEL TWO

ACTIVITY LESSON

Activity 28A: Colorea (*Color*)

Materials: Cassette player; Activity Cassette 2, Side A; Blackline Master 28A; and red, pink, orange, yellow, green, blue, brown, purple, and black crayons or markers.

Preparation: Make a copy of Blackline Master 28A for each child.

Make sure that children know what the illustrations represent. Then explain that **la maestra** is going to tell them what to **colorea** (*color*) the clothes. She will say each direction two times. Add that you will stop the tape to allow children time to color. Point out that there are more kinds of clothes than crayons, so the class will use some colors more than once. Remind children that it is not necessary to color the entire item. There will be time later to finish the coloring. Be sure to allow this time.

Activity 28B: What's in a name?

Materials: Cassette player; Activity Cassette 2, Side A; and Rosco flag(s).

Explain that **la maestra** is going to ask ¿**Cómo se llama?** (*What's his/her name?*). You will hand the Rosco flag to a child and the class should answer **Se llama** plus his or her name. **La maestra** will ask each question two times. Since **la maestra** only asks about four children, repeat this activity if possible.

Activity 28C: How are numbers alike and different?

Materials: Hundred Chart or chalkboard and chalk.

Preparation: Display a Hundred Chart or reproduce this chart on the chalkboard.

	1	2	3	4	5
10	11	12	13	14	15
20	21	22	23	24	25
30	31	32	33	34	35
40	41	42	43	44	45
50					

Discuss how numbers are alike or different in English and in Spanish. Help children find relationships between numbers. Focus on sounds first. Show children how ones and teens can begin with the same sound in English (*three/thirteen* and *four/fourteen*) and also in Spanish (**dos/doce** and **tres/trece**). Now show the opposite, some ones and teens that do not begin with the same sound in English (*one/eleven*) and in Spanish (**uno/once** and **cinco/quince**).

Do the same thing for ones and tens. In English *three/thirty; four/forty;* and *five/fifty* and in Spanish **tres/treinta; cuatro/cuarenta;** and **cinco/cincuenta** begin with the same sound. **Dos** and **veinte** in Spanish do not begin with the same sound.

You can continue the comparison with the end sounds [tē] in English (*twenty, thirty, forty,* etc.) and [ah] in Spanish (**treinta, cuarenta, cincuenta**).

Then talk about how the numbers 21–50 are named in a similar manner in both languages—by naming the tens and then the ones.

23	*twenty-three*	veintitrés
33	*thirty-three*	treinta y tres
37	*thirty-seven*	treinta y siete
47	*forty-seven*	cuarenta y siete

CLOSING

Tell the children that Spanish class is finished for today. In the next video, they are going to sing the new song about the seasons and go shopping with **la maestra** again.

Some children find sound relationships interesting. They help children notice new relations between numbers. Since the difficulty of this activity depends on your class's math skills, it will also appear in another lesson. In this way, you will have more flexibility discussing this math-related topic.

IF YOU HAVE TIME...

Materials: Cassette player; Activity 19B on Activity Cassette 1, Side B; Spanish calendar; Rosco and Dora hand puppets; and Gold Flashcards 41–47.

You may want to use this activity in a small group while other children finish coloring Blackline Master 28A.

Explain that doña Elena is going to ask some familiar questions and children should repeat after her. Then play the cassette once. Replay the cassette and stop after children repeat each question. Have volunteers ask the appropriate question and tell classmates to give answers that relate to the current day and/or weather.

After the question has been asked a couple of times, encourage shy children to use the puppets to ask it.

Lesson Twenty-Eight

Lesson 29

Materials to gather

- VCR and Video Lesson 29 on Tape 8
- Cassette player
- Activity Cassettes 1 and 2
- Blackline Masters 9C-1, 9C-2, 9C-3 (times of day)
- Spanish calendar
- Book, backpack, clock, ruler, scissors, pencil, globe or picture of one
- Blackline Master 29A (seasons)
- Gold Flashcards 41–47
- Scissors or paper cutter
- Tagboard or 6 sheets of paper
- Tape or glue
- *Optional materials:* Number Cards 1–9, 20, 30; 18 sheets of paper; and marker

OBJECTIVES

Language
- Name weather expressions that match seasons

Culture
- Recall that the weather changes that come with each season determine the type of clothing we wear

Review
- Respond to **¿Qué tiempo hace?** (*What is the weather like?*)
- Practice names for the seasons
- Sing **"Las estaciones"** (*"The Seasons"*)

Vocabulary
No new vocabulary is introduced in this lesson.

Warm-up

Materials: Blackline Masters 9C-1, 9C-2, 9C-3 (times of day); and a Spanish calendar.

Exchange greetings with the class for the current time of day. Then show a Blackline Master for another time of day and exchange the appropriate greetings for then (T = Teacher, C = class):

T: Buenos días/Buenas tardes/Buenas noches, clase.
Good morning/Good afternoon/Good evening, class.

C: Buenos días/Buenas tardes/Buenas noches, Maestro/Maestra.
Good morning/Good afternoon/Good evening, Teacher.

Display the calendar, then have volunteers ask and answer the question ¿Cuál es la fecha? (*What is the date?*). For numbers 1–31, see Activity 20C.

Review

Materials: Cassette player; Activity 6C on Activity Cassette 1, Side A; and a book, backpack, clock, ruler, scissors, pencil, globe.

Ask volunteers to name each classroom item as you hold it up. Point out that you want the whole class to practice saying **Necesito** (*I need*), so no one has the pictures Mr. Hale mentions. Then explain that he is going to ask ¿Quién necesita? (*Who needs?*) and the name of a classroom object. You will hold up the item, and everyone should answer **Necesito** and its name.

Introduce the video

Explain that children are going to use weather expressions, name the seasons, and understand more of the shopping trip.

Months of the year:

enero	*January*
febrero	*February*
marzo	*March*
abril	*April*
mayo	*May*
junio	*June*
julio	*July*
agosto	*August*
septiembre	*September*
octubre	*October*
noviembre	*November*
diciembre	*December*

Classroom items:

el libro	*book*
la mochila	*backpack*
el reloj	*clock*
la regla	*ruler*
las tijeras	*scissors*
el lápiz	*pencil*
el globo	*globe*

> **FYI** **Ustedes** means *you* for more than one person.

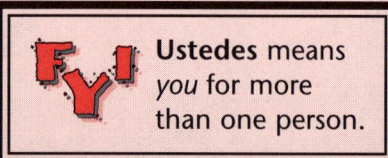

Video Lesson

1. Saying the opening conversation

Using **buenos días** (*good morning*) as a greeting, **la maestra** has the opening conversation with the children. She then adds:

Estoy muy bien porque estoy aquí con ustedes, con mis amigos.	*I'm very well because I'm here with you, with my friends.*

2. Reviewing expressions for the weather

La maestra models **¿Qué tiempo hace?** (*What's the weather like?*), answers the questions, and then asks the class to respond.

Hace frío.	*It's cold.*
Llueve.	*It's raining.*
Hace sol.	*It's sunny.*
Hace buen tiempo.	*It's good weather.*
Hace calor.	*It's hot.*
Hace viento.	*It's windy.*
Hace mal tiempo.	*It's bad weather.*
Nieva.	*It's snowing.*

3. Using "Las estaciones" ("The Seasons") to review

La maestra models names for the seasons by singing lines from "Las estaciones" and asks the class to sing the song with her.

En el invierno, en el invierno,	*In the winter, in the winter,*
diciembre, enero, febrero.	*December, January, February.*
La primavera, la primavera,	*The spring, the spring,*
marzo, abril y mayo.	*March, April, and May.*
En el verano, en el verano,	*In the summer, in the summer,*
junio y julio y agosto.	*June and July and August.*
Viene septiembre, octubre, noviembre,	*Come September, October, November,*
para el otoño.	*for the autumn.*

Next, children repeat the names of the seasons after **la maestra**, who also discusses typical weather for different seasons.

4. Integrating weather and the seasons

La maestra and the class say the names of the seasons. Next, she asks children to suggest weather that fits the different seasons.

En el invierno, hace frío y nieva.	*In winter, it's cold and it snows.*

LEVEL TWO

En la primavera, hace buen tiempo y llueve.	*In spring, it's good weather and it rains.*
En el verano, hace sol y hace calor.	*In summer, it's sunny and it's hot.*
En el otoño, hace viento.	*In autumn, it's windy.*

5. Naming clothes needed in different seasons

La maestra asks children about the clothing they need for various seasons.

En el invierno, ¿qué necesitas?	*In winter, what do you need?*
En el invierno, ¿necesitas el sombrero?	*In winter, do you need a hat?*
Sí, necesito el sombrero.	*Yes, I need a hat.*
En el verano, ¿qué necesitas?	*In summer, what do you need?*
En el verano, ¿necesitas un traje de baño?	*In summer, do you need a bathing suit?*
Sí, necesito un traje de baño.	*Yes, I need a bathing suit.*

6. Going shopping for clothes

Here are some excerpts from **la maestra**'s shopping trip.

Aquí está un sombrero de color rojo.	*Here's a red hat.*
No me gusta.	*I don't like it.*
Aquí está un sombrero de color negro con flores.	*Here's a black flowered hat.*
¿Me gusta o no me gusta?	*Do I or don't I like it?*
Sí, me gusta.	*Yes, I like it.*
Pero yo necesito una chaqueta.	*But I need a jacket.*
Chaqueta ... Aquí está una chaqueta perfecta.	*A jacket ... Here's a perfect jacket.*
¿Y qué más necesito?	*And what else do I need?*
Necesito una falda.	*I need a skirt.*

7. Closing

La maestra says **Adiós** (*Good-bye*) and **Hasta luego** (*See you later*) to the class.

EN ESPAÑOL

Children now know how to say **Necesito** (*I need*), **Me gusta** (*I like*), and **No me gusta** (*I don't like*). Point out that they can use these expressions every day.

FYI

el sombrero *the hat*
un sombrero *a hat*
la chaqueta *the jacket*
una chaqueta *a jacket*

Un and **una** mean *a, an*.
Uno means *one*.

After viewing the video, praise the children for their good listening and watching skills.

Lesson Twenty-Nine

Blackline Master 29A

ACTIVITY LESSON

Activity 29A: Where's winter?

Materials: Cassette player; Activity Cassette 2, Side A; Blackline Master 29A; and scissors or paper cutter.

Preparation: Make a copy of Blackline Master 29A for each child. You may wish to cut up the pictures with a paper cutter instead of having children do it with scissors.

Ask children to name the season that each picture represents. Then tell them to follow **la maestra**'s directions to **muéstrame** (*show me*) the picture of a particular season. She will say each direction two times.

Activity 29B: When is the weather bad?

Materials: Cassette player; Activity Cassette 2, Side A; Gold Flashcards 41–47; Blackline Master 29A; tagboard or 6 sheets of paper; and tape or glue.

Preparation: Use Blackline Master 29A to make flashcards of the seasons. First, copy the seasons onto separate sheets of paper—one apiece for spring and autumn and two apiece for winter and summer. Enlarge the pictures, so that they are easy to see. Second, mount the pictures on separate sheets of paper or on six pieces of tagboard approximately the size of flashcards. Save these "flashcards" of the seasons, as they will be a part of other activities. Display the Gold Flashcards for weather in random order where everyone can see them.

In this activity, children will match seasons with appropriate weather conditions. Hold up a flashcard for each season (winter through autumn), and ask a volunteer and then the whole class to name it. Tell children that **la maestra** is going to tell them to **pon** (*put*) the seasons on particular kinds of weather. Distribute the season flashcards to volunteers. Point out that you will stop the tape briefly after each command.

Replay this activity a couple of times if possible. Rearrange the weather cards each time. A summary of which season should be on top of each weather Flashcard follows. Leave the cards as is for use in Activity 29C.

el invierno	winter
Hace frío./Nieva.	It's cold./It snows.
la primavera	spring
Llueve.	It rains.
el verano	summer
Hace calor./Hace sol.	It's hot./It's sunny.
el otoño	autumn
Hace viento.	It's windy.

> You may want to point out that *It's bad weather* does not have any season on it. **La maestra** evidently likes all the seasons. Ask volunteers which season they might put **Hace mal tiempo** on. Accept all reasonable answers.

LEVEL TWO

Activity 29C: Organize seasons and weather

Materials: Gold Flashcards 41–47; season flashcards from Activity 29B; cassette player (optional); and Activity 29A on Activity Cassette 2, Side A (optional).

Preparation: If the two sets of flashcards from Activity 29B are in position, no preparation is needed. If not, put the appropriate pairs of cards together as shown on the chart in Activity 29B. Then display the pairs in random order.

The goal of this activity is for children to organize the seasons and weather expressions into the categories shown on the chart in Activity 29B. The order of the weather expressions within each category does not matter.

First, ask the class to help you put the weather flashcards for the same season together. Encourage children to use Spanish as much as possible, for example, by naming **el verano** and **hace calor** and also **el verano** and **hace sol**.

Next, have the class name the order of the seasons as they are sung in **"Las estaciones"** (*"The Seasons"*)— **el invierno** (*winter*), **la primavera** (*spring*), **el verano** (*summer*), **el otoño** (*autumn*). If children have difficulty doing this, you may want to play the beginning of Activity 29A in which **la maestra** names each season in English and in Spanish. After each season is named have volunteers move the flashcards into season order.

If you feel comfortable doing so, remind children how to say *in* (**en**) with each season—**en el invierno, en la primavera, en el verano,** and **en el otoño**. If not, ask volunteers do so. Tell the class to repeat each phrase. Then move the season flashcards, so that each season is to the left of its weather expression. Have volunteers "read" the cards.

En el invierno, hace frío.	*In winter, it's cold.*
En el invierno, nieva.	*In winter, it snows.*
En la primavera, llueve.	*In spring, it rains.*
En el verano, hace sol.	*In summer, it's sunny.*
En el verano, hace calor.	*In summer, it's hot.*
En el otoño, hace viento.	*In autumn, it's windy.*

CLOSING

Tell the children that Spanish class is finished for today. In the next class, they are going to learn how to say *I'm sorry* to Rosco.

This activity follows the lyrics in the song, so that children have a consistent ordering for the seasons.

IF YOU HAVE TIME . . .

Materials: Number Cards for 1–9, 20, 30; 18 sheets of paper; a marker; and tape (optional).

Preparation: Write 21–29 and 31–39 on separate sheets of paper. Order the numbers in rows of 1–9, 21–29, and 31–39 as on a Hundred Chart. Display them where everyone can see them. You may wish to pin them on a bulletin board or tape them on the wall.

Divide the class in half. In turn have children from each group touch and name any number they choose. When an answer is correct, the child keeps the number. Play continues until all the numbers have been named. Keep these numbers for use in more activities.

Lesson Twenty-Nine

Lesson 30

Materials to gather

- VCR and Video Lesson 30 on Tape 8
- Cassette player
- Activity Cassette 2
- Song Cassette
- Rap rolls from Activity 10C
- Gold Flashcards 41–45, 48–64
- Season flashcards from Activity 29B
- Rosco hand puppet
- **Estoy muy mal** (*I feel very bad*) masks from Activity 9B

OBJECTIVES

Language

- Use **necesito** (*I need*) to answer questions
- Learn to say **Lo siento** (*I'm sorry*) when someone isn't feeling well

Culture

- Compare the words *pajamas* and **pijama**

Review

- Name the seasons
- Sing **"Las estaciones"**(*"The Seasons"*) and **"La ropa"** (*"Clothing"*)
- Practice vocabulary for clothing

Vocabulary

Lo siento.   *I'm sorry.*

Warm-up

Materials: Cassette player; "Months Rap" on Song Cassette, Side B; and rap rolls from Activity 10C.

Play the "Months Rap" through once. Ask children to follow along on their rap rolls and say the words to themselves. Remind them to listen for any words that they do not know. Then play the song again and have sing them along. For lyrics to the rap, see Lesson 12, Video Lesson, section 4.

Review

Materials: Gold Flashcards 48–50 and 62–64; season Flashcards from Activity 29B.

Preparation: Make a copy of each month on a separate sheet of paper if you have not done so for an earlier activity.

Turn the month cards facedown. Display the season flashcards at wide intervals from each other where everyone can see them.

Ask volunteers to select a month card, turn it face up, show it to the class, and name it in Spanish. Then volunteers should put the month card next to the season in which it belongs and name the season. If children make mistakes or cannot name a month or season, have classmates help them. Emphasize that children should help one another as Rosco and Dora do. For seasons and months, see Lesson 28, Review section.

Introduce the video

Explain that children are going to learn how to say *I'm sorry* to Rosco.

EN ESPAÑOL

If you feel comfortable, use these expressions after children respond.

Muy bien.	*Very good.*
Excelente.	*Excellent.*

VIDEO LESSON

1. Saying the opening conversation

Using **buenos días** as a greeting, **la maestra** has the opening conversation with the class.

2. Finding and consoling a sick Rosco

After finding Rosco and learning that he has a cold, **la maestra** teaches the class how to tell him **Lo siento** (*I'm sorry*) because he's feeling sick.

3. Using *necesito* (*I need*) with weather and clothing

La maestra discovers why Rosco has a cold.

Necesitas una chaqueta cuando hace frío.	*You need a jacket when it is cold.*
Sí, necesito una chaqueta cuando hace frío.	*Yes, I need a jacket when it is cold.*
Cuando hace frío, ¿necesitas el traje de baño?	*When it's cold, do you need a bathing suit?*
No necesito el traje de baño cuando hace frío.	*I don't need a bathing suit when it's cold.*
¿Qué ropa necesitas cuando hace frío?	*What clothing do you need when it's cold?*
Necesito los zapatos/ la camisa/la chaqueta/ el sombrero.	*I need shoes/a shirt/a jacket/ a hat.*

Then **la maestra** asks the class what they need.

¿Necesitas ___?	*Do you need ___?*
Sí, necesito ___.	*Yes, I need ___.*

4. Reviewing the seasons

La maestra asks Rosco and the class to name the seasons. For seasons, see Lesson 28, Video Lesson, section 4.

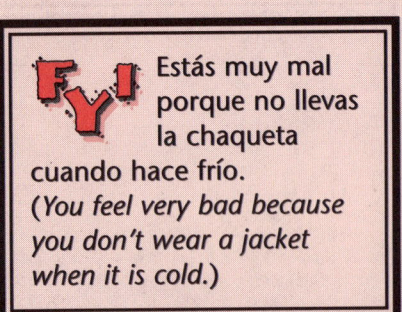

¿Qué estación es?	*What season is it?*
Es ___.	*It's ___.*

5. Singing "Las estaciones" (*"The Seasons"*)

At Rosco's request, **la maestra** invites the class to sing with her. For song lyrics, see Lesson 27, Video Lesson, section 7.

6. Integrating clothing and the seasons

La maestra asks Rosco to tell when to wear different clothing.

¿Qué es?	*What is it?*
Es ___.	*It's ___.*

FYI

Estás muy mal porque no llevas la chaqueta cuando hace frío.
(*You feel very bad because you don't wear a jacket when it is cold.*)

¿En qué estación necesitas la chaqueta?	In what season do you need a jacket?
Necesito la chaqueta en el invierno.	I need a jacket in winter.

Next, **la maestra** and a flustered Rosco discuss who wears what (**M** = Maestra, **R** = Rosco):

R: La blusa es para las chicas. No necesito blusa.	Blouses are for girls. I don't need blouses.
M: No necesitas la blusa porque tú eres chico.	No, you don't need blouses because you are a boy.
R: Necesito la camisa. Las chicas llevan la blusa.	I need shirts. Girls wear blouses.
R: No necesito el vestido.	I don't need a dress.
M: No, es para las chicas.	No, it's for girls.
R: Es para Dora.	It's for Dora.
R: No necesito la falda. Es de Dora.	I don't need the skirt. It's Dora's.

7. Playing *Pon aquí* (*Put here*)

The mime demonstrates the meaning of **pon** (*put*). Then **la maestra** tells Rosco to put specific clothing on the seasons.

Pon el pijama en el invierno.	Put the pajamas on winter.
Pon el traje de baño en el verano.	Put the bathing suit on summer.
Pon la chaqueta en el otoño.	Put the jacket on autumn.
Pon los pantalones en la primavera.	Put the pants on spring.

8. Singing "La ropa" ("Clothing")

La maestra adds two new verses to the song. For lyrics to the rest of the song, see the *If you have time . . .* activity in this lesson.

Ésta es mi chaqueta.	This is my jacket.
Ésta es mi chaqueta.	This is my jacket.
Ésta es mi chaqueta.	This is my jacket.
Tra la la la la.	Tra la la la la.
Éste es mi pijama.	These are my pajamas.
Éste es mi pijama.	These are my pajamas.
Éste es mi pijama.	These are my pajamas.
Tra la la la la.	Tra la la la la.

9. Closing

La maestra says **Adiós** (*Good-bye*) to the class.

FYI En el verano necesitas la ropa de verano, ¿sí? (*In summer you need summer clothing, don't you?*) Necesitas el pijama en todas las estaciones. (*You need pajamas during every season.*)

FYI In English and Spanish *pants* are considered plural—*pants* and **los pantalones**. In English, *pajamas* is plural, but in Spanish **el pijama** is singular.

EN ESPAÑOL Rosco exclaims **¡Un momento!** (*Just a second!*) when he can't keep up with **la maestra**. You may want to use this expression in the class.

FYI **Hay que** means *have to* or *must*. Cuando hace frío, hay que llevar la chaqueta. (*When it's cold, you have to wear a jacket.*)

After viewing the video, praise the children for their good listening and watching skills.

Lesson Thirty

After children have practiced this activity, you may want to replay the end of section 6 of the Video Lesson a couple of times, so that children better understand the humor in Rosco's remarks about not needing a dress or a skirt.

ACTIVITY LESSON

Activity 30A: What do you need?

Materials: Cassette player; Activity Cassette 2, Side A; and Gold Flashcards 51–61.

During this activity, **la maestra** is going to ask the class about twelve pieces of clothing. Watch the children, and if you see that their attention is starting to wander, stop and give them a short rest before continuing with the activity.

Put Gold Flashcards 51–61 in numerical order and have them handy. Explain that **la maestra** is going to ask ¿**Necesitas** ___? (*Do you need* ___?) and name an item of clothing. At the same time, you will show a Gold Flashcard of this item. **La maestra** will say each question two times. Children should answer **Necesito** (*I need*) and name the clothing. The answers are in this order: hat, pants, shirt, socks, shoes, blouse, sweater, dress, skirt, jacket, pajamas, bathing suit.

At the end of this activity, congratulate children on their persistence. This exercise has required them to focus on and speak Spanish longer than any other cassette activity so far.

Activity 30B: What should I wear?

Materials: Cassette player; Activity Cassette 2, Side A; and Gold Flashcards 41–45, 51, 56–57, 59, 61.

Tell the class that **la maestra** wants pairs of children to stand up. One child will have a Flashcard showing the weather. The other child will have a Flashcard showing clothing that is good to wear in that kind of weather. Then give the Flashcards to volunteers.

Reiterate that **la maestra** is going to say two commands with **párate** (*stand up*): **párate** with an article of clothing and **párate** with a weather picture. She will say each command two times. Two children should stand up. Repeat this activity with different children if possible.

LEVEL TWO

Activity 30C: *Lo siento* (*I'm sorry*)

Materials: Estoy muy mal (*I feel very bad*) masks from Activity 9B; hand puppet Rosco.

Discuss with children why and how **la maestra** said *I'm sorry* (**Lo siento**) to Rosco. Practice saying the expression a few times with the class.

Then using a Rosco hand puppet and a sick feeling mask, say, or have a volunteer say, **Estoy muy mal** (*I feel very bad*) and tell the class to answer **Lo siento**. Do this several times.

Repeat this scenario between volunteers. In each pair, the first child, who is holding the sick feeling mask, should say **Estoy muy mal** (*I feel very bad*); the second child should respond **Lo siento**. Point out that the "sick" child should always say **gracias** (*thank you*) in return.

Finally, have pairs of volunteers ask each other how they are. The "sick" child should continue to use the mask. Remind children that they must say **¿Y tú?**, not **¿Y usted?** to each other (C1 = first child, C2 = second child):

C1: ¿Cómo estás tú?	How are you?
C2: Muy bien, gracias. ¿Y tú?	Very well, thank you. And you?
C1: Muy mal.	Very bad.
C2: Lo siento.	I'm sorry.
C1: Gracias.	Thank you.

Volunteers may have difficulty getting through the entire dialogue the first few times. Encourage classmates to help them complete it.

Closing

Tell the children that Spanish class is finished for today. Explain that in the next video children are going to answer many questions and practice many numbers.

IF YOU HAVE TIME...

Materials: Cassette player; "La ropa" ("Clothing") on Song Cassette, Side A; and Gold Flashcards 51–54, 57.

Display the Gold Flashcards—hat, pants, shirt, shoes, dress—in random order. Play "La ropa" once, stopping after each verse for a volunteer to move the appropriate Flashcard into song order at the left. Then replay the song and have children sing it.

Esto es mi sombrero.
(*This is my hat.*)
Esto es mi sombrero.
(*This is my hat.*)
Esto es mi sombrero.
(*This is my hat.*)
Tra la la la la.
Éstos son mis pantalones.
(*These are my pants.*)
Ésta es mi camisa.
(*This is my shirt.*)
Éstos son mis zapatos.
(*These are my shoes.*)
Esto es mi vestido.
(*This is my dress.*)

Lesson 31

Materials to gather

- VCR and Video Lesson 31 on Tape 8
- Cassette player
- Activity Cassette 2
- Gold Flashcards 1–2
- **Estoy muy mal** (*I feel very bad*) masks from Activity 9B
- Rosco flag
- List of children's birthdays
- Children's birthday calendar art from Activity 21C
- Hundred Chart or chalkboard and chalk
- *Optional materials:* as many balls as groups of children

OBJECTIVES

Language
- Name individual numbers between 10 and 50
- Identify similarities and differences in the sounds for the names of English and Spanish numbers to 50

Culture
- Discuss similarities and differences between the English and Spanish organization of numbers to 50

Review
- Answer questions about the date and the weather
- Sing the "Months Rap"
- Answer ¿Cuándo es tu cumpleaños? (*When is your birthday?*) and ¿Cuántos años tienes (tú)? (*How old are you?*)
- Practice the numbers 11–20
- Practice counting to 50 by tens

Vocabulary

No new vocabulary is introduced in this lesson.

Warm-up

Materials: Gold Flashcards 1–2.

Say the opening conversation with your class if you feel comfortable doing so. If not, ask a volunteer to play the part of the teacher, using Gold Flashcard 1 or 2, as may be appropriate.

Review

Materials: **Estoy muy mal** (*I feel very bad*) masks from Activity 9B.

Remind children that **la maestra** said *I'm sorry* (**Lo siento**) to Rosco when he said he felt **muy mal** (*very bad*). Have pairs of volunteers ask each other how they are. The first child starts the conversation and should answer **muy mal** and use the feeling bad mask when asked how he/she feels. The second child should respond **Lo siento**. Point out that the sick child should also say thank you (**gracias**). Remind children that they must say ¿Y tú?, not ¿Y usted? (C1 = first child, C2 = second child):

C1: ¿Cómo estás tú?	*How are you?*
C2: Muy bien, gracias. ¿Y tú?	*Very well, thank you. And you?*
C1: Muy mal.	*Very bad.*
C2: Lo siento.	*I'm sorry.*
C1: Gracias.	*Thank you.*

Introduce the video

Tell the class they are going to talk about birthdays and numbers.

> **FYI** In English the date may be expressed two ways—as December 9 or the ninth of December, for example. In Spanish the date may only be expressed as the [number] of [month], as in **el nueve de diciembre**.

VIDEO LESSON

1. Saying the opening conversation

La maestra greets the class and then Rosco with **Buenas tardes** (*Good afternoon*) and they have the opening conversation.

2. Reviewing the calendar and weather

La maestra asks questions that Rosco and the class answer.

¿Qué tiempo hace en enero?	What's the weather like in January?
¿Qué día es?	What day of the week is it?
¿Cuál es la fecha?	What is the date?

3. Singing the "Months Rap"

La maestra sings the "Months Rap." For lyrics to the rap, see Lesson 12, Video Lesson, section 4.

4. Reviewing how to ask and answer about birthdays

La maestra models questions and answers for birthdays. Then she, Rosco, and the class answer with made-up dates (**M** = Maestra, **R** = Rosco, **C** = class):

| ¿Cuándo es tu cumpleaños? | When is your birthday? |
| Mi cumpleaños es el ___ de ___. | My birthday is ___. |

R: el siete de julio	July 7
M: el veintiuno de enero	January 21
R: el dieciséis de septiembre	September 16
el veinte de diciembre	December 20
C: el veintiuno de febrero	February 21
el once de marzo	March 11

5. Expressing age

La maestra models questions and answers for age.

| ¿Cuántos años tienes (tú)? | How old are you? |
| Tengo ___ años. | I am ___ years old. |

6. Reviewing numbers 11 to 20

La maestra models each number and the class repeats it. Then she asks the class **¿Qué número es?** (*What number is it?*) about various numbers and models the answers.

11	once	16	dieciséis
12	doce	17	diecisiete
13	trece	18	dieciocho
14	catorce	19	diecinueve
15	quince	20	veinte

7. Reviewing numbers to 50 by tens

La maestra models each number and the class repeats them. Next, she and the class play **Muéstrame ___** (*Show me ___*) with these numbers. Then she asks the class **¿Qué número es?** about them.

10	diez	40	cuarenta
20	veinte	50	cincuenta
30	treinta		

Lastly, **la maestra** shows children a series of numbers, asks **¿Qué número es?**, and models the responses.

11	once	13	trece
21	veintiuno	18	dieciocho
20	veinte	40	cuarenta
15	quince	50	cincuenta

8. Closing

La maestra talks about how the children are all growing to become the people they will be as adults. She points out that as amazing as it seems, some day they will say **Tengo quince años** (*I am 15 years old*) about themselves.

After viewing the video, praise the children for their good listening and watching skills.

Lesson Thirty-One

ACTIVITY LESSON

Activity 31A: ¿Cuántos años tienes tú? (*How old are you?*)

Materials: Cassette player; Activity Cassette 2, Side A; and Rosco flag.

Explain that in this cassette activity, **la maestra** is going to ask **¿Cuántos años tienes tú?** (*How old are you?*). Stop the tape at the sound of the harp and hand the Rosco flag to someone, so children know who should answer next. Since **la maestra** only asks the question three times, repeat this activity if possible, so that many children may answer.

Activity 31B: ¿Cuándo es tu cumpleaños? (*When is your birthday?*)

Materials: Cassette player; Activity Cassette 2, Side A; list of children's birthdays; and children's birthday calendars from Activity 21C, if possible.

If children did not make calendars showing their birthdays for Activity 21C, you may want to have the class make them now.

Tell the class that **la maestra** is going to ask **¿Cuándo es tu cumpleaños?** (*When is your birthday?*) in this activity. If children have calendars for the activity, ask them to show the dates when they respond orally to the questions. For months, see Lesson 29, Warm-up section. For numbers 1–31, see Activity 20C. Repeat this activity, if possible, since **la maestra** only asks the question three times.

IF YOU HAVE TIME...

Materials: As many balls as groups.

Divide the class into two or more groups and give each one a ball. Tell the class that they are going to count from **once** (*11*) to **veinte** (*20*) as they bounce the ball to one another. The first child says **once**. Each time a child bounces the ball, he or she should name the next number. After children count to *20*, have them count by tens to *50*. Repeat the activity if there is time.

Activity 31C: How are numbers alike and different?

Materials: Hundred Chart or chalkboard and chalk.

Preparation: Display a Hundred Chart or write these numbers on the chalkboard.

	1	2	3	4	5	6	7	8	9
10	11	12	13	14	15	16	17	18	19
20	21	22	23	24	25	26	27	28	29
30	31	32	33	34	35	36	37	38	39
40	41	42	43	44	45	46	47	48	49
50									

Discuss how numbers are alike or different in English and in Spanish. Focus on sounds first.

Show children how both in English and in Spanish ones can help them remember teens.

6 (six)	16 (sixteen)	6 (seis)	16 (dieciséis)
7 (seven)	17 (seventeen)	7 (siete)	17 (diecisiete)
8 (eight)	18 (eighteen)	8 (ocho)	18 (dieciocho)
9 (nine)	19 (nineteen)	9 (nueve)	19 (diecinueve)

Then demonstrate how <u>end sounds</u> in English and <u>beginning sounds</u> in Spanish help remember succeeding numbers.

13	thir<u>teen</u>		
14	four<u>teen</u>		
15	fif<u>teen</u>		
16	six<u>teen</u>	16	<u>dieci</u>séis
17	seven<u>teen</u>	17	<u>dieci</u>siete
18	eigh<u>teen</u>	18	<u>dieci</u>ocho
19	nine<u>teen</u>	19	<u>dieci</u>nueve

Then talk about how the numbers 21–50 are named in a similar manner in both languages—by naming the tens and then the ones. Ask volunteers to name samples—both within a ten, such as 24, 25, and 26, and across the tens, such as 24, 34, and 44. For numbers 1–31, see Activity 20C.

> If your class completed Activity 28C, start here. If not, you may wish to finish it before starting this one.

> *Numbers 32–39, 41–49:*
>
> 32 treinta y dos
> 33 treinta y tres
> 34 treinta y cuatro
> 35 treinta y cinco
> 36 treinta y seis
> 37 treinta y siete
> 38 treinta y ocho
> 39 treinta y nueve
> 41 cuarenta y uno
> 42 cuarenta y dos
> 43 cuarenta y tres
> 44 cuarenta y cuatro
> 45 cuarenta y cinco
> 46 cuarenta y seis
> 47 cuarenta y siete
> 48 cuarenta y ocho
> 49 cuarenta y nueve

CLOSING

Tell the children that Spanish class is finished for today. Next time they are going to learn names for people who work in schools.

Lesson Thirty-One

Lesson 32

Materials to gather

- VCR and Video Lesson 32 on Tape 8
- Cassette player
- Activity Cassette 2
- Song Cassette
- **Estoy muy mal** (*I feel very bad*) mask from Activity 9B
- Hand puppets Rosco and Dora
- Blackline Master 22A (rooms in school plus **la maestra**)
- Scissors
- Rosco flag(s)
- Gold Flashcards 48–50, 62–64
- Season flashcards from Activity 29B
- Tape
- *Optional materials:* Gold Flashcards 1–2; Number Cards 1–9, 30, 40; 18 sheets of paper; and marker

Objectives

Language
- Learn vocabulary for school personnel

Culture
- Use expressions of politeness, such as **Lo siento** (*I'm sorry*) and **Gracias** (*Thank you*)

Review
- Respond to questions about numbers, weather, and seasons
- Review the numbers 10, 20, 30, 40, 50
- Sing **"Las estaciones"** (*"The Seasons"*)
- Practice vocabulary for places in a school

Vocabulary

la maestra	(*female*) teacher
el maestro	(*male*) teacher
la directora	(*female*) principal
el director	(*male*) principal
la secretaria	(*female*) secretary
el secretario	(*male*) secretary
el enfermero	(*male*) nurse
la enfermera	(*female*) nurse

Warm-up

Materials: **Estoy muy mal** (*I feel bad*) mask from Activity 9B; Rosco and Dora hand puppets; and Gold Flashcards 1–2 (optional).

Ask children what **la maestra** said when Rosco was sick—*I'm sorry* (**Lo siento**). If you feel comfortable, use the face mask to say **Estoy muy mal** (*I feel bad*) and have a child respond with **Lo siento.** If a volunteer takes your place, have him/her use a Gold Flashcard to indicate the role of teacher. Repeat the process as Dora and then Rosco, and have the class answer.

Review

Materials: **Estoy muy mal** (*I feel bad*) mask; Gold Flashcards 1–2 (optional).

Explain that you are going to say you feel **muy mal** (*very bad*) in this opening conversation. Remind children to say **lo siento** in return and you will say thanks (**gracias**) to them. If you feel uncomfortable in this role, ask a volunteer to take your part. Tell him or her to use a Flashcard to denote his or her role as teacher (**T** = Teacher, **C** = child):

T: Buenos días/Buenas tardes, clase.	*Good morning/Good afternoon, class.*
C: Buenos días/Buenas tardes, Maestro/Maestra.	*Good morning/Good afternoon, Teacher.*
T: ¿Cómo estás tú?	*How are you?*
C: Muy bien, gracias. ¿Y usted?	*Very well, thank you. And you?*
T: Muy mal.	*Very bad.*
C: Lo siento.	*I'm sorry.*
T: Gracias.	*Thank you.*

Introduce the video

Explain that children are going to learn names for people who work in a school.

VIDEO LESSON

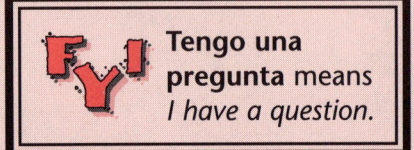

1. Greeting the class

Using **buenos días** as a greeting, **la maestra** has the opening conversation with Jorge and then with the class. She ends it by saying **Estoy muy bien porque estoy aquí con ustedes y con mi amigo Jorge.** (*I am very well because I am here with you and with my friend Jorge.*)

2. Reviewing numbers, weather, and seasons

La maestra asks a series of questions, and Jorge and the class answer.

¿Qué número es?	*What number is it?*
quince	*15*
catorce	*14*
treinta y ocho	*38*
¿Qué tiempo hace?	*What's the weather like?*
Hace frío. Nieva.	*It's cold. It's snowing.*
Hace viento.	*It's windy.*
¿Qué estación es?	*What season is it?*
el invierno	*winter*
el verano	*summer*

3. Playing *Muéstrame* ___ (*Show me* ___) with numbers to 50

La maestra models each number and plays **Muéstrame** ___. Then she asks **¿Qué número es?** (*What number is it?*) about them.

10	diez	*40*	cuarenta
20	veinte	*50*	cincuenta
30	treinta		

4. Singing "Las estaciones" (*"The Seasons"*)

La maestra asks the class to sing along to **"Las estaciones."** For song lyrics, see Lesson 27, Video Lesson, section 7.

FYI **Tengo una pregunta** means *I have a question.*

5. Integrating seasons and weather

La maestra asks the class to identify each season, and then she comments on it.

¿Qué estación es?	What season is it?
El invierno—En el invierno hace frío.	Winter—In winter, it's cold.
La primavera—En la primavera hace buen tiempo.	Spring—In spring, it's good weather.
El verano—En el verano hace calor.	Summer—In summer, it's hot.
El otoño—En el otoño hace viento.	Autumn—In autumn, it's windy.

6. Reviewing vocabulary for places in a school

La maestra describes actions in English and Jorge tells her in Spanish which place in a school one would go to perform that action.

7. Revisiting the school

La maestra takes the class on another tour of the school.

8. Playing ¿Dónde está la maestra? (Where is the teacher?)

La maestra models the names for places in a school. Then doña Elena asks the class to name each location in which they see **la maestra**.

la biblioteca	library
la cafetería	cafeteria
la oficina	office
el baño	bathroom
la clase	classroom
el patio	playground

9. Introducing vocabulary for school personnel

La maestra models each word and children repeat after her.

la maestra	(female) teacher
el maestro	(male) teacher
la directora	(female) principal
el director	(male) principal
la secretaria	(female) secretary
el secretario	(male) secretary
el enfermero	(male) nurse
la enfermera	(female) nurse

10. Closing

La maestra says **Adiós** (Good-bye) to the class.

After viewing the video, praise the children for their good listening and watching skills.

Lesson Thirty-Two

Blackline Master 22A

Answers:

el patio	playground
la cafetería	cafeteria
la biblioteca	library
la oficina	office
el baño	bathroom
la clase	classroom

LEVEL TWO

ACTIVITY LESSON

Activity 32A: Did *la maestra* say where she was going?

Materials: Cassette player; Activity Cassette 2, Side A; Blackline Master 22A; and scissors.

Preparation: Make a copy of Blackline Master 22A for each child.

Have children cut out the playing piece of **la maestra.** Then make sure that the class knows what each picture represents. Explain that the cassette teacher is going to tell children to **pon** (*put*) **la maestra** in different rooms.

Activity 32B: Where would you go . . . ?

Materials: Cassette player; Activity Cassette 2, Side A; Blackline Master 22A; and Rosco flag(s).

Preparation: If possible, reuse the Blackline Masters from Activity 22A. If not, make a copy for each child.

If you have time to do this activity more than once, first ask the whole class to respond. The second time, have volunteers answer or ask individuals to respond. Use the Rosco flag(s) to identify players in the activity.

Explain that children are going to play the same game with **la maestra** that Jorge did. She is going to describe places in school where children can do a particular thing. The class should name each place in Spanish.

Activity 32C: Sing a song of seasons

Materials: Cassette player; **"Las estaciones"** (*"The Seasons"*) on Song Cassette, Side A; Gold Flashcards 48–50, 62–64; season flashcards from Activity 29B; and tape.

Preparation: Copy each month onto a separate sheet of paper if you have not already done so.

Organize the season flashcards in a stack with winter on the top. Display the Gold Flashcards for December through November in groups according to their seasons on the chalkboard ledge. For lyrics to **"Las estaciones"** (*"The Seasons"*), see Lesson 27, Video Lesson, section 7.

Emphasize how much the class already knows in this song and have children name the months in Spanish. Then ask children to listen to the song as you play it once.

Next, play the first pair of lines, and ask the class to sing them. Have one volunteer explain what the children have just sung. Ask another volunteer to tape the flashcard for **el invierno** above **diciembre, enero,** and **febrero** and then draw lines from winter to each month to show that these three months are all part of winter. Follow the same process for **en la primavera** (*in spring*), **en el verano** (*in summer*), and **en el otoño** (*in autumn*).

Once you're done with this process, have the class sing the entire song once more straight through.

CLOSING

Tell the children that Spanish class is finished for today. In the next class, they are going to practice numbers and the words for people who work at a school.

Throughout this activity, hold up the relevant season card or point to the appropriate month Gold Flashcard as it is mentioned in **"Las estaciones."** The visuals help children to associate words and meaning.

IF YOU HAVE TIME...

Materials: Number Cards for 1–9, 30, 40; 18 sheets of paper; a marker; and tape (optional). If you did the *If you have time...* activity in Lesson 29, you may have "number cards" for 31–39.

Preparation: Write numbers 31–39 and 41–49 on separate sheets of paper. Order the numbers in rows of 1–9, 31–39, and 41–49 as on a Hundred Chart. Display them where everyone can see them.

Before beginning the game, you may want to have the entire class read all or some of the numbers on the chalkboard aloud as you point to them.

Divide the class in half. In turn, have children from each group touch and name any number they choose. When an answer is correct, the child keeps the number. Play continues until all the numbers have been named.

Lesson 33

Materials to gather

- VCR and Video Lesson 33 on Tape 9
- Cassette player
- Activity Cassette 2
- Song Cassette
- Gold Flashcards 1, 2, and 65–67
- Number Cards 10–50
- Blackline Master 33B (male and female cutouts)
- Hand puppet Dora
- *Optional materials:* laminating equipment; sticks or straws for mounting paper figures; drawing paper and crayons

OBJECTIVES

Language
- Practice vocabulary for school personnel

Culture
- Understand that names for occupations in Spanish indicate whether the person is male or female

Review
- Recall vocabulary for numbers 10–50

Vocabulary

No new vocabulary is introduced in this lesson.

Warm-up

Materials: Gold Flashcards 1, 2, and 65–67.

Hold up Flashcards 1 and 2 and ask the children to name them (**la maestra, el maestro**). Then ask the children to name some of the other people who work at their school, such as the principal, the secretary, and the nurse. Hold up Flashcards 65–67 to show these jobs.

Review

Materials: Number Cards for 10, 20, 30, 40, 50.

Tell the children that **la maestra** is going to review some numbers today. Then hold up the Number Cards one at a time. If you are comfortable doing so, ask **¿Qué número es?** (*What number is it?*).

10	diez
20	veinte
30	treinta
40	cuarenta
50	cincuenta

Introduce the video

Tell the children that **la maestra** and Dora are going to help them practice some names for people who work at their school.

Video Lesson

1. Greeting Dora and the children

La maestra holds the opening conversation with the children, then with Dora (**M** = Maestra, **D** = Dora, **C** = class):

M:	Buenos días, clase/ Dora.	*Good morning, class/ Dora.*
C/D:	Buenos días, Maestra.	*Good morning, Teacher.*
M:	¿Cómo estás tú?	*How are you?*
C/D:	Muy bien, gracias. ¿Y usted?	*Very well, thank you. And you?*
M:	Muy bien, gracias.	*Very well, thank you.*

2. Reviewing numbers

La maestra asks the children **¿Qué número es?** (*What number is it?*) and holds up number cards 10 (**diez**), 11 (**once**), 15 (**quince**), 16 (**dieciséis**), and 18 (**dieciocho**) for Dora and the class to read.

3. Practicing vocabulary for school personnel

La maestra models the vocabulary for school personnel. As part of the practice, she introduces and contrasts the difference between the male and female forms of the nouns. **La maestra** then plays a game of **¿Quién es?** (*Who is it?*) as she holds up Flashcards of school personnel for Dora to name.

4. Practicing more numbers

La maestra holds up number cards to review **diez** (*10*), **once** (*11*), **doce** (*12*), **trece** (*13*), **catorce** (*14*), **quince** (*15*), **dieciséis** (*16*), **diecisiete** (*17*), **dieciocho** (*18*), **diecinueve** (*19*), **veinte** (*20*), **treinta** (*30*), **cuarenta** (*40*), and **cincuenta** (*50*). She then shows the children the **números grandes** (*big numbers*) 10–50, whose names she asks them to repeat (**repite**). **La maestra** plays a game of **Muéstrame ___** (*Show me ___*) with these numbers, asking the children to point to the numbers she names. She then plays **¿Qué número es?** (*What number is it?*).

School personnel:

la maestra	(*female*) *teacher*
el maestro	(*male*) *teacher*
la directora	(*female*) *principal*
el director	(*male*) *principal*
la secretaria	(*female*) *secretary*
el secretario	(*male*) *secretary*
el enfermero	(*male*) *nurse*
la enfermera	(*female*) *nurse*

EN ESPAÑOL

You may want to use the command **repite** (*repeat*) during classwork with the children.

LEVEL TWO

5. Playing a game

Me gusta contar (*I like to count*), says Dora, and **la maestra** agrees by saying, **Me encanta contar** (*I love to count*). **La maestra** plays **¿Qué número es?** (*What number is it?*) by holding up number cards in this order for Dora and the children to name:

48	cuarenta y ocho
31	treinta y uno
33	treinta y tres
29	veintinueve
25	veinticinco
50	cincuenta
47	cuarenta y siete

La maestra says that the children will keep on practicing numbers because they are so useful.

6. Practicing new vocabulary

¡Vamos a jugar! (*Let's play!*) says **la maestra** before reviewing the names of school personnel. She and the children then play **Muéstrame ___** (*Show me ___*) with pictures of these employees. Holding up Flashcards, she then asks Dora and the children to answer **sí o no** (*yes or no*) to the following questions:

¿Es ___?	Is it ___?
¿Es ___ o es ___?	Is it ___ or is it ___?

7. Closing

La maestra and Dora bid the class **Adiós** (*Good-bye*).

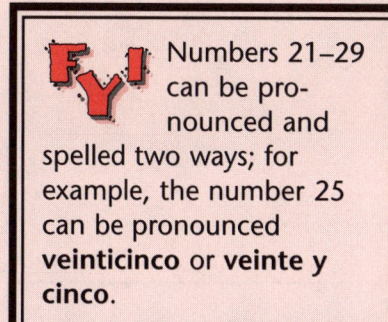

FYI Numbers 21–29 can be pronounced and spelled two ways; for example, the number 25 can be pronounced **veinticinco** or **veinte y cinco**.

FYI **Éstas son las personas que trabajan en la escuela** means *These are the people who work at the school.*

After viewing the video, praise the children for their good listening and watching skills.

Lesson Thirty-Three

ACTIVITY LESSON

Activity 33A: *Anda, corre, salta* (*Walk, run, jump*)

Materials: Cassette player; Activity Cassette 2, Side A; and Gold Flashcards 1, 2, 65–67.

Display the Flashcards where the children can see and reach them. Tell the children that **la maestra** is going to ask individual children to walk (**anda**), run (**corre**), or jump (**salta**) to the Flashcard she names and then to touch it (**toca**). Explain that you will point to a child, and he or she is to do what **la maestra** says.

La maestra calls out the picture names in the following order: **el maestro, la directora, la secretaria, la maestra.**

Activity 33B: Male or female?

Materials: Cassette player; Activity Cassette 2, Side A; Blackline Master 33B; *optional:* laminating equipment; sticks or straws for mounting figures.

Preparation: Duplicate Blackline Master 33B so that each child has one male and one female figure. You may want to laminate the figures for use throughout the program and mount them on sticks or straws.

Remind the children that the words they have learned for people who work at their school can name either female or male people. For example, **el maestro** refers to a *male teacher* and **la maestra** to a *female teacher*. Tell the children that **la maestra** is going to say some of these words. If the word refers to a female person, they should hold up the female figure. If the word refers to a male person, they should hold up the male figure.

La maestra calls out the names in the following order: **la secretaria** (*female*), **el maestro** (*male*), **la enfermera** (*female*), **el director** (*male*), **el secretario** (*male*).

Blackline Master 33B

✓ Observe the children's responses to be sure they grasp the distinction between male and female nouns.

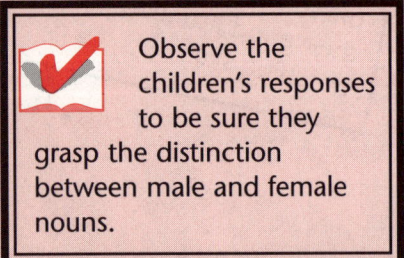

You may want to ask the class to say **sí** or **no** to show whether they agree with their classmates' choice of Flashcards.

Activity 33C: Sing a favorite song

Materials: Cassette player; Song Cassette.

Brainstorm with the children the names of some of the songs they have learned in Spanish, such as **"Las estaciones"** (*"The Seasons"*), **"Uno, dos, tres burritos"** (*"One, Two, Three Little Burros"*), **"Vengan a ver mi rancho"** (*"Come See My Ranch"*), and **"Español para ti"** (*"Spanish Is for You, and for Me"*). Have them vote on and then sing their favorite song.

CLOSING

Tell the children that Spanish class is finished for today. In the next class they will go to a school and visit some of the people who work there. Then ask a volunteer to put on the hand puppet Dora for the closing conversation with the class (**D** = Dora, **C** = class):

D: Adiós, clase.   *Good-bye, class.*
C: Adiós, Dora.   *Good-bye, Dora.*

IF YOU HAVE TIME...

Materials: Drawing paper and crayons for each child.

Encourage each child to draw a picture of a teacher, the principal, the secretary, or the nurse in their school. When they have finished, display the pictures on the bulletin board. Then point to each picture and ask **¿Quién es?** or *Who is it?* The children should reply using one of the words from this lesson: **es el maestro** or **la maestra** (*it is the* [male or female] *teacher*); **es el director** or **la directora** (*it is the* [male or female] *principal*), **es el enfermero** or **la enfermera** (*it is the* [male or female] *nurse*), or **es la secretaria** or **el secretario** (*it is the* [female or male] *secretary*).

Lesson Thirty-Three

Lesson 34

Materials to gather

- VCR and Video Lesson 34 on Tape 9
- Cassette player
- Activity Cassette 2
- Song Cassette
- Gold Flashcards 1, 2, and 65–67
- Blackline Master 34A (seasons and weather)
- A pencil for each child

OBJECTIVES

Language

- Understand sustained conversation in Spanish about the work of school personnel

Culture

- Understand the important role of the people who work at school

Review

- Recall the names of the seasons
- Recall phrases expressing weather
- Recall vocabulary related to school personnel and where they work
- Sing **"Español para ti"** (*"Spanish Is for You, and for Me"*) and **"Las estaciones"** (*"The Seasons"*)

Vocabulary

No new vocabulary is introduced in this lesson.

Warm-up

Remind the children that when they don't know what a word means, they can listen and look for clues. Offer this sentence as an example: *In the summer the foliage on the trees is green.* Ask what *foliage* means. Lead the children to conclude that words such as *trees* and *green* tell them that it means *leaves*.

Review

Point out to the children that they know many words that name things they see in school every day. Hold up or point to various items and, if you are comfortable doing so, ask **¿Qué es?** (*What is it?*). Otherwise, simply point to various objects and encourage the children to name them.

Introduce the video

Tell the children that in this lesson they are going to hear a lot of conversation in Spanish. Suggest that listening carefully and watching what people are doing will help them understand.

la bandera	*flag*
el calendario	*calendar*
el escritorio	*desk*
el globo	*globe*
el lápiz	*pencil*
el libro	*book*
el mapa	*map*
la mesa	*table*
el papel	*paper*
la pizarra	*chalkboard*
la regla	*ruler*
el reloj	*clock*
la silla	*chair*
la tiza	*chalk*

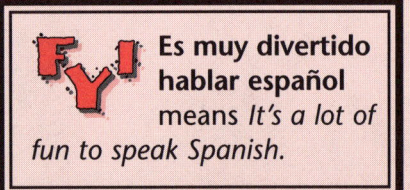

> **Es muy divertido hablar español** means *It's a lot of fun to speak Spanish.*

Months of the year:

enero	January
febrero	February
marzo	March
abril	April
mayo	May
junio	June
julio	July
agosto	August
septiembre	September
octubre	October
noviembre	November
diciembre	December

VIDEO LESSON

1. Greeting Rosco and the children

La maestra says **buenos días** (*good morning*) to Rosco. Using face masks as cues she asks him, **¿Estás muy mal o estás muy bien?** (*Do you feel very bad or are you fine?*) Rosco replies, **Estoy muy bien** (*I'm fine*). **La maestra** and the children then have the opening conversation (M = Maestra, C = class):

M: Buenos días, niños.	*Good morning, children.*
C: Buenos días, Maestra.	*Good morning, Teacher.*
M: ¿Cómo estás tú?	*How are you?*
C: Muy bien, gracias. ¿Y usted?	*Very well, thank you. And you?*
M: Muy bien, gracias.	*Very well, thank you.*

2. Singing a song

La maestra and Rosco sing "**Español para ti**" (*"Spanish Is for You, and for Me"*). For song lyrics, see Lesson 3, Video Lesson, section 3.

3. Reviewing months and seasons

Asking **¿Qué mes es?** (*What month is it?*) and **¿Qué estación es?** (*What season is it?*), **la maestra** reviews the seasons and months of the year as well as weather associated with some of them.

la primavera	*spring*
el verano—hace calor	*summer—it's hot*
el otoño—hace viento	*fall—it's windy*
el invierno—hace frío	*winter—it's cold*

4. Singing another song

La maestra leads the children in singing "**Las estaciones**" (*"The Seasons"*). For song lyrics, see Lesson 27, Video Lesson, section 7. She then shows Rosco pictures depicting times of the year and asks **¿Qué estación es?** (*What season is it?*).

5. Looking for Rosco

Rosco is missing! **¿Dónde está Rosco?** (*Where is Rosco?*), asks **la maestra. Estoy aquí** (*Here I am*), answers Rosco as he comes out of hiding.

LEVEL TWO

6. Reviewing rooms in the school

La maestra then plays **¿Dónde está ___?** (*Where is ___?*) with Rosco by showing Flashcards of school personnel and asking where the person is.

La maestra (el maestro) está en la clase.	*The (female) teacher [(male) teacher] is in the classroom.*
La directora está en la oficina.	*The (female) principal is in the office.*
La secretaria está en la oficina.	*The (female) secretary is in the office.*
El enfermero está en la oficina.	*The (male) nurse is in the office.*

7. Playing ¿Dónde está la maestra? (*Where is the teacher?*)

"Let's have some fun," says **la maestra**, prompting the children to say whether **la maestra está en la biblioteca** (*the teacher is in the library*), **el baño** (*the bathroom*), **la oficina** (*the office*), **la cafetería** (*the cafeteria*), **el patio** (*the playground*), or **la clase** (*the classroom*).

8. Visiting a school

La maestra leads the children on a tour of a school, where she chats with **la secretaria** (*the secretary*), who has **muchas cosas que hacer** (*a lot to do*); **la enfermera** (*the nurse*), who **es muy importante cuando los niños en la escuela están mal** (*is very important when the children in the school don't feel well*); **una maestra** (*a teacher*), in whose class **los niños trabajan mucho** (*the children work a lot*); and **la directora** (*the principal*), who says that **los niños son lo más importante en el mundo** (*the children are the most important things in the world*).

> **FYI** After leaving the school **la maestra** exclaims **¡Qué divertido fue!** which means *That was a lot of fun!*

9. Playing ¿Cuál falta? (*What's missing?*)

La maestra asks the children which of several pictures of school personnel is missing.

10. Closing

La maestra asks Rosco why the people she spoke with work at the school. He answers, **porque les gustan los niños** (*because they like children*). **La maestra** and Rosco then say **Adiós**.

> After viewing the video, praise the children for their good listening and watching skills.

Lesson Thirty-Four

Blackline Master 34A

ACTIVITY LESSON

Activity 34A: What's the weather?

Materials: Cassette player; Activity Cassette 2, Side A; Blackline Master 34A; and pencils.

Preparation: Duplicate Blackline Master 34A so that each child has a copy. Give each child a pencil.

Ask the children to name the weather represented by the pictures in the first column (*hot, cold, raining, windy*). Then ask them to name the seasons represented by the pictures in the second column (*winter, spring, summer, fall*). Tell them that **la maestra** is going to tell them the weather that goes with a certain season. They are to draw a line from the weather shown in the first column to the season it goes with in the second column.

Activity 34B: ¿Quién es? (*Who is it?*)

Materials: Cassette player; Activity Cassette 2, Side A; and Gold Flashcards 1, 2, and 65–67.

Arrange the Flashcards in numerical order. Tell the children that you are going to hold up the pictures of people who work in the school, one at a time. As you hold up each picture, **la maestra** is going to ask ¿Quién es? (*Who is it?*) twice. After the second time, they are to name the person in the picture in Spanish. Use **la maestra's** cues to hold up the pictures in order. For added practice, you may want to play the activity two or more times.

Activity 34C: Sing along

Materials: Cassette player; **"Español para ti"** (*"Spanish Is for You, and for Me"*) and **"Las estaciones"** (*"The Seasons"*) on the Song Cassette.

Encourage the children to sing along with these songs. For song lyrics, see Lesson 3, Video Lesson, section 3 and Lesson 27, Video Lesson, section 7, respectively.

You may want to play each song once before asking the children to sing along.

LEVEL TWO

Closing

Tell the children that **la clase de español** is finished for today. In the next class they will review some expressions for feelings as well as other vocabulary.

> **If You Have Time...**
>
> Materials: VCR and Video Lesson 34 on Tape 9.
>
> Replay **la maestra**'s visit to the school in the Video Lesson, stopping the tape after each conversation with a school employee. During each pause, lead a discussion about the conversation. Did **la maestra** use **tú** or **usted** with the person? Why? What did **la maestra** say when she shook someone's hand? (**Mucho gusto.**) What do they think this means? (*Pleased to meet you.*) What did the children learn about each person's job?

Lesson Thirty-Four

Lesson 35

Materials to gather

- VCR and Video Lesson 35 on Tape 9
- Cassette player
- Activity Cassette 2
- Song Cassette
- Hand puppet Dora
- Blackline Master 35A (pictures of school personnel)
- Scissors
- Gold Flashcards 41–47

- **Optional materials:** paper cutter

OBJECTIVES

Language
- Match appropriate expressions containing **tener** with pictures showing weather
- Associate items of clothing with weather

Culture
- Understand that weather determines what clothes we wear

Review
- Recall vocabulary for items of clothing
- Understand vocabulary for school personnel
- Recall the names of months and seasons
- Sing **"Las estaciones"** (*"The Seasons"*) and **"La ropa"** (*"Clothing"*)

Vocabulary

Tengo frío.	*I'm cold.*
Tengo calor.	*I'm hot.*

Warm-up

Use the hand puppet Dora to have the opening conversation with the children (**D** = Dora, **C** = class):

D: Buenos días, clase.	*Good morning, class.*
C: Buenos días, Dora.	*Good morning, Dora.*
D: ¿Cómo estás tú?	*How are you?*
C: Muy bien (Muy mal; Así, así), gracias. ¿Y tú?	*Fine (Very bad, So-so), thanks. And you?*
D: Muy bien, gracias.	*Fine, thank you.*

Review

Review the other greetings by asking the children how to greet someone in the afternoon (**Buenas tardes**) and evening (**Buenas noches**).

Introduce the video

Invite the children to listen and watch as **la maestra** and Dora talk about seasons, weather, and clothing.

> You may want to ask a volunteer to play the part of Dora.

VIDEO LESSON

1. Greeting Dora and the children

Using **Buenas tardes** (*Good afternoon*) as the greeting, **la maestra** has the opening conversation with Dora and then with the children. **La maestra**'s statement **Estoy perfecta porque estoy aquí con ustedes y con nuestra amiga, Dora** means *I'm just great because I'm here with you and with our friend, Dora.*

> **FYI:** **Ustedes** is used as the plural form of both **tú** and **usted** (singular *you*).

2. Singing a song

Vamos a cantar (*Let's sing*), says Dora. **La maestra** then sings "**Las estaciones**" ("*The Seasons*"). For the song lyrics, see Lesson 27, Video Lesson, section 7.

3. Playing ¿Qué estación es? (What season is it?)

La maestra and Dora review the four seasons and associated weather expressions.

¿Qué tiempo hace en ... ?	*What is the weather in . . . ?*
Hace buen tiempo en la primavera.	*The weather is good in the spring.*
Hace calor en el verano.	*It's hot in the summer.*
Hace viento en el otoño.	*It's windy in the fall.*
Hace frío en el invierno.	*It's cold in the winter.*

> **FYI:** In talking about winter, Dora says **Hace frío y nieva** (*It's cold and it snows*).

4. Reviewing weather expressions

Vamos a jugar (*Let's play*), says Dora. **La maestra** continues to review the names of seasons and expressions of weather.

5. Reviewing expressions of physical feelings

Vamos a mirar (*Let's look*), says **la maestra**. The mime then demonstrates the expressions **Tengo calor** (*I'm hot*) and **Tengo frío** (*I'm cold*). **La maestra** ties these in with weather expressions: **En el invierno, cuando hace frío, tengo frío.** (*In winter, when it's cold, I'm cold.*) **Cuando hace calor, tengo calor.** (*When it's hot, I'm hot.*)

6. Reviewing vocabulary for clothing

Noting that the weather determines what clothes we wear, **la maestra** begins a review of vocabulary for clothing. She asks Dora, **¿Qué necesitas cuando dices, "Tengo frío?"** (*What do you need when you say, "I'm cold"?*). Dora answers, **Necesito una chaqueta** (*I need a jacket*). **La maestra** then sings "**La ropa**" ("*Clothing*") and holds up Flashcards to review the names of articles of clothing. For the lyrics to "**La ropa**," see Lesson 30, Video Lesson, section 8.

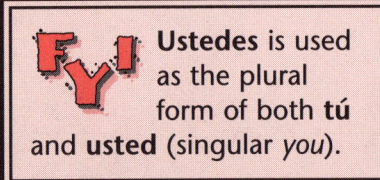

Vocabulary practiced:

la chaqueta	*jacket*
el pijama	*pajamas*
la blusa	*blouse*
el vestido	*dress*

7. Reviewing vocabulary for school personnel

Asking ¿**Quién es?** (*Who is it?*) as she holds up Flashcards, **la maestra** reviews the names of school personnel in this order:

el enfermero	*(male) nurse*
la maestra	*(female) teacher*
el maestro	*(male) teacher*
la directora	*(female) principal*
la secretaria	*(female) secretary*

8. Playing ¿*Cuál falta?* (*What's missing?*)

La maestra asks the children which of several pictures of school personnel is missing.

9. Singing "Las estaciones" (*"The Seasons"*)

La maestra reviews the seasons and months by singing "**Las estaciones**" (*"The Seasons"*). For song lyrics, see Lesson 27, Video Lesson, section 7.

10. Playing ¿*Quién es?* (*Who is it?*)

Using Flashcards showing school personnel, **la maestra** asks Dora, ¿**Quién es?** (*Who is it?*). She then asks the children, ¿**Es ___ o es ___?** (*Is it ___ or is it ___?*). Finally, she names the Flashcards and asks the children to **repite** (*repeat*).

11. Closing

After reviewing some of the topics covered in today's lesson, **la maestra** reminds the children that they have learned many things in Spanish. She and Dora then say **Adiós** (*Good-bye*).

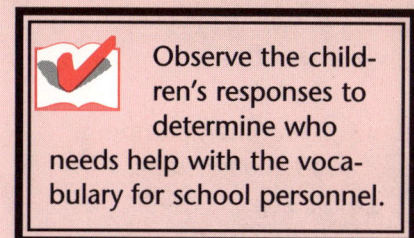

Observe the children's responses to determine who needs help with the vocabulary for school personnel.

After viewing the video, praise the children for their good listening and watching skills.

Lesson Thirty-Five

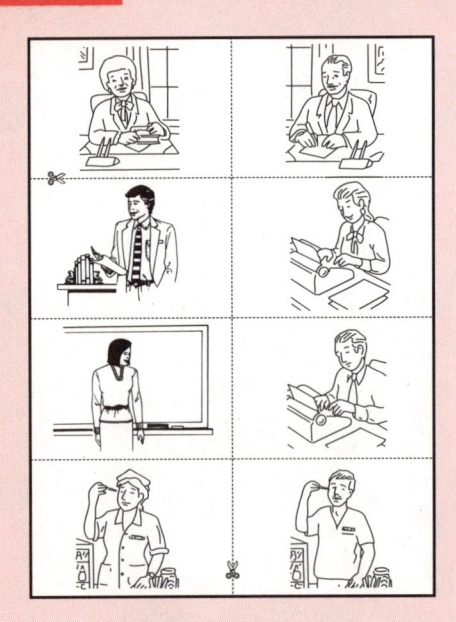

Blackline Master 35A

Flashcards:

41 Hace sol. Hace calor.
    It's sunny. It's hot.
42 Hace frío.
    It's cold.
43 Hace buen tiempo.
    It's good weather.
44 Llueve.
    It's raining.
45 Nieva. Hace frío.
    It's snowing. It's cold.
46 Hace viento.
    It's windy.
47 Hace mal tiempo.
    It's bad weather.

EN ESPAÑOL

You may want to introduce Activity 35C by saying, **¡Vamos a cantar!** (*Let's sing!*).

ACTIVITY LESSON

Activity 35A: School personnel

Materials: Cassette player; Activity Cassette 2, Side B; Blackline Master 35A; and scissors or paper cutter.

Preparation: Duplicate Blackline Master 35A so that each child has a copy. Then give a pair of scissors to each child or pair of children and have them cut out the pictures or cut them yourself with a paper cutter.

Tell the children that **la maestra** is going to ask them to hold up each picture that she names. Warn them that they will have to listen carefully so that they know whether to hold up a picture of a man or a picture of a woman. Monitor the activity to be sure children are responding correctly. You may want to repeat the activity.

Activity 35B: Talk about the weather

Materials: Gold Flashcards 41–47.

Display the Flashcards. Begin by reviewing the weather expressions depicted on each Flashcard: **¿Qué tiempo hace?** (*What's the weather like?*). Then ask the children in English to say which is their most and least favorite season. Encourage them to use the Spanish words for the seasons—**la primavera** (*spring*); **el verano** (*summer*); **el otoño** (*fall*); **el invierno** (*winter*).

Activity 35C: Let's sing

Materials: Cassette player; Song Cassette.

After playing **"Las estaciones"** (*"The Seasons"*) and **"La ropa"** (*"Clothing"*), lead the children in singing these songs. For lyrics, see Lesson 27, Video Lesson, section 7 and Lesson 30, Video Lesson, section 9, respectively. Alternatively, you may want to divide the class in half and assign one of the songs for each group to sing.

LEVEL TWO

CLOSING

Tell the children that Spanish class is finished for today. In the next class they will review the names of the months as well as sing a song about some of the months.

IF YOU HAVE TIME...

Materials: pictures from Blackline Master 35A.

Preparation: Divide the class into pairs. Be sure that each child has a set of pictures, randomly divided. Let the children play a matching game. Holding her or his pictures as if they were playing cards, each child in a pair should take turns drawing from the other player's hand. The goal is to get as many matching pictures as possible. As each picture is matched, the child should name the person shown. The child who matches all of her or his pictures first is the winner.

Lesson Thirty-Five

Lesson 36

Materials to gather

- VCR and Video Lesson 36 on Tape 9
- Cassette player
- Activity Cassette 2
- Calendar with large, easy-to-read dates
- Blackline Master 36A (pictures of dates and months)
- Gold Flashcards 1, 2, 65–67
- *Optional materials:* Song Cassette

OBJECTIVES

Language
- Respond to questions about the calendar
- Understand that **rápido** means *quickly* and **despacio** means *slowly*

Culture
- Sing "**Uno de enero**" (*"January First"*)

Review
- Recall vocabulary for days of the week and months of the year
- Demonstrate understanding of vocabulary for colors
- Recall the meanings of several commands combined with the adverbs **rápido** (*quickly*) and **despacio** (*slowly*)
- Recall numbers 1–10
- Understand vocabulary for school personnel

Vocabulary

rápido	*quickly*
despacio	*slowly*

Warm-up

Materials: Calendar with large, easy-to-read dates.

Ask a volunteer to point to a day of the week and name the date in English. Then name several holidays, point to them on the calendar, and ask the children to name their dates.

Review

Point out that a birthday is an important day in the year for most people. Review birthday expressions by asking a volunteer *How old are you?* in English, or in Spanish, if you feel comfortable (**¿Cuántos años tienes tú?**). If necessary, remind the child to reply, **Tengo ___ años** (*I'm ___ years old*). Then ask the children to pair up and take turns asking and answering the same question.

Introduce the video

Invite the children to listen and watch as **la maestra** and Rosco review the names of days of the week and months of the year.

Holidays you might name are New Year's Day (January 1), Independence Day (July 4th), Valentine's Day (February 14th), and May Day (May 1).

EN ESPAÑOL

You may want to use some of the following birthday expressions from Level 1 in your discussion of birthdays: **el cumpleaños** (*birthday*), **la fiesta** (*party*), **feliz cumpleaños** (*happy birthday*), **el regalo** (*gift*), **el globo** (*balloon*), and **la piñata** (*piñata*).

VIDEO LESSON

1. Greeting Rosco and the children

La maestra has the opening conversation with Rosco and then with the children (**M** = Maestra, **R** = Rosco, **C** = class):

M:	Buenos días, Rosco/clase.	*Good morning, Rosco/class.*
R/C:	Buenos días, Maestra.	*Good morning, Teacher.*
M:	¿Cómo estás tú?	*How are you?*
R/C:	Muy bien, gracias. ¿Y usted?	*Very well, thank you. And you?*
M:	Muy bien, gracias.	*Very well, thank you.*

2. Reviewing the calendar

La maestra asks **¿Qué es esto?** (*What is this?*) as she shows **el calendario** (*calendar*). After reviewing the days of the week she says, **Vamos a practicar los días de la semana** (*Let's practice the days of the week*) and recites the "Calendar Rap." For lyrics to the rap, see Lesson 12, Video Lesson, section 3.

3. Playing ¿Qué día es? (*What day is it?*)

La maestra and Rosco review some of the days of the week, saying **¡Olé!** (*Hurray!*) after each response from the children.

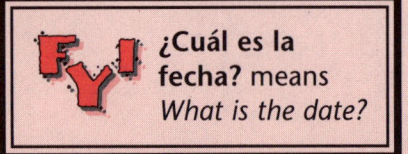

4. Reviewing colors

Showing colored **sombreros**, **la maestra** asks, **¿De qué color es?** (*What color is it?*). She reviews these colors: **anaranjado** (*orange*), **azul** (*blue*), **verde** (*green*), **rosado** (*pink*), and **amarillo** (*yellow*).

5. Reviewing the names of the months

La maestra asks **¿Qué mes es?** (*What month is it?*) as she shows pictures representing the names of the months.

6. Singing "Uno de enero" (*"January First"*)

La maestra says **Vamos a cantar** (*Let's sing*) before reviewing the names of the first seven months by singing **"Uno de enero"** (*"January First"*). For song lyrics, see Lesson 8, Video Lesson, section 3.

7. Reviewing dates

La maestra combines numbers and pictures representing months to review dates while she and Rosco sing **"Uno de enero."**

Days of the week:

lunes	Monday
martes	Tuesday
miércoles	Wednesday
jueves	Thursday
viernes	Friday
sábado	Saturday
domingo	Sunday

Months:

enero	January
febrero	February
marzo	March
abril	April
mayo	May
junio	June
julio	July
agosto	August
septiembre	September
octubre	October
noviembre	November
diciembre	December

FYI ¿Cuál es la fecha? means *What is the date?*

8. Reviewing commands

Vamos a mirar (*Let's look*), says **la maestra**. The mime demonstrates the words **anda** (*walk*) and **salta** (*jump*). **La maestra** ties these words in with the adverbs **rápido** (*quickly*) and **despacio** (*slowly*) and asks Rosco to **anda rápido** (*walk quickly*) and **salta despacio** (*jump slowly*).

9. Reviewing numbers 1 to 10

Vamos a contar rápido (*Let's count quickly*), invites **la maestra**. She then asks Rosco and the class to **cuenta rápido** (*count quickly*) and **cuenta despacio** (*count slowly*) from 1 to 10.

10. Reviewing vocabulary for school personnel

Asking **¿Quién es?** (*Who is it?*) as she holds up Flashcards, **la maestra** reviews the names of school personnel in this order: **la directora** (*female principal*), **la secretaria** (*female secretary*), **el enfermero** (*male nurse*), **la maestra** (*female teacher*), **el maestro** (*male teacher*). Then she says **Vamos a jugar** (*Let's play*), and plays a game of **¿Cuál falta?** (*What's missing?*) with pictures of school personnel.

11. Reviewing items of clothing and colors

Using Flashcards showing school personnel and pointing to articles of their clothing, **la maestra** asks Rosco and the children the following questions:

¿De qué color es la camisa del maestro? (azul)	*What color is the teacher's shirt? (blue)*
¿De qué color son los pantalones del maestro? (gris)	*What color are the teacher's pants? (gray)*
¿De qué color es la camisa del enfermero? (azul)	*What color is the nurse's shirt? (blue)*
¿De qué color son los pantalones del enfermero? (blanco)	*What color are the nurse's pants? (white)*
¿De qué color es la chaqueta de la directora? (azul)	*What color is the principal's jacket? (blue)*

12. Closing

After reviewing some of the topics covered in today's lesson, **la maestra** and Rosco say **Adiós** (*Good-bye*) and **Hasta la vista** (*Until we meet again*).

Numbers 1–10:

uno	one
dos	two
tres	three
cuatro	four
cinco	five
seis	six
siete	seven
ocho	eight
nueve	nine
diez	ten

After viewing the video, praise the children for their good listening and watching skills.

Lesson Thirty-Six

el 14 de	♥card
el 4 de	fireworks
el 17 de	shamrock
el 25 de	snowman

Blackline Master 36A

ACTIVITY LESSON

Activity 36A: ¿Cuál es la fecha? (*What is the date?*)

Materials: Cassette player; Activity Cassette 2, Side B; and Blackline Master 36A.

Preparation: Duplicate Blackline Master 36A so that each child has a copy.

Point out that the activity sheet has incomplete dates in the first column and pictures representing months in the second column. Explain that **la maestra** is going to ask them to put together each incomplete date and picture to make a complete date. After you review the names of the months represented by the pictures (*February*—**febrero**; *July*—**julio**; *March*—**marzo**; *December*—**diciembre**), play the activity. You may want to repeat it.

Activity 36B: Quickly and slowly

Materials: Cassette player; Activity Cassette 2, Side B; and Gold Flashcards 1, 2, and 65–67.

After you distribute the Flashcards among the children, ask each child to name the Flashcard he or she is holding. Tell them that **la maestra** is going to ask each child to **salta** (*jump*), **anda** (*walk*), or **corre** (*run*) **rápido** (*quickly*) or **despacio** (*slowly*) with each Flashcard she names. You may want to redistribute the Flashcards and play the activity several times.

LEVEL TWO

Activity 36C: Male or female?

Point out that the word **director** means a *male principal* and ask what the word is for a female principal (**directora**). Then tell them that **la maestra** is going to say some words for men who do certain jobs. After each word, the children should say the word that means that a woman does that job.

The teacher gives words in the following order (the answers follow in parentheses): **el maestro** (**la maestra**), **el director** (**la directora**), **el secretario** (**la secretaria**), **el enfermero** (**la enfermera**).

CLOSING

Tell the children that Spanish class is finished for today. In the next class they will visit a ranch with **la maestra**.

IF YOU HAVE TIME . . .

Materials: Cassette player; Song Cassette, Side A.

Play **"Uno de enero"** (*"January First"*) before asking the children to sing along. For song lyrics, see Lesson 8, Video Lesson, section 3.

Lesson 37

Materials to gather

- VCR and Video Lesson 37 on Tape 10
- Cassette player
- Activity Cassette 2
- Song Cassette
- Feeling masks from Activity 9B
- Gold Flashcards 20–27
- Drawing paper and crayons

- *Optional materials:* a large map of South America; pictures of llamas

OBJECTIVES

Language

- Learn vocabulary for animals
- Understand sustained conversation about several different animals

Culture

- Recognize that certain animals live in different parts of the world
- Understand that seasons are different in other countries

Review

- Recall vocabulary for seasons and weather
- Recall expressions of feeling containing **tengo**
- Sing **"Vengan a ver mi rancho"** (*"Come See my Ranch"*)

Vocabulary

el caballo	*horse*
el cerdo	*pig*
el conejo	*rabbit*
la gallina	*chicken, hen*
el gallo	*rooster*
el gato	*cat*
el perro	*dog*
la vaca	*cow*

Warm-up

Hold up the hand puppet Dora and ask the children what kind of animal Dora is (**una vaca**—*a cow*). Encourage the children to talk about their favorite animals, including farm animals, zoo animals, ranch animals, and pets. What are some of the reasons they like the animals?

Review

Materials: Feeling masks from Activity 9B.

As you hold each of the feeling masks in front of your face, ask the children what you would answer if someone asked you, **¿Cómo estás?** (*How are you?*).

Introduce the video

Invite the children to listen and watch as **la maestra** and Dora talk about different kinds of animals and **la maestra** visits animals on a ranch.

Possible replies:

Estoy muy bien.
I am (feeling) fine.

Estoy muy mal.
I am (feeling) very bad.

Estoy así, así.
I am (feeling) so-so.

VIDEO LESSON

1. Greeting Dora and the children

La maestra has the opening conversation with Dora and then with the children (**M** = Maestra, **D** = Dora, **C** = class):

M: Buenos días, Dora/ clase.	*Good morning, Dora/ class.*
D/C: Buenos días, Maestra.	*Good morning, Teacher.*
M: ¿Cómo estás tú?	*How are you?*
D/C: Muy bien, gracias. ¿Y usted?	*Very well, thank you. And you?*
M: Muy bien, gracias.	*Very well, thank you.*

La maestra says that she heard someone say that they feel **muy mal** (*very bad*), and Dora says **Lo siento** (*I'm sorry*).

2. Discussing weather and seasons

La maestra points out that people feel different in different weather. Using Flashcards representing different weather, she and Dora review weather expressions.

3. Reviewing the seasons

La maestra points out that weather depends on the seasons and that the seasons are different in different parts of the world. She asks **¿Qué estación es?** (*What season is it?*) to review the names of the seasons and the weather associated with each: **En ___ hace ___** (*In ___ it is ___*). She asks the children to **repite** (*repeat*) the names of the seasons.

4. Introducing the names of animals

After reminding the children that animals have feelings, **la maestra** uses Flashcards to introduce the names of some animals—**el caballo** (*horse*), **la gallina** (*chicken, hen*), **el conejo** (*rabbit*), **el cerdo** (*pig*), **el gallo** (*rooster*), **la vaca** (*cow*), **el gato** (*cat*), and **el perro** (*dog*).

5. Visiting a ranch

Vamos al rancho (*Let's go to the ranch*), says Dora. On the ranch **la maestra** visits and comments on several animals.

Los caballos son muy bonitos.	*The horses are very pretty.*
¿Qué ponen las gallinas? ¡Huevos!	*What do chicken lay? Eggs!*
El cerdo es muy grande y muy gordo pero es muy simpático.	*The pig is very big and very fat but it is very nice.*

EN ESPAÑOL

Lo siento literally means *I feel it*. You may want to encourage the children to use this phrase instead of *I'm sorry*.

Weather expressions:

Hace frío.	It's cold.
Hace sol.	It's sunny.
Llueve.	It's raining.
Hace mal tiempo.	It's bad weather.
Hace buen tiempo.	It's good weather.
Hace viento.	It's windy.
Nieva.	It's snowing.

Vocabulary for the seasons:

En el invierno hace frío.
(*It's cold in the winter.*)

En la primavera hace buen tiempo.
(*The weather is good in the spring.*)

En el verano hace calor.
(*It's hot in the summer.*)

En el otoño hace viento.
(*It's windy in the fall.*)

FYI **Ponen** in **ponen huevos** (*lay eggs*) comes from the verb **poner**, which usually means *to put*. In this case it is part of an idiomatic expression.

La cabra es de color negro, de color blanco y de color café.	The goat is black, white, and brown.
La llama vive en Sudamérica.	The llama lives in South America.

6. Discussing animals from different places

La maestra explains that some animals such as **la llama** come from different parts of the world but can be brought to other places to live. She explains that **la llama** is usually found in the Andes Mountains of **Sudamérica** (*South America*).

7. Playing a game

La maestra initiates a game about animal names by asking **¿Es el/la ___ o es el/la ___?** (*Is it the ___ or is it the ___?*). Answer: **Es el/la ___.** (*It is the ___.*) She also plays **¿Quién dice ___?** (*Who says ___?*) with the cow (**mu**), the cat (**miau**), and the dog (**guau**).

8. Singing a song

After observing that **el rancho es muy divertido** (*the ranch is a lot of fun*), **la maestra** says **Vamos a cantar** (*Let's sing*). She then sings "**Vengan a ver mi rancho**" ("*Come See my Ranch*").

Vengan a ver mi rancho, que es hermoso.	*Come see my ranch which is beautiful.*
Vengan a ver mi rancho, que es hermoso.	*Come see my ranch which is beautiful.*
Y el perro dice así, "guau, guau".	*And the dog says "bow-wow."*
Y el perro dice así, "guau, guau".	*And the dog says "bow-wow."*
A rin tin tin, a rin tin tin, a rin tin tin tin tan.	
A rin tin tin, a rin tin tin, a rin tin tin tin tan.	
Y el cerdo dice así, "truc-truc".	*And the pig says "oink, oink."*
Y el caballo dice así, "ji, jii, jiii".	*And the horse says "neigh, neigh."*
Y la gallina dice así, "clo-clo".	*And the chicken says "cluck, cluck."*
Y la vaca dice así, "mu, mu".	*And the cow says "moo, moo."*

9. Closing

La maestra and Dora say **Adiós** (*Good-bye*).

HERITAGE SPEAKERS

Encourage Spanish-speaking children in your class to talk about animals typical to the countries they came from. Children from other cultures and parts of the United States may also want to join in the discussion.

After viewing the video, praise the children for their good listening and watching skills.

Lesson Thirty-Seven

ACTIVITY LESSON

Activity 37A: Animals

Materials: Cassette player; Activity Cassette 2, Side B; Gold Flashcards 20–27.

Preparation: Arrange the Flashcards in numerical order.

Tell the children that you will hold up some pictures of animals, one at a time. **La maestra** will say the name of each animal and ask the children to repeat each name after her.

You may want to ask a volunteer to hold up the Flashcards.

Activity 37B: Sing "Vengan a ver mi rancho" (*"Come See my Ranch"*)

Materials: Cassette player; Song Cassette; Gold Flashcards 20–22 and 24–27.

Play the song **"Vengan a ver mi rancho"** (*"Come See my Ranch"*) at least once and encourage the children to sing along. Point out that the verses can be sung in a different order, with the cow coming first, then the horse, and so on. Then tell the children that you will hold up Flashcards to show them in what order to sing the verses. Hold up the Flashcards in any order you choose.

Activity 37C: Illustrate the seasons

Materials: Drawing paper; crayons.

Begin by brainstorming scenes and pleasures that the children associate with each season, such as swimming in the summer, building snowmen in the winter, and so on. Then encourage the children to illustrate a scene from their favorite season. When they have finished, ask the children to name in Spanish the season they have illustrated and to describe the scene, using as much Spanish as possible. Post their drawings on the bulletin board.

Vocabulary for seasons:

la primavera	spring
Hace buen tiempo.	The weather is good.
Está lloviendo or llueve.	It's raining.
Hace sol.	It's sunny.
el verano	summer
Hace calor.	It's hot.
el otoño	fall
Hace viento.	It's windy.
el invierno	winter
Hace frío.	It's cold.
Hace mal tiempo.	The weather is bad.
Está nevando or nieva.	It's snowing.

LEVEL TWO

CLOSING

Tell the children that Spanish class is finished for today. In the next class they will talk more about animals and visit a very interesting animal that lives in water.

IF YOU HAVE TIME...

Materials: A large map of South America; pictures of llamas.

Display pictures of llamas and point to South America and the Andes Mountains on a map before leading a discussion about llamas. You may want to tell the children that the llama is a relative of the camel, that it lives in herds owned by the Indians of the Andes, and that it is used to carry heavy loads as well as for food, milk, and wool. Encourage children who have seen llamas to describe them.

Lesson Thirty-Seven

Lesson 38

Materials to gather

- VCR and Video Lesson 38 on Tape 10
- Cassette player
- Activity Cassette 2
- Blackline Master 38A (pictures of animals)
- Gold Flashcards 20–33
- Scissors or a paper cutter
- *Optional materials:* Song Cassette

OBJECTIVES

Language

- Learn expressions for feelings
- Understand sustained conversation about animal habitats

Culture

- Understand that different animals live in different parts of the world and in different environments

Review

- Recall expressions of feelings containing **tengo**
- Recall vocabulary for animals
- Sing **"Vengan a ver mi rancho"** (*"Come See my Ranch"*)

Vocabulary

Tengo sed.	*I'm thirsty.*
Tengo hambre.	*I'm hungry.*
Tengo miedo.	*I'm afraid.*
Tengo sueño.	*I'm sleepy.*

Warm-up

Point out to the children that all the animals they have talked about so far live on land. Ask where else animals live. If necessary, remind the children that some animals live in the water and ask for examples of such animals.

Review

Materials: Gold Flashcards 20–27.

Show Flashcards 20–27, and ask children to say the names of the animals they've been studying.

Introduce the video

Invite the children to listen and watch as **la maestra** and Jorge talk more about animals, including one very special animal that lives in the water. Remind the children that listening and watching carefully will help them understand what **la maestra** says.

Animals:

el caballo	horse
el cerdo	pig
el conejo	rabbit
la gallina	chicken
el gallo	rooster
el gato	cat
el perro	dog
la vaca	cow

Video Lesson

1. Greeting Jorge and the children

La maestra has the opening conversation with Jorge and then with the children (M = Maestra, J = Jorge, C = class):

M: Buenos días, Jorge/clase.	Good morning, Jorge/class.
J/C: Buenos días, Maestra.	Good morning, Teacher.
M: ¿Cómo estás tú?	How are you?
J/C: Muy bien, gracias. ¿Y usted?	Very well, thank you. And you?
M: Muy bien, gracias.	Very well, thank you.

La maestra uses feeling masks to review the responses **Así, así** (*So-so*) and **Muy mal** (*Very bad*).

2. Discussing feelings

Using Flashcards, **la maestra** asks how the horse, cow, and cat would answer if asked **¿Cómo estás tú?** (*How are you?*) They would answer **Tengo calor** (*I'm hot*), **Tengo sed** (*I'm thirsty*), and **Tengo frío** (*I'm cold*).

3. Reintroducing expressions for feelings

Using Flashcards of animals, **la maestra** reintroduces more expressions for feelings containing **tengo**:

El perro dice, "Tengo hambre".	The dog is saying, "I'm hungry."
El cerdo dice, "Tengo miedo".	The pig is saying, "I'm afraid."
La gallina dice, "Tengo sueño".	The chicken is saying, "I'm sleepy."

> **FYI:** Expressions containing **tengo** literally mean *I have . . .*

4. Reviewing names of animals

Asking **¿Quién es?** (*Who is it?*), **la maestra** reviews the names of animals: **el caballo** (*horse*), **la vaca** (*cow*), **el gato** (*cat*), **el perro** (*dog*), **el cerdo** (*pig*), **el conejo** (*rabbit*), **la gallina** (*chicken*), **el gallo** (*rooster*). She then reviews both names of animals and expressions of feeling by asking **¿Qué dice el ___?** (*What is the ___ saying?*), **Tengo ___, dice ___** (*I'm ___, says the ___*), and **¿Quién dice "___"?** (*Who is saying "___"?*).

5. Singing a song

Vamos a cantar (*Let's sing*), says **la maestra**. She then sings "Vengan a ver mi rancho" (*"Come See my Ranch"*). For song lyrics, see Lesson 37, Video Lesson, section 8.

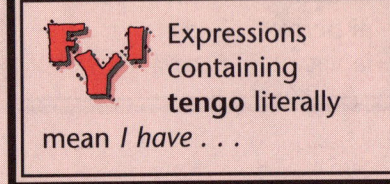

> **FYI:** La maestra's comment to Jorge **Te gusta cantar** means *You like to sing.*

6. Playing a game

After reminding the children that some animals come from other places, **la maestra** points out that **Jorge es una jirafa** (*Jorge is a giraffe*) and that giraffes come from the plains of **África** (*Africa*). She then asks ¿**Es el/la ___ o es el/la ___?** (*Is it the ___ or is it the ___?*) and ¿**Qué dice el/la ___?** (*What is the ___ saying?*) to review the names of animals and expressions of feelings.

7. Visiting a ranch

Vamos al rancho (*Let's go to the ranch*) says **la maestra.** Once again, the children accompany her while she visits and remarks on different animals.

Tara Lynn es un caballo grande.	*Tara Lynn is a large horse.*
Ginger es un caballo pequeño.	*Ginger is a small horse.*
¿Tienes hambre? Sí, tienes hambre.	*Are you hungry? Yes, you're hungry.*
¿Cuántos huevos hay?	*How many eggs are there?*
Las gallinas son muy importantes.	*Chickens are very important.*
Ahora el cerdo duerme. Tiene sueño.	*Now the pig is sleeping. He's sleepy.*
La llama es de color negro y de color café.	*The llama is black and brown.*

8. Discussing animal habitats

La maestra repeats that animals live in different places—**jirafas** (*giraffes*) like Jorge in Africa, **la llama** in **Sudamérica** (*South America*), and other animals in the water.

9. Visiting dolphins

La maestra takes the children to visit some dolphins. She explains that **los delfines viven en el agua, pero no son peces** (*dolphins live in the water, but they are not fish*). Other comments about dolphins: **Nadan en el agua y saltan también** (*They swim in the water and they also jump*); **Son muy inteligentes** (*They are very intelligent*).

10. Closing

La maestra points out that although dolphins look like fish, they are mammals, and reminds the children that every animal is different and lives in a different place. She and Jorge then say **Adiós** (*Good-bye*).

FYI **La maestra** says **El conejo no dice nada,** which means *The rabbit doesn't say anything.*

LANGUAGE ACROSS THE CURRICULUM

In a science project, help the children examine the relationship between what an animal looks like and its habitat. You might begin by asking how the giraffe manages to live on the dry plains of Africa. Then help the children discover that the giraffe's long neck enables it to eat the leaves from the tall trees. The children might also want to study the llama, whose thick fur helps it keep warm in the cold Andes Mountains.

FYI In Spanish, nouns that denote the whole of a class or kind take the definite article (in this case **los**—*the*), as in **los delfines** and **los animales** (*dolphins* and *animals*).

After viewing the video, praise the children for their good listening and watching skills.

Lesson Thirty-Eight

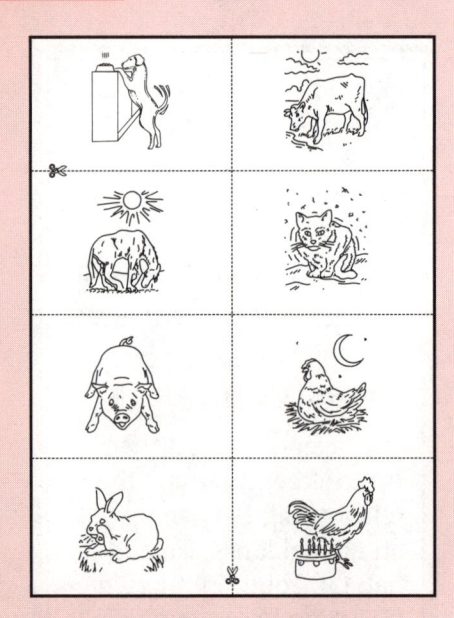

Blackline Master 38A

You may want to repeat Activity 38A, this time asking volunteers to take turns saying **Muéstrame** and naming each picture.

Feelings containing tengo:	
Tengo frío.	I'm cold.
Tengo calor.	I'm hot.
Tengo hambre.	I'm hungry.
Tengo sed.	I'm thirsty.
Tengo miedo.	I'm afraid.
Tengo sueño.	I'm sleepy.

ACTIVITY LESSON

Activity 38A: *Muéstrame* ___ (*Show me* ___)

Materials: Cassette player; Activity Cassette 2, Side B; Blackline Master 38A; and scissors or paper cutter.

Preparation: Duplicate Blackline Master 38A so that each child has a copy. Give scissors to each child or pair of children and have them cut out the pictures, or cut them yourself with a paper cutter.

Tell the children that doña Elena is going to name an animal and ask them to show its picture to her. They are to hold up the picture that she names. She names them in the following order: **el gallo** (*rooster*), **la vaca** (*cow*), **el cerdo** (*pig*), **el caballo** (*horse*), **el conejo** (*rabbit*).

Activity 38B: Stand and sit

Materials: Cassette player; Activity Cassette 2, Side B; and Gold Flashcards 28–33.

Distribute the Flashcards. Then tell the children that doña Elena is going to say **Párate con** (*Stand with*) and then name a feeling. The child holding the Flashcard that shows that feeling should stand up. When doña Elena says **siéntate**, he or she should sit down. To give more children a chance to participate, hand out the Flashcards to different children and play the activity again.

LEVEL TWO

Activity 38C: Discuss mammals

Brainstorm with the children all the facts they know about mammals. If necessary, remind them that the babies of mammals are born alive rather than hatched from eggs; that they are fed milk by their mothers; that they all have at least some hair or fur; and that they are warm-blooded—that is, that their bodies stay at about the same temperature regardless of the temperature of their surroundings. Ask the children to name the animals they have talked about in their Spanish lessons that are mammals—**el caballo** (*horse*), **el conejo** (*rabbit*), **la vaca** (*cow*), **el cerdo** (*pig*), **el gato** (*cat*), **el perro** (*dog*). You could also mention **la cabra** (*goat*), **el delfín** (*dolphin*), and **la llama**.

CLOSING

Tell the children that Spanish class is finished for today. In the next class they will learn more about the various places animals live.

IF YOU HAVE TIME . . .

Materials: Cassette player; Song Cassette.

Play the song **"Vengan a ver mi rancho"** (*"Come See my Ranch"*) while the children sing along. Then play the song again, asking volunteers to make the sounds of the different animals. For song lyrics, see Lesson 37, Video Lesson, section 8.

Lesson Thirty-Eight

Lesson 39

Materials to gather

- VCR and Video Lesson 39 on Tape 10
- Cassette player
- Activity Cassette 2
- Song Cassette
- Gold Flashcards 1, 2, 5, 6, and 20–22
- Gold Flashcards 20–27
- Gold Flashcards 28–33
- **Optional materials:** an encyclopedia

Objectives

Language
- Associate expressions with **tener** with visual cues
- Understand sustained conversation about dolphins

Culture
- Understand that animals live in different types of environments

Review
- Recall expressions of feelings containing **tengo**
- Recall vocabulary for animals
- Sing **"Vengan a ver mi rancho"** (*"Come See my Ranch"*)

Vocabulary

Tengo dolor.　　　　　　　　　*I'm hurt.*

Warm-up

Remind the children that in the last lesson they visited dolphins with **la maestra** and ask them where dolphins live (in **el agua**—*water*). Encourage them to think of some other places that animals can live, such as in deserts, forests, and mountains.

Review

Materials: Gold Flashcards 1, 2, 5, 6, and 20–22.

Remind the children to use **usted** (*formal you*) when talking to adults they do not know well, and **tú** (*informal you*) when talking to animals, friends, classmates, and family members. Then hold up each Flashcard and ask the children whether they would say **tú** or **usted** to each person or animal pictured. Answers: 1. **usted**; 2. **usted**; 5. **tú**; 6. **tú**; 20–22. **tú**.

Introduce the video

Invite the children to listen and watch as **la maestra** and Ñico talk more about animals and where they live and **la maestra** visits the dolphins again. Remind the children that listening and watching carefully will help them understand what **la maestra** says.

VIDEO LESSON

1. Greeting Ñico

Using **Buenos días** (*Good morning*) as the greeting, **la maestra** has the opening conversation with Ñico. Holding up feeling masks, **la maestra** reviews the responses **Muy mal** (*Very bad*), **Así, así** (*So-so*), and **Muy bien** (*Very well*). For the opening conversation, see Lesson 38, Video Lesson, section 1.

2. Reviewing expressions for feelings

Pointing out that there are other ways of answering ¿Cómo estás tú?, **la maestra** uses Flashcards to review expressions for feelings containing **tengo**:

El caballo dice, "Tengo calor".	*The horse is saying, "I'm hot."*
La vaca dice, "Tengo sed".	*The cow is saying, "I'm thirsty."*
El gato dice, "Tengo frío".	*The cat is saying, "I'm cold."*
El perro dice, "Tengo hambre".	*The dog is saying, "I'm hungry."*
El cerdo dice, "Tengo miedo".	*The pig is saying, "I'm afraid."*
La gallina dice, "Tengo sueño".	*The chicken is saying, "I'm sleepy."*

3. Reviewing expressions for feelings

La maestra says **Vamos a jugar** (*Let's play*). She reviews expressions for feelings before initiating a game of ¿**Cuál falta?** (*What's missing?*) with pictures representing expressions of feeling containing **tengo**.

4. Reviewing other expressions with *tengo*

La maestra asks Ñico ¿**Cuántos años tienes tú?** (*How old are you?*). Ñico answers **Tengo siete años** (*I'm seven years old*). **La maestra** then explains another way of answering ¿Cómo estás tú?—**Tengo dolor** (*I'm hurt*). Ñico replies, **Lo siento** (*I'm sorry*).

5. Playing a game

La maestra says **Vamos a jugar más** (*Let's play some more*). She reviews expressions of feelings and then plays ¿**Cuál falta?** (*What's missing?*) with pictures representing expressions of feelings containing **tengo**. She reminds the children that animals have feelings, too, and must be taken care of.

In this context, **la maestra's** statement **Buenas noches** means *Good night.*

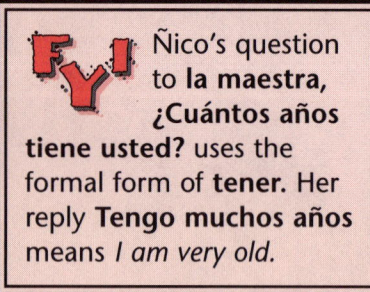

FYI

Ñico's question to **la maestra**, ¿**Cuántos años tiene usted?** uses the formal form of **tener**. Her reply **Tengo muchos años** means *I am very old.*

LEVEL TWO

6. Discussing animal habitats

La maestra asks Ñico where he lives. Ñico replies that he lives **en el bosque** (*in the jungle* or *forest*). **La maestra** reminds the children that animals can live **en el rancho** (*in the ranch*), **en el bosque**, **en la casa** (*in the jungle or forest* or *at home*), and **en el agua** (*in the water*).

7. Singing a song

Vamos a cantar del rancho (*Let's sing about the ranch*), says **la maestra**. She then sings "**Vengan a ver mi rancho**" ("*Come See my Ranch*"). For song lyrics, see Lesson 37, Video Lesson, section 8.

8. Visiting the dolphins

After commenting that **el rancho es muy divertido** (*the ranch is a lot of fun*), **la maestra** reviews animal habitats and reminds the children that dolphins look like fish but are really mammals. She says **Vamos a visitar los delfines** (*Let's visit the dolphins*) before visiting an indoor and outdoor aquarium. She comments on the dolphins.

Estoy aquí con unos amigos muy especiales.	I'm here with some very special friends.
Son de color gris y de color blanco.	They are gray and white.
Son nuestros amigos que viven en el agua.	They are our friends who live in the water.
Son muy bonitos.	They are very pretty.
Juegan, y saltan y nadan.	They play, and jump, and swim.
¿Hablan? ¡Sí, hablan!	Do they talk? Yes, they talk!

9. Closing

La maestra reminds the children that animals live **en el bosque** (*in the jungle* or *forest*), **en el rancho** (*on the ranch*), and **en el agua** (*in the water*). She and Ñico then say **Adiós** (*Goodbye*) and **Hasta luego** (*See you later*).

At the end of the lesson, you may want to point out that dolphins talk by clicking, creaking, whistling, and making other types of sounds.

After viewing the video, praise the children for their good listening and watching skills.

Lesson Thirty-Nine

EN ESPAÑOL

Here and elsewhere, continue to praise the children by saying **Muy bien** (*Very well*), **Fantástico** (*Fantastic*), **Perfecto** (*Perfect*), and **Excelente** (*Excellent*).

"Let's March #2"

Tengo sueño.	I'm sleepy.
Tengo frío.	I'm cold.
Tengo dolor.	I'm hurt.
Tengo sed.	I'm thirsty.
Tengo calor.	I'm hot.
Tengo hambre.	I'm hungry.
Tengo miedo.	I'm afraid.

ACTIVITY LESSON

Activity 39A: ¿Quién es? (*Who is it?*)

Materials: Cassette player; Activity Cassette 2, Side B; and Gold Flashcards 20–27.

Arrange the Flashcards in numerical order. Tell the children that you are going to hold up Flashcards while doña Elena asks **¿Quién es?** (*Who is it?*) twice. After the second time, they should answer **Es el** (*It is the*) and the name of the animal. Then play the activity, holding up each Flashcard in order when doña Elena says **¿Quién es?**

Activity 39B: "Let's March #2"

Materials: Cassette player; Song Cassette, Side A; and Gold Flashcards 28–33.

Have the children sit in a large circle. Then distribute the Flashcards. Tell the children that each child holding a Flashcard that shows one of the feelings in the song should stand and march inside the circle when their "feeling" is called. Then play the song several times, redistributing the Flashcards so that all the children get a chance to march.

Activity 39C: Where do animals live?

Brainstorm with the children some of the kinds of animals they know and where the animals live. You might begin by writing the following headings on the chalkboard: *water, woods, jungle, desert*. Then write as many animal names as the children can think of under each heading. Remind the children to use Spanish words whenever possible.

CLOSING

Tell the children that Spanish class is finished for today. In the next class they will learn more about the various places animals live.

> **IF YOU HAVE TIME...**
>
> Materials: An encyclopedia.
>
> Read about dolphins in an encyclopedia and share the information with the children. You may want to emphasize dolphins' ability to communicate and their family relationships. If you are comfortable using Spanish words, do so whenever possible.

Lesson Thirty-Nine

Lesson 40

Materials to gather

- VCR and Video Lesson 40 on Tape 9
- Cassette player
- Activity Cassette 2
- Song Cassette
- Feeling masks from Activity 9B
- Number Cards 10–100
- *Optional materials:* index cards; pencils

OBJECTIVES

Language
- Learn new expressions for feelings
- Learn new vocabulary for numbers 60, 70, 80, 90, 100

Culture
- Sing **"Vamos a contar"** (*"Let's Count"*)

Review
- Recall vocabulary for numbers 10, 20, 30, 40, and 50

Vocabulary

Estoy contento/contenta.	*I am happy.*
Estoy enojado/enojada.	*I am angry.*
Estoy triste.	*I am sad.*
sesenta	*sixty*
setenta	*seventy*
ochenta	*eighty*
noventa	*ninety*
cien	*one hundred*

Warm-up

Materials: Feeling masks from Activity 9B.

Hold up the feeling masks and ask the children to explain the feeling associated with each. Encourage the children to discuss other feelings, such as fear, sadness, and anger, and describe when they might experience such feelings.

Review

Remind the children that **la maestra** has described the colors of some of the animals she has visited on the ranch and at the aquarium. Review colors by pointing to objects and articles of clothing and asking ¿**De qué color es?** or *What color is it?*

Introduce the video

Tell the children that **la maestra**, Dora, and Rosco are going to talk about some new feelings and how to express them.

Colors:

amarillo	*yellow*
anaranjado	*orange*
azul	*blue*
blanco	*white*
café	*brown*
gris	*gray*
morado	*purple*
negro	*black*
rojo	*red*
rosado	*pink*
verde	*green*

Video Lesson

1. Greeting the children

La maestra holds the opening conversation with the children. She asks Dora **¿Cómo estás tú?** (*How are you?*). Dora answers **Muy bien** (*Very well*). For the opening conversation, see Lesson 38, Video Lesson, section 1.

2. Introducing new expressions for feelings

La maestra points out that Dora could also have answered **Estoy contenta** (*I am happy*). A boy, on the other hand, would answer **Estoy contento**. Rosco appears on the scene to demonstrate by saying **Estoy contento**. **La maestra** encourages the **niñas** (*girls*) in the class to say **Estoy contenta** and then the **niños** (*boys*) to say **Estoy contento**.

Vamos a mirar (*Let's look*), says **la maestra**. The mime demonstrates the statement **Estoy contento**, and then **la maestra** shows a Flashcard of a boy who looks **contento**.

La maestra explains that another way to answer the question **¿Cómo estás tú?** is to say **Estoy enojado** or **Estoy enojada** (*I am angry*). She then asks the girls and boys to say the appropriate statement. After the mime demonstrates **Estoy enojado**, **la maestra** shows a Flashcard of a boy who looks **enojado**.

Next, **la maestra** explains that both girls and boys would say **Estoy triste** (*I am sad*). The children repeat this statement, and **la maestra** reviews **Estoy contento/contenta** and **Estoy enojado/enojada**. The mime then demonstrates **Estoy triste**, and **la maestra** shows a Flashcard of a girl who looks **triste**.

After using the Flashcards to review the three expressions of feeling, **la maestra** reminds the children that people cannot always be happy because sometimes they are sad or angry.

3. Reviewing numbers

Vamos a contar (*Let's count*), says **la maestra** and asks the children **¿Cómo se dice diez, veinte, treinta, cuarenta, cincuenta?** (*How do you say 10, 20, 30, 40, 50?*). She reviews these numbers with the children and asks them to **repite** (*repeat*) them.

4. Practicing numbers 10, 20, 30, 40, and 50

La maestra plays a game of **Muéstrame ___** (*Show me ___*) and **¿Qué número es?** (*What number is it?*) to review the numbers.

FYI In general, an adjective ending in **-a** indicates feminine gender, an adjective ending in **-o** indicates masculine gender, and an adjective ending in **-e** indicates either.

5. Singing a song

Vamos a cantar (*Let's sing*), says **la maestra** before singing "**Vamos a contar**" ("*Let's Count*").

Dos y dos son cuatro.	*Two and two are four.*
Cuatro y dos son seis.	*Four and two are six.*
Seis y dos son ocho.	*Six and two are eight,*
Y ocho dieciséis.	*And eight, sixteen.*
Dieciséis y ocho	*Sixteen and eight*
Veinticuatro son.	*Are twenty-four.*
Vienticuatro y ocho	*Twenty-four and eight*
Treinta y dos nos dan.	*Give us thirty-two.*
Treinta y dos nos dan.	*Give us thirty-two.*
Treinta y dos nos dan.	*Give us thirty-two.*

6. Introducing more numbers

La maestra reviews the expressions of feeling **Estoy contenta** (*I am happy*) and **Estoy enojado** (*I am angry*), joking that Rosco is **enojado** because he wants to do numbers that are **más grandes** (*bigger*). **La maestra** then reviews the numbers 10, 20, 30, 40, and 50 and introduces the numbers 60, 70, 80, 90, and 100, asking the children to repeat them. For new numbers, see the Vocabulary section of this lesson.

7. Playing a game

La maestra plays a game of **Muéstrame ___** (*Show me ___*), asking the children to point to the numbers she names.

8. Reviewing new expressions for feelings

La maestra uses Flashcards to review the expressions **Estoy contento** (*I am happy*), **Estoy enojado** (*I am angry*), and **Estoy triste** (*I am sad*).

9. Closing

La maestra, Dora, and Rosco say **Adiós** (*Good-bye*) and **Hasta luego** (*See you later*).

LANGUAGE ACROSS THE CURRICULUM

Use a math activity to reinforce Spanish numbers 10, 20, 30, 40, and 50. Give several groups of children 50 of some small item, such as paper clips. Have them rearrange the items in groups of 10, 20, 30, 40, and 50, naming each group in Spanish.

FYI **Cuando juego con los números grandes estoy contenta** means *When I play with big numbers I am happy.*

After viewing the video, praise the children for their good listening and watching skills.

Lesson Forty

ACTIVITY LESSON

Activity 40A: Happy, sad, or angry?

Materials: Cassette player; Activity Cassette 2, Side B.

Tell the children that **la maestra** is going to say the Spanish expressions that mean *I am happy, I am sad,* and *I am angry.* They should make a face and gesture to show the feeling she expresses. Before playing the activity, you may want to demonstrate how to pantomime these feelings.

> Observe the children's responses to be sure they understand the phrases.

Activity 40B: *Salta, anda, corre* (*Jump, walk, run*)

Materials: Cassette player; Activity Cassette 2, Side B; and Number Cards 10–100.

Display the Number Cards where the children can see and reach them. Tell the children that **la maestra** is going to ask individual children to jump (**salta**), walk (**anda**), or run (**corre**) to the Number Card she names and then to touch it (**toca**). Explain that you will point to a child, and he or she is to do what **la maestra** says.

Point to different children at appropriate times during the activity. Play the activity at least twice to give more children a chance to participate.

> You may want to ask the class to say **¡Olé!** (*Hurray!*) to show that they agree with their classmates' choice of Number Cards.

Activity 40C: Sing a song

Materials: Cassette player; "**Vamos a contar**" ("*Let's Count*") on the Song Cassette, Side A.

Preparation: On the chalkboard, write the song in the form of equations, as in the video (2 + 2 = 4; 4 + 2 = 6; 6 + 2 = 8; 8 + 8 = 16; 16 + 8 = 24; 24 + 8 = 32).

Play the song at least once while the children listen. Then play it again while the children sing along, using the equations you have written on the board to guide them.

> Before they sing, remind the children to say **y** (*and*) instead of *plus* and **son** (*are*) instead of *equals.*

LEVEL TWO

Closing

Tell the children that Spanish class is finished for today. In the next class they will meet another interesting animal and sing a song about it.

IF YOU HAVE TIME...

Materials: 6 index cards for each child; a pencil for each child.

Preparation: Give each child the index cards and a pencil. Erase the answers to the equations on the chalkboard.

Ask the children to write each equation on an index card. Then have them write the answers to the equations and compare their answers with a partner.

Lesson Forty

Lesson 41

Materials to gather

- VCR and Video Lesson 41 on Tape 11
- Cassette player
- Activity Cassette 2
- Song Cassette
- Encyclopedia
- Gold Flashcards 20–22, 24–27, 28–33
- *Optional Materials:* Gold Flashcards 1, 2, 65–67

OBJECTIVES

Language
- Learn the name of a new animal friend

Culture
- Understand the role of the donkey in Latin America
- Sing **"Dulce canta el burro"** (*"Sweetly Sings the Donkey"*)

Review
- Recall phrases expressing feelings
- Recall names of animals
- Recall vocabulary related to school personnel and rooms in the school
- Recall different ways of expressing animal sounds

Vocabulary

el burro　　　　　　　　　　*donkey*

Warm-up

Have the opening conversation with the children, encouraging them to answer the question *How are you?* with the phrase that tells exactly how they feel (**T** = Teacher, **C** = class):

T: Buenos días, clase.	*Good morning, class.*
C: Buenos días, Maestra.	*Good morning, Teacher.*
T: ¿Cómo estás tú?	*How are you?*
C: [Muy bien/Así, así/ Muy mal]. ¿Y usted?	*[Fine/So-so/Very bad]. And you?*
T: Muy bien, gracias.	*Very well, thank you.*

Review

Materials: Gold Flashcards 20–22, 24–27.

Remind the children that they have learned how to express the sounds that some animals make. Review these sounds by holding up Flashcards 20–22 and 24–27 one at a time and asking the children to make the sound of the animal. Then encourage the children to name the animals.

Introduce the video

Tell the children that **la maestra** is going to introduce them to a new animal friend and teach them a song about it.

Animal sounds:

el perro—*guau-guau*
(*dog—bow-wow*)

el gato—*miau, miau*
(*cat—meow, meow*)

la gallina—*clo-clo*
(*chicken—cluck, cluck*)

el gallo—*qui-qui-ri-quí*
(*rooster—cock-a-doodle-doo*)

la vaca—*mu, mu*
(*cow—moo, moo*)

el cerdo—*truc-truc*
(*pig—oink, oink*)

el caballo—*ji, ji, jiii*
(*horse—neigh, neigh*)

VIDEO LESSON

1. Greeting the children and Rosco

Using **Buenos días** (*Good morning*) as the greeting, **la maestra** has the opening conversation with the children. When she asks Rosco ¿**Cómo estás tú?** (*How are you?*), he answers **Estoy enojado** (*I'm angry*). **La maestra** replies **Lo siento** (*I'm sorry*), and Rosco answers **Tengo hambre y estoy enojado** (*I'm hungry and I'm angry*). Using Flashcards as cues, **la maestra** reviews expressions for feelings by saying to Rosco ¿**No estás contento?** (*Aren't you happy?*), ¿**Estás enojado?** (*Are you angry?*), ¿**No estás triste?** (*Aren't you sad?*). For the opening conversation, see Lesson 38, Video Lesson, section 1.

> **FYI** **Estás enojado cuando tienes hambre** means *You get angry when you are hungry.*

2. Reviewing expressions for feelings

La maestra reminds the children that there are many ways to answer the question ¿**Cómo estás tú?** (*How are you?*):

Muy bien.	*Very well.*
Tengo frío.	*I'm cold.*
Tengo calor.	*I'm hot.*
Estoy contento.	*I'm happy.*

La maestra then asks the boys and girls to say **Estoy contento** or **Estoy contenta** (*I'm happy*) and **Estoy enojado** or **Estoy enojada** (*I'm angry*) appropriately. She reminds the children that both boys and girls say **Estoy triste** (*I'm sad*).

3. Reviewing names of animals

La maestra initiates a game of ¿**Quién es?** (*Who is it?*) with Flashcards. Answers: **el caballo** (*horse*), **la vaca** (*cow*), **el gato** (*cat*), **el perro** (*dog*), **el cerdo** (*pig*), **la gallina** (*chicken*). **La maestra** asks how the horse would answer the question ¿**Cómo estás tú?** (*Tengo calor—I'm hot*).

4. Introducing a new animal friend

La maestra introduces **el burro** (*donkey*). She explains that the donkey works hard in many Spanish-speaking countries because he carries loads to market and sometimes carries children on his back. She then reviews the sounds some animals make by asking Rosco ¿**Qué dice el gato?** (*miau*), ¿**Qué dice el perro?** (*guau*), ¿**Qué dice la vaca?** (*mu*), ¿**Qué dice el burro?** (*cají, cajó, cajá*).

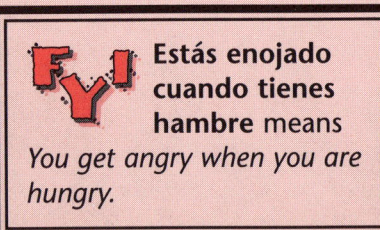

> **FYI** After the lesson, you may want to point out to the children that in English, *burro* means the same as *donkey*. It is one of many Spanish words that the English language has adopted. If necessary, remind the children to trill the **r** in the Spanish word **burro**.

LEVEL TWO

5. Introducing a new song

La maestra says **Vamos a cantar** (*Let's sing*) before introducing "**Dulce canta el burro**" ("*Sweetly Sings the Donkey*").

Dulce canta el burro	*Sweetly sings the donkey*
Al ir a comer.	*When he comes to eat.*
Si no lo cuidamos	*If we don't take care of him,*
Él rebuznará.	*He will bray.*
Cají, cajó, cajá.	*Cají, cajó, cajá.*
Cají, cajó, cajá.	*Cají, cajó, cajá.*
Cají, cajó, cajá.	*Cají, cajó, cajá.*
Cají, cajó, cajá.	*Cají, cajó, cajá.*

Saying **Me toca a mí** (*It's my turn*), Rosco repeats the chorus. **La maestra** says to Rosco **Cantas muy bien** (*You sing very well*).

6. Reviewing vocabulary for school personnel

La maestra points out that singing is a good way to learn and that many people at school like to sing. She asks the children to **repite** (*repeat*) the names of school personnel: **la maestra/el maestro** (*teacher*), **la enfermera/el enfermero** (*nurse*), **la secretaria/el secretario** (*secretary*), and **la directora/el director** (*principal*).

7. Reviewing rooms in the school

La maestra asks Rosco, "If you wanted to find **la maestra**, where in your school would you look?" Rosco replies, "**En la clase**" (*In the classroom*). Asking similar questions, **la maestra** reviews **la oficina** (*the office*), **la biblioteca** (*the library*), **el patio** (*the playground*), **el baño** (*the bathroom*), and **la cafetería** (*the cafeteria*). **La maestra** then plays ¿**Dónde está la maestra?** (*Where is the teacher?*) to review rooms in the school. The children should reply **La maestra está en ___** (*The teacher is in the ___*), adding the name of the room.

> Observe the children to be sure they are responding appropriately.

8. Singing and playing

La maestra leads the children in singing "**Dulce canta el burro**" ("*Sweetly Sings the Donkey*"). For song lyrics, see section 5 of this Video Lesson. She then plays ¿**Qué dice el/la ___?** (*What does the ___ say?*) to review the sounds of **el gato**—*the cat*—**miau, miau**), **el perro**—*the dog* (**guau, guau**), **el cerdo**—*the pig* (**truc-truc**), **la gallina**—*the chicken* (**clo-clo**), and **el burro**—*the donkey* (**cají, cajó, cajá**).

10. Closing

La maestra and Rosco say **Adiós** (*Good-bye*) and **Hasta luego** (*See you later*).

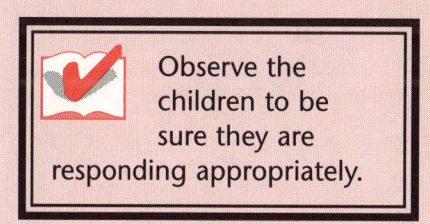

> After viewing the video, praise the children for their good listening and watching skills.

Lesson Forty-One

ACTIVITY LESSON

Activity 41A: How are you?

Materials: Cassette player; Activity Cassette 2, Side B; and Gold Flashcards 28–33.

Preparation: Arrange the Flashcards in numerical order.

Tell the children that in this activity **la maestra** will ask them **¿Cómo estás tú?** (*How are you?*). They will answer by saying **Tengo** and adding the feeling shown on the Flashcard that you are holding up. Show each Flashcard in turn when prompted by **la maestra**.

Activity 41B: Animals that help

Materials: An encyclopedia.

Lead the children in a discussion of animals around the world that work for people. Some animals you might want to discuss are: llama, elephant, sheepdog, guide dog, horse, ox, and donkey. Have the children vote on which animal they would like to know more about. Then help the children use an encyclopedia to find out more about the animal.

Activity 41C: Sing "Dulce canta el burro" (*"Sweetly Sings the Donkey"*)

Materials: Cassette player; **"Dulce canta el burro"** (*"Sweetly Sings the Donkey"*) on Side A of the Song Cassette.

Let the children listen to the song once; then encourage them to sing along with **la maestra**, making the gesture that expresses the donkey's wagging ears. You may want to replay the section in the Video Lesson in which **la maestra** sings the song as a round. Then divide the class into two groups so that they can sing the song the same way. For the lyrics to the song, see section 5 of this Video Lesson.

LEVEL TWO

CLOSING

Tell the children that Spanish class is finished for today. In the next class they will review weather expressions as well as other vocabulary.

IF YOU HAVE TIME...

Materials: Gold Flashcards 1, 2, 65–67.

Let the children take turns holding up each Flashcard and asking **¿Quién es?** (*Who is it?*) Encourage the rest of the children to answer **Es el/la ___** (*It is the ___*).

School personnel:

la maestra	*female teacher*
el maestro	*male teacher*
la directora	*female principal*
la secretaria	*female secretary*
el enfermero	*male nurse*

Lesson Forty-One

Lesson 42

Materials to gather

- VCR and Video Lesson 42 on Tape 11
- Cassette player
- Activity Cassette 2
- Song Cassette
- Blackline Master 42A (numbers)
- Scissors
- Gold Flashcards 41–47
- Gold Flashcards 48–50 and 62–64

Objectives

Language

- Learn new vocabulary for numbers
- Understand that **Busca** means *Search for*
- Respond to visual cues to answer questions about the weather

Culture

- Understand that different cultures celebrate different holidays
- Understand that in many Latin American and European countries the number 7 is written with a line through it

Review

- Recall the names of the months and seasons
- Recall the weather associated with different seasons
- Recall vocabulary for numbers
- Sing **"Dulce canta el burro"** (*"Sweetly Sings the Donkey"*) and **"Las estaciones"** (*"The Seasons"*)

Vocabulary

sesenta y tres	*sixty-three*
noventa y dos	*ninety-two*
ochenta y ocho	*eighty-eight*
cincuenta y uno	*fifty-one*
setenta y cinco	*seventy-five*
Busca ___.	*Search for, look for ___.*

Warm-up

Have the opening conversation with the children. At the point in the conversation where they answer the question ¿**Cómo estás tú?** (*How are you?*), ask each of several children to give a different answer (**T** = Teacher, **C** = class):

T: Buenos días, clase.	*Good morning, class.*
C: Buenos días, Maestro/ Maestra.	*Good morning, Teacher.*
T: Cómo estás tú?	*How are you?*
C: [Muy bien, Estoy contento/contenta, Tengo hambre, etc.] ¿Y usted?	*[Answers will vary.] And you?*
T: Muy bien, gracias.	*Very well, thanks.*

Review

Ask the children what the weather is like. If you are comfortable doing so, ask the question in Spanish—¿**Qué tiempo hace?** Ask the children to use as many weather expressions as possible in their answers.

Introduce the video

Encourage the children to listen and watch as **la maestra** talks more about the weather and teaches them a new expression that will help them play a new game.

Weather expressions:

Hace buen tiempo.
It's good weather.

Hace mal tiempo.
It's bad weather.

Hace calor.	*It's hot.*
Hace frío.	*It's cold.*
Hace sol.	*It's sunny.*
Hace viento.	*It's windy.*
Llueve.	*It's raining.*
Nieva.	*It's snowing.*

Video Lesson

1. Greeting Jorge and the children

La maestra says **buenas tardes** (*good afternoon*) and **¿Cómo estás tú?** (*How are you?*) to Jorge, who answers **muy bien** (*very well*). **La maestra** asks Jorge **¿Estás contento?** (*Are you happy?*), and Jorge answers **Sí, estoy contento** (*Yes, I am happy*). Continuing to use **buenas tardes** as the greeting, **la maestra** then has the opening conversation with the class.

2. Reviewing expressions of feelings

La maestra and Jorge review some ways to answer **¿Cómo estás tú?**, such as **Estoy contento/contenta**, **tengo frío** (*I'm cold*), and **Estoy muy bien** (*I'm very well*).

3. Singing a song

After reviewing **¿Qué dice el burro?** (*What does the donkey say?*—**Cají, cajó, cajá**), **la maestra** teaches the children and Jorge to sing **"Dulce canta el burro"** (*"Sweetly Sings the Donkey"*) line by line. She explains that the song says that if we don't take care of **el burro**, he will bray. She then sings the entire song. For song lyrics, see Lesson 41, Video Lesson, section 5.

4. Reviewing months and seasons

After reminding the children that in Spanish-speaking countries donkeys carry loads to market every month of the year, **la maestra** reviews the names of the months with Flashcards.

5. Singing another song

After saying **Vamos a cantar** (*Let's sing*), **la maestra** leads the children in singing the "Months Rap." For rap lyrics, see Lesson 12, Video Lesson, section 4.

6. Reviewing descriptions of weather

La maestra asks Jorge **¿Qué tiempo hace en ___?** (*What's the weather like in ___?*), adding the month of the year. Responses: **En enero hace frío y nieva** (*In January it's cold and it snows*). **En agosto hace calor** (*In August it's hot*). **En octubre hace viento** (*In October it's windy*). **La maestra** also reminds the children that the weather is not the same everywhere, that it depends on where one lives.

7. Reviewing seasons and weather

La maestra reminds the children that all the months of the year fit into the seasons and that different seasons have different weather. Asking Jorge **¿Qué tiempo hace en ___?** (*What is the weather like in ___?*), she reviews that **En el**

Months of the year:

enero	January
febrero	February
marzo	March
abril	April
mayo	May
junio	June
julio	July
agosto	August
septiembre	September
octubre	October
noviembre	November
diciembre	December

Heritage Speakers

Point out that Valentine's Day, St. Patrick's Day, the Fourth of July, and Thanksgiving are some holidays associated with certain months. Encourage heritage speakers to describe some holidays associated with certain months in their culture.

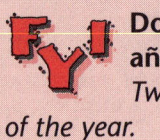

FYI **Doce meses del año** means *Twelve months of the year.*

invierno hace frío (*In the winter it is cold*); **En la primavera hace buen tiempo** or **llueve** (*In the spring the weather is good* or *it rains*); **En el verano hace calor** (*In the summer it is hot*); **En el otoño hace viento** (*In the fall it is windy*).

8. Singing a song

Vamos a cantar (*Let's sing*), says **la maestra** and sings "**Las estaciones**" (*"The Seasons"*). For song lyrics, see Lesson 27, Video Lesson, section 7.

9. Reviewing numbers

La maestra reminds the children that they have been learning other important things, such as **los números pequeños** (*small numbers*) and **los números grandes** (*big numbers*). Using Number Cards and asking **¿Qué número es?** she reviews the numbers 10, 20, 30, 40, and 50.

10. Playing *Muéstrame* ___ (*Show me* ___)

After asking the children to **repite** (*repeat*) the large numbers 10–100, **la maestra** invites them to play **Muéstrame** ___ (*Show me* ___).

11. Practicing numbers

La maestra holds up number cards and asks Jorge and the children **¿Qué número es?** (*What number is it?*). For the numbers, see the Vocabulary Section in this lesson.

12. Introducing a new command

La maestra introduces a new command, **busca** ___ (*search for* ___), by asking the mime to **busca** Rosco in a bag.

13. Playing *Busca* ___ (*Search for* ___)

La maestra asks Jorge to **busca** (*search for*) certain numbers in an envelope. For the names of the numbers, see the Vocabulary Section. She then asks Jorge **¿Qué número es?** (*What number is it?*).

14. Singing a song

La maestra reviews the topics covered in today's lesson before singing "**Dulce canta el burro**" (*"Sweetly Sings the Donkey"*) and reminding the children that we are all responsible for our animal friends, including our pets.

15. Closing

La maestra and Jorge say **Adiós** (*Good-bye*).

Numbers:

diez	10
veinte	20
treinta	30
cuarenta	40
cincuenta	50

sesenta	60
setenta	70
ochenta	80
noventa	90
cien	100

Explain to the children that in many Latin American and European countries, the number 7 is written with a line through the middle to distinguish it from the number 1.

FYI La maestra's statement to Jorge **Te ayudo** means *I'll help you.*

After viewing the video, praise the children for their good listening and watching skills.

Lesson Forty-Two

22	46
35	12
57	70
61	89

Blackline Master 42A

ACTIVITY LESSON

Activity 42A: *Busca* ___ (*Search for* ___)

Materials: Cassette player; Activity Cassette 2, Side B; Blackline Master 42A; and scissors.

Preparation: Duplicate Blackline Master 42A so that each child has a copy. Give each child or pair of children a pair of scissors.

Ask the children to cut out the numbers on the activity sheets and arrange them on their desks in any order they choose. Then tell them that doña Elena is going to say some numbers, one at a time. They are to look for each number she names. When they find it, they should say ¡Olé! (*Hurray!*).

Activity 42B: *¿Qué tiempo hace?* (*What is the weather like?*)

Materials: Cassette player; Activity Cassette 2, Side B; and Gold Flashcards 41–47.

Arrange the Flashcards in numerical order. Tell the children that you are going to hold up some pictures showing weather, one at a time. As you hold up each picture, doña Elena is going to ask ¿Qué tiempo hace? (*What is the weather?*) twice. After the second time, they should describe the weather shown in the picture. As you play the activity, use doña Elena's cues to hold up the pictures in order. For added practice, you may want to play the activity two or more times.

Activity 42C: Sing along

Materials: Cassette player; "Months Rap" on the Song Cassette, Side A; and Gold Flashcards 48–50 and 62–64.

Preparation: Arrange the Flashcards in numerical order.

Encourage the children to sing along with the Song Cassette while you hold up the Flashcards illustrating the months. For the lyrics to the rap, see Lesson 12, Video Lesson, section 4.

> You may want to play the song once before asking the children to sing along.

LEVEL TWO

CLOSING

Tell the children that Spanish class is finished for today. In the next class they will learn a new game.

> **IF YOU HAVE TIME...**
>
> Materials: **"Dulce canta el burro"** (*Sweetly Sings the Donkey"*) and **"Las estaciones"** (*The Seasons"*) on the Song Cassette.
>
> Divide the class into two groups. Help each group learn one of the songs from the cassette. Then let them sing it by themselves to the rest of the class. For the lyrics to the songs, see Lesson 41, Video Lesson, section 5 and Lesson 27, Video Lesson, section 7, respectively.

Lesson Forty-Two

Lesson 43

Materials to gather

- VCR and Video Lesson 43 on Tape 11
- Cassette player
- Activity Cassette 2
- Song Cassette
- Blackline Masters 43A (numbers) and 43B (letters)
- Pencils
- Scissors
- Sturdy blank cards
- Black marker

OBJECTIVES

Language

- Learn to pronounce vowel sounds in Spanish

Culture

- Understand that vowels are pronounced differently in English and Spanish

Review

- Recall some different ways to express feelings
- Recall vocabulary for numbers
- Review the meaning of **Busca** ___ (*Search for* ___)
- Recall the meanings of **despacio** (*slowly*) and **rápido** (*quickly*)

Vocabulary

No new vocabulary is introduced in this lesson.

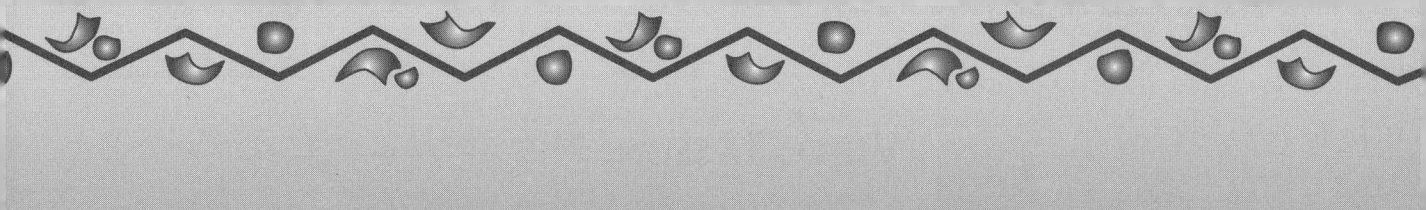

Warm-up

Ask the children to name the vowels (*a, e, i, o, u*). After you write them on the chalkboard, say some words and ask the children which vowel each contains. For example, *sat, hen, pin, top, pup.*

Review

Review some **números pequeños** (*small numbers*) by writing several simple equations on the chalkboard and asking individual children to state them in Spanish and then to solve them.

Introduce the video

Encourage the children to listen and watch as **la maestra** talks about vowel sounds in Spanish and how they are different from vowel sounds in English.

Examples of equations:

3 + 2 = [5]
Tres y dos son [cinco].

1 + 4 = [5]
Uno y cuatro son [cinco].

6 + 2 = [8]
Seis y dos son [ocho].

Video Lesson

1. Greeting Rosco and the children

Using **buenos días** as the greeting, **la maestra** has the opening conversation with Rosco and the children.

2. Reviewing expressions of feelings

La maestra and Rosco review some ways to answer ¿**Cómo estás tú?**, such as **Así, así** (*So-so*), **Muy mal** (*Very bad*), **Tengo frío** (*I'm cold*), **Tengo hambre** (*I'm hungry*), and **Tengo dolor** (*I'm hurt*).

3. Reviewing new expressions for feelings

After **la maestra** points out that there are other ways to answer the question ¿**Cómo estás tú?**, the mime demonstrates the meanings of **Estoy contento** (*I'm happy*), **Estoy triste** (*I'm sad*), and **Estoy enojado** (*I'm angry*). **La maestra** then plays a game of **Muéstrame** ___ (*Show me* ___) in which Rosco and the children pantomime these expressions.

4. Reviewing numbers

Asking Rosco ¿**Qué número es?**, **la maestra** reviews the numbers **cincuenta** (*50*), **setenta y cuatro** (*74*), **cuarenta y seis** (*46*), **cuarenta** (*40*), **treinta y ocho** (*38*), **veintiuno** (*21*), and **cincuenta y tres** (*53*). She then tells the children **Te toca a ti** (*It's your turn*) and reviews the numbers **sesenta y tres** (*63*), **cincuenta y uno** (*51*), **noventa y dos** (*92*), **ochenta y ocho** (*88*), and **setenta y cinco** (*75*), reminding the children that in some Latin American and European countries the number 7 is written with a line through it. Rosco exclaims ¡**Qué bueno!** (*That's good!*) when **la maestra** says that someone answered faster than he did.

5. Reviewing *Busca* ___ (*Search for* ___)

The mime illustrates the meaning of the command.

6. Playing *Busca* ___ (*Search for* ___)

Rosco responds to **la maestra**'s commands to **busca** (*search for*) Flashcards illustrating the expressions **Estoy contento** (*I'm happy*), **Estoy triste** (*I'm sad*), and **Estoy enojado** (*I'm angry*).

FYI

La maestra says ¡**Ay, tengo dolor!** ¡**Ay!** is an exclamation that means *Ouch!* She also tells Rosco **Siempre tienes hambre** (*You are always hungry*).

After the lesson, you may want to ask the children if they remember why the number 7 is written with a line through it. (to distinguish it from the number 1)

LEVEL TWO

7. Introducing *las vocales* (*vowels*)

La maestra introduces written letters in Spanish. She explains that while the letters look the same, some of them are pronounced differently in Spanish and in English. She then explains the sounds of the vowels in Spanish:

- a—[ah], as in **papa**
- e—[eh], as in **Pepe**
- i—[ee], as in **Lili**
- o—[oh], as in **Mono**
- u—[oo], as in **Lulu**

La maestra says **Vamos a mirar** (*Let's watch*). The mime then shows the position of the mouth and lips while the vowels are being pronounced.

8. Reviewing *despacio* (*slowly*) and *rápido* (*rapidly*)

Showing a video of slow-moving traffic, **la maestra** reviews the meaning of **despacio** (*slowly*). She then says **Vamos a decir las vocales despacio** (*Let's say the vowels slowly*). A game of ¿**Es ___ o es ___?** (*Is it ___ or is it ___?*) follows, in which Rosco and the children match vowel sounds with the printed vowels that represent them. After reviewing the meaning of **rápido** (*quickly*), she says **Vamos a decir las vocales rápido** (*Let's say the vowels rapidly*). This is followed by another game of ¿**Es ___ o es ___?** (*Is it ___ or is it ___?*).

9. Singing a song

La maestra tells the children that vowels are used in lots of things, including songs. She illustrates with the song "**Español para ti**" ("*Spanish Is for You, and for Me*"). For song lyrics, see Lesson 3, Video Lesson, section 3. She points out that we use vowel sounds in everything we speak and sing and gives the example of the [ah] sound in the word **para** (*for*).

10. Closing

La maestra says **Adiós**, emphasizing the [ah] sound. She promises that she and the children will get together again soon for more fun.

After viewing the video, praise the children for their good listening and watching skills.

Lesson Forty-Three

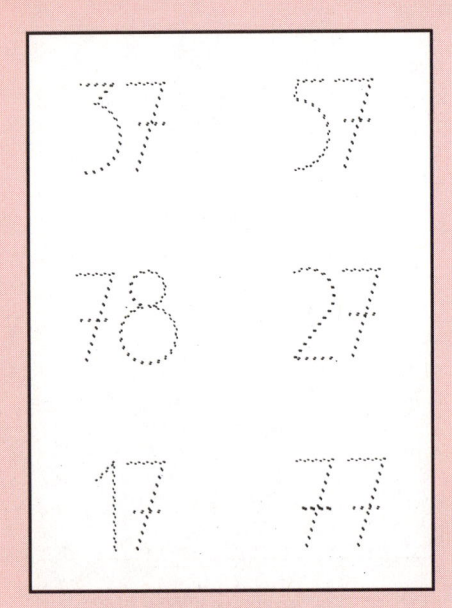

Blackline Master 43A

Numbers:

treinta y siete	37
cincuenta y siete	57
setenta y ocho	78
veintisiete	27
diecisiete	17
setenta y siete	77

Blackline Master 43B

LEVEL TWO

ACTIVITY LESSON

Activity 43A: Trace numbers

Materials: Blackline Master 43A; a pencil for each child.

Preparation: Duplicate Blackline Master 43A so that each child has a copy. Give each child a pencil.

Point out that each number on the activity sheet has a 7 in it. Remind the children that in many countries in Latin America and Europe, the number 7 is written with a line through it to distinguish it from the number 1. Then ask the children to trace each number on the activity sheet. When they have finished, ask volunteers to take turns reading the numbers in Spanish.

Activity 43B: *Busca* ___ (*Search for* ___)

Materials: Cassette player; Activity Cassette 2, Side B; five sturdy blank cards; a black marker; Blackline Master 43B; and scissors.

Preparation: Print one vowel on each of the cards. Place them together where the children can see them. Duplicate Blackline Master 43B so that each child has a copy. Give each child or pair of children a pair of scissors.

Ask the children to cut out the letters on the activity sheet and arrange them faceup on their desks in any order they choose. Then tell them that doña Elena is going to say the letters, one at a time. They are to look for (**busca**) each letter she names. When they find it they should pronounce it. As the children pronounce each letter, point to the appropriate letter card that you have made. For added practice, you may want to play the activity more than once.

Save the vowel cards for future use.

Activity 43C: Fast and slow

Materials: Cassette player; Activity Cassette 2, Side B.

Inform the children that doña Elena is going to say the vowel sounds and tell them to mouth them either quickly or slowly. Offer the example of the mime and let the children practice mouthing various words or sounds. Then play the tape. You may want to repeat the activity, this time asking the children to say the vowel sounds out loud.

CLOSING

Tell the children that Spanish class is finished for today. In the next class they will practice recognizing vowel sounds.

> **IF YOU HAVE TIME...**
>
> Materials: Cassette player; **"Español para ti"** (*"Spanish Is for You, and for Me"*) on the Song Cassette, Side A.
>
> Play the song once for the children to listen to. Then encourage them to sing along with **la maestra**. For song lyrics, see Lesson 3, Video Lesson, section 3.

Lesson Forty-Three

Lesson 44

Materials to gather

- VCR and Video Lesson 44 on Tape 11
- Cassette player
- Activity Cassette 2
- Song Cassette
- Blackline Master 29A (seasons)
- Scissors
- Blackline Master 44B (incomplete words)
- Pencils
- Vowel cards from Activity 43B
- Blackline Master 43A (numbers)

OBJECTIVES

Language

- Recognize vowel sounds in words
- Respond to visual cues to answer questions about the weather
- Show comprehension of **rápido** (*quickly*) and **despacio** (*slowly*) by performing actions appropriately

Culture

- Notice the difference between the plural **ustedes** and the singular **tú** to mean *you*

Review

- Recall expressions for feelings
- Practice expressions relating to the calendar
- Practice vowel sounds
- Recall the names of the months and seasons
- Recall the weather associated with different seasons
- Recall vocabulary for numbers

Vocabulary

No new vocabulary is introduced in this lesson.

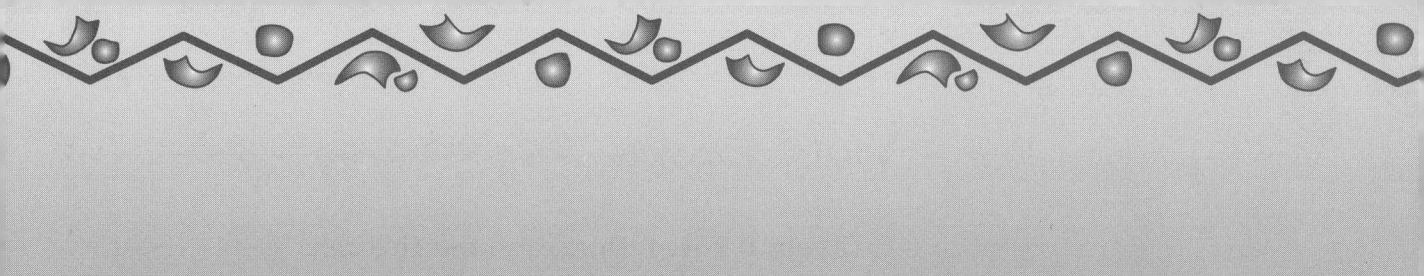

Warm-up

Materials: Cassette player; **"Uno, dos, tres niñitos"** (*"One, Two, Three Little Children"*) on the Song Cassette, Side A.

Before you play the song, choose ten children and ask them to stand up one at a time as each number is sung from 1 to 10 and sit down one at a time as each number is sung from 10 to 1. Then play the song while the children just listen. Play it again while the children sing along and carry out the actions you have explained. For song lyrics, see Lesson 14, Video Lesson, section 6.

Review

Review questions and answers relating to names. Divide the class into pairs and have the partners ask and tell each other their names. Then have the partners ask and tell each other the name of someone else in the class.

Introduce the video

Encourage the children to listen and watch as **la maestra**, Rosco, and Dora review questions and answers about the calendar.

You may want to play the tape again, this time asking different children to raise and lower their hands while the numbers are counted.

Questions and answers relating to names:

¿Cómo te llamas?
(*What is your name?*)

Me llamo ___.
(*My name is ___.*)

¿Cómo se llama?
(*What is his/her name?*)

Se llama ___.
(*His/Her name is ___.*)

VIDEO LESSON

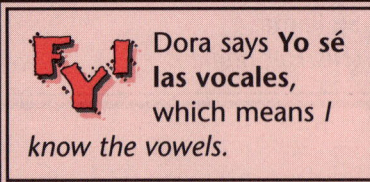

1. Greeting Rosco, Dora, and the children

La maestra says **buenas tardes** (*good afternoon*) and **¿Cómo están ustedes?** (*How are you [plural]?*) to Dora and Rosco. She continues the opening conversation with the puppets and then with the children.

2. Reviewing expressions of feelings

La maestra reviews some ways to answer **¿Cómo estás tú?**, such as **Tengo hambre** (*I'm hungry*) and **Estoy contento/a** (*I'm happy*). **La maestra** asks Rosco **¿Estás contento?** (*Are you happy?*). He answers No, **tengo hambre. La maestra** replies **Siempre tiene hambre y no está contento** (*He is always hungry and he is not happy*).

3. Reviewing the calendar

Showing a large calendar, **la maestra** begins by asking **¿Qué mes es?** (*What month is it?*). She then reviews the names of the months and the days. Months: **enero** (*January*), **febrero** (*February*), **marzo** (*March*), **abril** (*April*), **mayo** (*May*), **junio** (*June*), **julio** (*July*), **agosto** (*August*), **septiembre** (*September*), **octubre** (*October*), **noviembre** (*November*), **diciembre** (*December*). After asking **¿Qué día es?** (*What day is it?*) she reviews the names of the days of the week with the "Calendar Rap." For rap lyrics, see Lesson 12, Video Lesson, section 3. She also reviews **¿Qué número es?** (*What number is it?*) and **¿Cuál es la fecha?** (*What is the date?*) and the appropriate response to the latter: **(Es) el ___ de ___** (*It is the ___ of ___*).

4. Reviewing *las vocales* (*vowels*)

Holding up vowel cards, **la maestra** reminds the children that vowels are needed to speak and sing. She asks **¿Cuáles son?** (*What are they?*) and then reviews the vowel sounds: **a**—[ah], **e**—[eh], **i**—[ee], **o**—[oh], **u**—[oo].

5. Playing a game

La maestra reinforces the sounds of the vowels by showing vowel cards to Rosco and Dora and asking **¿Es ___ o es ___?** (*Is it ___ or is it ___?*).

6. Practicing vowel sounds

La maestra takes away the vowel cards one at a time and asks which one is missing. She then says **Vamos a mirar** (*Let's watch*). The mime shows the proper position of the mouth and lips while the vowels are being pronounced. **La maestra** reviews vowel sounds again by removing vowel cards one at a time and repeating the entire series.

FYI

La maestra says to Rosco and Dora **Hablan muy bien el español** (*You speak Spanish very well*). Note that the plural subject (Rosco and Dora) is implied in the plural verb form **hablan**.

FYI

Dora says **Yo sé las vocales**, which means *I know the vowels*.

LEVEL TWO

7. Helping the children listen for vowel sounds and reviewing the seasons

La maestra reminds the children that they use vowel sounds whenever they speak Spanish. She asks **¿Qué estación es?** (*What season is it?*) and reviews the names of the seasons, beginning with **el invierno** (*winter*). After pointing out the [ee] and [oh] sounds in **invierno**, she continues with **la primavera** (*spring*), **el verano** (*summer*), and **el otoño** (*fall*). She points out the several [oh] sounds in **otoño** and reviews the questions **¿Qué estación es?** (*What season is it?*) and **¿Qué tiempo hace en ___?** (*What is the weather like in ___?*) as well as some responses to the latter question: **Hace frío y nieva en el invierno** (*It is cold and it snows in the winter*); **Hace buen tiempo en la primavera** (*The weather is good in the spring*); **Hace calor y hace sol en el verano** (*It is hot and sunny in the summer*); **Hace viento en el otoño** (*It is windy in the fall*).

8. Singing a song

After saying **Vamos a cantar** (*Let's sing*), **la maestra** leads the children in singing "**Las estaciones**" ("*The Seasons*"). For song lyrics, see Lesson 27, Video Lesson, section 7.

9. Reviewing numbers

Rosco says **Me gusta contar** (*I like to count*). **La maestra** says **Vamos a contar** (*Let's count*) and points to the **números grandes** (*big numbers*) 10–100. She then presents the video showing slow-moving traffic to review **despacio** (*slowly*) and says **Vamos a contar despacio** (*Let's count slowly*). Rosco and the children count the numbers slowly and play a short game of **¿Qué número es?** (*What number is it?*). **La maestra** then shows the video of fast-moving traffic to illustrate **rápido** (*quickly*) and says **Vamos a contar rápido** (*Let's count quickly*). After Rosco and the children have counted quickly, **la maestra** points at number cards and asks **¿Qué número es?** (*What number is it?*).

10. Closing

La maestra reviews the topics presented in today's lesson. She and Rosco then say **Adiós**.

FYI: **Me gusta esa canción** means *I like that song.* **Me gusta cantar** means *I like to sing.* **A los niños les gusta cantar** means *The children like to sing.*

Numbers:

diez	10
veinte	20
treinta	30
cuarenta	40
cincuenta	50
sesenta	60
setenta	70
ochenta	80
noventa	90
cien	100

FYI: **La maestra** tells Rosco **Te gusta cuando contamos rápido** (*You like it when we count quickly*).

After viewing the video, praise the children for their good listening and watching skills.

Lesson Forty-Four

Blackline Master 29A

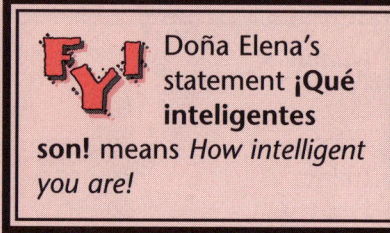

Doña Elena's statement ¡Qué inteligentes son! means *How intelligent you are!*

a e i o u
1. __m__go
2. R__sc__
3. D__r__
4. Jorg__
5. j__li__

Blackline Master 44B

ACTIVITY LESSON

Activity 44A: The seasons

Materials: Cassette player; Activity Cassette 2, Side B; Blackline Master 29A; and scissors.

Preparation: Duplicate Blackline Master 29A so that each child has a copy. Give each child or pair of children a pair of scissors and have the children cut out the pictures on the activity sheets.

Ask the class to arrange the pictures on their desks in any order they choose. Then explain that doña Elena is going to ask them to show her the picture of each season as she names it.

You may want to perform the activity several times, each time asking a different child to play the part of doña Elena by saying **Muéstrame** (*Show me*) and naming the seasons: **la primavera** (*spring*), **el verano** (*summer*), **el otoño** (*fall*), **el invierno** (*winter*).

Activity 44B: *Las vocales* (Vowels)

Materials: Cassette player; Activity Cassette 2, Side B; Blackline Master 44B; pencils; vowel cards from Activity 43B.

Preparation: Duplicate Blackline Master 44B so that each child has a copy. Give each child a pencil.

Point out that each of the words on the activity sheet is missing at least one vowel. Tell the children that doña Elena will say each word. If they listen closely, they will be able to hear the sound of each missing vowel. They should write each vowel they hear in the correct blank. As doña Elena gives each answer, you may want to point to or hold up the appropriate vowel card. Missing vowels: 1. **a**, **i** (**amigo**); 2. **o**, **o** (**Rosco**); 3. **o**, **a** (**Dora**); 4. **e** (**Jorge**); 5. **u**, **o** (**julio**).

Activity 44C: Arrange numbers

Materials: Blackline Master 43A; scissors.

Preparation: Give a pair of scissors to each child or pair of children and ask them to cut up Blackline Master 43A into six separate numbers.

Ask each child to arrange the six numbers in order, starting with the smallest. When they have finished, let them discuss their conclusions with a partner, saying the names of the numbers in Spanish. You may want to repeat the activity, this time asking the partners to mix up the numbers and then arrange them from largest to smallest.

Answers: 17 (**diecisiete**); 27 (**vientisiete**); 37 (**treinta y siete**); 57 (**cincuenta y siete**); 77 (**setenta y siete**); and 78 (**setenta y ocho**).

LEVEL TWO

Closing

Tell the children that Spanish class is finished for today. In the next class they will learn how to answer the telephone in Spanish.

Family Connection

To foster a friendly link between home and school, you may want to send out Family Letter 3 (see the Teacher's Resource Book). This letter suggests how families can be involved in their children's learning of Spanish.

If You Have Time...

Materials: Cassette player; "Calendar Rap" and **"Las estaciones"** (*"The Seasons"*) on the Song Cassette, Side A.

Play each song as the children listen; then encourage them to sing along. Instead of the children clapping during "Calendar Rap," you may want to ask them to tap their feet or tap a pencil or pen on the desk. For rap lyrics, see Lesson 12, Video Lesson, section 3; and for song lyrics, see Lesson 27, Video Lesson, section 7.

Lesson Forty-Four

Lesson 45

Materials to gather

- VCR and Video Lesson 45 on Tape 12
- Cassette player
- Activity Cassette 2
- Song Cassette
- An encyclopedia
- Blackline Master 45A (telephone)
- Scissors
- Drawing paper
- Crayons
- *Optional materials:* laminating machine

OBJECTIVES

Language

- Learn a new game reinforcing vowel sounds
- Learn new vocabulary relating to the telephone
- Learn new vocabulary relating to the home

Culture

- Understand that people all over the world live in different kinds of homes
- Understand that there are different ways of answering the phone in Spanish

Review

- Recall expressions for feelings
- Practice expressions relating to the calendar
- Practice vowel sounds
- Show comprehension of **rápido** (*quickly*)

Vocabulary

Vocabulary for the telephone:

el teléfono	*telephone*
Diga.	*Hello.*
Adiós.	*Good-bye.*
Hasta luego.	*See you later.*
Hasta mañana.	*Until tomorrow.*

Vocabulary for the home:

la casa	*house*
la sala	*living room*
el comedor	*dining room*
el baño	*bathroom*
el cuarto	*bedroom*
la cocina	*kitchen*

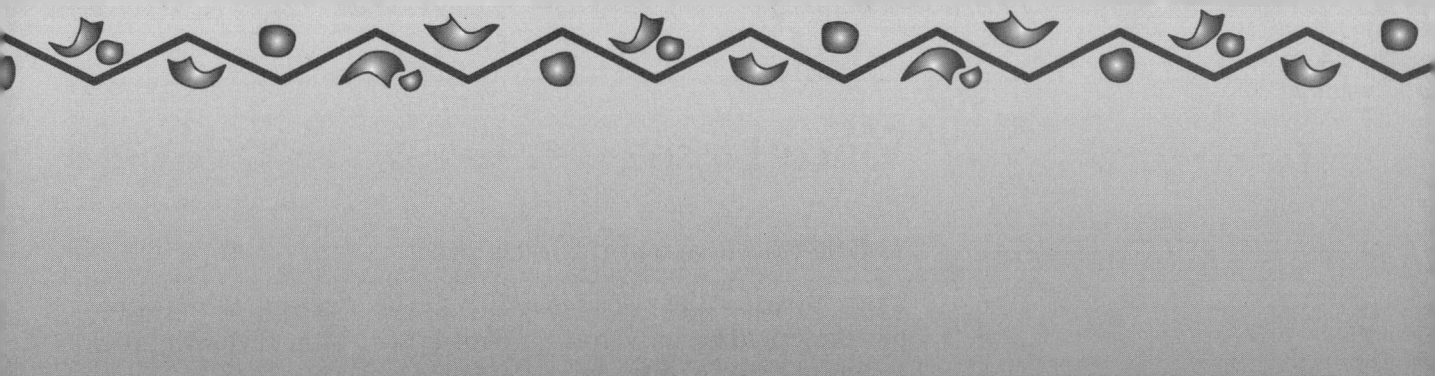

Warm-up

Lead the children in a discussion about the telephone. Why is it such an important invention? What does it enable people to do that they couldn't do otherwise? What do people say when they answer the phone? What do they say before they hang up?

Review

Ask the children to tell you the Spanish words for the actions you pantomime. Then pantomime commands such as the following: *jump* (**salta**), *walk* (**anda**), *run* (**corre**), *sit* (**siéntate**), *touch ___* (**toca ___**), *look for ___* (**busca ___**), *color* (**colorea**).

Introduce the video

Encourage the children to listen and watch as **la maestra** and Rosco teach them how to answer the telephone in Spanish.

VIDEO LESSON

1. Greeting Rosco and the children

Using **Buenos días** (*Good morning*) as the greeting, **la maestra** has the opening conversation with Rosco. After reviewing the response **Estoy contento/a** (*I'm happy*), she has the conversation with the children.

2. Reviewing expressions of feelings

La maestra reviews some ways to answer **¿Cómo estás tú?** (*How are you?*), such as **Estoy contento/a** (*I'm happy*), **Estoy triste** (*I'm sad*), and **Estoy enojado/a** (*I'm angry*). She reminds the children that **niños** (*boys*) and other males answer **Estoy contento** and **Estoy enojado**; **niñas** (*girls*) and other females answer **Estoy contenta** and **Estoy enojada**, and both males and females answer **Estoy triste**.

3. Reviewing the calendar

Showing a large calendar, **la maestra** points to a couple of days and asks Rosco **¿Qué día es?** (*What day is it?*) Rosco replies **Es viernes** (*It's Friday*) and **Es martes** (*It's Tuesday*).

4. Singing a song

La maestra says **Vamos a cantar** (*Let's sing*). She reviews the names of the days of the week with the "Calendar Rap." For rap lyrics, see Lesson 12, Video Lesson, section 3.

5. Reviewing the names of the months

La maestra asks **¿Qué mes es?** (*What month is it?*). Using pictures that represent the twelve months, she reviews their names. Finally, she holds up a card showing the number 12 to indicate that **Hay doce meses del año** (*There are twelve months in the year*).

6. Singing another song

La maestra sings the "Months Rap." For rap lyrics, see Lesson 12, Video Lesson, section 4. Afterwards she says **¡Qué divertido fue!** (*What fun that was!*).

7. Reviewing *las vocales* (*vowels*)

La maestra reminds the children that when we speak and sing we use special sounds called vowels. Holding up vowel cards, she reviews the vowel sounds: **a**—[ah], **e**—[eh], **i**—[ee], **o**—[oh], **u**—[oo]. Integrating the phrase **más rápido** (*faster*), she teaches the children a vowel game in which they do the following while saying the vowel sounds: A—touch nose; E—touch shoulders; I—snap fingers; O—clap hands, U—slap thighs.

FYI La maestra says **Vamos a practicar los días de la semana** (*Let's practice the days of the week*) and **Hay siete días de la semana** (*There are seven days in the week*).

Days of the week:

lunes	Monday
martes	Tuesday
miércoles	Wednesday
jueves	Thursday
viernes	Friday
sábado	Saturday
domingo	Sunday

Months of the year:

enero	January
febrero	February
marzo	March
abril	April
mayo	May
junio	June
julio	July
agosto	August
septiembre	September
octubre	October
noviembre	November
diciembre	December

LEVEL TWO

8. Answering the telephone

Brrring! It's the telephone! **La maestra** says **Busco el teléfono—aquí está** (*I'm looking for the telephone—here it is*). She answers it by saying **Diga**, which is equivalent to *Hello*. No one responds, and **la maestra** says **No hay nadie** (*There's no one there*). She then asks the children to pretend that they are answering the telephone by saying **Diga**. The phone rings again—**otra vez**. This time it's doña Elena calling **la maestra** to say **Quiero invitarla a visitar mi casa** (*I want to invite you to visit my house*)—**mañana** (*tomorrow*)! **La maestra** agrees, saying **Me gusta la idea** (*I like the idea*).

9. Introducing vocabulary relating to the home

La maestra explains that she is excited about visiting doña Elena at her house **porque la casa de doña Elena es muy bonita** (*because doña Elena's house is very pretty*). Wondering what some of the rooms in the house will be, she shows pictures of a home and its rooms. After naming each room, she asks the children to **repite** (*repeat*). For the names of the rooms, see the Vocabulary Section.

10. Practicing vocabulary for rooms of the home

La maestra tells Rosco **Voy a visitar la casa de doña Elena** (*I'm going to visit doña Elena's house*). She and Rosco review the purpose of each room: cooking—**la cocina** (*kitchen*), sleeping—**el cuarto** (*bedroom*), sitting and visiting with company or watching television—**la sala** (*living room*), sitting at a table for a meal—**el comedor** (*dining room*), bathing and showering—**el baño** (*bathroom*).

11. Practicing with the telephone

La maestra helps the children practice saying **teléfono** and **Diga** (*Hello*) to answer the phone.

12. Saying good-bye

La maestra and Rosco teach the children some ways of ending a phone conversation: **Adiós** (*Good-bye*), **Hasta luego** (*See you later*), and **Hasta mañana** (*Until tomorrow*). She reminds the children that tomorrow she will visit doña Elena and says **¡Qué divertido será!** (*What fun it will be!*).

13. Closing

La maestra and Rosco say **Adiós**, and **la maestra** reminds the children to answer the phone by saying **Diga** (*Hello*).

FYI **Diga** literally means *Speak* or *Talk*. Other ways to answer the phone in various Spanish-speaking countries are **Dígame** (*Speak to me*) and **Oigo** (*I'm listening*) in Spain and **Bueno**, which is probably short for **Buenos días**, in Mexico. **Hola** (*Hi*) is understood in all Spanish-speaking countries. Doña Elena ends the conversation by saying **Hasta entonces**, which means *Until then*.

La maestra tells Rosco **Duermes en el cuarto** (*You sleep in the bedroom*) and **Comes en el comedor** (*You eat in the dining room*).

If necessary, lead the children in pronouncing **teléfono** with the accent on the second syllable, as the accent mark makes clear.

After viewing the video, praise the children for their good listening and watching skills.

Lesson Forty-Five

Blackline Master 45A

You may want to laminate the children's pictures of telephones for use in future activities and games.

Use this opportunity to point out that different people live in different kinds of homes, such as apartment buildings, houses, town houses, and condominiums. Help the children use an encyclopedia to expand the discussion to include people in cultures all over the world.

LEVEL TWO

ACTIVITY LESSON

Activity 45A: Talk on the telephone

Materials: Cassette player; Activity Cassette 2, Side B; Blackline Master 45A; and scissors.

Preparation: Duplicate Blackline Master 45A so that each child has a copy. Divide the class into pairs. Give each pair of children a pair of scissors. Ask them to cut out the picture of the telephone.

Tell the children that **la maestra** is going to remind them how to answer the telephone in Spanish and then give them a chance to answer their make-believe telephones.

For the second part of this activity, explain that one of the children in each pair should imitate the sound of a telephone ringing. The other child should answer the make-believe phone by saying **Diga** (*Hello*). The first child should then say **Buenos días** (*Good morning*) to initiate the opening conversation between the partners.

Activity 45B: Draw pictures

Materials: Drawing paper; crayons.

Preparation: Distribute drawing paper and crayons to each child.

Ask the children to draw pictures relating to their homes. For example, they could draw the outside of their house or apartment building, their favorite room in the home, or a family member doing a certain activity, such as cooking or reading, in one of the rooms. When they have finished, ask the children to describe their pictures. Then mount them on the bulletin board or encourage the children to take them home.

Activity 45C: Sing

Materials: Cassette player; "Months Rap" and **"Las vocales"** (*"The Vowels"*) on Side A of the Song Cassette.

Play the "Months Rap" as the children listen; then encourage them to sing along. For song lyrics, see Lesson 12, Video Lesson, section 4. Next, help the children learn a song that will give them practice in saying the vowel sounds in Spanish—**"Las vocales"** (*"The Vowels"*). Play the song several times before encouraging them to sing along.

"**Las vocales**" (*"The Vowels"*)

A, E, I, O, U.
A, mapa.
E, Pepe.
I, Lili.
O, rojo.
U, cucú.
A, E, I, O, U.

Closing

Tell the children that Spanish class is finished for today. In the next class they will go with **la maestra** as she visits doña Elena at her home.

IF YOU HAVE TIME...

Materials: The make-believe telephones from Activity 45A.

Give the children a chance to practice dialing their home telephone numbers. If they don't know their numbers, encourage them to find out what they are. In the meantime, write a telephone number on the board that they can pretend to dial, such as 555-4287. Ask the children to say the numbers softly to themselves in Spanish while they are pretending to dial.

LANGUAGE ACROSS THE CURRICULUM

Use the children's practice with talking on the telephone as a jumping-off point for a history lesson. Help them use an encyclopedia to research the inventor of the telephone, Alexander Graham Bell, what the first telephone looked like, the first words spoken over the telephone, and so on.

Lesson Forty-Five

Lesson 46

Materials to gather

- VCR and Video Lesson 46 on Tape 12
- Cassette player
- Activity Cassette 2
- Song Cassette

- *Optional materials:* make-believe telephones from Activity 45A

- *Prepare ahead:* cut out (and laminate) pictures illustrating a house and the rooms of the house (Activity 46A)

OBJECTIVES

Language
- Understand sustained conversation about the home
- Recognize vowel sounds in words
- Respond to visual cues to answer questions about the seasons and weather

Culture
- Review the custom of greeting a friend by kissing her or him on both cheeks

Review
- Recall expressions for feelings
- Practice vowel sounds
- Recall meaning of **rápido** (*quickly*) and **despacio** (*slowly*)
- Recall the names of the seasons
- Recall weather expressions associated with different seasons
- Practice vocabulary related to the telephone
- Practice vocabulary related to the home

Vocabulary
No new vocabulary is introduced in this lesson.

Warm-up

Remind the children that **la maestra** is going to visit her friend doña Elena today. Encourage them to recall what friends in Spanish-speaking countries do to greet each other (kiss each other on both cheeks). Ask them to watch to see if **la maestra** and doña Elena carry out this custom when they meet.

Review

Remind the children that in the last lesson they learned the Spanish names for rooms of the home. Ask them to recall what other rooms they have learned about in Spanish class (rooms of the school). Review the vocabulary for rooms of the school by asking questions like these: Where does the school secretary work? (**la oficina**—*the office*) Where would you go to look for a book? (**la biblioteca**—*the library*) Where do you eat lunch? (**la cafetería**—*the cafeteria*) Where do you go to wash your hands? (**el baño**—*the bathroom*) Where do you go to play outside? (**el patio**—*the playground*) Where can you usually find your teacher? (**la clase**—*the classroom*)

Introduce the video

Encourage the children to listen and watch as **la maestra** pays a visit to doña Elena at her home. Remind them that listening carefully and watching what people do while speaking will help them understand the conversation.

273

VIDEO LESSON

1. Greeting Rosco and the children

Using **Buenos días** (*Good morning*) as the greeting, **la maestra** has the opening conversation with the children. She says that she is **muy contenta** (*very happy*). When Rosco asks **¿Por qué?** (*Why?*), she replies **Porque estoy aquí con ustedes** (*Because I'm here with you* [*plural*]). **La maestra** asks Rosco **¿Estás contento?** He replies **Sí, estoy muy contento** (*Yes, I'm very happy*), and **la maestra** asks him **¿No estás enojado?** (*Aren't you angry?*) and **¿No estás triste?** (*Aren't you sad?*).

2. Reviewing *las vocales* (*vowels*)

La maestra reminds the children of the body game based on the vowel sounds. Integrating the words **más rápido** (*faster*) and **despacio** (*slowly*), she leads the game by doing the following while saying the vowel sounds: A—touch nose; E—touch shoulders; I—snap fingers; O—clap hands; U—slap thighs.

3. Helping the children listen for vowel sounds and reviewing the seasons

La maestra points out to the children that they can hear vowel sounds in everything they say, including the names of the seasons: **el invierno** (*winter*), **la primavera** (*spring*), **el verano** (*summer*), **el otoño** (*fall*). She points out the [oh] sounds in **otoño**.

4. Reviewing weather expressions

After pointing out that different seasons have different weather, **la maestra** reviews the question **¿Qué tiempo hace?** (*What is the weather like?*). Using Flashcards showing weather conditions she reviews weather expressions: **Hace viento** (*It is windy*), **Hace calor y hace sol** (*It is hot and sunny*), **Hace buen tiempo** (*The weather is good*), **Hace frío y nieva** (*It is cold and it's snowing*), **Hace frío** (*It is cold*), **Llueve y hace mal tiempo** (*It's raining and it's bad weather*), **Llueve** (*It's raining*).

5. Practicing weather expressions with names of seasons

Asking **¿Qué estación es?**, **la maestra** reviews the names of the seasons combined with weather expressions: **En el invierno hace frío** (*In the winter it's cold*), **En la primavera hace buen tiempo** (*In the spring it's good weather*), **En el verano hace calor** (*In the summer it's hot*), **En el otoño hace viento** (*In the fall it's windy*).

6. Singing a song

Rosco says **Vamos a cantar** (*Let's sing*), to which **la maestra** replies **Pues, sí** (*Of course*). She leads the children in singing "**Las estaciones**" ("*The Seasons*"). For song lyrics, see Lesson 27, Video Lesson, section 7.

La maestra's statement **Es muy divertido** means *It's a lot of fun.*

You may want to point out that in some ways Spanish is easier to read than English. With only a few exceptions, each Spanish vowel has only one sound, while English vowels can have a long or short sound.

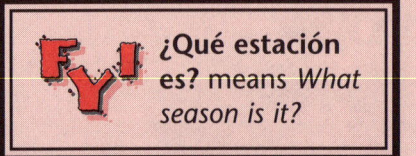

FYI **¿Qué estación es?** means *What season is it?*

LEVEL TWO

7. Practicing vocabulary

La maestra tells Rosco that every **estación del año** (*season of the year*) is a good season to visit friends. She reminds him of her upcoming visit to doña Elena's house and tells him that the house has a lot of rooms. She reviews vocabulary relating to the home, which she asks the children to **repite** (*repeat*): **la casa** (*house*), **la sala** (*living room*), **el comedor** (*dining room*), **el baño** (*bathroom*), **el cuarto** (*bedroom*), **la cocina** (*kitchen*).

She tells the children that these are **todas las partes de la casa** (*all the areas of the house*).

8. Reviewing expressions for the telephone

Before going to doña Elena's house **la maestra** reviews expressions for the telephone and points out that the telephone lets us talk to people who are far away.

9. Visiting doña Elena's house

Arriving at **la casa de doña Elena** (*doña Elena's house*), **la maestra** greets her friend by kissing her on both cheeks. Doña Elena is holding a baby, her **hija** (*daughter*). **La niña se llama Elenita** (*The little girl's name is Elenita*). The hand puppet Rosco is nearby; doña Elena explains of her daughter: **Le encanta jugar con Rosco** (*She loves to play with Rosco*).

Doña Elena takes **la maestra** on a tour of her house. Remarks in their conversation include: **La sala es grande** (*The living room is big*), **La cocina es pequeña** (*The kitchen is small*), **El comedor es muy bonito** (*The dining room is very pretty*), **La hija tiene sueño** (*The child is sleepy*), **A ella le gusta mucho su cuarto** (*She likes her room a lot*), the **colores** (*colors*) in **el baño** (*bathroom*) are **blanco, rosado y negro** (*white, pink, and black*).

After showing **la maestra** her home, doña Elena says **Gracias por visitarnos** (*Thanks for visiting us*). **La maestra** replies **Es un placer** (*It is a pleasure*), and doña Elena says **Vuelva pronto** (*Come back soon*).

10. Playing games

La maestra reviews vocabulary relating to the home by playing **Muéstrame ___** (*Show me ___*) and the choice game **¿Es ___ o es ___?** (*Is it ___ or is it ___?*) For vocabulary, see section 7 of this lesson.

11. Closing

La maestra remarks about the game they just played **¡Qué divertido fue!** (*What fun that was!*). She and Rosco say **Adiós**.

FYI Besides being a common word for *bedroom*, **cuarto** is a generic word for *room*. Other words for *bedroom* are **recámara**, **habitación**, and **dormitorio**.

Telephone expressions:

Diga.   Hello.
Adiós. Good-bye.

FYI Note that in Spanish, the possessive is indicated by **de** (*of*) rather than by an apostrophe, as in English. Thus, **la casa de doña Elena**—*the house of doña Elena* or *doña Elena's house*.

After viewing the video, praise the children for their good listening and watching skills.

Lesson Forty-Six

ACTIVITY LESSON

Activity 46A: Walk, jump, run

Materials: Cassette player; Activity Cassette 2, Side B; and visuals illustrating vocabulary relating to the home.

Preparation: Cut out magazine or newspaper pictures showing a house and its rooms (living room, dining room, bathroom, bedroom, and kitchen) or create them yourself. You may want to laminate the pictures for future use. Display them where children can reach them.

Tell the children that you are going to point to individual children and that **la maestra** is going to ask that child to **anda** (*walk*), **salta** (*jump*), or **corre** (*run*) to the picture she names and to touch it (**toca**). Then play the activity, choosing different children as prompted by **la maestra**.

> You may want to play the activity more than once. As a variation, ask each child who touches a picture to choose the next child.

Activity 46B: Talk about communication

Lead a discussion about ways people keep in touch with each other, such as writing letters, telephoning, faxing, using e-mail, and so on. How many of these methods have the children used? What do they like and dislike about them? What are some of the advantages and disadvantages of each? If possible, arrange a visit to the office of your school, where the secretary can demonstrate and explain the communication devices school employees use.

Activity 46C: Sing along

Materials: Cassette player; "**Las estaciones**" ("*The Seasons*") and "**Las vocales**" ("*The Vowels*") on the Song Cassette, Side A.

Encourage the children to sing the songs. For song lyrics, see Lesson 27, Video Lesson, section 7 and Lesson 45, Activity 45C, respectively. After you say the name of each season, help the children name each vowel sound they hear. Vowel sounds: **primavera** (*spring*)—[ee], [ah], [eh], [ah]; **verano** (*summer*)—[eh], [ah], [oh]; **otoño** (*fall*)—[oh], [oh], [oh]; **invierno** (*winter*)—[ee], [ee], [eh], [oh].

> **HERITAGE SPEAKERS**
>
> If you have heritage speakers in your class, you might ask them to take turns saying the names of the seasons several times before the rest of the children name the vowel sounds.

LEVEL TWO

Closing

Tell the children that Spanish class is finished for today. In the next class they will learn some new phrases in Spanish.

> **If You Have Time...**
>
> Materials: The make-believe telephones from Activity 45A.
>
> Divide the class into pairs. Ask the partners to take turns pretending they are **la maestra** and doña Elena. **La maestra** is to call doña Elena to talk about her pleasant visit. Encourage the children to discuss the rooms of doña Elena's house, using Spanish words and phrases whenever possible. Remind the children to use **Diga** (*Hello*) and **Adiós** (*Good-bye*) during the conversation.

Lesson 47

Materials to gather

- VCR and Video Lesson 47 on Tape 12
- Cassette player
- Activity Cassette 2
- Song Cassette
- Pictures of rooms you gathered for Activity 46A
- Blackline Master 47A (rooms of the home)
- Scissors

Objectives

Language
- Learn new conversational phrases
- Understand sustained conversation about the home
- Learn vocabulary for family members

Culture
- Recognize similarities and differences in families and homes

Review
- Practice vowel sounds
- Recall the expressions **más rápido** (*faster*) and **más despacio** (*slower*)
- Practice the expressions **¿Dónde está ... ?** (*Where is . . . ?*) and **Aquí está** (*Here he/she/it is*)
- Practice vocabulary relating to the home

Vocabulary

¿Qué haces?	*What are you doing?*
Hablo por teléfono.	*I'm talking on the telephone.*
la mamá	*mother*
el papá	*father*
la hija	*daughter*
el hijo	*son*
el abuelo	*grandfather*
la abuela	*grandmother*

Warm-up

Remind the children that in the last lesson **la maestra** went to visit her friend doña Elena. Ask them to pretend that **la maestra** is coming to visit their homes. Encourage them to discuss whom she might meet there and what they would like to show her.

Review

Materials: Pictures you gathered for Activity 46A showing rooms of the home.

Review colors by pointing to various items in the pictures and asking **¿De qué color es?** or *What color is it?* Encourage the children to answer you with the sentence **Es de color ___** (*It is ___*).

Introduce the video

Tell the children that in today's video they will see a repeat of **la maestra**'s visit to doña Elena's house and learn vocabulary for family members.

Colors:

amarillo	*yellow*
anaranjado	*orange*
azul	*blue*
blanco	*white*
café	*brown*
gris	*gray*
morado	*purple*
negro	*black*
rojo	*red*
rosado	*pink*
verde	*green*

FYI Presenting episodes containing sustained conversation more than once gives the children added exposure to Spanish as it is spoken in real life at the same time that it gives them practice in using context clues to figure out meaning. During the second viewing the children will probably understand much more of the conversation between **la maestra** and doña Elena than they did during the first viewing.

> **FYI** **Rápido** can mean either *quickly* or *quick/fast*. When it is used as an adjective to mean *quick*, its ending must reflect the gender and number of the word it describes:
>
> **el** coche rápid**o**
> *the fast car*
>
> **la** motocicle**ta** rápid**a**
> *the fast motorcycle*
>
> When it is used as an adverb to mean *quickly*, its ending does not change:
>
> **Los** niñ**os** corren rápido.
> *The children run quickly.*

> **FYI** The present progressive in English (*I'm studying; I'm talking*) can be rendered in Spanish by the simple present tense. Thus, **estudio** can mean either *I study* or *I am studying* and **hablo** either *I speak* or *I am speaking*, depending on the context.

> **LANGUAGE ACROSS THE CURRICULUM**
>
> Now that the children are familiar with the names of rooms of the home, encourage them to draw maps of their homes. You might begin by helping them draw a map showing, for example, how to get from their classroom to the bathroom or cafeteria. Then ask them to draw a map showing how to get from their front door to each of the rooms on the same floor.

VIDEO LESSON

1. Greeting Rosco and the children

La maestra is talking on the telephone about her visit to doña Elena's house. Rosco interrupts her to tell her that she has a class. Using **Buenos días** (*Good morning*) as the greeting, **la maestra** has the opening conversation with the children and Rosco.

2. Asking and answering questions

La maestra tells Rosco that she's been having a lot of fun. **Hablo por teléfono** (*I'm talking on the telephone*), she explains and then asks Rosco **¿Qué haces tú?** (*What are you doing?*). Rosco answers **No hablo por teléfono—no me gusta.** (*I'm not talking on the telephone—I don't like it*).

3. Reviewing *las vocales* (*vowels*)

La maestra tells Rosco that she has something for him to do—practice the vowel sounds. Integrating the phrases **más rápido** (*faster*) and **más despacio** (*slower*), she plays the body game by doing the following while saying the vowel sounds: A—touch nose; E—touch shoulders; I—snap fingers; O—clap hands, U—slap thighs.

4. Reviewing questions and answers

La maestra asks Rosco **¿Dónde está Dora?** (*Where is Dora?*). Rosco replies **Un momento** (*Just a moment*) and leaves to find her. Dora appears, and in response to her question **¿Qué haces?** (*What are you doing?*) **la maestra** answers **Hablo por teléfono y juego con las vocales** (*I'm talking on the telephone and playing with vowels*). **La maestra** asks Dora **¿Qué haces?** and Dora answers **Estudio español** (*I'm studying Spanish*). **La maestra** explains that to ask someone what he or she is doing, one says **¿Qué haces?**

La maestra asks the children to repeat **¿Qué haces?** and to pretend to talk on the phone and say **Hablo por teléfono** (*I'm talking on the telephone*).

La maestra informs Dora that she had a telephone call from doña Elena and that she went to visit doña Elena and her **hija** (*daughter*), Elenita, **en su casa** (*at her home*).

5. Visiting doña Elena's house

La maestra's visit to doña Elena's house is shown again. Some of the remarks during the visit are:

¡Qué bonita es la hija!	*How pretty your daughter is!*
La bebé es preciosa.	*The baby is precious.*
Elenita tiene hambre.	*Elenita is hungry.*

Este es el cuarto de Elenita. *This is Elenita's room.*
Te dejamos en tu cuarto. *We'll leave you in your room.*

When **la maestra** says **Me gusta tu casa** (*I like your house*), doña Elena replies **Es tuya** (*It is yours*), which in many Spanish-speaking countries is a statement of courtesy comparable to *Make yourself at home.*

6. Playing a game

Vamos a jugar (*Let's play*) says **la maestra** before initiating a game of **Muéstrame ___** (*Show me ___*) and the choice game **¿Es ___ o es ___?** (*Is it ___ or is it ___?*) to practice vocabulary relating to the home.

7. Playing another game

La maestra asks **¿Dónde está Rosco?** (*Where is Rosco?*) and **¿Dónde está Dora?** Receiving the reply **Aquí estoy** (*Here I am*) from both, she says **Vamos a jugar** (*Let's play*), initiating a game of **¿Dónde está la maestra?** (*Where is the teacher?*) to review vocabulary relating to the home. The appropriate form of the response to the question is **Está en ___** (*She is in ___*). **La maestra** emphasizes that each room has a different purpose by asking Rosco where he would go to wash his hands (**el baño**—*bathroom*), eat (**la cocina** or **el comedor**—*kitchen* or *dining room*), and sleep (**el cuarto**—*bedroom*). She also points out that every house is a little different because every **familia** (*family*) is different. A family can be **pequeña** (*small*) or **grande** (*big*), and each family is made up of different members.

8. Introducing vocabulary for members of the family

Showing Flashcards representing family members and naming them, **la maestra** asks the children to **repite** (*repeat*)—**la mamá** (*mother*), **el papá** (*father*), **la hija** (*daughter*), **el hijo** (*son*), **el abuelo** (*grandfather*), **la abuela** (*grandmother*). **La maestra** points out that every **familia** (*family*) needs to be celebrated.

9. Singing a song

La maestra suggests that they celebrate the lesson by singing "**Español para ti**" ("*Spanish Is for You, and for Me*") and then says **Vamos a cantar** (*Let's sing*). For song lyrics, see Lesson 3, Video Lesson, section 3.

10. Closing

After **la maestra** expresses her wish that everyone in the children's **familia** (*family*) and **casa** (*house*) is well, she and Rosco say **Adiós**.

Vocabulary relating to the home:

la casa	*house*
la sala	*living room*
el comedor	*dining room*
el baño	*bathroom*
el cuarto	*bedroom*
la cocina	*kitchen*

HERITAGE SPEAKERS

The extended family plays an important role in the lives of many Hispanic families. Divide the class into small groups and encourage the children to discuss their families. Get them started with such questions as: Who lives in your house with you? Do your grandparents, aunts, uncles, or cousins live nearby? Do you see these family members often? When they have finished talking, ask one member of each group to summarize the discussion. Encourage the children to note similarities and differences in the family lives of their classmates.

After viewing the video, praise the children for their good listening and watching skills.

Lesson Forty-Seven

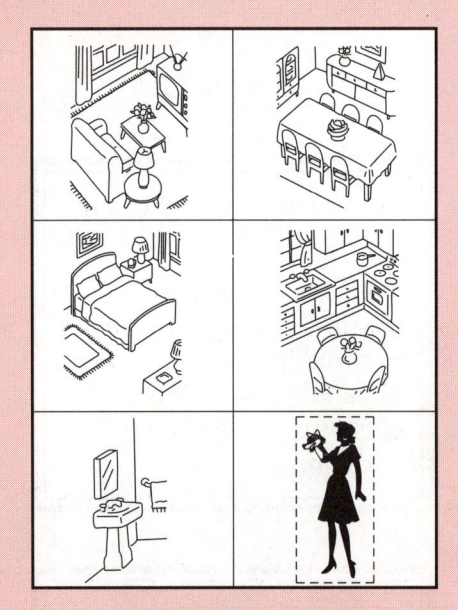

Blackline Master 47A

You may want to play Activity 47A more than once. As a variation, divide the class into pairs and ask partners to take turns asking each other to **toca** (*touch*) certain pictures.

Activity Lesson

Activity 47A: *Toca* ___ (Touch ___)

Materials: Blackline Master 47A; Cassette player; and Activity Cassette 2, Side B.

Preparation: Duplicate Blackline Master 47A so that each child has a copy.

Ask the children to name each room shown on the activity sheet (**la sala**—*living room*; **el comedor**—*dining room*; **el cuarto**—*bedroom*; **la cocina**—*kitchen*; **el baño**—*bathroom*). Tell the children that they are to touch the picture of each room that **la maestra** names.

Activity 47B: *Pon la maestra en ...* (Put the teacher in . . .)

Materials: Cassette player; Activity Cassette 2, Side B; Blackline Master 47A; and scissors.

Preparation: Distribute Blackline Master 47A, one per child or pair of children. Give scissors to each child or pair of children and ask them to cut out the picture of **la maestra** along the dotted line.

Tell them that **la maestra** is going to ask them to put (**pon**) the picture of the teacher in the rooms of the house that she names.

Activity 47C: Sing

Materials: Cassette player; "**Español para ti**" ("*Spanish Is for You, and for Me*") on the Song Cassette, Side A.

After the children sing the song, lead them in a discussion of the **nueva sensación** (*new sensation* or *feeling*) that speaking Spanish gives them. (The children may comment that it feels different to speak and hear words that are totally new to them; they may also remark that it is fun to be able to speak to each other in a language that other people may not understand.) For song lyrics, see Lesson 3, Video Lesson, section 3.

LEVEL TWO

CLOSING

Tell the children that Spanish class is finished for today. In the next class they will talk about ways of going places.

> **IF YOU HAVE TIME...**
>
> Materials: Blackline Master 47A; scissors.
>
> Preparation: Divide the class into pairs. Give two copies of Blackline Master 47A and scissors to each pair of children.
>
> Ask the partners to cut out the pictures of rooms. Encourage them to use the pictures in a game of concentration. The players should arrange one set of pictures faceup, study them for a minute or two, and then turn them facedown. The partner who is holding the other set of pictures should draw from the pictures on the desk to try to match them with the ones he or she is holding in as few draws as possible. When the first player has matched all the pictures, the players should rearrange the pictures before the second player takes a turn. The player who matches the pictures in the fewest draws is the winner.

Ask the children to name the rooms in Spanish as they play the game in *If you have time...*

Lesson Forty-Seven

Lesson 48

Materials to gather

- VCR and Video Lesson 48 on Tape 12
- Cassette player
- Activity Cassette 2
- Song Cassette
- Gold Flashcard 69
- Gold Flashcards 35–40
- *Optional materials:* crayons, drawing paper

OBJECTIVES

Language
- Learn vocabulary relating to transportation
- Understand conversational statements about transportation

Culture
- Understand the role of grandparents in many Spanish-speaking families
- Recall the donkey as a means of transportation in many Spanish-speaking countries

Review
- Practice vocabulary for family members
- Sing **"Dulce canta el burro"** (*"Sweetly Sings the Donkey"*) and **"Fray Felipe"** (*"Friar Phillip"*)

Vocabulary

el transporte	*transportation*
el autobús	*bus*
el coche	*car*
el avión	*airplane*
el tren	*train*
el jipi	*jeep*
la bicicleta	*bicycle*
la motocicleta	*motorcycle*
el taxi	*taxi*
el bote	*boat*
Voy en ___.	*I'm going by ___.*

Warm-up

Materials: Gold Flashcard 69.

Display the Flashcard and ask the children to name the kinds of transportation shown (bus, car, plane, train). Encourage them to discuss which of these kinds of transportation they have used, where they went, and what they remember about each means of travel.

Review

Materials: Gold Flashcard 69.

Encourage the children to use the words **rápido** (*fast*) and **despacio** (*slow*) to compare the means of transportation shown on the Flashcard. You might begin by pointing to the bus and the plane and asking the children which of the two is more **rápido** and which is more **despacio**.

Introduce the video

Encourage the children to listen and watch as **la maestra** and Rosco talk about families and ways people travel to visit family members.

Video Lesson

1. Greeting Rosco and the children

Using **Buenos días** as the greeting, **la maestra** has the opening conversation with Rosco and the children.

2. Reviewing vocabulary for family members

La maestra tells Rosco that she's been thinking about **la familia** (*the family*). She says to Rosco, **Tu familia es grande** (*Your family is big*) and **Mi familia es pequeña** (*My family is small*). Then she uses Flashcards to review the names of family members: **la mamá** (*mother*), **el papá** (*father*), **la hija** (*daughter*), **el hijo** (*son*), **el abuelo** (*grandfather*), **la abuela** (*grandmother*).

3. Discussing the role of grandparents

La maestra explains that in Spanish-speaking families grandmothers and grandfathers often live in the same house as their children and grandchildren.

4. Singing a song

La maestra asks Rosco why he has a **campana** (*bell*). Rosco replies **Vamos a cantar** (*We're going to sing*). Together they sing "**Fray Felipe**" ("*Friar Phillip*") as Rosco rings the bell at the appropriate time.

Fray Felipe, Fray Felipe.	*Friar Phillip, Friar Phillip.*
¿Duermes tú?	*Are you sleeping?*
¿Duermes tú?	*Are you sleeping?*
Toca la campana, toca la campana.	*Ring the bell, ring the bell.*
Tan, tan, tan. Tan, tan tan.	*Ding, ding, dong. Ding, ding, dong.*

5. Introducing vocabulary for transportation

La maestra points out that people can travel to visit family members in many ways, such as by plane, train, and boat if they are far away, and by car, bus, and taxi if they are close. She then shows Flashcard 69, which depicts four ways of traveling: **autobús** (*bus*), **coche** (*car*), **avión** (*airplane*), and **tren** (*train*). She introduces the phrase **Voy en** ___ (*I'm going by* ___).

HERITAGE SPEAKERS

It is even more common for grandparents to live with their children and grandchildren when one of the grandparents has been widowed. The grandparents often participate in the raising and nurturing of their grandchildren and are respected members of the family. Encourage heritage speakers in your class to describe their grandparents' roles and duties in their families.

In Spanish, **v** is pronounced like *b*. This is especially evident when **v** is at the beginning of a word, such as **voy** (*I'm going* or *I go*).

LEVEL TWO

6. Traveling

Vamos a mirar (*Let's watch*), says **la maestra**. She asks ¿**Qué es esto?** (*What is this?*) and models words for **muchas formas de transporte** (*many forms of transportation*). For transportation vocabulary, see the Vocabulary Section of this lesson. Then she illustrates some of these words, beginning each trip by pointing to two pictures on Flashcard 69 and asking Rosco ¿**Es el ___ o es el ___?** (*Is it the ___ or is it the ___?*). When Rosco answers correctly she says **Voy en ___** (*I'm going by ___*).

Some of **la maestra**'s remarks are: **Estoy aquí con muchos autobuses** (*I'm here with many buses*); **Este autobús es un autobús de la escuela** (*This bus is a school bus*); **El autobús tiene luces** (*The bus has lights*); **Aquí viene el autobús amarillo y negro** (*Here comes the yellow and black bus*); ¿**Quién está en el autobús? ¡Es Rosco!** (*Who is on the bus? It's Rosco!*); **Aquí viene el coche** (*Here comes the car*); ¿**Adónde voy?** (*Where am I going?*); **Doña Elena y yo vamos al restaurante en coche** (*Doña Elena and I are going to the restaurant by car*); **Es la piloto** (*She is the pilot*); **Es un avión pequeño** (*It's a small plane*); **Estoy en la estación de los trenes** (*I am at the train station*); **Voy de viaje en tren** (*I'm going on a train trip*); **Tengo mi maleta** (*I have my suitcase*).

7. Discussing *el burro* (*donkey*)

La maestra remarks that traveling is a wonderful way to have fun and learn new things. She reminds Rosco that in some Spanish-speaking countries, people and children can travel by donkey.

8. Singing a song

Vamos a cantar (*Let's sing*), says **la maestra**. She sings "**Dulce canta el burro**" (*"Sweetly Sings the Donkey"*). For song lyrics, see Lesson 41, Video Lesson, section 5.

9. Practicing

La maestra remarks that it would be fun to sing the song while riding on a donkey. **Voy en burro** (*I'm going by donkey*), Rosco says. **La maestra** asks the children to repeat some other travel phrases: **Voy en autobús** (*I'm going by bus*), **Voy en coche** (*I'm going by car*), **Voy en avión** (*I'm going by plane*), **Voy en tren** (*I'm going by train*).

10. Closing

La maestra repeats that travel is a wonderful way to learn new things and meet fun people. She and Rosco say **Adiós**.

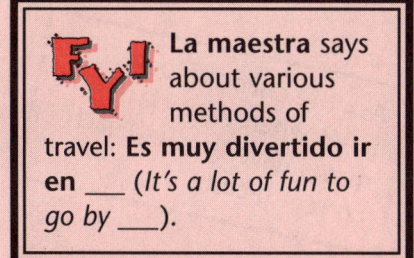

FYI **La maestra** says about various methods of travel: **Es muy divertido ir en ___** (*It's a lot of fun to go by ___*).

FYI The plural **autobuses** has no accent, in contrast to the singular **autobús**.

HERITAGE SPEAKERS

In Cuba, Puerto Rico, and the Canary Islands, **guagua** is the common word for *bus*. In Chile and Bolivia, the same word is used to refer to young children or babies. Ask heritage speakers in your class the word for *bus* in the countries they came from.

After viewing the video, praise the children for their good listening and watching skills.

Lesson Forty-Eight

Ask the children to say ¡Olé! when their classmates have touched each correct picture.

HERITAGE SPEAKERS

Some of your students may have traveled to Spanish-speaking countries to visit relatives. Encourage them to describe their journeys.

ACTIVITY LESSON

Activity 48A: *Toca* ___ (*Touch* ___)

Materials: Gold Flashcards 35–40; Cassette player; and Activity Cassette 2, Side B.

Arrange the Flashcards in numerical order where you and the children can see and reach them. Tell the children that **la maestra** is going to help them review the names of family members. She will ask children chosen by you to touch the picture of the family member she names. You may want to play the activity more than once, choosing different children each time.

Activity 48B: Talk about families

Optional materials: Crayons, drawing paper.

Lead the children in a discussion about visits to family members, encouraging them to speak Spanish as much as possible. How far away do their relatives live? What means of travel do they use to visit them? You may want to ask the children to draw a picture showing such a trip.

Activity 48C: Sing

Materials: Cassette player; **"Dulce canta el burro"** (*"Sweetly Sings the Donkey"*) on the Song Cassette, Side A.

After the children sing the song, lead them in a discussion of what they think riding on a donkey would be like. Point out that it may be similar to riding on a horse and invite children who have ridden horseback to describe the experience. For song lyrics, see Lesson 41, Video Lesson, section 5.

LEVEL TWO

CLOSING

Tell the children that Spanish class is finished for today. In the next class they will talk more about transportation.

> **IF YOU HAVE TIME...**
>
> Encourage the children to discuss means of transportation owned by people in their families, such as cars, bicycles, motorcycles, tricycles, Big Wheels, skates, skateboards, and so on. Which are good for short trips? Which are for longer trips? Which are for young children? Which are for older children? Which are for adults?

Lesson Forty-Eight

Lesson 49

Materials to gather

- VCR and Video Lesson 49 on Tape 13
- Cassette player
- Activity Cassette 2
- Song Cassette
- Gold Flashcard 69
- Gold Flashcards 20–27
- Crayons, drawing paper
- *Optional materials:* vowel cards made for Activity 43B

OBJECTIVES

Language

- Associate vocabulary for transportation with appropriate visuals
- Understand conversational statements about transportation

Culture

- Sing "**Uno, dos, tres niñitos**" (*"One, Two, Three Little Children"*)

Review

- Practice vocabulary for school personnel
- Recall the vowel sounds and the vowel game
- Practice vocabulary for transportation

Vocabulary

No new vocabulary is introduced in this lesson.

Warm-up

Materials: Gold Flashcard 69.

Display the Flashcard while you ask the children questions like the following: Which would you take to go to the mall? (car, bus) Which would you take to travel to a different part of the country? (bus, car, plane, train) Which would you take to go across the ocean? (plane) Encourage them to use Spanish words whenever possible.

Review

Materials: Gold Flashcards 20–27.

Remind the children that they have been learning the names of family members. Point out that some people think of their pets as members of the family. Then review vocabulary for animals by showing Gold Flashcards 20–27 and asking the children to name them. Ask the children to discuss which of the animals make good pets, and why.

Introduce the video

Encourage the children to listen and watch as **la maestra** sings a song with them and talks more about ways of traveling.

Transportation vocabulary:

el coche	*car*
el autobús	*bus*
el avión	*plane*
el tren	*train*

Vocabulary for animals:

el perro	*dog*
el gato	*cat*
la gallina	*chicken*
el conejo	*rabbit*
el gallo	*rooster*
la vaca	*cow*
el cerdo	*pig*
el caballo	*horse*

Video Lesson

1. Greeting the children and Rosco

Using **Buenos días** as the greeting, **la maestra** has the opening conversation with the children. To the question **¿Cómo está usted?** she answers **Muy bien, perfecta, muy contenta** (*Very well, perfect, very happy*). She asks Rosco **¿Estás contento? ¿Tienes hambre?** (*Are you happy? Are you hungry?*). When Rosco answers **No tengo hambre** (*I'm not hungry*), **la maestra** says **¡Pues, qué sorpresa!** (*Well, what a surprise!*). Rosco answers **Tengo sueño, pero me gusta jugar** (*I'm sleepy but I like to play*).

2. Reviewing vocabulary for school personnel

Showing Flashcards, **la maestra** asks Rosco **¿Quién es?** (*Who is it?*). She and Rosco review male and female counterparts in each profession in this order: **la directora/el director** (*female/male principal*), **la secretaria/el secretario** (*female/male secretary*), **el enfermero/la enfermera** (*male/female nurse*); **el maestro/la maestra** (*male/female teacher*). La maestra points out that we can say **Buenos días, ___** (*Good morning, ___*) to people in each of these professions.

3. Singing a song

After pointing out that **los niños** (*children*) are the most important people **en la escuela** (*in the school*), **la maestra** says **Vamos a cantar** (*Let's sing*) and leads the children in singing "Uno, dos, tres niñitos" (*One, Two, Three Little Children*). For song lyrics, see Lesson 14, Video Lesson, section 6.

4. Reviewing vowels

La maestra reminds the children that we use **vocales** (*vowels*) in everything we say and sing **en español** (*in Spanish*). Rosco says the names of the vowels: **a** [ah], **e** [eh], **i** [ee], **o** [oh], **u** [oo]. **La maestra** then asks Rosco what vowel sounds are in **niñitos** (*little children*—[ee] and [oh]) and **tres** (*three*—[eh]). She shows the appropriate vowel cards as he gives the correct responses.

Integrating the terms **más rápido** (*faster*) and **despacio** (*slowly*), **la maestra** plays the vowel game: A—touch nose, E—touch shoulders, I—snap fingers, O—clap hands, U—slap thighs. She next makes the hand motions while the children say the appropriate vowel sounds and then asks the children to make the motions while she says the sounds. Rosco says **No puedo** (*I can't*) to indicate that he can't make the hand motions.

> Observe the children to determine whether they are saying the appropriate vowel sounds. For added practice with the sounds, you may want to play the vowel game independently of the video.

LEVEL TWO

5. Reviewing vocabulary relating to transportation

La maestra tells the children that they will review ways of getting from one place to another and will hear all of the vowel sounds—[ah], [eh], [ee], [oh], [oo]. She asks **¿Qué es esto?** (*What is this?*) as she points to pictures of forms of **el transporte** (*transportation*).

After modeling the words, she introduces each form of transportation with a picture of Rosco. As she takes various forms of transportation to different places, **la maestra** makes the following remarks: **Voy al parque en bicicleta. ¿Por qué? Porque hace calor y hace sol. Es muy divertido ir al parque en bicicleta.** (*I'm going to the park by bicycle. Why? Because it's hot and sunny. It's a lot of fun to go to the park by bicycle.*) **El señor conduce el taxi. ¿Adónde voy? Voy en taxi de compras. Pago al señor.** (*The man is driving the taxi. Where am I going? I'm going shopping by taxi. I am paying the man.*) **Aquí viene el jipi. Es el jipi de mi amigo. Voy en jipi al supermercado.** (*Here comes the jeep. It's my friend's jeep. I'm going by jeep to the supermarket.*) **Estoy en el bote y el bote está en el lago. Hace sol y hace buen tiempo.** (*I'm on the boat and the boat is on the lake. It's sunny and the weather is good.*) **Me gusta la moto. Voy en moto a la escuela.** (*I like the motorcycle. I'm going by motorcycle to the school.*) Note that **motocicleta** is often shortened to **moto**.

La maestra's remarks reinforce the phrase **Voy en ___** (*I'm going by ___*). She also introduces a variation: **A veces voy en ___** (*Sometimes I go by ___*).

6. Closing

After reminding the children that they can use **Voy en ___** (*I'm going by ___*) with all of the forms of transportation they have been learning, **la maestra** and Rosco say **Adiós**.

Transportation vocabulary:

el transporte	transportation
el autobús	bus
el coche	car
el avión	airplane
el tren	train
el jipi	jeep
la bicicleta	bicycle
la motocicleta	motorcycle
el taxi	taxi
el bote	boat
Voy en ___.	I'm going by ___.

After viewing the video, praise the children for their good listening and watching skills.

Lesson Forty-Nine

ACTIVITY LESSON

Activity 49A: Male and female

Materials: Cassette player; Activity Cassette 2, Side B.

Tell the children that **la maestra** is going to help them review the names of men and women who have particular jobs. She may say the name of a man who has a certain job and ask them to say the name of a woman who has the same job. Or she may say the name of a woman who has a certain job and ask them to say the name of a man who has the same job. Then play Activity 49A. You may want to play the activity more than once.

Activity 49B: Draw forms of transportation

Materials: Crayons, drawing paper.

Remind the children of the forms of transportation they have learned to say in Spanish. For the vocabulary, see section 5 of this lesson. Then ask the children to draw their favorite one. When they have finished, ask volunteers to show their drawings to the class and explain their choices.

Activity 49C: Sing

Materials: Cassette player; "Uno, dos, tres niñitos" ("*One, Two, Three Little Children*") on Side A of the Song Cassette.

Play the song once while the children listen. Then play it again while ten children you have chosen perform some activity, such as stand up one by one during the first verse and sit down one by one during the second verse. Finally, play the song a third time while the whole class sings along. For song lyrics, see Lesson 14, Video Lesson, section 6.

CLOSING

Tell the children that Spanish class is finished for today. In the next class they will listen to a new story about Rosco.

IF YOU HAVE TIME...

Materials: Vowel cards made for Activity 43B.

Arrange the vowel cards where the children can see them. Say a few of the words naming forms of transportation and ask the children to name the vowel sounds they hear in each. As they say each sound, point to the correct vowel card.

HERITAGE SPEAKERS

You may want to ask a heritage speaker in your class to say the names of the vowels.

Lesson Forty-Nine

Lesson 50

Materials to gather

- VCR and Video Lesson 50 on Tape 13
- Cassette player
- Activity Cassette 3
- Blackline Master 50A (Rosco and transportation)
- Scissors

- *Optional materials:* Song Cassette, vowel cards from Activity 43B

OBJECTIVES

Language

- Pantomime vowel sounds
- Learn a new phrase relating to transportation
- Listen to a story about transportation

Culture

- Understand the difference between a car, a taxi, and a jeep
- Recall that in Spanish the verb form indicates who performs the action

Review

- Practice vocabulary for numbers 1–100
- Recall the vowel sounds and the vowel game
- Practice vocabulary for forms of transportation

Vocabulary

Aquí viene ___.	Here comes ___.
Va en ___.	He/She goes by ___.

Warm-up

Lead the children in a discussion of the kinds of transportation they take almost every day, such as a car or bus to school, a bike to a friend's house, a car to the mall, and so on. Encourage them to use Spanish whenever possible. For transportation vocabulary, see the sidebar text for Lesson 49, Video lesson, section 5.

Review

Review **números pequeños** (*small numbers*) by writing numbers 1–10 on the chalkboard and asking volunteers to take turns coming to the board, naming a number in Spanish, and crossing it out. You may want to do the activity more than once to give more children a chance to participate. Numbers 1–10: **uno** (*1*), **dos** (*2*), **tres** (*3*), **cuatro** (*4*), **cinco** (*5*), **seis** (*6*), **siete** (*7*), **ocho** (*8*), **nueve** (*9*), **diez** (*10*).

> You may also want to review some **números grandes** (*large numbers*), such as **treinta** (*30*), **cincuenta** (*50*), **ochenta** (*80*), **cien** (*100*).

Introduce the video

Encourage the children to listen and watch as **la maestra** reviews numbers and forms of transportation, and doña Elena reads a new story about Rosco.

Video Lesson

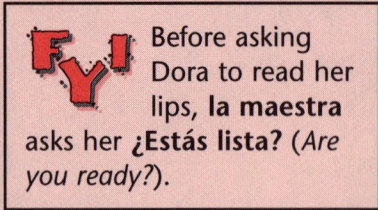

1. Greeting Dora and the children

Using **Buenas tardes** (*Good afternoon*) as the greeting, **la maestra** has the opening conversation with Dora and then with the children. She adds **Estoy muy contenta** (*I am very happy*).

> Be sure the children are not sliding too quickly over the **a** in **buenas**, which would result in an [uh] sound rather than the correct [ah] sound.

2. Reviewing numbers 10–100

La maestra begins the review by saying that one of her favorite things to do is to work with **los números** (*numbers*). **Me gusta contar** (*I like to count*), replies Dora. **Vamos a contar** (*Let's count*) says **la maestra**, adding that **estos son números grandes** (*these are big numbers*). **De diez en diez** (*By tens*), Dora explains. **La maestra** points to the numbers **diez** (*10*), **veinte** (*20*), **treinta** (*30*), **cuarenta** (*40*), **cincuenta** (*50*), **sesenta** (*60*), **setenta** (*70*), **ochenta** (*80*), **noventa** (*90*), and **cien** (*100*) while Dora and the children count.

3. Playing a game

La maestra asks Dora ¿**Qué número es?** as she points to the numbers *80* (**ochenta**), *40* (**cuarenta**), and *20* (**veinte**). She then says **Vamos a jugar** (*Let's play*) before reviewing the numbers and playing the same game with the children. **La maestra** ends the review by saying **Los números son muy divertidos** (*Numbers are a lot of fun*). Dora replies **Me encanta contar** (*I love to count*).

> **La maestra** says that she heard one of the children reply **muy rápido** (*very quickly*).

4. Reviewing vowels

La maestra asks Dora what vowel sounds she hears in the word **números**. Dora replies [oo], [eh], [oh].

5. Miming vowel sounds

La maestra shows how to position the mouth and lips while saying the vowels: **A** [ah], **E** [eh], **I** [ee], **O** [oh], **U** [oo]. She asks Dora which vowels she is miming—[oh] and [ah], Dora replies correctly. **La maestra** then says **Vamos a mirar** to introduce the mime, who repeats the demonstration while the children copy the position of his mouth and lips.

La maestra mimes saying the vowels while Dora and then the children say them out loud. Integrating the phrase **más rápido** (*faster*), **la maestra** then plays the vowel game: A—touch nose, E—touch shoulders, I—snap fingers, O—clap hands, U—slap thighs.

> **FYI** Before asking Dora to read her lips, **la maestra** asks her ¿**Estás lista?** (*Are you ready?*).

6. Reviewing vocabulary relating to *el transporte* (*transportation*)

La maestra shows pictures of Rosco traveling to review the names of forms of transportation combined with **Va en** ___ (*He is going by* ___), occasionally integrating the question ¿**De qué**

color es ___? (*What color is ___?*). She explains that when she is talking about herself taking transportation she says **(Yo) voy en ___** (*I am going by ___*) and that when she is talking about Rosco she says **Rosco va en ___** (*Rosco is going by ___*). She asks the children to **repite** (*repeat*) **Va en ___** (*He is going by ___*). **La maestra** explains that **un taxi** (*a taxi*) is a **coche** (*car*) that we pay someone to drive for us and that **un jipi** (*jeep*) is a special kind of **coche** that goes on rough terrain, such as mountains.

7. Playing a game

La maestra says **Vamos a jugar** (*Let's play*) before initiating a game of **Muéstrame ___** (*Show me ___*) with pictures of various forms of transportation, integrating the phrases **El/La ___ está aquí** (*The ___ is here*) and **Aquí está el/la ___** (*Here is the ___*).

8. Demonstrating with toys

Muchas formas de transporte (*Many forms of transportation*), says **la maestra**. She then uses toys representing **el autobús** (*bus*), **el coche** (*car*), **la moto** (*motorcycle*), **el avión** (*plane*), **el bote** (*boat*), and **el tren** (*train*) to introduce the phrase **Aquí viene ___** (*Here comes ___*).

9. Introducing a new story

La maestra tells the children that **doña Elena va a leer** (*doña Elena is going to read*). **Vamos a leer** (*Let's read*) says doña Elena, telling the children that **la historia se llama "Rosco va"** (*the story is called "Rosco Is Going"*). The story reinforces these constructions: **Rosco va ___** (*Rosco is going ___*), **¿Cómo va?** (*How is he going?*), and **Va en ___** (*He is going by ___*).

In the story, Rosco make the following trips: **al parque en bicicleta** (*to the park by bike*), **a la escuela en autobús** (*to school by bus*), **a la tienda en taxi** (*to the store by taxi*), **al supermercado en jipi** (*to the supermarket by jeep*), **al restaurante en coche** (*to the restaurant by car*), **al lago en bote** (*to the lake by boat*), **a México en avión** (*to Mexico by plane*), **de viaje en tren** (*on a trip by train*), **a su casa en moto** (*home by motorcycle*). At the end of the story doña Elena says **¡Qué divertido fue leer!** (*What fun it was to read!*).

10. Closing

La maestra points out that **Rosco va en muchas formas de transporte** (*Rosco is going by many forms of transportation*). She and Dora then say **Adiós** and **Hasta luego** (*See you later*).

Transportation vocabulary:

la bicicleta	bicycle
el autobús	bus
el taxi	taxi
el jipi	jeep
el coche	car
el bote	boat
el avión	airplane
el tren	train
la moto *or*	
la motocicleta	motorcycle

FYI Recall that in Spanish, the verb form indicates who is performing the action. Thus, subject nouns and pronouns are not necessary except for clarity or emphasis. For example, the subject *Rosco* or *he* is included in the verb **Va** in the phrase **Va en ___** (*He is going by ___*).

FYI The **x** in **México** and **mexicano** (*Mexican*) has the sound of Spanish **j**; that is, the sound of *h* pronounced with the back of the tongue raised.

After viewing the video, praise the children for their good listening and watching skills.

Lesson Fifty

Blackline Master 50A

To extend Activity 50B, you may want to divide the class into pairs and have each partner take turns saying **Aquí viene ___** (*Here comes ___*) while the other child moves the appropriate picture.

ACTIVITY LESSON

Activity 50A: Male and female

Materials: Cassette player; Activity Cassette 3, Side A; Blackline Master 50A; scissors.

Preparation: Duplicate Blackline Master 50A so that each child has a copy. Give scissors to each child or pair of children and ask them to cut out the picture of Rosco along the dotted line.

Tell the children that **la maestra** is going to help them review forms of transportation. She is going to say **Rosco va en ___** (*Rosco is going by ___*) and add the name of a form of transportation. They are to put the picture of Rosco over the picture of the transportation she names.

Activity 50B: *Aquí viene ___* (*Here comes ___*)

Materials: Cassette player; Activity Cassette 3, Side A; Blackline Master 50A; scissors.

Preparation: Give scissors to each child or pair of children. Ask them to cut out the pictures on the activity sheet.

Tell the children that **la maestra** will say the phrase that means *Here comes ___* and add the name of one of the forms of transportation shown in their pictures. Each time they hear the sentence, they are to move the correct picture across their desks.

Activity 50C: Discuss the story

Materials: VCR and Video Lesson 50 on Tape 13.

Preparation: Tell the children that you are going to replay doña Elena's reading of "**Rosco va**" ("*Rosco Is Going*") and that they should listen for as many details as possible. Then replay the video.

Basing your questions on the details of the story supplied in section 9 of the Video Lesson, ask the children questions like these, encouraging them to answer in Spanish:

How did Rosco get to the park? (**en bicicleta**)

How did he get to school? (**en autobús**)

How did he get to the lake? (**en bote**)

Closing

Tell the children that Spanish class is finished for today. In the next class they will talk about dates and go with **la maestra** as she takes various forms of transportation.

> ### IF YOU HAVE TIME...
>
> Materials: Cassette player; **"Las vocales"** ("*The Vowels*") on the Song Cassette, Side A; and the vowel cards from Activity 43B.
>
> Arrange the vowel cards where the children can see them. Point to the appropriate vowel cards while the children listen to the song. Then have them make the appropriate hand motions for the vowel game (see section 5 of the Video Lesson) while they sing along with **la maestra**.
>
> A, E, I, O, U.
> A, mapa.
> E, Pepe.
> I, Lili.
> O, rojo.
> U, cucu.
> A, E, I, O, U.

Lesson Fifty

Lesson 51

Materials to gather

- VCR and Video Lesson 51 on Tape 13
- Cassette player
- Activity Cassette 3
- Song Cassette
- Calendar
- Gold Flashcards 48–50 and 62–64
- Blackline Master 51A (dates)
- Rosco flag
- Vowel cards from Activity 43B
- *Optional materials:* crayons, drawing paper
- *Prepare ahead:* Find individual pictures or models of a car, bus, boat, and plane (Activity 51B)

OBJECTIVES

Language
- Complete sentences relating to forms of transportation
- Understand conversational statements about transportation

Culture
- Sing **"Uno de enero"** (*"January First"*) and **"Español para ti"** (*"Spanish Is for You, and for Me"*)

Review
- Recall statements of feeling
- Practice questions and answers about the calendar
- Recall that **Busca** ___ means *Search for* ___
- Practice vocabulary for forms of transportation

Vocabulary
No new vocabulary is introduced in this lesson.

Warm-up

Materials: A calendar.

Encourage a discussion of dates by asking volunteers to say what their birthdays are and find them on the calendar.

Review

Materials: A calendar; Gold Flashcards 48–50 and 62–64.

Review the names of the months by pointing to each month on the calendar and asking the children to name it in Spanish. As they name it, point to the appropriate picture on the Flashcards.

You may also want to review why each month is represented as it is on the Flashcards.

Introduce the video

Encourage the children to listen and watch as **la maestra** and Rosco talk about the calendar and **la maestra** takes different kinds of transportation.

Months of the year:

enero	*January*
febrero	*February*
marzo	*March*
abril	*April*
mayo	*May*
junio	*June*
julio	*July*
agosto	*August*
septiembre	*September*
octubre	*October*
noviembre	*November*
diciembre	*December*

VIDEO LESSON

1. Greeting Rosco and the children

Using **Buenos días** as the greeting, **la maestra** has the opening conversation with Rosco. Rosco answers **Estoy muy contento** (*I am very happy*); **la maestra** replies **Estoy muy contenta** (*I am very happy*). She then has the conversation with the children.

2. Reviewing statements of feeling

La maestra points out that there are many ways to answer the question **¿Cómo estás tú?**, including **así, así** (*so-so*) and **muy contento/contenta** (*very happy*).

3. Reviewing questions and answers about the calendar

La maestra begins a review of the calendar by asking **¿Qué es esto?** (*What is this?*). Rosco replies **el calendario** (*the calendar*). She asks **¿Qué mes es?** (*What month is it?*), **¿Qué día es?** (*What day of the week is it?*), and **¿Cuál es la fecha?** (*What is the date?*).

4. Reviewing the months of the year

Referring to the months of the year, **la maestra** asks **¿Cuántos son?** (*How many are there?*). Rosco replies **doce** (*12*), and **la maestra** adds **Hay doce meses del año** (*There are 12 months in the year*). **La maestra** uses the Flashcards to review the names of the months. For the months, see the Review section of this lesson.

5. Asking the date

La maestra asks Rosco **¿Cuál es la fecha?** (*What is the date?*). The correct response is **El ___ de ___** (*The ___ of ___*). To prompt Rosco's responses, **la maestra** shows Flashcards representing months and adds number cards. After answering a question correctly Rosco says **Soy muy inteligente** (*I'm very intelligent*).

6. Singing a song

La maestra says **Vamos a cantar** (*Let's sing*) before singing "Uno de enero" (*"January First"*) to review the first seven months of the year. For song lyrics, see Lesson 8, Video Lesson, section 3. She explains the meaning of the last verse: **El que la ha roto la pagará** (*He who broke the tambourine will pay for it*).

7. Reviewing vocabulary for transportation

Before reviewing the vocabulary **la maestra** points out that every day of the month and year, people search for things. She says **Vamos a mirar** (*Let's watch*) to introduce the mime's demonstration of the meaning of **Busca ___** (*Search for ___*).

She and Rosco then take turns telling each other to **Busca ___** (*Search for ___*) several toy vehicles and then identifying each: **Busca el/la ___. ¿Es el/la ___? Sí, es el/la ___.** (*Search for the ___. Is it the ___? Yes, it is the ___.*)

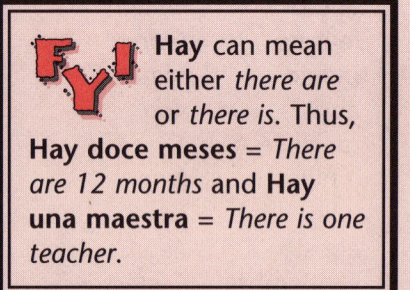

FYI

Hay can mean either *there are* or *there is*. Thus, **Hay doce meses** = *There are 12 months* and **Hay una maestra** = *There is one teacher.*

Answers:

el veintiuno de febrero (*February 21st*)

el once de diciembre (*December 11th*)

el diez de enero (*January 10th*)

Names of toy vehicles:

el coche	car
el avión	plane
el bote	boat
el autobús	bus
la moto	motorcycle

LEVEL TWO

La maestra then shows Rosco the toys and asks him to complete the phrase **Aquí viene** ___ (*Here comes___*) with the name of each. During their conversation she also reviews the phrases **Voy en** ___ (*I am going by* ___), **¿De qué color es?** (*What color is it?*), and **Es de color** ___ (*It is* ___).

8. Traveling

A video shows **la maestra** taking different forms of transportation. Some of **la maestra's** remarks are:

Aquí viene el autobús amarillo y negro.	*Here comes the yellow and black bus.*
¿Quién está en el autobús? ¡Es Rosco!	*Who is on the bus? It's Rosco!*
Voy al parque en bicicleta. ¿Por qué?	*I'm going to the park by bicycle. Why?*
Porque hace calor y hace sol.	*Because it's hot and sunny.*
Estoy en el bote y el bote está en el lago.	*I'm on the boat and the boat is on the lake.*
Hace sol y hace buen tiempo.	*It's sunny and the weather is good.*
Aquí viene el taxi. Voy en taxi.	*Here comes the taxi. I'm going by taxi.*
Estoy en la estación de los trenes.	*I'm at the train station.*
Voy de viaje en tren. Tengo mi maleta.	*I'm going on a train trip. I have my suitcase.*

Then she says **Aquí viene** ___ (*Here comes___*) and **Voy en** ___ (*I'm going by* ___) with **el jipi** (*jeep*), **la moto** (*motorcycle*), **el avión** (*plane*), and **el coche** (*car*).

Forms of transportation:

el autobús	bus
la bicicleta	bicycle
el bote	boat
el tren	train
el taxi	taxi
el jipi	jeep
la moto	motorcycle
el avión	plane
el coche	car

9. Asking questions

La maestra reviews some types of transportation by showing toy vehicles to Rosco and asking **¿Qué es esto?** (*What is this?*). **La maestra** here adds a model of a **tren** (*train*).

10. Singing another song

Vamos a cantar (*Let's sing*), suggests **la maestra**. She and Rosco sing "**Español para ti**" (*"Spanish Is for You, and for Me"*). For song lyrics, see Lesson 3, Video Lesson, section 3.

11. Closing

La maestra says **¡Qué bueno, qué divertido!** (*How great, what a lot of fun!*) before reminding the children that they have learned a lot. She and Rosco say **Adiós**.

After viewing the video, praise the children for their good listening and watching skills.

Lesson Fifty-One

el 21 de	❄
el 8 de	⛱
el 30 de	🚌
el 22 de	🎃

Blackline Master 51A

Answers for Activity 51A:

el veintiuno de enero
(*January 21st*)

el ocho de agosto
(*August 8th*)

el treinta de septiembre
(*September 30th*)

el veintidós de noviembre
(*November 22nd*)

ACTIVITY LESSON

Activity 51A: What is the date?

Materials: Cassette player; Activity Cassette 3, Side A; and Blackline Master 51A.

Preparation: Duplicate Blackline Master 51A so that each child has a copy.

Tell the children that **la maestra** is going to ask them what the date is. To answer, they will read each incomplete statement on their activity sheets and add the name of the month that each picture represents.

Activity 51B: *Busca* ___ (*Search for* ___)

Materials: Cassette player; Activity Cassette 3, Side A; Rosco flag; and the individual pictures or models of a car, bus, boat, and plane that you have gathered.

Preparation: Hide each picture or model in a different place in the classroom.

Tell the children that they are going to play a game called **Busca** ___ (*Search for* ___). Inform them that you have hidden pictures (or models) of a car, bus, boat, and plane somewhere in the classroom. **La maestra** will say which picture or model to search for, and you will give the Rosco flag to a child to indicate which child is to search. Tell the children that you will say **sí** or **no** to indicate whether the child who is searching is getting warm or cold. Make sure you pause the tape at the harp sound until the item is found. You may want to play the activity more than once to give more children a chance to participate.

Activity 51C: Sing

Materials: Cassette player; "**Uno de enero**" ("*January First*") and "**Las vocales**" ("*The Vowels*") on the Song Cassette, Side A; and the vowel cards from Activity 43B.

Divide the class into two groups and give each group time to practice one of the songs. You may want to let the children vote on which song they want to sing. Then let the groups take turns singing their song to the other children. During the singing of "**Las vocales**" ("*The Vowels*"), ask a member of the audience to hold up the appropriate vowel cards. For song lyrics, see Lesson 8, Video Lesson, section 3, and Activity 45C respectively.

LEVEL TWO

Closing

Tell the children that Spanish class is finished for today. In the next class they will learn the names of parts of the body and sing a new song.

> **IF YOU HAVE TIME...**
>
> Materials: Crayons; drawing paper.
>
> Ask the children to make drawings of different kinds of transportation, including a train, a motorcycle, and a bicycle. When they have finished, hide each picture and repeat Activity 51B, this time encouraging volunteers to take turns playing the part of **la maestra** by saying **Busca ___** (*Search for ___*) and adding the name of one of the forms of transportation whose pictures you have hidden. For transportation vocabulary, see sidebar for section 8 of this Video Lesson.

Lesson Fifty-One

Lesson 52

Materials to gather

- VCR and Video Lesson 52 on Tape 13
- Cassette player
- Activity Cassette 3
- Song Cassette
- Gold Flashcards 9–12, 14–16, 19
- Gold Flashcards 28–33
- Blackline Master 52A (weather)
- Scissors
- *Optional materials:* crayons, drawing paper

OBJECTIVES

Language
- Associate new vocabulary with parts of the face and body
- Understand that **dale** means *give him/her*

Culture
- Sing the song **"Ojos, orejas, boca, nariz"** (*"Eyes, Ears, Mouth, Nose"*)
- Understand that weather is different in different parts of the world

Review
- Practice weather expressions for different months of the year
- Recall that **dame** means *give me*
- Review expressions and vocabulary relating to transportation

Vocabulary

el señor Papa	*Mr. Potato Head*
el pelo	*hair*
los ojos	*eyes*
la boca	*mouth*
las orejas	*ears*
la nariz	*nose*
las manos	*hands*
los brazos	*arms*
los pies	*feet*
Dale.	*Give him/her.*

Warm-up

Materials: Gold Flashcards 9–12, 14–16, 19.

Ask the children to name in English the parts of the face and body highlighted on the Flashcards. Then encourage a discussion by asking the children what each of these parts of the body is used for.

Review

Materials: Gold Flashcards 28–33.

Point out to the children that we use parts of the body to show how we feel. Review expressions of feeling by asking the children to name the feeling depicted on each of the Flashcards.

Introduce the video

Encourage the children to listen and watch as **la maestra**, Rosco, and Dora talk about the weather and introduce the names of some parts of the body.

Just for fun, you may want to lead the children in a physical activity in which they shake their hands, arms, legs, and feet, open their eyes and mouth wide, and shake their hair.

Expressions of feeling:

Tengo frío.	I'm cold.
Tengo calor.	I'm hot.
Tengo hambre.	I'm hungry.
Tengo sed.	I'm thirsty.
Tengo miedo.	I'm afraid.
Tengo sueño.	I'm sleepy.

Video Lesson

1. Greeting the children, Rosco, and Dora

Using **Buenos días** as the greeting, **la maestra** has the opening conversation with the children. She says **Estoy muy contenta porque estoy aquí con mis amigos** (*I am very happy because I am here with my friends*) and adds **Rosco y Dora están muy contentos también** (*Rosco and Dora are very happy, too*).

2. Reviewing weather expressions

Using Flashcards representing weather and asking **¿Qué tiempo hace?** (*What's the weather like?*), **la maestra** reviews weather expressions: **Hace sol y hace calor** (*It's sunny and hot*), **Hace frío** (*It's cold*), **Hace buen tiempo** (*It's good weather*). **La maestra** asks **¿Hace frío en agosto o hace frío en diciembre?** (*Is it cold in August or is it cold in December?*). Rosco answers **Hace frío en diciembre** (*It's cold in December*). She next asks "In what months can we say **Hace viento**?" The puppets answer **En octubre y en abril** (*In October and in April*). Finally, **la maestra** reminds the children that during each month of the year, the weather is different in different parts of the world.

3. Introducing vocabulary for parts of the face and body

La maestra asks **¿Quién es?** (*Who is it?*) and **¿Recuerdas al señor Papa?** (*Do you remember Mr. Potato Head?*) to introduce **el señor Papa**. She says **Con el señor Papa nosotros podemos recordar las partes de la cara y las partes del cuerpo** (*With Mr. Potato Head we can remember the parts of the face and the parts of the body*).

Pointing to Mr. Potato Head's features while singing "**Ojos, orejas, boca, nariz**" (*"Eyes, Ears, Mouth, Nose"*), **la maestra** reviews the parts of the face: **los ojos** (*eyes*), **las orejas** (*ears*), **la boca** (*mouth*), and **la nariz** (*nose*). She sings the song again, encouraging the children to point to the appropriate parts:

Ojos, orejas, boca, nariz,	*Eyes, ears, mouth, nose,*
Boca, nariz, boca, nariz,	*Mouth, nose, mouth, nose,*
Ojos, orejas, boca, nariz,	*Eyes, ears, mouth, nose,*
Son las partes de la cara.	*Are the parts of the face.*

La maestra next uses Mr. Potato Head to demonstrate the vocabulary for some parts of the body—**las manos** (*hands*), **el pelo** (*hair*), **los brazos** (*arms*), and **los pies** (*feet*). She asks **¿De qué color es el pelo del señor Papa?** (*What color is Mr. Potato Head's hair?*) and Dora answers **Es anaranjado** (*It's orange*). Finally, **la maestra** reviews all the new vocabulary for parts of the face and body.

4. Reviewing *Dame* ___ (*Give me* ___)

La maestra says **Vamos a mirar** (*Let's watch*). Then the mime illustrates the meaning of **Dame** ___ (*Give me* ___). She then asks Rosco to give her various parts of **el señor Papa**'s body:

FYI Notice that **papa** (*potato*) and **papá** (*father*) are pronounced differently. **Papa** is stressed on the first syllable while **papá** is stressed on the second syllable, as indicated by the accent mark.

Also, notice that in Spanish the definite article (**el/la/los/las**) is always used before the title of a person who is being talked about, even when the title precedes a name. Thus, **el señor Papa, la señora Rodríguez, las señoritas Brown, el profesor O'Toole, la doctora San José**.

FYI Note that although **mano** appears to be a masculine noun because it ends in **-o**, it is really feminine and so takes the feminine definite article **la** (plural **las**).

Dame el pelo.	*Give me his hair.*
Dame los ojos.	*Give me his eyes.*
Dame la boca.	*Give me his mouth.*
Dame la nariz.	*Give me his nose.*
Dame las orejas.	*Give me his ears.*

5. Introducing a new command

La maestra again says **Vamos a mirar** (*Let's watch*) to introduce the mime, who this time illustrates the meaning of **dale** (*give him/her*). She then reviews some transportation vocabulary by telling Rosco and Dora to **dale/dame** various toy vehicles.

For example, **Dale el autobús a Dora** (*Give the bus to Dora*) and **Dame el autobús** (*Give me the bus*).

6. Reviewing expressions related to transportation

La maestra uses the toy vehicles to illustrate the sentence **Aquí viene ___** (*Here comes ___*). Using pictures of Rosco she also explains that when she is taking transportation she says **Voy en ___** (*I am going by ___*) and when he or she is taking transportation she says **Va en ___** (*He/She is going by ___*). For a complete list of the transportation vocabulary, see the sidebar for section 7 below.

7. Playing a game

Vamos a jugar (*Let's play*), says **la maestra**. She reviews transportation vocabulary before initiating a game of **¿Cuál falta?** (*What's missing?*).

8. Playing another game

La maestra reviews the names of parts of the body (see the Vocabulary Section) before removing parts of **el señor Papa**'s body and asking **¿Cuál falta?** (*What's missing?*).

9. Singing a song

La maestra sings "**Ojos, orejas, boca, nariz**" (*"Eyes, Ears, Mouth, Nose"*) to review the names of parts of the face. For song lyrics, see section 3 above.

10. Closing

La maestra promises the children that they will have more fun practicing **las formas del transporte y las partes de la cara** (*forms of transportation and parts of the face*). She, Rosco, and Dora say **Adiós** and **Hasta luego** (*See you later*).

FYI In Spanish, the definite article is always used with parts of the body. Possession of parts of the body is indicated by context or by verb forms known as the reflexive. For example, when talking about Mr. Potato Head, **Dame el pelo** means *Give me his hair*. **Me duelen los pies** means *My feet hurt*.

Toy vehicles:

el autobús	bus
el bote	boat
la moto	motorcycle
el coche	car
el avión	airplane

Transportation vocabulary:

el jipi	jeep
la bicicleta	bicycle
la moto	motorcycle
el autobús	bus
el bote	boat
el taxi	taxi
el avión	plane
el tren	train
el coche	car

After viewing the video, praise the children for their good listening and watching skills.

Lesson Fifty-Two

Blackline Master 52A

Weather conditions:

From left to right:

Hace buen tiempo.
It's good weather.

Hace frío.
It's cold.

Hace calor.
It's hot.

(Fourth picture is not named in tape.)

Llueve.
It's raining.

Nieva.
It's snowing.

Hace viento.
It's windy.

Hace mal tiempo.
It's bad weather.

LEVEL TWO

ACTIVITY LESSON

Activity 52A: What is the weather like?

Materials: Cassette player; Activity Cassette 3, Side A; Blackline Master 52A; and scissors.

Preparation: Duplicate Blackline Master 52A so that each child has a copy. After you review the weather conditions shown in each picture, divide the class into pairs and give scissors to each group of children. Have them cut out each picture along the lines.

Tell the children that doña Elena is going to name certain weather conditions. During the first half of the game, one of the children will give the pictures that show that weather to her or his partner; during the second half, the other child will do the giving. Doña Elena will tell them when to switch roles.

Activity 52B: *Simón dice* (*Simon says*)

Materials: Cassette player; Activity Cassette 3, Side A; and Gold Flashcards 10, 11, 14, 16, 19.

Display the Flashcards where the children can see them. Review the names of the parts of the body shown on the Flashcards: **la boca** (*mouth*), **la nariz** (*nose*), **el pelo** (*hair*), **las manos** (*hands*), **los pies** (*feet*). Then tell the children that doña Elena is going to play a game of **Simón dice** (*Simon says*) with them. She will say **Simón dice toca ___** (*Simon says touch ___*) and add the name of one of the parts of the body that they have just reviewed. They are to touch the part of the body that doña Elena names.

Activity 52C: Sing

Materials: Cassette player; "Ojos, orejas, boca, nariz" ("*Eyes, Ears, Mouth, Nose*") on the Song Cassette, Side A.

After the children listen to the song once, encourage them to sing along as they touch the parts of the face named in the song. For song lyrics, see section 3 in this Video Lesson.

CLOSING

Tell the children that Spanish class is finished for today. In the next class they will learn some new words about street and traffic safety.

IF YOU HAVE TIME...

Materials: Crayons, drawing paper.

Ask the children to make drawings of imaginary creatures whose most noticeable features are one or more of the body parts whose names they learned today. When they have finished, encourage them to describe their drawings to the class, using Spanish as much as possible. For body parts, see the Vocabulary Section of this lesson.

LANGUAGE ACROSS THE CURRICULUM

Incorporate the words for the parts of the body into a science unit. Talk about the five senses and which parts of the body are used for each sense. For the sense of taste you will need one more vocabulary word: **la lengua** (*tongue*).

Lesson Fifty-Two

Lesson 53

Materials to gather

- VCR and Video Lesson 53 on Tape 14
- Cassette player
- Activity Cassette 3
- Song Cassette
- Sheets of red, yellow, and green construction paper
- Scissors
- Blackline Master 53A (traffic light)
- Green, red, and yellow crayons
- *Optional materials:* laminating machine

OBJECTIVES

Language

- Learn jingles reinforcing vowel sounds and ways to express feelings
- Learn vocabulary relating to street safety

Culture

- Compare rules of street safety in different cultures

Review

- Recall expressions for the telephone
- Practice vowel sounds
- Show comprehension of **rápido** (*quickly*) and **despacio** (*slowly*)
- Recall vocabulary for parts of the face
- Recall vocabulary for feelings of happiness, sadness, and anger
- Sing "**Ojas, orejas, boca, nariz**" ("*Eyes, Ears, Mouth, Nose*")

Vocabulary

la calle	*street*
las luces del tráfico	*traffic lights*
Verde: ¡Sigue!	*Green: Go!*
Amarillo: ¡Espera!	*Yellow: Wait!*
Rojo: ¡Alto!	*Red: Stop!*

Warm-up

Materials: Sheets of red, yellow, and green construction paper; scissors.

Preparation: Cut a large circle out of each sheet of construction paper.

Lead the children in a discussion about colors. Hold up the red circle and ask the children what the color red means to them. (danger; stop) Then hold up each of the other circles and ask the same question. Summarize the discussion by pointing out that some colors can send a message without the need for words.

Review

Begin a review of color words by asking the children to name the colors of each of the circles you have been discussing (**verde**—*green*, **rojo**—*red*, **amarillo**—*yellow*). Then review other color words by holding up or pointing to objects in the classroom and asking ¿**De qué color es?** or *What color is it?*

Introduce the video

Encourage the children to listen and watch as **la maestra** and Dora review vowel sounds and talk about how to stay safe while crossing the street.

Color words:

negro	*black*
azul	*blue*
anaranjado	*orange*
blanco	*white*
café	*brown*
rosado	*pink*
gris	*gray*
morado	*purple*

VIDEO LESSON

1. Greeting Dora and the children

Using **Buenos días** as the greeting, **la maestra** has the opening conversation with Dora.

2. Reviewing telephone expressions

Dora asks **¿Qué es?** (*What is it?*). **La maestra** replies **Es el teléfono. Hablo por teléfono.** (*It's the telephone. I'm talking on the telephone.*). When Dora asks **¿Qué haces?** (*What are you doing?*), **la maestra** repeats **Hablo por teléfono.** After suggesting that the children pretend to have telephones, she has the opening conversation with the class.

Dora next asks **¿Cómo se dice Hello?** (*How do you say "Hello"?*). **La maestra** answers **Diga** and adds that one can say **Adiós** to say *Good-bye*. She adds that when we learn to speak Spanish, we can talk to our friends at home, **en la escuela** (*at school*), and **por teléfono** (*on the telephone*).

3. Reviewing *las vocales* (vowels)

La maestra reviews **las vocales** (*vowels*). After playing the vowel game she says **Vamos a hacerlo rápido** (*Let's say it quickly*). She then asks the children to play the game **despacio** (*slowly*).

La maestra says a jingle integrating vowel sounds and ways to express feelings:

A E I O U	A E I O U
Estoy contento/a.	I am happy.
¿Cómo estás tú?	How are you?
A E I O U	A E I O U

La maestra then introduces the mime's demonstration of **Estoy contento** (*I'm happy*). To point out the different endings she reminds the children that **las niñas dicen estoy contenta** (*girls say I'm happy* [f]) and **los niños dicen estoy contento** (*boys say I'm happy* [m]). **La maestra** then repeats the jingle. After the mime demonstrates **Estoy triste** (*I'm sad*) and **Estoy enojado/a**, she repeats the jingle substituting these statements.

4. Reviewing vocabulary for parts of the face

La maestra brings out **el Señor Papa** (*Mr. Potato Head*) and reviews words and statements describing feelings: **contento** (*happy*); **no está enojado** (*he is not angry*); and, as she turns Mr. Potato Head's mouth upside-down, **triste** (*sad*). She then points out Mr. Potato Head's facial features and sings "**Ojos, orejas, boca, nariz**" ("*Eyes, Ears, Mouth, Nose*") to review vocabulary for parts of the face. For song lyrics, see Lesson 52, Video Lesson, section 3.

La maestra then invites the children to sing along with her and Dora as she points to Mr. Potato Head's features.

FYI After saying **Diga** (*Hello*), the person answering the phone may say **¿Quién es?** (*Who is it?*), **¿Quién habla?** (*Who is speaking?*), or **¿De parte de quién?** (*Who is calling?*; literally, *On the part of whom?*). The person calling may respond **Soy** [name] (*I am* [name]) or **Habla** [name] ([name] *is speaking*).

Vowel sounds:

a—[ah], **e**—[eh], **i**—[ee], **o**—[oh], **u**—[oo]

Vowel game:

A—touch nose;
E—touch shoulders
I—snap fingers
O—clap hands
U—slap thighs

A E I O U
(*A E I O U*)
Estoy triste (enojado/a).
(*I am sad [angry].*)
¿Cómo estás tú?
(*How are you?*)
A E I O U
(*A E I O U*)

La maestra quickly reviews expressions of feeling by again straightening Mr. Potato Head's mouth to reflect that **él no está triste—está contento** (*He isn't sad—he's happy*).

5. Reviewing vocabulary for transportation

La maestra asks Dora to complete the phrase **Aquí viene ___** (*Here comes___*) with the words naming toy vehicles.

6. Introducing vocabulary for street safety

La maestra points out that all the vehicles Dora has named ride on streets or railroad tracks and help us get to many fun places. She adds that it is **importante** (*important*) to know the rules of the road because vehicles can be dangerous. Using a Flashcard she introduces **calle** (*street*) and **las luces del tráfico** (*traffic lights*). She asks **¿De qué colores son?** (*What colors are they?*). Dora answers **Verde, amarillo,** and **rojo** (*Green, yellow,* and *red*).

Saying **Vamos a mirar** (*Let's watch*), **la maestra** next introduces the colors and commands of the traffic lights (see the Vocabulary Section) and pantomimes how to follow the commands. **La maestra** and Dora agree that **son muy importantes** (*they are very important*).

After reviewing the colors of traffic lights, **la maestra** demonstrates how to pantomime each command and asks the children to pantomime them.

7. Playing a game

La maestra introduces a choice game using traffic-light colors and commands. Pointing to a green light she asks **¿Es ¡Sigue! o es ¡Alto!?** (*Is it Go! or is it Stop!?*). Dora answers **Es ¡Sigue!** (*It's Go!*). Pointing to a yellow light she asks **¿Es ¡Alto! o es ¡Espera!?** (*Is it Stop! or is it Wait!?*). Dora answers **Es ¡Espera!** (*It's Wait!*). Pointing to a red light she asks **¿Es ¡Alto! o es ¡Sigue!?** (*Is it Stop! or is it Go!?*). Dora answers **Es ¡Alto!** (*It's Stop!*).

8. Playing another game

Vamos a jugar (*Let's play*) says **la maestra**, introducing an association game using traffic-light colors and commands. She asks children to complete these statements: **Verde es ___** (*Green is ___*); **Amarillo es ___** (*Yellow is ___*); **Rojo es ___** (*Red is ___*). Answers: **¡Sigue!** (*Go!*), **¡Espera!** (*Wait!*), **¡Alto!** (*Stop!*).

9. Closing

La maestra says **Mis alumnos son muy inteligentes** (*My students are very smart*). She reminds the children that it's important to be safe and that they should obey traffic lights and crossing guards and be careful on the streets. She and Dora say **Adiós** and **Hasta la vista** (*Until we meet again*).

Toy vehicles:

el coche	car
el autobús	bus
la moto	motorcycle
el tren	train

FYI **La maestra** says **Hay tres luces del tráfico** (*There are three traffic lights*).

Traffic-light colors:

Verde	Green
Amarillo	Yellow
Rojo	Red

FYI **Sigue** literally means *keep going*. **Espera** can mean either *wait* or *hope*; in the context of a traffic light it means *wait*.

After viewing the video, praise the children for their good listening and watching skills.

Lesson Fifty-Three

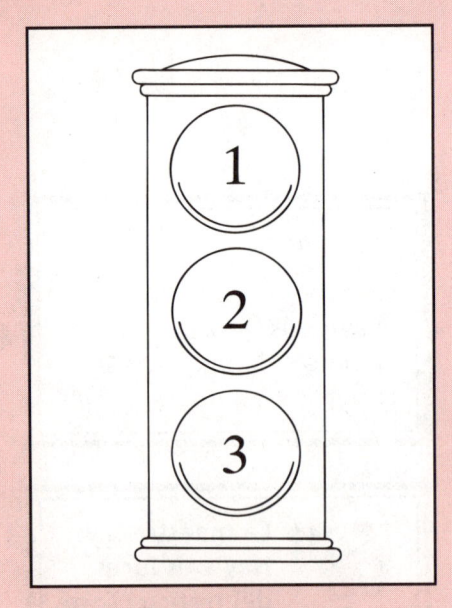

Blackline Master 53A

You may want to laminate the children's traffic lights for use in future activities and games.

Heritage Speakers

Invite heritage speakers in your class to discuss street safety in the countries they came from. Are the rules the same as in the United States? How are they different?

ACTIVITY LESSON

Activity 53A: Traffic lights

Materials: Blackline Master 53A; Cassette player; Activity Cassette 3, Side A; and green, red, and yellow crayons.

Preparation: Duplicate Blackline Master 53A so that each child has a copy. Give each child a green, red, and yellow crayon.

Tell the children that **la maestra** is going to ask them to color the traffic lights with their crayons. She will tell them which color to use on each light. Make sure you pause the tape at the harp sound to give the children time to color.

For the second part of the activity, tell the children that **la maestra** is going to ask them to touch (**toca**) each light that gives the command that she names.

Activity 53B: Discuss traffic lights

Encourage the children to discuss the purpose of traffic lights and what would happen if there were no traffic lights or if people did not obey them.

Activity 53C: *Vamos a cantar* (*Let's sing*)

Materials: Cassette player; **"Ojos, orejas, boca, nariz"** (*"Eyes, Ears, Mouth, Nose"*) and **"Las vocales"** (*"The Vowels"*) on the Song Cassette.

Play each song as the children sing along. Lead them in touching each part of the face as it is mentioned in the first song and in playing the vowel game (see sidebar for section 3 in this Video Lesson) while singing the second. For song lyrics, see Lesson 52, Video Lesson, section 3 and Activity 45C, respectively.

LEVEL TWO

CLOSING

Tell the children that Spanish class is finished for today. In the next class they will learn more words that name parts of the body and also more expressions relating to street safety.

IF YOU HAVE TIME...

Materials: Traffic lights from Activity 53A.

Let the children practice pantomiming the command of each street light—**Verde: ¡Sigue!** (*Green: Go!*), **Amarillo: ¡Espera!** (*Yellow: Wait!*), **Rojo: ¡Alto!** (*Red: Stop!*). Ask the children to stand up, with one child standing before the group. That child should hold up his/her traffic light and point to each different color at random while the rest of the children pantomime the action that goes with it.

Lesson Fifty-Three

Lesson 54

Materials to gather

- VCR and Video Lesson 54 on Tape 14
- Cassette player
- Activity Cassette 3
- Song Cassette
- Feeling masks from Activity 9B
- Blackline Master 53A (traffic light)
- Green, red, and yellow crayons
- *Prepare ahead:* cover numbers from traffic light in Blackline Master 53A before copying it

OBJECTIVES

Language

- Learn vocabulary relating to the face and body
- Learn a new rule for street safety

Culture

- Sing "**Dulce canta el burro**" (*"Sweetly Sings the Donkey"*) and "**Las vocales**" (*"The Vowels"*)

Review

- Recall vocabulary for parts of the face and body
- Practice vowel sounds
- Recall vocabulary for street safety

Vocabulary

la cara	*face*
la cabeza	*head*
los dedos	*fingers*
las piernas	*legs*

Warm-up

Lead the children in a discussion about traffic safety. Why is it important? What are some ways to stay safe while crossing the street? If there are crossing guards near your school, ask the children what the rules are for crossing the street.

Review

Materials: Feeling masks from Activity 9B.

Review expressions of feeling by having the opening conversation using the feeling masks. As the children participate in the conversation, ask them to hold up the feeling mask that reflects their statement of how they feel, and you do the same (T = Teacher; C = class):

T: Buenos días, clase.	*Good morning, class.*
C: Buenos días, Maestro/Maestra	*Good morning, Teacher.*
T: ¿Cómo estás tú?	*How are you?*
C: Muy bien/Así, así/Muy mal, gracias. ¿Y usted?	*Very well/So-so/Very bad, thank you. And you?*
T: [*Response will vary*], gracias.	*[Response will vary], thank you.*

Introduce the video

Encourage the children to listen and watch as **la maestra** and Dora talk about new words for parts of the face and body and a new rule for street safety.

Video Lesson

1. Greeting Dora and the children

Using **Buenos días** as the greeting, **la maestra** has the opening conversation with Dora and then with the children.

2. Singing a song

La maestra says **Vamos a cantar** (*Let's sing*), inviting the children to sing "**Ojos, orejas, boca, nariz**" (*"Eyes, Ears, Mouth, Nose"*) while she points to her facial features. For song lyrics, see Lesson 52, Video Lesson, section 3. She says **Aquí están las orejas de Dora** (*Here are Dora's ears*) and **¿Cuántas son?** (*How many are there?*). Dora replies **Dos—uno, dos** (*Two—one, two*). Still referring to Dora, **la maestra** adds **Y una boca de color rosado** (*And a pink mouth*). Dora says **Muy bonita** (*Very pretty*).

3. Reviewing vocabulary for parts of the face and body

Using Flashcards, **la maestra** reviews **las partes del cuerpo y las partes de la cara** (*parts of the body and parts of the face*). She asks the class to **repite** (*repeat*) all the words they've learned.

4. Reviewing *las vocales* (vowels)

La maestra reminds the children that they use **las vocales** (*vowels*) every time they speak and sing in Spanish. The mime shows the position of the mouth and lips while the vowels are pronounced. After reviewing the vowel sounds, **la maestra** asks *How would you say ___?* as she shows Dora each vowel card.

La maestra then leads Dora and the children in saying the jingle integrating vowel sounds with an expression of feeling:

A E I O U	A E I O U
Estoy contento/a.	I am happy.
¿Cómo estás tú?	How are you?
A E I O U	A E I O U

She reminds the children that boys say **contento** and girls say **contenta** and then says the same jingle substituting the statements **Estoy triste** (*I am sad*) and **Estoy enojado/a** (*I am angry*), pointing out that boys say **enojado** and girls say **enojada**.

5. Reviewing vocabulary for street safety

Pointing to a Flashcard, **la maestra** reviews **las luces del tráfico—verde, amarillo, rojo** (*traffic lights—green, yellow, red*). She repeats **rojo** and asks Dora what vowel sound she hears in the word: **¿Es ___?** (*Is it ___?*). Dora replies **Es [oh]** (*It's [oh]*). **La maestra** then repeats the colors of traffic lights.

6. Reviewing traffic light colors and commands

La maestra tells the children that traffic lights are **muy importante** (*very important*) because they tell us what to do. She reviews their colors and their commands. She then introduces a

---

Parts of the face and body:

la cara	face
los ojos	eyes
la boca	mouth
la nariz	nose
las orejas	ears
la cabeza	head
los brazos	arms
las manos	hands
los dedos	fingers
las piernas	legs
los pies	feet

FYI Referring to **los dedos** (*fingers*), **la maestra** asks **¿Cuántos son?** (*How many are there?*) and counts to ten: **uno** (*1*), **dos** (*2*), **tres** (*3*), **cuatro** (*4*), **cinco** (*5*), **seis** (*6*), **siete** (*7*), **ocho** (*8*), **nueve** (*9*), **diez** (*10*).

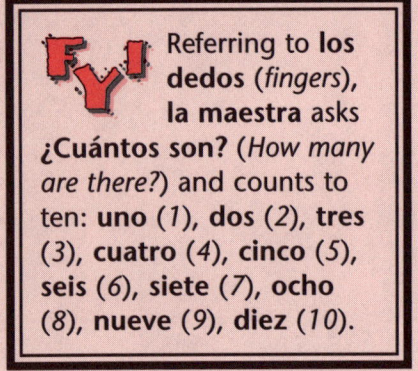

Vowel sounds:

a—[ah], **e**—[eh], **i**—[ee], **o**—[oh], **u**—[oo].

video of herself reviewing traffic-light colors and commands and pantomiming the action of each.

Back in the classroom **la maestra** initiates a game of choice by pointing green and asking Dora ¿Es ¡Sigue! o es ¡Espera!? (*Is it Go! or is it Wait!?*). Dora answers ¡Sigue! (*Go!*). Pointing to red **la maestra** asks ¿Es ¡Alto! o es ¡Espera!? (*Is it Stop! or is it Wait!?*). Dora answers ¡Alto! (*Stop!*). **La maestra** points to yellow and asks ¿Es ¡Espera! o es ¡Sigue!? (*Is it Wait! or is it Go!?*). Dora answers ¡Espera! (*Wait!*). **La maestra** then asks the children to **repite** (*repeat*)—**Verde:** ¡Sigue! (*Green: Go!*), **Amarillo:** ¡Espera! (*Yellow: Wait!*), **Rojo:** ¡Alto! (*Red: Stop!*).

7. Playing another game

La maestra says **Vamos a mirar** (*Let's watch*) to introduce a video of herself playing the association game with traffic-light colors and commands: **Verde es __** (*Green is __*); **Amarillo es __** (*Yellow is __*); **Rojo es __** (*Red is__*). Back in the classroom she reviews these commands.

8. Discussing new vocabulary

La maestra points out that we should cross the street safely by paying close attention to **las luces del tráfico** (*traffic lights*). She then asks what we should do when there are no traffic lights. To answer the question she introduces the following statement while pantomiming the actions:

Miro a la derecha,	*I look to the right,*
miro a la izquierda,	*I look to the left,*
y cruzo la calle.	*and I cross the street.*

After asking the children to **repite** (*repeat*) the statement, she introduces a video of herself crossing a street after looking to the right and left. Back in the classroom she repeats the statement and then reviews street vocabulary and commands.

Next, saying **Miro una luz del tráfico que es __** (*I'm looking at a traffic light that is __*) she names each of the colors of a traffic light, pantomimes the appropriate command, and asks Dora and the children to name the command. Finally, she pantomimes each step in crossing the street (see above) and asks Dora and the children to state it in words.

9. Singing a song

Vamos a cantar (*Let's sing*), says **la maestra**. She and the children sing "Dulce canta el burro" (*"Sweetly Sings the Donkey"*). For song lyrics, see Lesson 41, Video Lesson, section 5.

10. Closing

La maestra and Dora say **Adiós, Hasta la vista** (*Until we meet again*), and **Hasta luego** (*See you later*).

Traffic-light colors:

verde	green
amarillo	yellow
rojo	red

Traffic-light commands:

¡Sigue!	Go!
¡Espera!	Wait!
¡Alto!	Stop!

Answers:

¡Sigue!	Go!
¡Espera!	Wait!
¡Alto!	Stop!

In section 9, encourage the children to move their hands to suggest the donkey's floppy ears.

After viewing the video, praise the children for their good listening and watching skills.

Lesson Fifty-Four

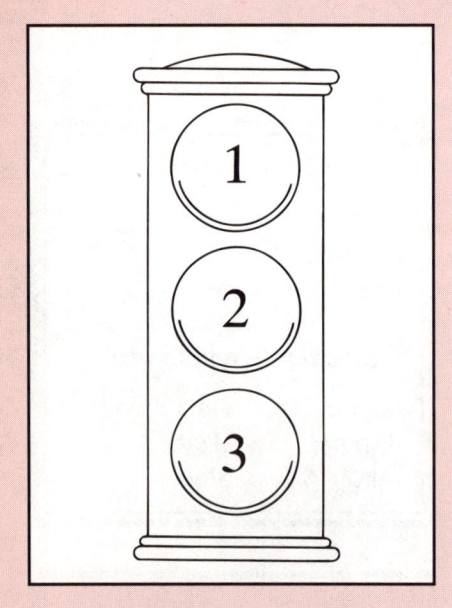

Blackline Master 53A

ACTIVITY LESSON

Activity 54A: *Muéstreme* ___ (*Show me* ___)

Materials: Cassette player; Activity Cassette 3, Side A; Blackline Master 53A; and a red, yellow, and green crayon.

Preparation: Color the numbers on Blackline Master 53A and make three copies. Color the top light on one of the copies red, the middle light on another copy yellow, and the bottom light on the third copy green. Arrange the traffic lights where the children can see and reach them. Then review the pantomimes that go with each light: stopping, folding the arms and waiting, and a walking motion.

Tell the children that **la maestra** will review the command that each of the lights gives. She will then ask a child to show her the light that gives the command that she names and to pantomime the action that goes with it. You will choose each child who is to participate. Be sure to pause the tape at the harp sound. You may want to play the activity more than once to give more children a chance to participate.

Activity 54B: Pantomime traffic light commands

Materials: Cassette player; Activity Cassette 3, Side A.

Ask the children to stand up. Tell them that **la maestra** is going to ask them to pantomime the traffic light command that she names—stop, wait, or go. Then play the activity. You may want to carry out the activity more than once. For variety, ask volunteers to take turns giving the commands in Spanish: ¡Alto!, ¡Espera!, or ¡Sigue! (*Stop!*, *Wait!*, or *Go!*)

Activity 54C: Sing

Materials: Cassette player; "**Dulce canta el burro**" ("*Sweetly Sings the Donkey*") and "**Las vocales**" ("*The Vowels*") on the Song Cassette, Side A.

Divide the class in half so that they can sing the first song as a round. While they are singing the second song lead them in playing the vowel game (A—touch nose; E—touch shoulders; I—snap fingers; O—clap hands; U—slap thighs). For song lyrics, see Lesson 41, Video Lesson, section 5 and Activity 45C, respectively.

LEVEL TWO

Closing

Tell the children that Spanish class is finished for today. In the next class they will review vowel sounds and street safety and meet a police dog.

> **IF YOU HAVE TIME . . .**
>
> Materials: The red and green traffic lights from Activity 54A.
>
> Have the children use the gym or playground to play Traffic Light. Ask them to line up at the starting line, with one child, the leader, standing with her or his back to the group about 50 feet away and holding the traffic lights. The children should start to walk toward the leader. When the leader turns around and shows the red light, the group should stop. If the leader catches anyone moving, that child must return to the starting line.
>
> Play resumes when the leader shows the green light and turns around. Whoever tags the leader first becomes the leader for the next game.

Lesson 55

Materials to gather

- VCR and Video Lesson 55 on Tape 14
- Cassette player
- Activity Cassette 3
- Song Cassette
- Gold Flashcards 41–47
- Blackline Master 55A (incomplete words)
- Vowel cards from Activity 43B
- Pencils
- Gold Flashcard 68
- *Optional materials:* pencils, writing paper

OBJECTIVES

Language
- Learn new vocabulary relating to street safety
- Name vowel sounds in spoken words

Culture
- Discuss how being able to speak Spanish helps in police work
- Sing **"Ojos, orejas, boca, nariz"** (*"Eyes, Ears, Mouth, Nose"*) and **"Español para ti"** (*"Spanish Is for You, and for Me"*)

Review
- Practice vowel sounds
- Recall vocabulary for parts of the face and body
- Recall the meanings of **rápido** (*quickly*) and **despacio** (*slowly*)
- Review vocabulary and rules for street safety

Vocabulary

el perro policía	*police dog*
la policía	*(female) police officer*
el policía	*(male) police officer*

Warm-up

Lead the children in a discussion about police officers. How do they help us? Why are they important? Share an experience in which a police officer has helped you and encourage volunteers to do the same. Then share a riddle with the children: I can be a special helper to a police officer. I can also be a pet. What am I? (a police dog)

Review

Materials: Gold Flashcards 41–47.

Point out that police officers have to work in all kinds of weather. Then review weather expressions by holding up each Flashcard and asking the children to name the weather it shows.

Introduce the video

Encourage the children to listen and watch as **la maestra** and the puppets review vowel sounds, vocabulary for parts of the face and body, and talk more about street safety.

Weather expressions:

Hace sol.
(*It's sunny.*)

Hace buen tiempo.
(*It's good weather.*)

Hace frío.
(*It's cold.*)

Hace calor.
(*It's hot.*)

Llueve *or* Está lloviendo.
(*It's raining.*)

Nieva.
(*It's snowing.*)

Hace viento.
(*It's windy.*)

Hace mal tiempo.
(*It's bad weather.*)

Vowel sounds:

a—[ah], e—[eh], i—[ee],
o—[oh], u—[oo]

Vowel game:

A—touch nose
E—touch shoulders
I—snap fingers
O—clap hands
U—slap thighs

Parts of the body:

la cabeza	head
los brazos	arms
las manos	hands
los dedos	fingers
las piernas	legs
los pies	feet

Video Lesson

1. Greeting Ñico and the children

Using **Buenos días** as the greeting, **la maestra** has the opening conversation with Ñico. Ñico says **Estoy contento** (*I'm happy*) and **la maestra** says **Yo estoy contenta. La maestra** then has the conversation with the children. She says that she heard a boy say **Estoy contento** and a girl say **Estoy contenta** and that she also heard **Tengo hambre** (*I'm hungry*) and **Muy bien** (*Very well*).

2. Reviewing *las vocales* (*vowels*)

La maestra reminds the children that they use the vowel sounds every time they sing and speak **en español**. She reviews the vowel sounds and then asks Ñico which vowel sounds are in his name. Ñico replies **i** [ee] and **o** [oh].

3. Playing the vowel game

Integrating **rápido** (*fast*), **más rápido** (*faster*), and **despacio** (*slow*), **la maestra** plays the vowel game.

4. Reviewing vocabulary for parts of the body

Using Flashcards, **la maestra** reviews the names of parts of the body. After pointing out the [ah] and [eh] sounds in **cabeza** (*head*), she asks the children to **repite** (*repeat*) the words. She then says **Vamos a mirar** (*Let's watch*) to introduce the mime, who reveals these body parts one by one.

5. Singing a song

La maestra sings "**Ojos, orejas, boca, nariz**" ("*Eyes, Ears, Mouth, Nose*") while pointing to her **cara** (*face*). For song lyrics, see Lesson 52, Video Lesson, section 3. She then asks the children to **repite** (*repeat*) as she uses Flashcards to review the same vocabulary plus **pelo** (*hair*). She then says **Vamos a mirar** (*Let's watch*) before the mime points to each of these features as she names it.

6. Reviewing vocabulary for street safety

Dora appears on the scene, and **la maestra** asks her when it is especially **importante** (*important*) to use two **partes de la cara** (*parts of the face*): **ojos** (*eyes*) and **orejas** (*ears*). Dora says **Con luces del tráfico** (*With traffic lights*) and **la maestra** adds **Y también cuando cruzo la calle** (*And also when I cross the street*). She reminds the children to use **las orejas** to listen for traffic and **los ojos** to watch what's happening.

7. Discussing helpers

La maestra points out that we have an important helper **en la calle** (*on the street*)—**la policía** (*[female] police officer*). Dora introduces a new puppet, **el perro policía** (*police dog*), and **la maestra** points out that because he is not female, he is called **el policía** (*[male] police officer*).

LEVEL TWO

8. Reviewing traffic light colors and commands

La maestra reviews traffic light colors and commands: **Verde: ¡Sigue!** (*Green: Go!*), **Amarillo: ¡Espera!** (*Yellow: Wait!*), **Rojo: ¡Alto!** (*Red: Stop!*). She next names the color of each light, pantomimes its command, and asks the children to state the command in words. She then reviews other street vocabulary: **la calle** (*street*), **la policía** (*[female] police officer*), **el policía** (*[male] police officer*), **el perro policía** (*police dog*). Finally, she once again reviews the color and command of each light.

9. Playing a game

La maestra says **Vamos a mirar** (*Let's watch*) to **el perro policía** (*the police dog*). **La maestra** on the video reviews vocabulary for street safety: **la calle** (*street*); **la policía** (*[female] police officer*); **las luces del tráfico** (*traffic lights*); and **el policía** (*[male] police officer*). After saying **Vamos a jugar** (*Let's play*), **la maestra** initiates a game of **Muéstrame ___** (*Show me ___*) with this vocabulary.

10. Reviewing a safety rule

After reminding **el perro policía** (*the police dog*) that it's important to watch the colors of traffic lights, **la maestra** says **Vamos a mirar** (*Let's watch*) to introduce the association game with traffic light colors and commands: **Verde es ___** (*Green is ___*); **Amarillo es ___** (*Yellow is ___*); **Rojo es ___** (*Red is ___*).
La maestra then reviews the rule for crossing the street when there is no light. She shows the video of herself crossing a street while stating this rule and carrying out the actions:

Miro a la derecha,	*I look to the right,*
miro a la izquierda,	*I look to the left,*
y cruzo la calle.	*and I cross the street.*

11. Singing another song

Vamos a cantar (*Let's sing*), says **la maestra**. She and the children sing "**Español para ti**" ("*Spanish Is for You, and for Me*"). For song lyrics, see Lesson 3, Video Lesson, section 3.

12. Reviewing traffic-light colors and commands

La maestra invites **el perro policía** (*the police dog*) to come back again. She then reviews the commands and actions associated with **las luces del tráfico** (*traffic lights;* see section 8) and the rule for crossing the street when there are no lights (see section 10). **La maestra** then reminds the children that it will take time and practice to learn all the safety rules.

13. Closing

La maestra and Dora say **Adiós** and **Hasta luego** (*See you later*).

LANGUAGE ACROSS THE CURRICULUM

If possible, invite a police officer to visit your class to talk about traffic safety and how it applies to pedestrians and bicycle riders. The officer could also talk about whether he or she was required to learn Spanish during police training and how it has been useful. You might also ask the officer to talk about the role of the police department and of individual officers.

Answers:

¡Sigue!	Go!
¡Espera!	Wait!
¡Alto!	Stop!

After viewing the video, praise the children for their good listening and watching skills.

Lesson Fifty-Five

Blackline Master 55A

| a | e | i | o | u |

1. r__j__
2. v__rd__
3. m__m__´
4. abu__l__
5. aut__b__´s
6. bl__s__

Blackline Master 55A

As they do Activity 55A, circulate among the children to evaluate how well they understand the vowel sounds in Spanish.

You may want to carry out Activity 55B more than once. For variety, ask volunteers to take turns giving the above commands and naming the items in Spanish: **la policía** (*female police officer*), **las luces del tráfico** (*traffic lights*), **la calle** (*street*).

ACTIVITY LESSON

Activity 55A: *Muéstrame ___* (*Show me ___*)

Materials: Cassette player; Activity Cassette 3, Side A; Blackline Master 55A; vowel cards from Activity 43B; and pencils.

Preparation: Duplicate Blackline Master 55A so that each child has a copy. Arrange the vowel cards where the children can see them. Make sure that each child has a pencil.

Point out that each word on the activity sheet is missing two vowels. Tell them that **la maestra** will read each word. They are to listen carefully and write in the vowel sounds they hear. Answers: 1. rojo; 2. verde; 3. mamá; 4. abuelo; 5. autobús; 6. blusa.

Activity 55B: Walk, jump, run

Materials: Cassette player; Activity Cassette 3, Side A; and Gold Flashcard 68.

Put the Flashcard where the children can see and reach it. Tell the children that **la maestra** is going to ask you to choose children to **anda** (*walk*), **salta** (*jump*), or **corre** (*run*) to the Flashcard and **toca** (*touch*) certain items in the picture. Then play the activity, pausing the tape at the harp sound and choosing different children as prompted by **la maestra**.

Activity 55C: Sing

Materials: Cassette player; "Ojos, orejas, boca, nariz" ("*Eyes, Ears, Mouth, Nose*") and "**Manos, dedos, piernas, pies**" ("*Hands, Fingers, Legs, Feet*") on the Song Cassette, Side A.

Divide the class in half so that they can sing the songs as a round. For lyrics to the first song, see Lesson 52, Video Lesson, section 3. Following are the lyrics to the second song:

Manos, dedos, piernas, pies,	*Hands, fingers, legs, feet,*
Piernas, pies, piernas, pies.	*Legs, feet, legs, feet.*
Manos, dedos, piernas, pies,	*Hands, fingers, legs, feet,*
Son las partes del cuerpo.	*Are the parts of the body.*

LEVEL TWO

Closing

Tell the children that Spanish class is finished for today. In the next class **la maestra** will talk about words that give commands.

If You Have Time...

Materials: Writing paper; pencils.

Preparation: Divide the class into pairs. Make sure each child has a pencil and a few sheets of paper.

Write the following words, or others of your own choosing, on the chalkboard. Encourage partners to take turns writing one of the words, leaving out at least one of the vowels. They should then show the word to their partner and challenge her or him to complete it, without looking at the board. You may want to ask heritage speakers to move about the room pronouncing the words for the children. Possible words: **rojo** (*red*), **calle** (*street*), **gato** (*cat*), **vaca** (*cow*), **cocina** (*kitchen*), **uno** (*1*), **taxi** (*taxi*), **moto** (*motorcycle*), **casa** (*house*).

Lesson Fifty-Five

Lesson 56

Materials to gather

- VCR and Video Lesson 56 on Tape 14
- Cassette player
- Activity Cassette 3
- Blackline Master 53A (traffic light)
- Red, yellow, and green crayons

OBJECTIVES

Language

- Understand positive and negative commands

Culture

- Sing "**Español para ti**" (*"Spanish Is for You, and for Me"*)
- Discuss gender of workers in different cultures

Review

- Recall expressions and vocabulary relating to transportation
- Recall vocabulary for street safety

Vocabulary

¡Anda! / ¡No andes!	Walk! / Don't walk!
¡Corre! / ¡No corras!	Run! / Don't run!
¡Salta! / ¡No saltes!	Jump! / Don't jump!
¡Toca! / ¡No toques!	Touch! / Don't touch!

Warm-up

Brainstorm with the children a list of the commands they frequently hear, such as *Pick up your clothes!*, *Feed the dog!*, *Please set the table!*, *No talking!*, or *Stop yelling!* Point out that some of these commands tell them to do something and some tell them not to do something.

Review

Remind the children that all the commands they have learned so far in Spanish tell someone to do something. Review some of these commands by asking the children to pantomime the following: **anda** (*walk*), **toca** (*touch*), **siéntate** (*sit down*), **colorea** (*color*), **dale** (*give him or her*), **busca** (*search for, look for*), **salta** (*jump*).

Introduce the video

Encourage the children to listen and watch as **la maestra** and Rosco talk about how to tell someone *not* to do something in Spanish.

Video Lesson

1. Greeting the children and Rosco

Using **Buenos días** as the greeting, **la maestra** has the opening conversation with the children. After saying **Estoy muy contenta** (*I am very happy*), **la maestra** asks Rosco ¿**Estás contento?** Rosco answers **Estoy contento** (*I am very happy*).

La maestra says that possibly one of the children said **Así, así** (*So-so*), **Tengo frío** (*I'm cold*), **Tengo calor** (*I'm hot*), or **Tengo hambre** (*I'm hungry*) in answer to the question ¿**Cómo estás tú?** (*How are you?*).

2. Singing a song

La maestra and Rosco lead the class in singing "**Español para ti**" ("*Spanish Is for You, and for Me*"). For song lyrics, see Lesson 3, Video Lesson, section 3. **La maestra** tells Rosco **Cantas muy bien** (*You sing very well*) and adds **Me gusta cantar** (*I like to sing*).

3. Reviewing traffic commands

La maestra reviews **las luces del tráfico** (*traffic lights*), which have **tres colores** (*three colors*). She asks Rosco ¿**Cuáles son?** (*What are they?*); together they review traffic-light commands while she pantomimes the actions associated with each.

4. Reviewing positive commands and introducing negative commands

La maestra says **Vamos a mirar** (*Let's watch*) to introduce the mime, who pantomimes the meaning of **Anda** (*Walk*). She points out that when she sees a light that is **verde** (*green*) she can say either ¡**Sigue!** (*Go!*) or ¡**Anda!** (*Walk!*). She then points out that when she sees **la luz de color rojo** (*the red light*) she can say ¡**Alto!** (*Stop!*), but that sometimes she needs to tell Rosco ¡**No andes!** (*Don't walk!*). This time the mime pantomimes obeying the command ¡**No andes!**

La maestra explains that sometimes she needs to tell Rosco both what to do and what not to do because she cares about him. After the mime demonstrates ¡**Corre!** (*Run!*) and ¡**No corras!** (*Don't run!*), **la maestra** says that sometimes teachers need to tell children what not to do, such as ¡**No corras en la biblioteca!** (*Don't run in the library!*) or **en la clase** (*the classroom*).

The mime then demonstrates the positive and negative commands ¡**Salta!**/¡**No saltes!** (*Jump!/Don't jump!*) and ¡**Toca!**/¡**No toques!** (*Touch!/Don't touch!*). **La maestra** next reviews these positive and negative commands once again.

FYI **La maestra** tells Rosco **Siempre tienes hambre** (*You're always hungry*).

Traffic-light commands:

Rojo: ¡Alto!
(*Red: Stop!*)

Amarillo: ¡Espera!
(*Yellow: Wait!*)

Verde: ¡Sigue!
(*Green: Go!*)

FYI Note that for the familiar *you* (**tú**), the negative form of the command is different from both the positive form of the command and the regular form of the second person singular. For example, **Tocas el tren** (*You are touching the train*) uses the simple present conjugation of the verb **tocar**. **Toca el tren** uses the imperative, or command, form of **tocar**. **No toques el tren** uses the negative imperative of **tocar**.

LEVEL TWO

5. Playing a game

Rosco says **Vamos a jugar** (*Let's play*). **La maestra** and Rosco play a game of **Simón dice** (*Simon says*) in which Rosco gives these commands: **¡Salta!/¡No saltes!** (*Jump!/Don't jump!*), **¡Anda!/ ¡No andes!** (*Walk!/Don't walk!*), **¡Siéntate!** (*Sit down!*), **¡Párate!** (*Stand up!*), and **¡Corre!/¡No corras!** (*Run!/Don't run!*). Finally, **la maestra** says **¡Bastante, Rosco!** (*Enough, Rosco!*).

La maestra tells the children that they need to listen for commands while looking at **las luces del tráfico** (*traffic lights*) and must pay attention to special helpers like **la policía** (*female police officer*) and **el policía** (*male police officer*).

6. Reading a story

Doña Elena next reads the story **Rosco va** (*Rosco Is Going*). The story (first read in Lesson 50) reinforces these constructions: **Rosco va ___** (*Rosco is going ___*), **¿Cómo va?** (*How is he going?*), and **Va en ___** (*He is going by ___*). In the story Rosco makes the following trips: **al parque en bicicleta** (*to the park by bicycle*), **a la escuela en autobús** (*to school by bus*), **a la tienda en taxi** (*to the store by taxi*), **al supermercado en jipi** (*to the supermarket by jeep*), **al restaurante en coche** (*to the restaurant by car*), **al lago en bote** (*to the lake by boat*), **a México en avión** (*to Mexico by plane*), **de viaje en tren** (*on a trip by train*), **a su casa en moto** (*home by motorcycle*).

7. Reviewing vocabulary for street safety

La maestra reviews **las luces del tráfico** (*traffic lights*) and their commands. She then introduces a video of herself using a traffic light to review these same commands.

8. Playing a game

La maestra initiates a game in which she asks Rosco to associate the correct command with the traffic-light color she names: **Verde: ___, Amarillo: ___, Rojo: ___.** She then introduces a video of herself pointing out colors on a traffic light and asking the children to complete these statements: **Verde es ___, Amarillo es ___, Rojo es ___.**

9. Reviewing traffic safety and commands

La maestra reviews the words **el policía** (*male police officer*) and **la policía** (*female police officer*) as well as positive and negative commands.

10. Closing

La maestra reminds the children to use the traffic lights and to look **a la derecha y a la izquierda** (*to the right and left*) before they **sigue** (*go*). She and Rosco then say **Adiós**.

HERITAGE SPEAKERS

Ask heritage speakers whether they remember seeing female police officers in the countries where they used to live. You may want to extend the discussion to other occupations as well, such as teaching, medicine, bus driving, and so on.

Answers:

¡Sigue!	Go!
¡Espera!	Wait!
¡Alto!	Stop!

After viewing the video, praise the children for their good listening and watching skills.

Lesson Fifty-Six

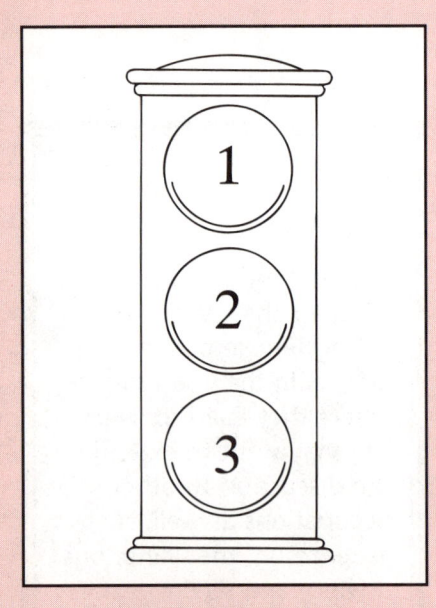

Blackline Master 53A

You may want to repeat Activity 56B, this time asking heritage speakers or other volunteers to give the commands: ¡Anda!/¡No andes! (*Walk!/Don't walk!*); ¡Salta!/¡No saltes! (*Jump!/Don't jump!*); ¡Corre!/¡No corras! (*Run!/Don't run!*); ¡Toca!/ ¡No toques! (*Touch!/Don't touch!*).

ACTIVITY LESSON

Activity 56A: Traffic light march

Materials: Cassette player; Activity Cassette 3, Side A; Blackline Master 53A; red, yellow, and green crayons.

Preparation: <u>Cover numbers</u> and duplicate Blackline Master 53A so that each child has a copy. Give each child a red, yellow, and green crayon.

Ask the children to use whichever crayon they want to color one of the traffic lights. Make sure they color the correct circle depending on the color they've chosen (top—red, middle—yellow, bottom—green). Then ask children to gather in a large circle.

Tell the children that **la maestra** is going to review the traffic lights and their commands. She is then going to give certain commands. Children holding the traffic light with the color that gives that command should march in the center of the circle.

You may want to repeat the activity after having the children exchange traffic lights so that they have one of a different color.

Activity 56B: *Simón dice* (*Simon says*)

Materials: Cassette player; Activity Cassette 3, Side A.

Tell the children that **la maestra** is going to play **Simón dice** (*Simon says*) using the commands they already knew and the ones they learned in this lesson. If Simon tells them to walk, run, jump, or touch, they should do it. If he tells them not to do it, they should stop. (Depending on available space, you may want to have the children pantomime the actions.)

LEVEL TWO

Activity 56C: Discuss safety

Discuss ways to stay safe while using different forms of transportation. You may want to begin by dividing the class into three groups and assigning one form of transportation to each, such as bus, car, and bicycle. Ask each group to work together to come up with as many safety tips as they can for people using that form of transportation. For example, *bus*: stay seated, don't throw things, don't bother the driver; *car*: fasten seatbelt, no fighting; *bicycle*: keep to the side of the road or on bicycle paths, obey traffic signals, don't ride on the sidewalk. Encourage the children to speak Spanish as much as possible.

CLOSING

Tell the children that Spanish class is finished for today. In the next class they will learn some new vocabulary for different places to go.

IF YOU HAVE TIME...

Materials: A red and green traffic light from Activity 56A.

Let the children play Traffic. In this game, some of the children will pretend to be vehicles, such as **un jipi** (*a jeep*), **un coche** (*a car*), **una moto** (*a motorcycle*), **una bicicleta** (*a bicycle*), or **un taxi** (*a taxi*). Other children will be pedestrians, and one child will be **una policía** or **un policía** (*a police officer*). Children who are "vehicles" should speed up and down an area designated as a street until **la policía** or **el policía** holds up the red traffic light and allows the "pedestrians" to cross. The "vehicles" should resume when the officer holds up the green light.

Lesson 57

Materials to gather

- VCR and Video Lesson 57 on Tape 15
- Cassette player
- Activity Cassette 3
- Song Cassette
- Blackline Master 57A (transportation)
- Scissors
- Drawing paper and crayons

Objectives

Language

- Understand **busca** (*look for, search for*) in combination with vocabulary for transportation
- Learn new vocabulary for destinations in the community
- Understand connected sentences about the beach

Culture

- Explore similarities between destinations in different cultures

Review

- Practice appropriate responses to questions about names
- Recall positive and negative commands
- Recall phrases and words relating to transportation

Vocabulary

el zoológico	*zoo*
la playa	*beach*
la piscina	*swimming pool*
el parque	*park*
la escuela	*school*
la tienda	*store*
el supermercado	*supermarket*
el restaurante	*restaurant*
el lago	*lake*
el aeropuerto	*airport*

Warm-up

Brainstorm with the children some of the places in their community where they like to go, such as the library, movie theater, swimming pool, skating rink, museum, or mall. What do they do in these places? What makes them fun or special?

Review

Point out that some places in the community are best visited during certain months and times of the year. For example, July is a good month to visit the beach. Name a month and then ask the children to name a place in the community that is good to visit during that month. (Elicit that most places are good to visit during more than one of the months and that some places, such as the library, are good to visit every month.) Then ask the children to name the months that make up each season.

Introduce the video

Encourage the children to listen and watch as **la maestra**, Dora, and **el perro policía** (*the police dog*) talk about safety and then **la maestra** and Dora talk about special and fun places to go in the community.

Seasons and months:

invierno: diciembre, enero, febrero
(*winter: December, January, February*)

primavera: marzo, abril, mayo
(*spring: March, April, May*)

verano: junio, julio, agosto
(*summer: June, July, August*)

otoño: septiembre, octubre, noviembre
(*fall: September, October, November*)

VIDEO LESSON

1. Greeting the children

Using **Buenos días** as the greeting, **la maestra** has the opening conversation with the children.

2. Reviewing questions and answers about names

Referring to **el perro policía** (*the police dog*), **la maestra** asks Dora **¿Cómo se llama?** (*What is his name?*). Dora answers **Se llama Pablo** (*His name is Pablo*). **La maestra** asks Pablo **¿Cómo te llamas?** (*What's your name?*). Pablo answers **Me llamo Pablo** (*My name is Pablo*). **La maestra** then reminds the children that when someone says **¿Cómo se llama?** he or she is asking someone else's name, and when someone says **¿Cómo te llamas?** he or she is asking our name, and we should answer **Me llamo ___**. She next asks the children **¿Cómo te llamas?** twice.

To review these statements, she points to Pablo and asks the children **¿Cómo se llama?** After the reply **Se llama Pablo**, she points to Dora and asks the same question.

3. Reviewing positive and negative commands

La maestra points out that it's the job of the police to keep people safe and that it goes with their job to tell people what to do and what not to do. She then says **Vamos a mirar** (*Let's watch*) to introduce the mime, who demonstrates the positive and negative commands **¡Anda!/¡No andes!** (*Walk!/Don't walk!*), **¡Corre!/¡No corras!** (*Run!/Don't run!*), **¡Salta!/¡No saltes!** (*Jump!/Don't jump!*), **¡Toca!/¡No toques!** (*Touch!/Don't touch!*). She once again reminds the children to listen when someone tells them not to do something because it may keep them from hurting themselves or causing damage.

4. Reviewing ¡Busca! (Search!)

La maestra asks Dora to **busca ___** (*search for ___*) each of the following toy vehicles: **el coche** (*car*), **el bote** (*boat*), **la moto** (*motorcycle*), **el autobús** (*bus*), **el avión** (*plane*). After Dora finds each, **la maestra** asks **¿Es el/la ___, clase?** (*Is it the ___, class?*). She encourages the children to answer **Sí, es el/la ___** (*Yes, it is the ___*).

5. Reviewing a sentence relating to travel

La maestra reminds the children to say **Voy en** (*I'm going by ___*) when they're going in one of these forms of transportation. She asks the children to complete this sentence with the name of the toy vehicle that she holds up: **Voy en ___** (*I am going by ___*). Holding up other toy vehicles she leads the children in stating these complete sentences: **Voy en moto** (*I'm going by motorcycle*), **Voy en autobús** (*I'm going by bus*), **Voy en avión** (*I'm going by plane*).

LEVEL TWO

6. Introducing new vocabulary for destinations

La maestra points out that we can use the sentence **Voy en ___** (*I'm going by ___*) while going to a lot of fun places in the community. Using the Flashcards showing destinations to illustrate, she next points out that we can say **Voy al zoológico** (*I'm going to the zoo*) and **Voy al zoológico en coche** (*I'm going to the zoo by car*). She then helps the children pronounce **zoológico** and models these sentences for them to say: **Voy a la playa** (*I'm going to the beach*), **Voy a la piscina** (*I'm going to the swimming pool*), and **Voy al parque** (*I'm going to the park*).

7. Visiting the beach

La maestra says **Vamos a mirar** (*Let's watch*) to introduce a video of herself at the beach. Some of her comments follow:

Estoy aquí en la playa.	I'm here at the beach.
Aquí todos se divierten.	Here everybody has a good time.
Y también hay palmas.	And there are also palm trees.
Yo llevo pantalones cortos.	I'm wearing shorts.
Llevo sandalias.	I'm wearing sandals.
Llevo unas gafas de sol.	I'm wearing sunglasses.
Esta toalla tiene un mapa.	This towel has a map.
Este mapa es de España.	This map is of Spain.
Me encanta la playa.	I love the beach.

8. Traveling with Rosco

La maestra points out that Rosco can go to a lot of fun places and that he can say **Voy en ___** (*I'm going by ___*) plus a form of transportation. He can also say **Voy a ___** (*I'm going to ___*) plus a destination.

9. Closing

Dora comments **Me encanta viajar** (*I love to travel*). **La maestra** agrees, and she and Dora say **Adiós**.

FYI In the Spanish of the Americas (Mexico, the Caribbean, and South America), **z** (as in **zoológico**) is pronounced exactly like **s**.

Also, note that when saying **Voy a** plus a destination that begins with **el**, the article contracts with **a** to become **al**, as in **Voy al zoológico** (*I'm going to the zoo*) and **Voy al parque** (*I'm going to the park*). However, if the article is **la**, it stays the same—**Voy a la piscina** (*I'm going to the pool*).

After viewing the video, praise the children for their good listening and watching skills.

Lesson Fifty-Seven

Blackline Master 57A

As a variation, repeat Activity 57A, this time asking a heritage speaker or another volunteer to play the part of doña Elena in saying **Busca ___** (*Search for ___*).

Heritage Speakers

Ask heritage speakers if they remember some favorite places to go in the towns and communities where they used to live. How were they like the places they discovered in their new communities? How were they different?

LEVEL TWO

Activity Lesson

Activity 57A: Transportation

Materials: Cassette player; Activity Cassette 3, Side A; Blackline Master 57A; scissors.

Preparation: Duplicate Blackline Master 57A so that each child has a copy. Hand out scissors to each child or pair of children. Ask the children to cut out the pictures along the lines and arrange them on their desks in any order they choose.

Tell the children that doña Elena is going to ask them to **busca ___** (*search for ___*) the picture that shows a certain kind of transportation. When they find the picture she names, they should name the form of transportation.

Transportation words: **la bicicleta** (*bicycle*), **el autobús** (*bus*), **el jipi** (*jeep*), **el coche** (*car*), **el bote** (*boat*), **el avión** (*plane*), **el tren** (*train*), **la moto** (*motorcycle*).

Activity 57B: Favorite places

Materials: Drawing paper; crayons.

Remind the children of their earlier discussion in which they talked about some of their favorite places to go in their neighborhoods and communities. Then encourage them to draw a picture of one of their favorite places. When they have finished, ask each child to describe her or his drawing and tell why that place is a favorite.

Activity 57C: Sing

Materials: Cassette player; Song Cassette, Side A.

Help the children think of some of the songs they have learned, such as **"Dulce canta el burro"** (*"Sweetly Sings the Donkey"*), **"Vengan a ver mi rancho"** (*"Come See My Ranch"*), **"Las estaciones"** (*"The Seasons"*), and **"Uno, dos, tres niñitos"** (*"One, Two, Three Little Children"*). After the children vote on their favorite song, lead them in singing it. For lyrics to the songs listed here, see Lesson 41, Video Lesson, section 5; Lesson 37, Video Lesson, section 8; Lesson 27, Video Lesson, section 7; and Lesson 14, Video Lesson, section 6, respectively.

CLOSING

Tell the children that Spanish class is finished for today. In the next class they will talk about how things in their lives change and learn a new command.

IF YOU HAVE TIME . . .

Materials: Transportation pictures from Activity 57A.

Divide the class into pairs. Let the children play a concentration game with their pictures. Have the partners sit facing each other with their pictures arranged facedown. (Tell the children to try to remember where they placed each picture.) The partners should take turns drawing from each other's pictures, naming the picture, and placing it on top of the picture they think it matches. When all the pictures have been drawn, they should check to see how many of their pictures match. The partner who has the most matching pictures wins.

Lesson 58

Materials to gather

- VCR and Video Lesson 58 on Tape 15
- Cassette player
- Activity Cassette 3
- Gold Flashcards 5–7
- Gold Flashcards 70 and 71
- Drawing paper and crayons
- *Optional materials:* Song Cassette

Objectives

Language

- Understand that the command **Cuenta** means *Count*
- Learn vocabulary relating to travel

Culture

- Understand that some changes happen because we want them to, and others just happen to us

Review

- Recall numbers 1–100
- Practice vowel sounds integrating **rápido** (*quickly*) and **despacio** (*slowly*)
- Recall jingles reinforcing vowel sounds and ways to express feelings
- Recall vocabulary for destinations in the community
- Understand connected sentences about the beach

Vocabulary

Cuenta.	*Count.*
¿Adónde vas (tú)?	*Where are you going?*
Voy a ___.	*I'm going to ___.*
¿Cómo vas?	*How are you going?*
Voy a ___ en ___.	*I'm going to ___ by ___.*

Warm-up

Lead the children in a discussion about changes. Encourage volunteers to name some changes in their lives during the past year, such as moving to a new home, a new baby in the family, a new friend, or even new shoes or other clothing because they outgrew the old.

Review

Materials: Gold Flashcards 5–7.

Point out to the children that our feelings might change frequently during the day, or even during an hour. Review expressions of feeling such as **Estoy contento/contenta** (*I'm happy*), **Estoy triste** (*I'm sad*), and **Estoy enojado/enojada** (*I'm angry*) by holding up each of the Flashcards and asking the children to name the feeling it shows.

Introduce the video

Encourage the children to listen and watch as **la maestra** and Rosco talk about change.

> You may want to ask the children to name some situations that can result in each of these feelings.

Video Lesson

1. Greeting Rosco and the children

Using **buenos días** as the greeting, **la maestra** has the opening conversation with Rosco and the children.

2. Discussing changes

La maestra asks Rosco if he notices anything **diferente** (*different*) today. Rosco replies **El pelo corto** (*Short hair*). **La maestra** says that she has had a haircut, and Rosco says **Mi pelo no está diferente** (*My hair is not different*).

La maestra points out that some changes, such as haircuts, come about because we want them to, and other changes, such as losing a tooth and getting taller, just happen.

3. Reviewing numbers

La maestra says **Busco un número** (*I'm looking for a number*). She then shows Rosco some number cards and asks **¿Qué número es?** (*What number is it?*). He replies **treinta y ocho** (*38*), **veintidós** (*22*), **quince** (*15*).

4. Introducing a new command

To introduce the command **¡Cuenta!** (*Count!*) **la maestra** says *Let's look*. The mime illustrates the command by counting his fingers. **La maestra** then says **Rosco, ¡cuenta!** (*Rosco, count!*). She and Rosco count from 1 to 10. She points out that we can also count by tens and tells Rosco to read these numbers.

5. Reviewing *las vocales* (vowels)

La maestra asks **¿Cuál es?** (*Which is it?*) as she shows the vowel cards. Rosco answers **a**—[ah], **e**—[eh], **i**—[ee], **o**—[oh], **u**—[oo].

6. Reviewing *rápido* (quickly) and *despacio* (slowly)

La maestra integrates the words **rápido** (*quickly*) and **despacio** (*slowly*) in the vowel game. She next asks her **alumnos** (*students*) to read the vowel cards she shows, and finally she reviews all the vowels.

7. Saying jingles

La maestra says the jingles integrating vowel sounds and ways to express feelings. She says that she heard boys say **enojado** (*angry*) and **contento** (*happy*) and girls say **enojada** and **contenta**.

8. Reviewing destinations in the community

Appearing in sunglasses, Rosco says **Quiero ir a la playa** (*I want to go to the beach*), and **la maestra** reveals that the reason for her haircut is that summer is coming and she wants to go to a

---

Numbers 1–10, 10–100:

1	uno	10	diez
2	dos	20	veinte
3	tres	30	treinta
4	cuatro	40	cuarenta
5	cinco	50	cincuenta
6	seis	60	sesenta
7	siete	70	setenta
8	ocho	80	ochenta
9	nueve	90	noventa
10	diez	100	cien

Vowel game:

A—touch nose; E—touch shoulders; I—snap fingers; O—clap hands; U—slap thighs.

Vowel jingles:

A E I O U
(*A E I O U*)
Estoy contento/a.
(*I am happy.*)
Estoy triste.
(*I am sad.*)
Estoy enojado/a.
(*I am angry.*)
¿Cómo estás tú?
(*How are you?*)
A E I O U
(*A E I O U*)

lot of places. Using Flashcards to illustrate, she names some of them: **la playa** (*beach*), **el zoológico** (*zoo*), **la piscina** (*swimming pool*), **el parque** (*park*).

9. Visiting the beach

Vamos a la playa (*Let's go to the beach*), says Rosco. **La maestra's** visit to the beach (first shown in Lesson 57) is shown again. Some other remarks of **la maestra** are: **Aquí en la playa hace calor y hace mucho sol.** (*Here at the beach it's hot and very sunny.*) **Yo me divierto mucho aquí en la playa porque hay arena, mucha arena.** (*I have a very good time here at the beach because there's sand, a lot of sand.*) **Me gusta la arena—es bonita.** (*I like sand—it's pretty.*) **Aquí en la playa, en esta silla, tengo una toalla.** (*Here at the beach, on this chair, I have a towel.*) **En España todos los niños hablan español y todos van a la playa y se divierten en la playa.** (*In Spain all the children speak Spanish and they all go to the beach and have a good time at the beach.*)

10. Playing a game

After commenting on Rosco's **gafas de sol** (*sunglasses*), **la maestra** shows Flashcards and asks the class to **repite** (*repeat*) the names of destinations (see section 8). She then says **Vamos a jugar** (*Let's play*). After asking **¿Adónde vas tú?** (*Where are you going?*) she points to scenes that illustrate the responses: **Voy al zoológico** (*I'm going to the zoo*), **Voy a la piscina** (*I'm going to the swimming pool*), **Voy al parque** (*I'm going to the park*), **Voy a la playa** (*I'm going to the beach*).

She then plays a game of **Muéstrame ___** (*Show me ___*) with pictures of these destinations and ends by reviewing the question **¿Adónde vas tú?** and the answer **Yo voy a ___**.

11. Reviewing questions and answers

La maestra asks Rosco **¿Adónde vas tú?** (*Where are you going?*) and points to scenes on the Flashcards showing destinations. Rosco replies **Voy (al zoológico, a la piscina, al parque)** (*I'm going to [the zoo, the swimming pool, the park]*). She next shows a toy **moto** (*motorcycle*) and a toy **coche** (*car*) and encourages Rosco to say **Voy a la playa en moto** (*I'm going to the beach by motorcycle*). **La maestra** next asks **Adónde vas tú y cómo vas?** (*Where are you going and how are you going?*). Rosco replies by combining pictures of destinations with the means of transportation she is showing to reply **Voy a ___ en ___** (*I'm going to ___ by ___*).

12. Closing

La maestra tells the children that they have done a wonderful job today and that they are learning a lot of Spanish. She and Rosco say **Adiós** and **Hasta la vista** (*Until we meet again*).

Referring to the picture of the swimming pool **la maestra** says **La chica lleva el traje de baño** (*The girl is wearing a bathing suit*).

FYI Referring to the picture of the zoo **la maestra** says **El tigre está allá** (*The tiger is there*).

FYI Although the interrogative **dónde** means *where*, it applies only to existing locations; for example, **¿Dónde está el perro?** (*Where is the dog?*). To ask where someone is going, use the interrogative **adónde**, which combines the words **a** (*to*) and **dónde** (*where*) and literally means *to where*.

After viewing the video, praise the children for their good listening and watching skills.

Lesson Fifty-Eight

ACTIVITY LESSON

Activity 58A: *Simón dice* (Simon says)

Materials: Cassette player; Activity Cassette 3, Side A.

Tell the children that doña Elena is going to play Simon says. Remind them that if Simon says to do something, they should do it. If he does not, they should not do it. Ask the children to listen for the following words during the game: **Anda** (*Walk*), **Salta** (*Jump*), **Corre** (*Run*), **Párate** (*Stand up*), and **Siéntate** (*Sit down*).

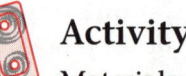

> You may want to repeat the activity by asking volunteers to play the part of **la maestra** in saying **Simón dice** ___ (*Simon says ___*).

Activity 58B: Can you draw a picture?

Materials: Cassette player; Activity Cassette 3, Side A; Gold Flashcards 70 and 71; drawing paper; and crayons.

Display the Flashcards and ask the children to name the places depicted on each: the zoo (**el zoológico**), the beach (**la playa**), the pool (**la piscina**), the park (**el parque**). Ask them to draw a picture of their favorite one of these places.

For the second part of the activity, tell the children that doña Elena is going to ask them to stand up with pictures showing certain places. When she names the place they have drawn, they should stand up with their pictures.

Activity 58C: Let's count

Materials: Cassette player; Activity Cassette 3, Side A.

Tell the children that doña Elena is going to ask them to count with her, first from 1 to 10, then from 20 to 30, and finally from 10 to 100 by tens. Then play the activity. For numbers 1–10 and 10–100 by tens, see section 4 of this Video Lesson.

Numbers 20–30:

20	veinte
21	veintiuno
22	veintidós
23	veintitrés
24	veinticuatro
25	veinticinco
26	veintiséis
27	veintisiete
28	veintiocho
29	veintinueve
30	treinta

LEVEL TWO

CLOSING

Tell the children that Spanish class is finished for today. In the next class they will learn a new song and talk more about places to go in the community.

IF YOU HAVE TIME...

Materials: Cassette player; **"Las vocales"** (*"The Vowels"*) on the Song Cassette, Side A.

Play the song while the children sing along. Then play it again, this time leading them in playing the vowel game (see section 6 of the Video Lesson) as they sing. For song lyrics, see Activity 45C.

Lesson Fifty-Eight

Lesson 59

Materials to gather

- VCR and Video Lesson 59 on Tape 15
- Cassette player
- Activity Cassette 3
- Handfuls of small items, such as paper clips or pebbles
- Sheets of paper with a number between 10 and 50 written on each
- Blackline Master 59A (destinations and vehicles)
- A large ball, such as a volleyball
- Drawing paper and crayons
- *Optional materials:* two sets of numbers 0–9 written on 8½" by 11" pieces of construction paper

OBJECTIVES

Language

- Understand connected sentences about travel to destinations in the community

Culture

- Sing **"Vamos a contar"** (*"Let's Count"*)

Review

- Recall that **cuenta** means *count*
- Practice counting
- Recall sentence constructions relating to travel
- Review vocabulary for destinations in the community

Vocabulary

No new vocabulary is introduced in this lesson.

Warm-up

Tell the children that in this lesson they will practice counting and sing a counting song. Encourage them to think about places in the community where they might need or want to count. For example, at a store they might need to count money; at the beach they might want to count seashells; at the zoo they might want to count the number of a certain kind of animal.

Review

Materials: Handfuls of small items, such as paper clips or pebbles; sheets of paper with a number between 10 and 50 written on each (one for each group).

Divide the class into small groups. Give each group several handfuls of the small items you have chosen and a sheet of paper with a number on it.

Review numbers by asking the children to make a pile of the items that consists of the number of items shown on the sheet of paper you have given them. Remind them to count the items in Spanish. For numbers, see the Video Lesson of this lesson.

To get more practice, give each group another sheet of paper with a different number on it, and have them repeat the process.

Introduce the video

Encourage the children to listen and watch as **la maestra** and Rosco talk about numbers and places in the community that are fun to visit.

Video Lesson

1. Greeting the children and Rosco

Using **Buenas tardes** (*Good afternoon*) as the greeting, **la maestra** has the opening conversation with the children and with Rosco. Rosco says **Estoy contento** (*I'm happy*), and **la maestra** says **Estoy contenta también** (*I'm happy too*).

2. Reviewing *Cuenta* (*Count*) integrating numbers

La maestra says **Vamos a mirar** to introduce the mime, who illustrates the command **Cuenta** (*Count*) by counting his fingers. **La maestra** then says **Rosco, ¡cuenta!** (*Rosco, count!*). She and Rosco count from 1 to 20 together. She points out that we can also count **de diez en diez** (*by tens*) and tells Rosco and the children to read numbers from 10 to 100 by tens.

3. Singing a song

Before singing "**Vamos a contar**" ("*Let's Count*"), **la maestra** explains that it is a song sung by Spanish-speaking children in the Caribbean. Afterwards, **la maestra** says **Me gusta cantar** (*I like to sing*) and Rosco says **Me gusta contar** (*I like to count*).

Dos y dos son cuatro.	Two and two are four.
Cuatro y dos son seis.	Four and two are six.
Seis y dos son ocho.	Six and two are eight.
Y ocho dieciséis.	And eight, sixteen.
Diez y seis y ocho	Sixteen and eight
Veinticuatro son.	Are twenty-four.
Vienticuatro y ocho	Twenty-four and eight
Treinta y dos nos dan.	Give us thirty-two.
Treinta y dos nos dan.	Give us thirty-two.
Treinta y dos nos dan.	Give us thirty-two.

4. Reviewing destinations in the community

La maestra points out that a lot of people like to sing and play games while traveling **en coche** (*by car*). Using Flashcards, she begins a review of places to visit in the community by saying **Voy a la playa** (*I'm going to the beach*), which she asks the children to **repite** (*repeat*). She and Rosco then offer some other ways of answering the question **¿Adónde vas?** or **¿Adónde vas tú?** (*Where are you going?*): **Voy al zoológico** (*I'm going to the zoo*); **Voy a la piscina** (*I'm going to the swimming pool*); **Voy al parque** (*I'm going to the park*).

5. Playing a game

La maestra says **Vamos a jugar** (*Let's play*). After asking **¿Adónde vas tú?** (*Where are you going?*) she points to scenes that illustrate the responses: **Voy al zoológico** (*I'm going to the zoo*); **Voy a la piscina** (*I'm going to the swimming pool*); **Voy al parque**

Numbers 1–20, 30–100:

1	uno
2	dos
3	tres
4	cuatro
5	cinco
6	seis
7	siete
8	ocho
9	nueve
10	diez
11	once
12	doce
13	trece
14	catorce
15	quince
16	dieciséis
17	diecisiete
18	dieciocho
19	diecinueve
20	veinte
30	treinta
40	cuarenta
50	cincuenta
60	sesenta
70	setenta
80	ochenta
90	noventa
100	cien

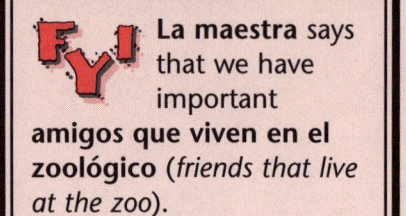

FYI — **La maestra** says that we have important **amigos que viven en el zoológico** (*friends that live at the zoo*).

(*I'm going to the park*); **Voy a la playa** (*I'm going to the beach*). She then plays a game of **Muéstrame** ___ (*Show me* ___) with pictures of these destinations and ends by reviewing their names.

6. Playing another game

La maestra plays a choice game with Rosco, pointing to places shown on the Flashcards and asking **¿Es ___ o es ___?** (*Is it ___ or is it ___?*).

7. Playing ¿Cuál falta? (*What's missing?*)

La maestra says **Vamos a jugar ¿Cuál falta?** (*Let's play What's missing?*). She plays the game with pictures of destinations in the community—**el zoológico** (*zoo*), **la piscina** (*swimming pool*), **la playa** (*beach*), **el parque** (*park*).

8. Practicing vocabulary relating to travel

La maestra asks Rosco **¿Cuál es?** as she holds up toy vehicles one by one to review **el coche** (*car*), **el autobús** (*bus*), and **el tren** (*train*). Combining the toys with pictures on the Flashcards she encourages Rosco to say **Voy a la piscina en autobús** (*I'm going to the swimming pool by bus*), **Voy al parque en coche** (*I'm going to the park by car*), **Voy al zoológico en tren** (*I'm going to the zoo by train*), and **Voy a la playa en autobús** (*I'm going to the beach by bus*). **La maestra** says sentences containing different combinations of these destinations and vehicles and asks the children to repeat them.

9. Traveling

Vamos a mirar (*Let's watch*), says **la maestra** to introduce a video showing herself going different places on different forms of transportation. Some of **la maestra**'s comments are:

¿Quién está en el autobús? ¡Es Rosco!	Who is on the bus? It's Rosco!
Es muy divertido ir al parque en bicicleta.	It's a lot of fun to go to the park by bicycle.
Estoy en el bote y el bote está en el lago.	I'm on the boat and the boat is on the lake.
Estoy en la estación de los trenes.	I'm at the train station.
Tengo mi maleta. Vamos en tren.	I have my suitcase. We're going by train.
Aquí viene el jipi. Voy en jipi.	Here comes the jeep. I'm going by jeep.

10. Closing

La maestra and Rosco tell the children **Adiós** and **Hasta la vista** (*Until we meet again*).

LANGUAGE ACROSS THE CURRICULUM

Tie a discussion about **la playa** (*the beach*) and what you might find there to a science lesson. If possible, bring in pictures of beaches, sea birds, and ocean animals. You might discuss the food chain at the beach as well as the effects of pollution, specifically of oil spills.

After viewing the video, praise the children for their good listening and watching skills.

Lesson Fifty-Nine

Blackline Master 59A

You may want to repeat Activity 59A, this time by asking heritage speakers or other volunteers to create oral sentences that pair the pictures in different ways.

Doña Elena says these numbers:

veintiuno—uno más: veintidós (*21—one more: 22*)

cuarenta—uno más: cuarenta y uno (*40—one more: 41*)

diecinueve—uno más: veinte (*19—one more: 20*)

cuarenta y ocho—uno más: cuarenta y nueve (*48—one more: 49*)

noventa y nueve—uno más: cien (*99—one more: 100*)

LEVEL TWO

ACTIVITY LESSON

Activity 59A: Let's go!

Materials: Cassette player; Activity Cassette 3, Side A; Blackline Master 59A; and scissors.

Preparation: Duplicate Blackline Master 59A so that each child has a copy. Give scissors to each child or pair of children and tell them to cut out the pictures along the lines.

Tell the children to arrange the pictures on their desks in any order they choose. Explain that doña Elena is going to name some destinations and some ways of getting there by saying, for example, "I am going to the *beach* by *bus*." They should put the destination she names, such as *beach*, and the transportation she names, such as *bus*, side by side.

Activity 59B: Can you count?

Materials: Cassette player; Activity Cassette 3, Side A; and a large ball, such as a volleyball.

Have the children stand in a large circle. Then tell them that during this activity they are going to bounce the ball to one another while doña Elena states a number and says **uno más** (*one more*). The child receiving the ball should add one to the number stated by doña Elena and name the resulting number. Then play the activity, bouncing the ball to one of the children while doña Elena states the first number and pausing the tape at the harp sound to give the child time to respond. Have the first child bounce the ball to the next child, and so on to the end of the activity.

Activity 59C: Let's draw!

Materials: Blackline Master 59A; drawing paper; and crayons.

Remind the children of the construction **Voy a ___ en ___** (*I'm going to ___ by ___*). Then ask them to use the pictures from Blackline Master 59 as a basis for their own pictures of these places and the different ways of getting there. When they have finished, have them use **Voy a ___ en ___** sentences to describe their pictures to the class.

CLOSING

Tell the children that Spanish class is finished for today. In the next class they will learn new vocabulary for activities.

IF YOU HAVE TIME...

Materials: Two sets of numbers 0–9 written on 8½" by 11" pieces of construction paper.

Divide the class into two teams and give one set of numbers to each team. Call out (or have a volunteer call out) two-digit numbers, one at a time. Challenge the teams to form the numbers using one member from each team, who should stand side by side holding their numbers in front of them.

Lesson 60

Materials to gather
- VCR and Video Lesson 60 on Tape 15
- Cassette player
- Activity Cassette 3
- Song Cassette

OBJECTIVES

Language
- Learn new vocabulary and constructions based on sports and other activities

Culture
- Understand that soccer and baseball are very popular in Spanish-speaking countries
- Understand that **el fútbol** is the Spanish name for the sport known in the United States as *soccer*

Review
- Review questions and answers about destinations in the community
- Recall vocabulary for forms of transportation
- Recall constructions relating to travel
- Sing "**Español para ti**" ("*Spanish Is for You, and for Me*")

Vocabulary

¿Qué vas a hacer?	*What are you going to do?*
Voy a saltar la cuerda.	*I'm going to jump rope.*
Voy a jugar al béisbol.	*I'm going to play baseball.*
Voy a jugar al fútbol.	*I'm going to play soccer.*
Voy a ir de campo.	*I'm going to go on a picnic.*
Voy a nadar.	*I'm going to swim.*
Voy a jugar.	*I'm going to play.*
Voy a jugar al vólibol.	*I'm going to play volleyball.*

Warm-up

Encourage the children to talk about some of their favorite sports and activities. Which of the activities can they do by themselves? Which are team sports? What kinds of teams have they played on?

Review

Point out that sports and other activities often require certain items or equipment, such as a ball, a bat, roller skates, or a helmet. Remind the children that school activities often require certain items, too. Review classroom items by holding them up or pointing to them and asking the children to name them.

Introduce the video

Encourage the children to listen and watch as **la maestra** and Ñico review forms of transportation and talk about different sports and activities.

Classroom items:

el libro	book
la mochila	book bag, backpack
el papel	paper
los colores	crayons
los lápices	pencils
la regla	ruler
las gomas	erasers
las tijeras	scissors
los bolis	pens
el cuaderno	notebook
el sacapuntas	pencil sharpener

Video Lesson

1. Greeting Ñico and the children

Using **buenos días** as the greeting, **la maestra** has the opening conversation with Ñico and the children. She and Ñico review alternative replies to the question ¿**Cómo estás tú?** (*How are you?*): **Tengo hambre** (*I'm hungry*), **Estoy muy mal** (*I'm very bad*), **Estoy así, así** (*I'm so-so*), **Estoy muy bien** (*I'm very good*). When Ñico asks ¿**Estás contenta?** (*Are you happy?*), **la maestra** replies **Estoy muy contenta de ver a mis amigos en las clases** (*I'm very happy to see my friends in the classes*).

2. Reviewing questions and answers

Using Flashcards, **la maestra** and Ñico review some responses to the question ¿**Adónde vas (tú)?** (*Where are you going?*), such as **Voy al parque** (*I'm going to the park*), **Voy a la playa** (*I'm going to the beach*), **Voy al zoológico** (*I'm going to the zoo*), and **Voy a la piscina** (*I'm going to the swimming pool*). **La maestra** says **Vamos a la playa cuando hace calor y hace sol** (*We go to the beach when it's hot and sunny*) and that at the zoo she will see **el león y la zebra** (*the lion and the zebra*).

3. Playing a game

La maestra says **Vamos a mirar** (*Let's watch*) to introduce a game of ¿**Cuál falta?** (*What's missing?*) to review the names of destinations in the community discussed in section 2.

4. Discussing activities

Referring to destinations, **la maestra** asks Ñico ¿**Cuál es tu favorito?** (*Which is your favorite?*). Ñico answers **Me gusta el parque** (*I like the park*). **La maestra** agrees, adding that she can say **Voy a jugar** (*I'm going to play*) when she is at the park and **Voy a nadar** (*I'm going to swim*) when she is at the swimming pool. She then says **Vamos a mirar** (*Let's watch*) to introduce the mime's demonstration of **nadar** (*to swim*).

5. Reviewing vocabulary for destinations and forms of transportation

La maestra reviews the question ¿**Qué vas a hacer?** (*What are you going to do?*) and the statement **Voy a nadar** (*I'm going to swim*). She then combines these constructions with vocabulary and constructions for destinations and transportation, resulting in these sentences:

Voy al parque en coche.	*I'm going to the park by car.*
Voy a jugar.	*I'm going to play.*
Voy a la piscina en autobús.	*I'm going to the swimming pool by bus.*

FYI Just as American English differs somewhat from British English, Spanish differs from country to country. Many words in Spanish derive from Arabic because the Moors invaded Spain in A.D. 711 and exerted an enormous influence until they left in A.D. 1492. Although **la piscina** is commonly used for *swimming pool*, **la alberca**, a word of Arabic origin, is used for *pool* in some Spanish-speaking countries.

Also, note that **Vamos**, as in **Vamos a la playa**, can mean either *We are going* or *Let's go*, depending on the context.

FYI The Spanish language has two words for *play*—**jugar**, which refers to sports and games, and **tocar**, which refers to musical instruments, as in **Toco el piano** (*I play the piano*).

LEVEL TWO

Voy a nadar.	*I'm going to swim.*
Voy al parque en moto.	*I'm going to the park by motorcycle.*
Voy a jugar al béisbol.	*I'm going to play baseball.*

6. Introducing vocabulary and constructions for activities

La maestra reviews the question **¿Qué vas a hacer?** (*What are you going to do?*) and introduces several activities that can be expressed with the construction **Voy a ___** (*I'm going to ___*):

Voy a saltar la cuerda.	*I'm going to jump rope.*
Voy a jugar al béisbol.	*I'm going to play baseball.*
Voy a jugar al fútbol.	*I'm going to play soccer.*
Voy a ir de campo.	*I'm going to go on a picnic.*
Voy a nadar.	*I'm going to swim.*
Voy a jugar.	*I'm going to play.*

7. Discussing *fútbol* (soccer)

In reviewing the question **¿Qué vas a hacer?** (*What are you going to do?*), **la maestra** explains that the game that in Spanish-speaking countries is called **fútbol** is called *soccer* in the United States. She also explains that in some Spanish-speaking countries **béisbol** (*baseball*) is the favorite sport. Using Flashcards, she then asks the children to **repite** (*repeat*) the sentences introduced in the preceding section.

8. Introducing a different sport

La maestra introduces the sentence **Voy a jugar al vólibol** (*I'm going to play volleyball*). She then says **Vamos a mirar** (*Let's watch*) to introduce a video showing a group of people, including herself, playing volleyball. She also reviews the question **¿Quién es?** (*Who is it?*) to ask Ñico whom she was playing volleyball with—doña Elena. She next reviews **Voy a ___** (*I'm going to ___*) combined with activities.

9. Singing a song

La maestra says **Vamos a cantar** (*Let's sing*). She and Ñico then sing "**Español para ti**" (*"Spanish Is for You, and for Me"*). For song lyrics, see Lesson 3, Video Lesson, section 3.

10. Closing

La maestra reminds the children that there are many wonderful places to go and many wonderful things to do. She and Ñico say **Adiós** and **Hasta luego** (*See you later*).

FYI In Spanish-speaking countries the game of *football* played in the United States is called **el fútbol americano**.

HERITAGE SPEAKERS

Soccer is less popular in the United States than it is in many other parts of the world. However, Spanish television stations often televise soccer matches, and soccer remains a popular sport among Spanish speakers in the United States. Invite heritage speakers in your class to talk about soccer and about their favorite teams and players. Have them bring in any pictures they or family members might have of famous players.

After viewing the video, praise the children for their good listening and watching skills.

Lesson Sixty

IF YOU HAVE TIME...

Materials: Cassette player; **"Español para ti"** (*"Spanish Is for You, and for Me"*) on the Song Cassette, Side A.

Encourage the children to sing along with the cassette. For song lyrics, see Lesson 3, Video Lesson, section 3.

ACTIVITY LESSON

Activity 60A: We are mimes!

Materials: Cassette player; Activity Cassette 3, Side A.

Tell the children that doña Elena is going to name some of the activities discussed in the lesson—jumping rope, playing baseball, and playing soccer. They should pantomime each activity that she names.

Activity 60B: Football and soccer

Encourage the children to compare and contrast football and soccer. In what ways are the games different? How are they alike? Ask them to think about such details as uniforms, the kind of ball used, the object of the games, and so on.

Activity 60C: Sing a song

Materials: Cassette player; **"El picnic"** (*"The Picnic"*) on the Song Cassette, Side A.

After you have played the song several times, encourage the children to sing along.

Hoy es lunes. Hoy es lunes.	*Today is Monday. Today is Monday.*
Lunes—pan. Todos tienen hambre.	*Monday—bread. Everyone is hungry.*
Vamos a comer.	*Let's eat.*
martes—mango	*Monday—mango*
miércoles—chile	*Tuesday—pepper*
jueves—tomate	*Thursday—tomato*
viernes—limón	*Friday—lemon*
sábado—queso	*Saturday—cheese*
domingo—jamón	*Sunday—ham*

LEVEL TWO

Closing

Tell the children that Spanish class is finished for today. In the next class they will talk more about sports and activities.

Lesson 61

Materials to gather

- VCR and Video Lesson 61 on Tape 16
- Cassette player
- Activity Cassette 3
- Song Cassette
- Blackline Master 61A (sports and Rosco)
- Scissors
- Gold Flashcards 72, 73

OBJECTIVES

Language

- Understand vocabulary and constructions based on destinations combined with sports and other activities

Culture

- Recognize that different parts of the world have different climates
- Understand that baseball is Puerto Rico's favorite sport

Review

- Recall vocabulary for weather and seasons
- Practice vocabulary for destinations in the community
- Recall constructions relating to travel
- Sing **"Las estaciones"** (*"The Seasons"*)

Vocabulary

No new vocabulary is introduced in this lesson.

Warm-up

If you have any Little Leaguers or baseball fans in the class, encourage them to talk about baseball. What do they like about the sport? Why do they think so many people like it? What makes a good player?

Review

Point out that many sports teams have uniforms of different colors. Ask Little League players in your class what color their uniforms are; then ask the colors of the uniforms of other sports teams the children know, both professional and amateur.

Introduce the video

Encourage the children to listen and watch as **la maestra**, Rosco, and Ñico talk more about different sports and activities.

FYI You may want to tell the children that Little League began in 1939 in Williamsport, Pennsylvania, with 30 boys playing on three teams. Today 3 million boys and girls from ages 5 to 18 play on 198,000 teams in 85 countries.

Colors:

morado	*purple*
gris	*gray*
blanco	*white*
rosado	*pink*
café	*brown*
negro	*black*
azul	*blue*
verde	*green*
rojo	*red*
anaranjado	*orange*
amarillo	*yellow*

Video Lesson

1. Greeting the children, Rosco, and Ñico

Using **buenos días** as the greeting, **la maestra** has the opening conversation with the children, Rosco, and Ñico, during which they review the response **Estoy muy contento/contenta**. **La maestra** says **Estoy contenta porque estoy aquí con todos mis amigos** (*I'm happy because I'm here with all my friends*).

2. Reviewing expressions for weather and seasons

La maestra asks **¿Qué tiempo hace?** (*What is the weather like?*). Using Flashcards, she and the puppets review the expressions **Hace sol** (*It's sunny*), **Hace calor** (*It's hot*), **Llueve** (*It's raining*), and **Hace frío** (*It's cold*).

La maestra reminds the children that different **estaciones** (*seasons*) have different weather in different parts of the world and in different parts of the country. She asks the children to **repite** (*repeat*) and asks **¿Qué tiempo hace?** to review some of the weather associated with the seasons: **el otoño—hace viento, hace buen tiempo, hace frío** (*fall—it's windy, it's good weather, it's cold*); **el verano—hace calor, hace sol, hace buen tiempo** (*summer—it's hot, it's sunny, it's good weather*); **el invierno—hace frío, nieva** (*winter—it's cold, it's snowing*); **la primavera—hace buen tiempo, hace sol, hace viento, llueve** (*spring—it's good weather, it's sunny, it's windy, it's raining*). Note that, eager for his turn to name some weather, Ñico says **Me toca a mí** (*It's my turn*); **la maestra** agrees, saying **Te toca a ti** (*It's your turn*).

3. Singing a song

La maestra reviews the names of **las cuatro estaciones** (*the four seasons*—see section 2) before Ñico says **Vamos a cantar** (*Let's sing*). **La maestra** then sings "**Las estaciones**" ("*The Seasons*"). For song lyrics, see Lesson 27, Video Lesson, section 7.

4. Reviewing seasons and activities

La maestra again reviews the names of **las cuatro estaciones** (*the four seasons*). Next, showing Flashcards **la maestra** asks **¿Qué vas a hacer?** (*What are you going to do?*) and reviews some seasonal responses:

En el otoño voy a jugar al fútbol.	*In the fall I'm going to play soccer.*
En el verano voy a saltar la cuerda.	*In the summer I'm going to jump rope.*
En el invierno voy a jugar al béisbol.	*In the winter I'm going to play baseball.*
En la primavera voy a ir de campo.	*In the spring I'm going to go on a picnic.*

La maestra reminds the children that when it's very cold they should wear winter clothing, such as **un abrigo** (*coat*), **unas botas** (*boots*), **una chaqueta** (*jacket*), **un sombrero** (*hat*).

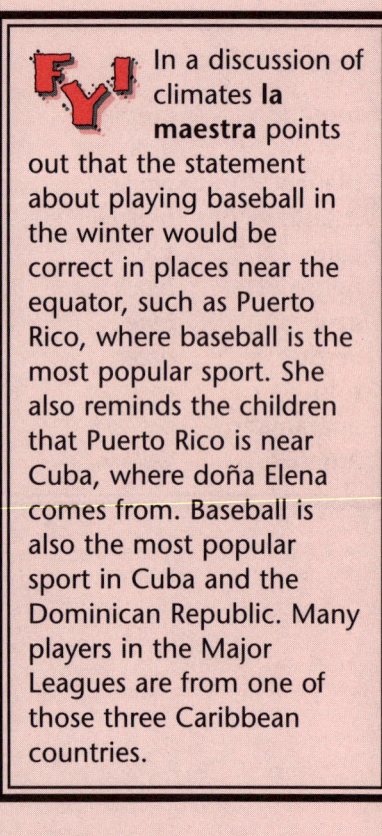

FYI In a discussion of climates **la maestra** points out that the statement about playing baseball in the winter would be correct in places near the equator, such as Puerto Rico, where baseball is the most popular sport. She also reminds the children that Puerto Rico is near Cuba, where doña Elena comes from. Baseball is also the most popular sport in Cuba and the Dominican Republic. Many players in the Major Leagues are from one of those three Caribbean countries.

LEVEL TWO

5. Reviewing Voy a ___ (I'm going to ___)

La maestra tells the children to **escucha** (*listen*) as she asks **¿Qué vas a hacer?** (*What are you going to do?*) to review the construction **Voy a ___** (*I'm going to ___*) to describe activities: **saltar la cuerda** (*jump rope*), **jugar al béisbol** (*play baseball*), **jugar al fútbol** (*play soccer*), **ir de campo** (*go on a picnic*), **nadar** (*swim*), **jugar** (*play*). She reminds the children that **jugar** can be used with any game.

6. Practicing vocabulary for activities and destinations

Using Flashcards and asking **¿Qué vas a hacer?** (*What are you going to do?*), **la maestra** reviews vocabulary for activities combined with vocabulary for destinations, based on the construction **Voy a ___** (*I'm going to ___*):

Voy a nadar. Voy a la piscina.	*I'm going to swim. I'm going to the pool.*
Voy a jugar. Voy al parque.	*I'm going to play. I'm going to the park.*
Voy a jugar al vólibol.	*I'm going to play volleyball.*

La maestra then shows the video of her, doña Elena, and others playing volleyball.

7. Closing

Referring to the volleyball game, **la maestra** says **¡Fue muy divertido!** (*It was a lot of fun!*). She then reviews activities and destinations expressed with **Voy a ___** (*I'm going to ___*) before she and the hand puppets say **Hasta luego** (*See you later*) and **Adiós**.

FYI Note that both the Spanish construction **Voy a** and its direct translation into English, *I'm going to*, can signal either an intention, as in **Voy a jugar** (*I'm going to play*), or a place, as in **Voy al parque** (*I'm going to the park*).

After viewing the video, praise the children for their good listening and watching skills.

Lesson Sixty-One

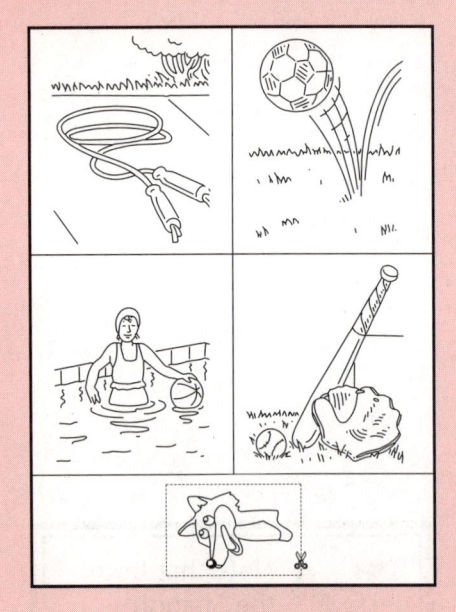

Blackline Master 61A

ACTIVITY LESSON

Activity 61A: Rosco likes sports

Materials: Cassette player; Activity Cassette 3, Side A; Blackline Master 61A; and scissors.

Preparation: Duplicate Blackline Master 61A so that each child has a copy. Give scissors to each child or pair of children and have them cut out the picture of Rosco along the dotted line.

Tell the children that Rosco is going to say **Voy a** ___ (*I'm going to* ___) and then name a sport or activity. They are to place Rosco on the picture of the activity he names.

Activity 61B: Walk, run, jump

Materials: Gold Flashcards 72 and 73.

Display the Flashcards where the children can see and reach them. Then tell the children that doña Elena will ask individual children to walk (**anda**), run (**corre**), or jump (**salta**) to the picture of the activity she names and to touch it (**toca**). You will choose each child who is to participate. Pause the tape at the harp sound and choose different children as prompted by doña Elena.

Activity 61C: Let's sing

Materials: Cassette player; "Las estaciones" (*"The Seasons"*) on the Song Cassette, Side A.

Have the children brainstorm some activities that go with each season, such as swimming and roller skating in the summer, ice skating in the winter, jumping rope in the spring, and so on. Point out that some of the activities can be done during more than one season. Then encourage them to sing along with **"Las estaciones"** (*"The Seasons"*). While they are singing each verse, ask them to pantomime one of the activities they discussed. For song lyrics, see Lesson 27, Video Lesson, section 7.

LEVEL TWO

CLOSING

Tell the children that Spanish class is finished for today. In the next class they will listen to a new story.

> **IF YOU HAVE TIME...**
>
> Materials: Cassette player; **"Buenos días a ti"** (*"Good Morning to You"*), **"Buenas tardes a ti"** (*"Good Afternoon to You"*), and **"Buenas noches a ti"** (*"Good Evening to You"*) on the Song Cassette, Side A.
>
> Have the children sing along with the cassette. For song lyrics, see Lesson 6, Video Lesson, section 3.

Lesson Sixty-One

Lesson 62

Materials to gather

- VCR and Video Lesson 62 on Tape 16
- Cassette player
- Activity Cassette 3
- Song Cassette
- Make-believe telephones from Activity 45A
- Gold Flashcards 70–73
- Scissors
- *Optional materials:* crayons and drawing paper

OBJECTIVES

Language
- Understand a story

Culture
- Understand that **perdón** (*pardon me*) is the word to use to apologize for coughing or sneezing

Review
- Recall vocabulary for colors
- Review vocabulary for destinations in the community
- Review constructions relating to travel
- Practice vocabulary and constructions relating to sports and activities
- Sing **"Español para ti"** (*"Spanish Is for You, and for Me"*)

Vocabulary
No new vocabulary is introduced in this lesson.

Warm-up

Encourage the children to discuss their school day. What are some of the activities, classes, and events—such as attendance, opening exercises, reading, arithmetic, lunch, recess—that happen almost every day? What are some special events that happen only once in a while?

Review

Materials: Make-believe telephones from Activity 45A.

Divide the class into pairs. Then have partners take turns pretending to call each other on the telephone to talk about school, games, sports, or anything else that interests them. Encourage them to use Spanish as much as possible and remind them to say **Diga** (*Hello*) at the beginning of the conversation and **Adiós** (*Good-bye*) at the end.

Introduce the video

Encourage the children to listen and watch as **la maestra**, Dora, and Jorge talk more about different sports and activities and doña Elena reads a new story about school.

VIDEO LESSON

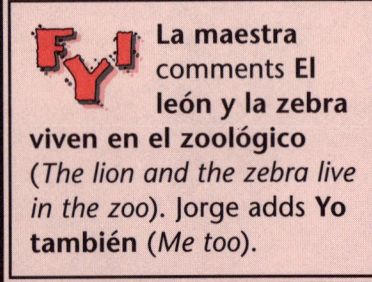

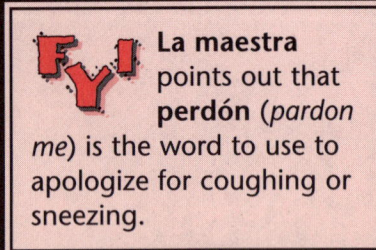

1. Greeting the children, Dora, and Jorge

Using **Buenas tardes** (*Good afternoon*) as the greeting, **la maestra** leads the opening conversation. She comments that **Jorge tiene dos colores. Jorge es de color amarillo y de color café** (*Jorge has two colors. Jorge is yellow and brown*) and that **Dora tiene tres colores** (*Dora has three colors*). **¿De qué colores es?** (*What color is she?*), she asks. Jorge answers **Es de color blanco, de color negro y de color rosado** (*She is white, black, and pink*).

Speaking of Dora, **la maestra** comments that **La boca es de color rosado** (*Her mouth is pink*).

2. Practicing vocabulary and constructions for destinations and transportation

Using Flashcards as prompts, **la maestra** asks the children to **repite** (*repeat*) the names of places. She asks Jorge and Dora **¿Adónde vas?** (*Where are you going?*) and prompts them to answer by combining **Voy a ___** (*I'm going to ___*) with the names of the places on the Flashcards that she points to: **el zoológico** (*zoo*), **la playa** (*beach*), **la piscina** (*swimming pool*), **el parque** (*park*). **La maestra** then follows the same procedure with the children.

FYI La maestra comments **El león y la zebra viven en el zoológico** (*The lion and the zebra live in the zoo*). Jorge adds **Yo también** (*Me too*).

To review the question **¿Cómo vas?** (*How are you going?*) **la maestra** places toy vehicles next to scenes on the Flashcards to prompt the following comments: **Voy a la playa en coche** (*I'm going to the beach by car*); **Voy al zoológico en autobús** (*I'm going to the zoo by bus*); **Voy a la piscina en moto** (*I'm going to the swimming pool by motorcycle*); **Voy al parque en avión** (*I'm going to the park by plane*).

3. Practicing vocabulary and constructions for activities

La maestra reviews several answers to the question **¿Qué vas a hacer?** (*What are you going to do?*). **Vamos a mirar** (*Let's watch*) says **la maestra**. She then introduces a lesson in which she asks the children to **escucha** (*listen*) and **repite** (*repeat*) as she points to scenes of activities, asking **¿Qué vas a hacer?** (*What are you going to do?*), and then answering: **Voy a saltar la cuerda** (*I'm going to jump rope*), **Voy a jugar al béisbol** (*I'm going to play baseball*), **Voy a jugar al fútbol** (*I'm going to play soccer*), **Voy a ir de campo** (*I'm going to go on a picnic*), **Voy a nadar** (*I'm going to swim*), **Voy a jugar** (*I'm going to play*).

FYI La maestra points out that **perdón** (*pardon me*) is the word to use to apologize for coughing or sneezing.

LEVEL TWO

4. Previewing a new book

La maestra explains that when she is going to do something she says **Voy a** ___ (*I'm going to* ___). She then points out that sometimes we want to talk about someone else and asks **¿Quién es?** (*Who is it?*) as she points to a picture of Antonito. **La maestra** remarks that to talk about Antonito she would say **Va a** ___ (*He is going to* ___), as in **Va a comer** (*He is going to eat*) and **Va a dormir** (*He is going to sleep*).

5. Introducing the book

La maestra says **Vamos a mirar** (*Let's watch*) to present doña Elena, who reads the book "**Un día feliz con Antonito**" ("*A Happy Day with Antonito*"). Some sentences from the book are:

Por la mañana Antonito se levanta.	*In the morning Antonito gets up.*
Toma su desayuno.	*He has breakfast.*
¿Qué toma? Toma leche con chocolate.	*What does he have? He has chocolate milk.*
Ahora mira el reloj. ¡Es tarde!	*Now he looks at the clock. It's late!*
Anda rápido a la escuela.	*He quickly walks to school.*
En la clase Antonito lee un libro y colorea en un papel.	*At school Antonito reads a book and colors on a piece of paper.*
Durante el recreo salta la cuerda.	*During recess he jumps rope.*
Por la tarde, después de la escuela, Antonito lleva sus libros y corre a casa.	*In the afternoon, after school, Antonito takes his books and runs home.*
Ahora Antonito duerme.	*Now Antonito is sleeping.*

6. Singing a song

After asking **¿Te gusta el libro?** (*Do you like the book?*), **la maestra** says **Vamos a cantar** (*Let's sing*). She and the puppets sing "**Español para ti**" ("*Spanish Is for You, and for Me*"). For song lyrics, see Lesson 3, Video Lesson, section 3.

7. Closing

La maestra says **Adiós** to the children.

After viewing the video, praise the children for their good listening and watching skills.

Activity Lesson

Activity 62A: Activities and places

Materials: Cassette player; Activity Cassette 3, Side A; Gold Flashcards 70–73; and scissors.

Preparation: Make a copy of each Flashcard and cut it in half, so each destination or activity will be on a separate page.

Distribute the Flashcard pictures to eight children, and tell the class that **la maestra** is going to name a place to go and an activity. The two children holding pictures showing the place and the activity that she mentions should stand up. Pause the tape at the harp sound to give the children time to stand up.

> For added practice, you may want to redistribute the Flashcard pictures and repeat the activity.

Activity 62B: Discuss Antonito's day

Play the section of the video in which doña Elena reads the story about Antonito's day at school. Then lead a discussion in which the children recall as much as they can about the story. You may want to prompt the children with questions based on the summary in section 5 of this Video Lesson.

Activity 62C: Sing

Materials: Cassette player; **"Español para ti"** (*"Spanish Is for You, and for Me"*) on the Song Cassette, Side A.

Play the song while the children sing along. Encourage children who want to sing the song as a duet, trio, or quartet to do so after giving them time to rehearse. For song lyrics, see Lesson 3, Video Lesson, section 3.

LEVEL TWO

CLOSING

Tell the children that Spanish class is finished for today. In the next class they will learn some new expressions for activities.

IF YOU HAVE TIME...

Materials: Crayons and drawing paper.

Lead the children in discussing how Antonito's day at school is like and unlike their day. Then ask them to draw pictures of their favorite part of the school day. When they have finished, ask volunteers to describe their drawings, using Spanish as much as possible.

Lesson Sixty-Two

Lesson 63

Materials to gather

- VCR and Video Lesson 63 on Tape 16
- Cassette player
- Activity Cassette 3
- Feeling masks from Activity 9B
- Gold Flashcards 5–7
- Blackline Master 63A (activities)
- 11 colored fish from Lesson 16
- Blackline Master 63C (Antonito)
- Crayons
- *Optional materials:* Song Cassette

OBJECTIVES

Language

- Learn new vocabulary for activities
- Discuss the story **"Un día feliz con Antonito"** (*"A Happy Day with Antonito"*)

Culture

- Understand the concept that **fútbol** (*soccer*) and American football are not the same
- Sing a favorite song

Review

- Practice vocabulary and constructions relating to sports and activities
- Recall vocabulary for colors

Vocabulary

Va a ___	*He/She is going to ___*
montar en bicicleta	*to ride a bicycle*
dormir	*to sleep*
leer	*to read*
hacer un viaje	*to take a trip*

Warm-up

Materials: Feeling masks from Activity 9B.

Review expressions of feeling by having the opening conversation using the masks. As the children participate in the conversation, ask them to hold up the feeling mask that reflects their statement of how they feel, and you do the same (T = Teacher, C = class):

T: Buenos días, clase.	*Good morning, class.*
C: Buenos días, Maestro/ Maestra.	*Good morning, Teacher.*
T: ¿Cómo estás tú?	*How are you?*
C: [*Responses will vary*: Muy bien; Así, así; Muy mal], gracias. ¿Y usted?	[*Responses will vary*: Very well; So-so; Very bad], thank you. And you?
T: [*Responses will vary*], gracias.	[*Responses will vary*], thank you.

Review

Materials: Gold Flashcards 5–7.

Have the children name the feeling shown on each Flashcard. Encourage them to discuss situations that might cause these feelings by asking questions like these: How would you feel if it was a beautiful day and you were going on a picnic? (**contento/a**—*happy*) How would you feel if it rained and you had to call off the picnic? (**triste**—*sad*) How would you feel if someone blamed you for something that you didn't do? (**enojado/a**—*angry*)

Introduce the video

Encourage the children to listen and watch as **la maestra**, Dora, and Rosco teach them new vocabulary for activities.

Feelings:

Estoy bien; estoy contento/a
(*I'm fine; I'm happy*)

Estoy mal; estoy triste
(*I'm not well; I'm sad*)

Estoy enojado/a
(*I'm angry*)

Video Lesson

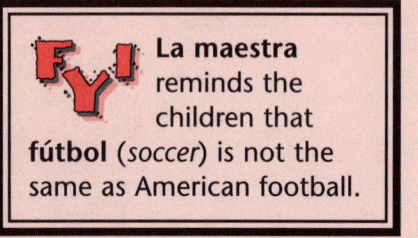

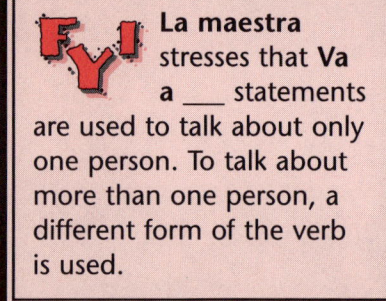

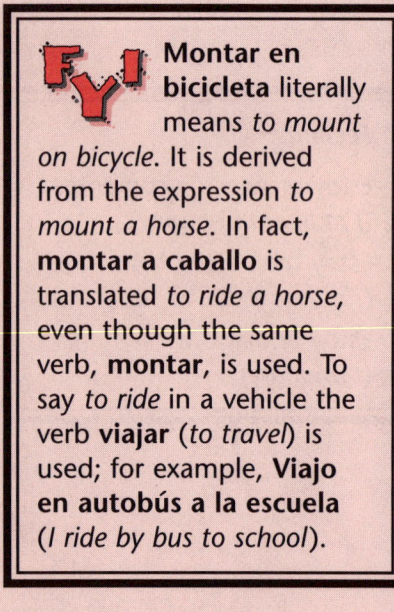

1. Greeting the children, Dora, and Rosco

Using **Buenos días** as the greeting, **la maestra** has the opening conversation with the children. She says **Estoy muy contenta porque Dora está aquí y Rosco está aquí** (*I'm very happy because Dora is here and Rosco is here*).

2. Reviewing vocabulary and constructions for activities

Using Flashcards and asking the children to **repite** (*repeat*), **la maestra** reviews **Voy a ___** (*I'm going to ___*) combined with activities: **Voy a saltar la cuerda** (*I'm going to jump rope*), **Voy a jugar al fútbol** (*I'm going to play soccer*), **Voy a ir de campo** (*I'm going to go on a picnic*), **Voy a jugar al béisbol** (*I'm going to play baseball*).

La maestra points out that to talk about someone else, such as Rosco or Dora, you say **Va a ___** (*He/She is going to ___*): **Rosco va jugar al fútbol** (*He is going to play soccer*); **Dora va a saltar la cuerda** (*Dora is going to jump rope*); **La maestra va a ir de campo** (*The teacher is going to go on a picnic*).

3. Introducing new vocabulary

Using Flashcards **la maestra** introduces new vocabulary for activities combined with **Voy a ___** (*I'm going to ___*):

montar en bicicleta	*to ride a bicycle*
leer	*to read*
dormir	*to sleep*
hacer un viaje	*to take a trip*

La maestra introduces a review of **Va a ___** (*He/She is going to ___*) statements combined with new and old vocabulary, including forms of transportation: **Va a dormir** (*He is going to sleep*), **Va a montar en bicicleta** (*He is going to ride a bicycle*), **Va a leer** (*He is going to read*), **Va a hacer un viaje en coche/en avión/en autobús** (*He/She is going to take a trip by car/by plane/by bus*).

La maestra next reviews some of the new vocabulary by asking **Si hablamos de este niño/esta niña, ¿qué va a hacer?** (*If we're talking about this boy/girl, what is he/she going to do?*)

FYI **La maestra** reminds the children that **fútbol** (*soccer*) is not the same as American football.

FYI **La maestra** stresses that **Va a ___** statements are used to talk about only one person. To talk about more than one person, a different form of the verb is used.

FYI **Montar en bicicleta** literally means *to mount on bicycle*. It is derived from the expression *to mount a horse*. In fact, **montar a caballo** is translated *to ride a horse*, even though the same verb, **montar**, is used. To say *to ride* in a vehicle the verb **viajar** (*to travel*) is used; for example, **Viajo en autobús a la escuela** (*I ride by bus to school*).

LEVEL TWO

4. Discussing *"Un día feliz con Antonito"* (*"A Happy Day with Antonito"*)

Through questions and answers like the following **la maestra** reviews the book:

¿Qué va a hacer?	What is he going to do?
Va a comer.	He is going to eat.
Está en su silla y a la mesa.	He is in his chair and at the table.
¿Adónde va?	Where is he going?
Va a la escuela.	He is going to school.
Tiene la mochila.	He has his backpack.
Cruza la calle.	He crosses the street.
¿De qué color es el autobús?	What color is the bus?
¿Dónde está?	Where is he?
Está en la clase.	He is in the classroom.
Va a leer el libro.	He is going to read the book.
¿De qué color es la pizarra?	What color is the chalkboard?
Antonito va a jugar.	Antonito is going to play.
Antonito va a saltar la cuerda con sus amigos.	Antonito is going to jump rope with his friends.
Está en el patio.	He is on the playground.
Va a casa.	He is going home.
Va a dormir.	He is going to sleep.

5. Reviewing vocabulary for colors

La maestra points out that we get a lot of pleasure from colors. She shows colored **sombreros** and asks ¿**De qué color es?** (*What color is it?*).

6. Playing a game

Continuing the review of colors, **la maestra** plays ¿**Cuál falta?** (*What's missing?*) with **muchos peces de muchos colores** (*many fish of many colors*).

7. Practicing new vocabulary

La maestra shows Flashcards to review the new vocabulary combined with **Va a ___** (*He/She is going to ___*). See section 3 of this lesson.

8. Closing

La maestra, Dora, and Rosco say **Adiós** and **Hasta luego** (*See you later*) to the children.

Colors:

anaranjado	*orange*
azul	*blue*
morado	*purple*
verde	*green*
gris	*gray*
blanco	*white*
amarillo	*yellow*
rosado	*pink*
negro	*black*
rojo	*red*
café	*brown*

After viewing the video, praise the children for their good listening and watching skills.

Lesson Sixty-Three

378

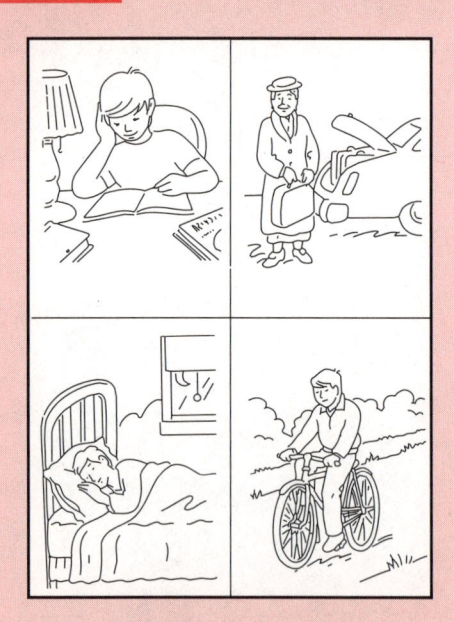

Blackline Master 63A

For added practice, you may want to repeat Activity 63A, asking heritage speakers or other volunteers to take turns playing the part of **la maestra**.

ACTIVITY LESSON

Activity 63A: Recognize activities

Materials: Cassette player; Activity Cassette 3, Side A; and Blackline Master 63A.

Preparation: Duplicate Blackline Master 63A so that each child has a copy.

Tell the children that **la maestra** is going to say **Va a ___** (*He/She is going to ___*) and then name an activity. They are to **toca** (*touch*) the picture showing the activity that she names.

Activity 63B: Favorite colors

Materials: 11 colored fish from Lesson 16.

Arrange the fish where the children can see and reach them. Tell the class that **la maestra** is going to show them how to say that they like a certain color. Explain that you will then choose children to go to the front of the room, choose any fish they like, and say that they like that color using the sentence that **la maestra** teaches them. For colors, see section 5 of this Video Lesson.

LEVEL TWO

Activity 63C: Let's color!

Materials: Blackline Master 63C; crayons.

Preparation: Duplicate Blackline Master 63C so that each child has a copy.

Give each child a set of crayons. Then ask the children to color the picture of Antonito in any colors they like. When they have finished, divide the class into pairs. Encourage the partners to take turns naming each color in their pictures.

CLOSING

Tell the children that Spanish class is finished for today. In the next class they will recall the names of family members and talk more about activities.

Blackline Master 63C

IF YOU HAVE TIME . . .

Materials: Cassette player; Song Cassette, Side A.

Brainstorm with the children the names of some of the songs they have learned this year, such as **"Las estaciones"** (*"The Seasons"*—Lesson 27, Video Lesson, section 7), **"Dulce canta el burro"** (*"Sweetly Sings the Donkey"*—Lesson 41, Video Lesson, section 5), and **"Vengan a ver mi rancho"** (*"Come See My Ranch"*—Lesson 37, Video Lesson, section 8). Ask them to vote on their favorite song. Then lead the children in singing it.

Lesson Sixty-Three

Lesson 64

Materials to gather

- VCR and Video Lesson 64 on Tape 16
- Cassette player
- Activity Cassette 3
- Gold Flashcards 72–75
- Gold Flashcards 70, 71
- *Optional materials:* Song Cassette

OBJECTIVES

Language

- Integrate vocabulary and constructions relating to destinations, transportation, and activities

Culture

- Review the concept that in Spanish-speaking families the grandparents often live with other family members
- Sing **"Fray Felipe"** (*"Friar Phillip"*)
- Understand that songs can travel from culture to culture

Review

- Recall vocabulary for family members
- Recall vocabulary and constructions for sports and activities
- Practice vocabulary and constructions relating to destinations and transportation

Vocabulary

No new vocabulary is introduced in this lesson.

Warm-up

Ask the children to talk about activities their families like to do together, such as take walks, go to the movies or favorite restaurants, go to the mall or a museum, play games, watch television, or visit friends and family members.

Review

Give the children a chance to review the names of rooms of the house (**la casa**) by asking where they or a family member would go to: eat breakfast (**la cocina**—*kitchen*), watch television (**la sala**—*living room*), take a shower (**el baño**—*bathroom*), eat supper (**el comedor**—*dining room*), and sleep (**el cuarto**—*bedroom*).

Introduce the video

Encourage the children to listen and watch as Dora and Rosco talk about family members and activities.

Video Lesson

1. Greeting Dora, Rosco, and the children

Using **Buenos días** as the greeting, **la maestra** has the opening conversation first with Dora and Rosco together, then with the children. She asks Dora and Rosco ¿**Cómo están ustedes?** (*How are you?*).

La maestra, Dora, and Rosco review the negative construction and expressions of feeling with the following comments: **No estoy enojada** (*I'm not angry*), **No estoy triste** (*I'm not sad*), **No tengo hambre** (*I'm not hungry*), **Estoy contenta** (*I'm happy*).

2. Reviewing names of family members

La maestra says **Mi papá va a visitarme** (*My father is going to visit me*). Using Flashcards she reviews the names of family members: **la mamá** (*mother*); **el papá** (*father*); **el hermano** (*brother*), who is also **el hijo** (*son*); **la hermana** (*sister*), who is also **la hija** (*daughter*); and **el abuelo y la abuela** (*grandfather and grandmother*), who in Spanish-speaking families often **viven con la familia en la casa** (*live with the family in the house*), along with aunts and uncles.

3. Reviewing vocabulary and constructions for activities

Using Flashcards, **la maestra** reviews activities. Integrating the names of family members with Flashcards showing activities, **la maestra** then asks Rosco and Dora to use their imagination to answer questions such as ¿**Qué va a hacer la mamá?** (*What is the mother going to do?*) and ¿**Qué va a hacer el papá?** (*What is the father going to do?*). **La maestra** combines Flashcards showing family members with Flashcards showing activities to prompt the sentences. For activities, see Lesson 63, Video Lesson, sections 2 and 3.

4. Playing a game

La maestra comments on what fun it is to construct our own ideas by combining things we know. She then says **Vamos a mirar** (*Let's watch*) to introduce a game of **Muéstrame** (*Show me*). She begins by reviewing the construction **Va a ___** (*He/She is going to ___*) combined with activities and then asks the children to show her the picture of the activity she names. She then points to a picture of an activity and asks the children **Es ___, ¿sí o no?** (*Is it ___, yes or no?*).

FYI

Because she is asking both Dora and Rosco how they are, **la maestra** uses the plural form of the verb **estar**, which is **están**, and the plural word for **tú** (*you*), which is **ustedes**. Note that **ustedes** is also the plural of the more formal word for *you*, **usted**.

Sentences in section 3:

La mamá va a saltar la cuerda.
(*The mother is going to jump rope.*)

El papá va a jugar al fútbol.
(*The father is going to play soccer.*)

El hermano va a jugar al béisbol.
(*The brother is going to play baseball.*)

La hermana va a ir de campo.
(*The sister is going to go on a picnic.*)

La abuela va a leer.
(*The grandmother is going to read.*)

El abuelo va a hacer un viaje.
(*The grandfather is going to take a trip.*)

LEVEL TWO

5. Reviewing names of family members and activities

La maestra combines Flashcards showing family members with those showing activities to prompt sentences that answer questions such as **El abuelo—¿Qué va a hacer?** (*The grandfather—What is he going to do?*).

6. Playing another game

La maestra says **Vamos a jugar** (*Let's play*) before initiating a game of **¿Cuál falta?** (*What's missing?*) with scenes showing activities. She then reviews the activities shown on the Flashcards. Next she points to the activities and asks the children **¿Qué va a hacer?** (*What is he/she going to do?*). The children answer by saying **Va a ___** (*He/She is going to ___*).

7. Integrating vocabulary for destinations, transportation, and activities

La maestra combines Flashcards with models of transportation to prompt sentences like these: **Voy al parque en coche. Voy a jugar al béisbol.** (*I'm going to the park by car. I'm going to play baseball.*) **Voy al parque en autobús. Voy a ir de campo.** (*I'm going to the park by bus. I'm going to go on a picnic.*) **Voy a la playa en moto. Voy a jugar al fútbol.** (*I'm going to the beach by motorcycle. I'm going to play soccer.*)

8. Singing a song

La maestra asks "Who could say **Voy a dormir** (*I'm going to sleep*)?" Rosco answers **Vamos a cantar** (*Let's sing*) because the answer is **Fray Felipe**. **La maestra** and the puppets sing the song.

Fray Felipe, Fray Felipe.	*Friar Phillip, Friar Phillip.*
¿Duermes tú? ¿Duermes tú?	*Are you sleeping? Are you sleeping?*
Toca la campana, toca la campana.	*Ring the bell, ring the bell.*
Tan, tan, tan. Tan, tan, tan.	*Ding, ding, dong. Ding, ding, dong.*

9. Closing

La maestra, Rosco, and Dora say **Adiós**.

Activities in section 4:

Va a dormir.
(*He is going to sleep.*)

Va a montar en bicicleta.
(*He is going to ride a bicycle.*)

Va a hacer un viaje en avión.
(*He is going to take a trip by plane.*)

Va a leer.
(*He is going to read.*)

La señora va a hacer un viaje en coche.
(*The lady is going to take a trip by car.*)

El señor va a hacer un viaje en autobús.
(*The gentleman is going to take a trip by bus.*)

EN ESPAÑOL

Again using the plural form of **estar**, **la maestra** asks Rosco and Dora **¿Están listos?** (*Are you ready?*). You may want to ask the children this question at appropriate times throughout the day, such as when they are getting ready to go outside or to the gym.

After viewing the video, praise the children for their good listening and watching skills.

Lesson Sixty-Four

> Call on individuals to pantomime the activities or ask the class to pantomime together.

ACTIVITY LESSON

Activity 64A: Pantomime activities

Materials: Cassette player; Activity Cassette 3, Side A.

Tell the children that **la maestra** is going to say **Voy a ___** (*I am going to ___*) and add the name of an activity. The children should pantomime the activity she names.

For added practice, you may want to ask volunteers or heritage speakers to express the same and other activities for the children to pantomime, such as **Voy a jugar al fútbol** (*I'm going to play soccer*), **Voy a ir de campo** (*I'm going on a picnic*), and **Voy a hacer un viaje** (*I'm going to take a trip*).

Activity 64B: Team up

Materials: Gold Flashcards 72–75.

Preparation: Pick four pairs of students, one for each Flashcard. Tell the boys to pretend that their name is Paco; girls should pretend that their name is Pepita.

Give the first Flashcard to the first pair of children. The first partner should say **Voy a ___** (*I'm going to ___*) and add the name of the first activity on the Flashcard. The second partner should repeat to the class **Paco** (or **Pepita**) **va a ___** (*Paco or Pepita is going to ___*). The partners should do the same with the second activity on the Flashcard, after which the other partners should take their turns.

#72:	Voy (Paco/Pepita va) a saltar la cuerda.	I'm going (Paco/Pepita is going) to jump rope.
	Voy (Paco/Pepita va) a jugar al fútbol.	I'm going (Paco/Pepita is going) to play soccer.
#73:	Voy (Paco/Pepita va) a ir de campo.	I'm going (Paco/Pepita is going) on a picnic.
	Voy (Paco/Pepita va) a jugar al béisbol.	I'm going (Paco/Pepita is going) to play baseball.
#74:	Voy (Paco/Pepita va) a dormir.	I'm going (Paco/Pepita is going) to sleep.
	Voy (Paco/Pepita va) a montar en bicicleta.	I'm going (Paco/Pepita is going) to ride a bike.
#75:	Voy (Paco/Pepita va) a leer.	I'm going (Paco/Pepita is going) to read.
	Voy (Paco/Pepita va) a hacer un viaje.	I'm going (Paco/Pepita is going) to take a trip.

Activity 64C: Go places

Materials: Gold Flashcards 70, 71.

To give the children practice in naming destinations, repeat the above activity with Gold Flashcards 70 and 71.

#70: Voy (Paco/Pepita va) al zoológico. — I'm going (Paco/Pepita is going) to the zoo.

Voy (Paco/Pepita va) a la playa. — I'm going (Paco/Pepita is going) to the beach.

#71: Voy (Paco/Pepita va) a la piscina. — I'm going (Paco/Pepita is going) to the pool.

Voy (Paco/Pepita va) al parque. — I'm going (Paco/Pepita is going) to the park.

Closing

Tell the children that Spanish class is finished for today. In the next class they will review some of the fun places they visited with **la maestra** during the past months.

IF YOU HAVE TIME...

Materials: Cassette player; Song Cassette, Side A.

Encourage the children to sing along with **"Fray Felipe"** (*"Friar Phillip"*). You may then want to have two groups of children sing the song as a round. For song lyrics, see section 8 of this Video Lesson.

Encourage children who know the song in English to sing it. If necessary, you may want to sing it yourself (see lyrics below) before pointing out that the song is also very popular in France (*"Frère Jacques"*) and that it may have been brought to the United States by American soldiers who learned it in France during World War I.

Are you sleeping, are you sleeping, Brother John, Brother John?

Morning bells are ringing, morning bells are ringing,

Ding, ding, dong. Ding ding, dong.

LESSON 65

Materials to gather

- VCR and Video Lesson 65 on Tape 17
- Cassette player
- Song Cassette
- Drawing paper and crayons
- Gold Flashcards 28–33

- *Optional materials:* writing paper; pencils

OBJECTIVES

Language
- Understand a story
- Understand consecutive sentences about animals

Culture
- Sing **"Dulce canta el burro"** (*"Sweetly Sings the Donkey"*)

Review
- Recall vocabulary for parts of the face and body
- Recall vocabulary for rooms of the school
- Review positive and negative commands
- Remember vocabulary for animals

Vocabulary
No new vocabulary is introduced in this lesson.

Warm-up

Tell the children that their Spanish lessons are almost over for this school year and that in the next two videos they will revisit some places with **la maestra**. Ask what their favorite places have been and what they remember most about them.

Review

Materials: Drawing paper and crayons.

Preparation: Give drawing paper and crayons to each child.

Review vocabulary for parts of the face and body by having the children name them one at a time as you point to them. Then ask the children to draw a picture of a real or imaginary animal. Their pictures should show as many as possible of the face and body parts whose names they have just reviewed. When they have finished, encourage the children to describe their drawings to the class.

Introduce the video

Encourage the children to listen and watch as **la maestra** once again takes them to visit some of their favorite friends—the animals on the ranch and the dolphins.

Parts of the face and body:

el pelo	*hair*
los ojos	*eyes*
la boca	*mouth*
las manos	*hands*
las orejas	*ears*
la nariz	*nose*
los brazos	*arms*
los pies	*feet*
la cara	*face*
la cabeza	*head*
los dedos	*fingers*
las piernas	*legs*

Video Lesson

1. Greeting the children, Dora, and Rosco

Using **Buenos días** as the greeting, **la maestra** has the opening conversation with the children and then with Dora and Rosco, whom she asks **¿Cómo están ustedes?** (*How are you* [plural]*?*). She and the hand puppets review some expressions of feeling: **Estoy muy contenta** (*I'm very happy*) and **Tengo hambre** (*I'm hungry*).

La maestra points out that there are only two more Spanish classes and tells the children that they will spend the classes remembering some of the things they have done and learned.

2. Playing a game

La maestra says **Vamos a jugar** (*Let's play*) to introduce the game of **¿Dónde está la maestra?** (*Where is the teacher?*) to review vocabulary for rooms of the school.

3. Reviewing positive and negative commands

After reviewing the commands **salta** (*jump*), **corre** (*run*), and **no toques** (*don't touch*), **la maestra** says **Vamos a mirar** (*Let's watch*) to present the mime, who demonstrates positive and negative commands: **siéntate** (*sit down*), **párate** (*stand up*), **toca** (*touch*), **no toques** (*don't touch*), **anda** (*walk*), **no andes** (*don't walk*), **corre** (*run*), **no corras** (*don't run*), **salta** (*jump*), **no saltes** (*don't jump*), **busca** (*look for*).

4. Reintroducing a book

Referring to the mime, **la maestra** asks **¿Quién es?** (*Who is it?*) to reintroduce the book "**Un día feliz con Antonito**" ("*A Happy Day with Antonito*"), first read in Lesson 62. Some more sentences from the book are:

Busca su ropa y se pone sus pantalones, su camisa y sus zapatos.	He looks for his clothes and puts on his pants, his shirt, and his shoes.
¿Le gusta la leche con chocolate? ¡Sí!	Does he like chocolate milk? Yes!
Mira el semáforo y cruza la calle con la luz verde.	He looks at the traffic light and crosses the street with the green light.
Está contento, y Antonito habla con sus amigos.	He is happy, and Antonito talks with his friends.
Por la noche Antonito tiene sueño pero está contento.	At night Antonito is sleepy but he is happy.
¿Por qué? Porque su día fue feliz.	Why? Because his day was happy.

Responses:

La maestra está en ...
The teacher is in . . .

la biblioteca	the library
el baño	the bathroom
la oficina	the office
la cafetería	the cafeteria
el patio	the playground
la clase	the classroom

5. Visiting the ranch

La maestra once again visits the ranch and talks about the animals she meets there.

Some of **la maestra**'s comments are:

Estoy aquí con unos amigos, los caballos.	*I'm here with some friends, the horses.*
Tara Lynn es un caballo grande.	*Tara Lynn is a big horse.*
Ginger es un caballo pequeño.	*Ginger is a small horse.*
Aquí estoy con unas gallinas—muchas gallinas de muchos colores.	*I'm here with some chickens—many chickens of many colors.*
¿Qué ponen las gallinas? ¡Huevos!	*What do hens lay? Eggs!*
Es nuestro amigo el cerdo.	*It's our friend the pig.*
Ahora el cerdo duerme.	*Now the pig is sleeping.*

6. Visiting the aquarium

La maestra points out that **unos amigos viven en el rancho y otros amigos viven en el agua** (*some friends live on the ranch and some friends live in the water*). She then revisits the aquarium.

Some of **la maestra**'s comments are: **Estoy aquí con unos amigos muy especiales—¡los delfines!** (*I'm here with some very special friends—the dolphins!*) **No son peces. Son nuestros amigos que viven en el agua.** (*They are not fish. They are our friends who live in the water.*) **Nadan en el agua y saltan también.** (*They swim in the water and they also jump.*)

8. Singing a song

Vamos a cantar (*Let's sing*) says **la maestra**, introducing the song "**Dulce canta el burro**" ("*Sweetly Sings the Donkey*"). After singing the song **la maestra** says **Es muy divertido cantar** (*It's a lot of fun to sing*). For song lyrics, see Lesson 41, Video Lesson, section 5.

9. Closing

La maestra, Rosco, and Dora say **Adiós** and **Hasta luego** (*See you later*).

After viewing the video, praise the children for their good listening and watching skills.

Lesson Sixty-Five

ACTIVITY LESSON

Activity 65A: Express feelings

Materials: Gold Flashcards 28–33.

Arrange the Flashcards where the children can see and reach them. Then call on volunteers to take turns holding up one of the Flashcards, stating the animal's feeling in the following form: **El/La ___ dice, "Tengo ___"** (*The ___ is saying, "I'm ___"*), and then turning the Flashcard over. After each statement, encourage the rest of the class to say ¡Olé! (*Hurray!*).

Activity 65B: Can you draw animals?

Materials: Drawing paper and crayons.

Preparation: Give drawing paper and crayons to each child.

Ask the children to draw a picture of their favorite animal from the video they have just seen. When they have finished, ask them to describe their drawings, using as much Spanish as possible. Why is that animal their favorite?

Activity 65C: Let's sing

Materials: Cassette player; **"Dulce canta el burro"** (*"Sweetly Sings the Donkey"*) on the Song Cassette, Side A.

Play the song while the children sing along. Then divide the class into three groups and ask them to sing the song as a round.

For song lyrics, see Lesson 41, Video Lesson, section 5.

Animals and expressions:

El gato dice, "Tengo frío".
(*The cat is saying, "I'm cold."*)

El caballo dice, "Tengo calor".
(*The horse is saying, "I'm hot."*)

El perro dice, "Tengo hambre".
(*The dog is saying, "I'm hungry."*)

La vaca dice, "Tengo sed".
(*The cow is saying, "I'm thirsty."*)

El cerdo dice, "Tengo miedo".
(*The pig is saying, "I'm afraid."*)

La gallina dice, "Tengo sueño".
(*The chicken is saying, "I'm sleepy."*)

LEVEL TWO

Closing

Tell the children that Spanish class is finished for today. In the next class they will revisit some more places with **la maestra**.

IF YOU HAVE TIME...

Materials: Gold Flashcards 28–33; writing paper; and pencils.

Display the Flashcards where the children can see them. Divide the class into pairs. Ask the partners to review each animal's expression of feeling. Then encourage them to choose one of the expressions and use it as the first line of a short story. In their stories, they may want to take into account why the animal has that feeling and what the animal does about it. When they have finished, ask the partners to share their stories with the class.

Lesson Sixty-Five

Lesson 66

Materials to gather

- VCR and Video Lesson 66 on Tape 17
- Cassette player
- Song Cassette
- Gold Flashcards 41–47
- Cut-out of Rosco from Blackline Master 61A
- Gold Flashcards 1, 68–71
- Writing paper
- Pencils or pens
- Colored markers

OBJECTIVES

Language

- Understand consecutive sentences about life situations, such as shopping and taking a trip
- Understand a story

Culture

- Sing **"Las estaciones"** (*"The Seasons"*), the "Months Rap," and **"Español para ti"** (*"Spanish Is for You, and for Me"*)

Review

- Recall vocabulary for school items
- Remember vocabulary for clothing
- Review vocabulary relating to street safety
- Recall vocabulary and constructions relating to travel

Vocabulary

No new vocabulary is introduced in this lesson.

Warm-up

Remind the children that the school year is coming to a close and that summer is on the way. Encourage them to talk about their plans for summer vacation. Point out that this is their last Spanish lesson of the school year, and that **la maestra** is planning a vacation, too.

Review

Materials: Gold Flashcards 41–47.

Arrange the Flashcards where the children can see them. Then tell the children that during the past months they have experienced many kinds of weather. Point to each Flashcard and ask the children to say the appropriate weather expression.

Introduce the video

Encourage the children to listen and watch as **la maestra** and Rosco revisit some stores.

Weather expressions:

Hace sol.
(*It's sunny.*)

Hace buen tiempo.
(*It's good weather.*)

Hace frío.
(*It's cold.*)

Hace calor.
(*It's hot.*)

Llueve *or* Está lloviendo.
(*It's raining.*)

Nieva.
(*It's snowing.*)

Hace viento.
(*It's windy.*)

Hace mal tiempo.
(*It's bad weather.*)

Video Lesson

1. Greeting the children and Dora

Using **Buenos días** as the greeting, **la maestra** has the opening conversation with the children and then with Dora. Dora says **Estoy muy contenta** (*I'm very happy*).

2. Singing a song

La maestra comments that she and the children have been watching the months, days, and seasons pass all year. She then says **Vamos a cantar** (*Let's sing*) before singing "**Las estaciones**" (*"The Seasons"*) and then the "Months Rap." For song lyrics, see Lesson 27, Video Lesson, section 7 and Lesson 12, Video Lesson, section 4, respectively.

3. Shopping with Rosco

La maestra and Rosco's shopping trip for school supplies is shown again. Rosco **necesita muchas cosas para la clase** (*needs a lot of things for class*), such as **colores** (*crayons*), **bolígrafos** (*pens*), **un cuaderno** (*notebook*), **papel** (*paper*), **una regla** (*ruler*), **lápices** (*pencils*), **gomas** (*erasers*), **un sacapuntas** (*pencil sharpener*)—everything but **tiza** (*chalk*), which **la maestra** buys for herself. Rosco says **gracias** (*thank you*) to **la maestra** for buying him school supplies, and she says **de nada** (*you're welcome*).

4. Saying good-bye to Dora

Dora says **Yo necesito ir de compras** (*I need to go shopping*)—**Voy a hacer un viaje** (*I'm going on a trip*). She and **la maestra** say **adiós**.

5. Shopping for clothes

La maestra's visit to a clothing store is shown again. She says **Voy de compras a la tienda** (*I'm going shopping at the store*). She visits **el departamento de los zapatos** (*the shoe department*), where, besides **zapatos de muchos colores** (*shoes of many colors*), she looks at **botas** (*boots*), both **largas y cortas** (*long and short*). She also shops for **un sombrero** (*hat*) and finds **un sombrero de color negro con flores** (*a black hat with flowers*).

En el departamento de ropa (*In the clothing department*) she finds **un suéter de color morado** (*a purple sweater*), **una chaqueta de color rojo** (*a red jacket*), **una falda muy larga** (*a very long skirt*), **pantalones** (*pants*), **una blusa de muchos colores** (*a blouse of many colors*), and **un abrigo de color azul** (*a blue coat*). After shopping she says **Es muy divertido ir de compras a la tienda** (*It's a lot of fun to go shopping at the store*) and **Tengo ropa para llevar a la escuela** (*I have clothes to wear to school*).

6. Reviewing street safety

Jorge appears to say good-bye because he is going to take a trip (**va a hacer un viaje**). Jorge says **Voy al zoológico** (*I'm going to the zoo*). **La maestra** reminds him to be careful crossing the street and reviews **las luces del tráfico** (*traffic lights*) and their commands. She then reviews the rules for crossing the street: **Miro a la derecha, miro a la izquierda, y cruzo la calle** (*I look to the right, I look to the left, and I cross the street*).

7. Reintroducing a book

Rosco appears. **La maestra** reintroduces doña Elena, who again reads the book "**Rosco va**" ("*Rosco Is Going*"). In the book Rosco **va al parque en bicicleta** (*goes to the park by bicycle*), **a la escuela en autobús** (*to school by bus*), **a la tienda en taxi** (*to the store by taxi*), **al supermercado en jipi** (*to the supermarket by jeep*), **al restaurante en coche** (*to the restaurant by car*), **al lago en bote** (*to the lake by boat*), **a México en avión** (*to Mexico by plane*), **de viaje en tren** (*on a trip by train*), and **a su casa en moto** (*home by motorcycle*).

8. Singing a song

La maestra says that it's almost time to say good-bye. Referring to Rosco she says **Vamos a hacer un viaje en avión** (*We are going to take a trip by plane*). **Vamos a visitar a mi familia** (*We are going to visit my family*). She and Rosco then sing "**Español para ti**" ("*Spanish Is for You, and for Me*") For song lyrics, see Lesson 3, Video Lesson, section 3.

9. Closing

La maestra and Rosco say **Adiós** and **Hasta luego** (*See you later*).

Traffic commands:

Verde: ¡Sigue!
(*Green: Go!*)

Amarillo: ¡Espera!
(*Yellow: Wait!*)

Rojo: ¡Alto!
(*Red: Stop!*)

After viewing the video, praise the children for their good listening and watching skills.

Lesson Sixty-Six

ACTIVITY LESSON

Activity 66A: Where is Rosco?

Materials: Cut-out of Rosco from Blackline Master 61A; Gold Flashcards 1, 68–71.

Arrange the Flashcards where the children can see and reach them and play ¿Dónde está Rosco? (*Where is Rosco?*). Ask volunteers to take turns putting the Rosco cut-out on one of the scenes shown on the Flashcards and asking ¿Dónde está Rosco? The children should answer Rosco está en ___ (*Rosco is on/in ___*). Responses: 1—Rosco está en la clase (*Rosco is in the classroom*); 68—Rosco está en la calle (*Rosco is on the street*); 69—Rosco está en el autobús/el coche/el avión/el tren (*Rosco is on the bus/in the car/on the plane/on the train*); 70—Rosco está en el zoológico/en la playa (*Rosco is at the zoo/on the beach*); 71—Rosco está en la piscina/en el parque (*Rosco is in the swimming pool/at the park*).

Activity 66B: Cooperative learning—Write a letter

Materials: Writing paper; pencils or pens; colored markers.

Have the children work in small groups and write letters to **la maestra** and doña Elena or to one of the puppets, such as Rosco, Dora, Jorge, or Ñico. Brainstorm a few ideas on what to mention in the letter, such as a favorite episode, a question, or an idea for what to include in future videos. Help the children draft the letters and then assign a volunteer in each group to write them. Have the other children decorate the letters. Post the final products on the bulletin board.

Activity 66C: Sing

Materials: Cassette player; Song Cassette, Side A.

Ask the children to pick one or two of their favorite songs to sing. Let them sing the songs with the cassette; then encourage them to sing by themselves.

LEVEL TWO

CLOSING

Tell the children that Spanish class is finished until the next school year. Congratulate them on the many things they have learned and tell them that **la maestra** is looking forward to teaching them more Spanish when they meet again after vacation.

FAMILY CONNECTION

To foster a friendly link between home and school, you may want to send out Family Letter 4 (see the Teacher's Resource Book). The letter fosters understanding of what the children are learning in Spanish and suggests enrichment and practice activities for outside of school. This final letter suggests some ways to continue the children's interest in Spanish over the summer.

IF YOU HAVE TIME...

Encourage the children to role-play some of the episodes from the videos; for example, they may want to pretend that they are **la maestra** and Rosco shopping for school supplies or **la maestra** visiting **el rancho**. Remind them to use as much Spanish as possible during their presentations.